Management for Professionals

More information about this series at http://www.springer.com/series/10101

Peter M. Haller • Ulrich Naegele •
Susan Berger

Bridging Cultural Barriers

How to Overcome Preconceptions in Cross-Cultural Relationships

Springer

Peter M. Haller
CCC Cross Culture Coaching©
Regensdorf, Switzerland

Ulrich Naegele
PMP®
International Project Management and Coach
Stuttgart, Germany

Susan Berger
SAB Translations
Berlin, Germany

ISSN 2192-8096 ISSN 2192-810X (electronic)
Management for Professionals
ISBN 978-3-030-17129-2 ISBN 978-3-030-17130-8 (eBook)
https://doi.org/10.1007/978-3-030-17130-8

Cover illustration: eStudio Calamar, Berlin/Figueres

This Springer imprint is published by the registered company Springer Nature Switzerland AG.
The registered company address is: Gewerbestrasse 11, 6330 Cham, Switzerland

To my mother Hilde and my companions in life: Anita, Mechthild, and Hanna

All life is suffering.
To overcome suffering
What is needed
Is compassion and patience
(I have chosen the sayings of Buddha, learned during an excursion in Myanmar, because to us Westerners the deeper meaning remains alien, but not to people living in a collective society.)

Preface

This is a book about experience-based learning—to gain experience, and more importantly, to process past experiences of encounters in other cultures which have remained unsolved and were not understood until this day.

In my 50 years as an expatriate manager of multinational businesses and thereafter as a facilitator and lecturer in Eastern and Western Europe, in Asia, and in Africa, I fell a thousand times into the trap of clichés and stereotypes, i.e., prejudices. Getting over these past experiences was the starting point and basic idea for my latter teachings as a cross-cultural coach and facilitator.

I was fortunate enough in my life to meet the right people at the right time helping me to find my way: Prof. Dr. Rolf Pfeiffer, at that time Dean of the Export Academy of the University Reutlingen, gave me a chance to start lecturing in other cultures about international marketing and intercultural management.

The approach to overcome cultural barriers is simple. It is based on the premise that every human being is unique and has strengths and weaknesses. The same is valid for every single culture in our world. None is alike. If I want to build a trustful relationship, be it with a person or within an alien culture, I will bank on the strengths and try to handle the weaknesses. And I will avoid comparing one to another as this may lead to polarization and end in a conflict with the risk of escalation.

At the beginning, the book contains the fundamental aspects for experience-based learning for you to gain an understanding or insights into an alien culture. It may even be an eye-opener for an experience already made in the past.

Nearly half of the book is devoted to specific cultures and nations, serving as exemplary models to give you some idea of how to approach a culture and to understand better the way its members think and act. As stated in the following acknowledgments, we have expanded the original German book with contributions from coauthors from Africa, the Arab and Islamic world, Canada, India, and the United Kingdom.

The book ends on a practical note, showing you how to put your learning into practice, and finally, if you are in international project management, you will get a lot of practical advice on how to master cross-cultural hurdles.

Last but not least, we have also put an emphasis on the role of women in four societies and cultures: Africa, the Arab and Islamic world, India, and Japan. The reason is that the Western view is often diametrically opposed to the view of the women living inside these cultures. We hope that this may lead to a differentiated perception of the women in these worlds, a better understanding, and many happy personal encounters without reservations.

Our book is designed as input and guidance not only for professionals but also for everyday life as an expat or a tourist. It includes a lot of case studies of experiences made to illustrate how to understand, accept, and respect people you may meet in a new environment.

I wish you many new, exciting, and enjoyable encounters with people from other worlds!

Regensdorf, Switzerland
November 2018

Peter M. Haller

Acknowledgments

I am immensely grateful to all those who contributed to this book. First of all, to my friend and colleague Ulrich Naegele without whose commitment the first original German edition would never have seen the light of day. His assistance during the proofreading of this present edition was invaluable. Then to Susan Berger, who took care of the translation of the rather complex German text into English. And thereafter to Vinita Balasubramanian for her advice and patience during the final editing.

Finally, my grateful acknowledgments go to the authors enriching the country sections: Adiza Ujo for Africa, Raeid Meri for the Arabic and Islamic World, Vinita Balasubramanian for India, and last but not least, my lifelong mentor and friend Mike Ferrier for the United Kingdom and Canada.

All this was in itself a cross-cultural experience in a never-ending lifelong process of learning for which I am truly grateful.

Contents

Contributors

Vinita Balasubramanian Hochdorf, Germany

Susan Berger SAB Translations, Berlin, Germany

Mike Ferrier Grand Cayman, Cayman Islands

Peter M. Haller CCC Cross Culture Coaching©, Regensdorf, Switzerland

Raeid Meri WalktheChange, Bonn, Germany

Ulrich Naegele PMP®, International Project Management and Coach, Stuttgart, Germany

Adiza Ujo Abuja, Nigeria

List of Figures

Why Another Intercultural Manual? 1

Summary
This chapter provides background information on our reasons for having written this work, for all those who are interculturally interested, personally involved or professionally engaged worldwide. We would like to point the way to understanding unusual thinking and behavior in foreign cultures. Finally, we explain how this work is structured and how you can best use it for yourself.

1.1 Communication as a Bridge Between Cultures

Every individual has his/her own strengths and weaknesses—no two people are the same. We are all unique individuals. To survive, we need the community. Comparing people can quickly lead to polarization, to verdicts of "good" or "bad" which lead on to communicative lapses. A positive relationship is established when we focus on the strengths of the other person and try to manage the weaknesses.

The same applies to cultures. All cultures are unique—none are alike. Each has its strengths and its weaknesses. For this reason, cultures cannot be compared with one another. Comparing a foreign culture to one's own perspective leads to polarization, misunderstandings, clichés and prejudices. This often results in insurmountable barriers to social interaction with one another.

We hypothesize that outcomes between people, positive or negative, is contingent upon positive or negative communicative interaction. When conflicts in our own cultural sphere are based on negative communication, how much more likely must it be in an unknown culture in which we can neither speak the language nor interpret non-verbal cues? The likelihood of misinterpreting is not only a challenge for

P. M. Haller et al., *Bridging Cultural Barriers*, Management for Professionals,
https://doi.org/10.1007/978-3-030-17130-8_1

business people and politicians in contact with other cultures, it is also a barrier for tourists who travel in a foreign country—limited to sightseeing, with no genuine contact with the local population, and no opportunity for enriching experiences and encounters with them.

Creating these positive experiences is not just a question of mastering the language, but also of personal attitude and perceptions of the other world. Our perceptions are based on our own social influences and our personal world view, which we convey positively or negatively to a stranger through body language despite language barriers.

Fundamental understanding and acceptance of otherness is the key to positive experiences, to the development of relationships, to personal development, and from a holistic perspective, to inner and outer peace, be it with a partner, in a community or between nations.

Let us begin with the Western view of the world. The West has been shaped by the Age of Enlightenment which ushered in the modern age around 250 years ago. Essentially, the "*Enlightenment*" means that all issues can be resolved on the basis of rational logic to create an ideal world that will make life more livable.

This focus on rationality led to a comprehensive framework of rules and regulations that captured and structured the world into systems. We want to be able to understand, shape and forecast with it. We want to disseminate knowledge and make it easier to acquire. Descartes' motto "*I think, therefore I am*" *(Cogitoergo sum)* summarizes this in a nutshell. Man can influence and shape the world. This view of the world permeates our Western cultures; indeed, it is the foundation of today's Western society.

The Enlightenment has brought us a long way. Over the years, Europe, the United States, the entire Western world have significantly influenced, shaped and characterized the history of the world in various ways. Countless inventions that improve our quality of life and extend our lives are part of that, but so are the negative outcomes of a false sense of mission, the conquest and oppression of entire continents and cultures, all of which have consequences to this day.

Western education is based on the principle of enlightenment, of reason. It is based on teaching and learning systems that offer a wide range of choices for educating rationally oriented people. It extends to the many forms of human resource development, vocational training and all types of professions, especially research. These Western qualification systems as a whole reflect the systematic thinking, learning of rules and abstract conceptual models which form the basis for a transfer of knowledge.

Despite their similarities, Western cultures show great differences from an insider's perspective. For example, people from the German culture, in contrast to other Europeans, tend to assume that projects with perfect planning and processes are automatically assured of smooth operation and an optimum result. Yet the French neighbor may approach projects much more pragmatically, often leading to conflicts in cooperation, as French team members may mistake German perfectionism for paternalism.

We can make certain generalizations about the West from our own point of view in the Western world and identify general differences i.e. with Asian cultures. When we look at the entire world with its manifold cultural diversity, the variety of their teaching and learning systems is ultimately infinite. It is obvious that besides the analytical, rational cause-and-effect principles serving as an educational basis in the West, another holistic world of thought and feeling must surely exist.

Due to the global shift in the balance of power and spheres of influence since the 1990s, we are now confronted on a daily basis with formerly distant cultures, such as those of Asia. They have learned to align their holistic educational systems successfully with rational, experimental learning. Hence, they are able to develop completely new ways of thinking from those in the West and transform them into action. And this is done with amazing success, as is evident in the development not only of Japan, Korea, India and the Southeast Asian countries, but particularly of China.

In this connection, the vague feeling intensifies that we in the West may not have reached the end of the story and that Western values and knowledge are not the only ones worthy of being exalted. The "*End of History*" as once proclaimed by the eminent American social scientist Francis Fukuyama is as unlikely as the end of the world was going to be in 2012 according to the Maya prophecies. It starts to dawn on us that perhaps the Western view of the world is not the only way and that something "*different*" does or will exist alongside it in future.

1.2 The Importance of Interculturalism in Our World Today

Internationalization, globalization and global networking in professional and private life are increasing. The world is changing. Digitization has made cross border communication easier, faster. The trans-national flow of information affects us not only hourly, but every minute, whether in business or at home. We spend our holidays abroad, in foreign cultures, because we are not only looking for recreation, but also for enrichment and new learning.

Practically every business today works across borders with the emerging markets in Asia, be it as a supplier, a customer or even a consumer, because Western markets are saturated and new markets usually bring expansion opportunities, growth and profit. The establishment of foreign branches and cross-border company acquisitions or partnerships creates cross-cultural working environments. This results in multinational companies increasingly having international teams working together across borders. Besides taking advantage of location and cost factors, culturally diverse skills can be of benefit to a company in terms of innovation and creativity. This involves a basic prerequisite: to be able to work together without biases, team members must understand and respect each other not only on a human, but also on a cultural level. From our consultancy practice we know that basic cultural understanding is often missing, as it is neither sought nor conveyed, and team members talk and work at cross purposes.

Intercultural issues become the focus of interest only when an intercultural encounter has already become heated. Disagreements on factual issues are attributed to cultural differences and become increasingly difficult to overcome. As a result, international projects are unable to meet their deadlines, or the final quality of the outcome is inferior, and the team can no longer be deployed for future projects. A scapegoat has to be found, and so the team is dissolved.

The consequences of expatriate failure are also serious when expatriate managers or employees have to return home prematurely due to lack of intercultural adaptation. Figures based on experiences of corporations, for example in Switzerland, estimate that this can affect around 15% of those who are posted abroad. The costs of family repatriation and possible follow-up costs such as severance pay can quickly amount to several hundred thousand Swiss francs, euros or dollars. Even greater damage is caused by frustrated employees and the subsequent monetary damage caused by failed business development. In these cases, a turnaround or the integration of the company acquired abroad may be delayed by months or even years.

When intercultural situations escalate, money and prestige are often at stake. In the authors' experience, intercultural training is often the penultimate option before a contact is completely severed. This also applies to preparations for postings abroad, which is, in our experience, only provided to a minority of expatriate employees and executives.

If the operational levels of expatriates sent abroad are given pre-departure training, manager of expatriates are often ignored. The result is frustration among employees in the field, as they are simultaneously dealing with a sense of helplessness and even hopelessness in their intercultural environment, and at the same time they are under pressure from their home country's management which is ignorant of their situation and concerns.

There are also rare and positive exceptions such as a German automotive company which interculturally trained all employees—from the secretary to the board—when it entered into a joint venture with a Japanese company.

1.3 What You Can Learn from This Manual and How to Use It

This manual is based on practical experience and is intended for daily cross-cultural practice. Its goal is to serve as a pragmatic basis and instrument for all those who want to experience other cultures, whether as a manager, a member of an international work team, a field worker, a student or a tourist in search of new encounters.

You can use this book for private study or in a study group with like-minded people who enjoy exploring foreign cultures. Advanced students can develop a program as instructors, using the same structure and procedure for both individual and group study. For instructions, please refer to Chap. 5 "*Bridging Cultures in Everyday Life*".

Here is how this manual is structured. Unlike what is suggested by Western thought, it is in our opinion futile attempting to understand other cultures rationally. Two examples from other cultures:

Russia

Who would grasp Russia with the mind?
For her no yardstick was created:
Her soul is of a special kind,
By faith alone appreciated.
(Fyodor Ivanovich Tyutchev 1803–1872).[1]

Japan

When a "Gaijin" (literally human from outside) enters Japan, nothing will happen anymore between the 2nd and 10th year.

Of course, we can and must acquire knowledge if we want to successfully communicate with other cultures. This knowledge, however, needs to be based on a profound acceptance of otherness and a high respect for other views and actions. Communicating this rationally would only scratch the surface. Cultures cannot be understood by using checklists and by storing knowledge cognitively onto our own hard disk.

Becoming familiar with cultures is based on building up knowledge, experiences and processing the experiences. This should lead to a positive approach to otherness which then results in positive interaction. When combined with real respect for otherness, it results in expanding one's knowledge and deepening one's understanding of foreign cultures.

This manual is structured as follows:

Chapter 1 serves to introduce you, the reader, to the subject matter of this manual.

Chapter 2 lays the groundwork. We define our understanding of culture and the impact of culture on everyday personal and business life. We define intercultural competence and explain the differences between experience-based, affective teaching and learning in the Orient and compare it to cognitive-rational education in the West. This is in a sense the philosophical basis for the following chapters of the handbook.

Chapter 3 describes ways and means to gain access to other cultures. We explain the key areas to gain competencies with history, geography and climatic conditions forming the basis. It includes the differences in applying and experiencing leadership and explains the differences in viewing and experiencing the world.

[1]https://en.wikipedia.org/wiki/Fyodor_Tyutchev. Last viewed July 8, 2018.

Finally, the influence of education, communication styles and behavior as well as the importance of relationships in an intercultural context are presented.

Chapter 4 throws light on cultures from all over the world: Africa, the Arab and Islamic cultures, China, France, Germany, India, Italy, Israel, Japan, Russia, Spain, the UK and the Spanish speaking world, South America, the USA, as well as some of the smaller countries such as Austria, Belgium, Central and Middle European countries and Switzerland. It deals with the basic cultural differences in family life and education, communication styles, relationship building and above all, how to avoid and resolve conflicts as illustrated in the case studies.

Chapter 5 is a guide on how to study a given culture and put the lessons from this book into day-to-day practice.

Chapter 6: For those involved in an international project at any level, this chapter provides not just the tools for effective cross-cultural project management, but also hints on how to avoid pitfalls and overcome cultural barriers. Case studies serve to elucidate the points.

The BookBackmatter contains CVs of the authors and Coauthors

▶ This manual uses a holistic, intuitive, and experience-based approach to explain the profound complexity of cultures. It attempts to show how understanding and trust can be built, resulting in strong intercultural relationships. It is intended as a source of inspiration, guidance and motivation which each reader is free to interpret for himself or herself.

The handbook does not claim to be an academically scientific work. We are trying to show the diversity and richness of cultures in a simple, accessible way. The aim is to share practical experiences and guidelines to be used by people in international contexts. If the focus on specific cultures tends to black and white portrayals to a certain extent it is because priority has been given to the core values of a given culture for immediate understanding and pragmatic access. As a result, the infinite variety of gray areas and nuances that cultures contain cannot always be done justice to in detail.

The structure and content of the book are based on decades of the authors' experience in international management, intercultural training, intercultural mediation, and handling a variety of intercultural encounters on a professional and personal level. The authors bring a cumulative international business experience of a century to this work. To all those who are open to foreign cultures and willing to recognize and respect the differences we trust that it will provide a source of inspiration.

2 Intercultural Competence as Intuitive Access to Alien Cultures

Summary
This chapter is based on a pragmatic definition of what culture means in general and what intercultural competence means for the individual. We will develop the manual on the following basic premises:

- A culture contains the fundamental values of every society.
- These values are vital to the ways we think and behave.
- Dealing with one's own and others' values decides on success or failure in intercultural cooperation.

We will explain the intuitive and experience-based access to other cultures and why this is a meaningful route to successful international cooperation.

2.1 What Does Culture mean?

The term culture comes from the Latin word "*cultura*". It originally means care of the body, primarily of the mind. According to one of the definitions in cultural anthropology, culture represents the complex of knowledge, beliefs, art, morality, law, customs, and all other skills and traditions that man has acquired as a member of society.

There is no universal term for culture. It can be defined according to one's own experience and personal view. We not only speak of national or a country's culture, but also of corporate culture, food culture, culture of conflict, cultural landscape and so on. In the context of this manual and in simplified terms, culture determines the behavior patterns essential for humans to make living together possible.

P. M. Haller et al., *Bridging Cultural Barriers*, Management for Professionals,
https://doi.org/10.1007/978-3-030-17130-8_2

Just as no two individuals are the same, no culture is the same as another. Besides, every culture is composed of innumerable subcultures—regional, tribal, and linguistic cultures, some of whom face difficulties as minorities.

2.1.1 Maslow's Teachings and Interculturalism

American psychologist Abraham Maslow uses a pyramid to depict five tiers of human needs. The basic message of this model is that lower-level needs must be satisfied before the upper-level needs become relevant (Fig. 2.1).

Especially in the Western world, but also i.e. in Saudi Arabia or the Emirates there are generally no deficits at the first stage of physical needs, such as food and drink. Similarly, the second and third stages of the pyramid, i.e. the safety needs, such as protection against danger or job security, and social needs, with the desire for good relationships with colleagues are often a given. However, whenever job security or political conditions become disrupted, the basic needs gain in salience.

Generally, people in individualistic Western cultures focus on their ego needs and self-actualisation, i.e. fulfillment of personal goals such as professional achievement and a corresponding status.

From a different perspective, we may also apply the first two levels of bodily needs and security to our inner selves. We need a sense of basic security to be able to act and to advance in our lives. This also includes the feeling of being safely embedded in our own culture, giving us thus security and clarity to act in culturally appropriate manner.

However, as soon as we find ourselves in another culture or deal with colleagues or people from an alien culture, we may even be thrown back to the basic needs of the first level:

– Eating or drinking may become problematic, affecting your physical well-being. Think of the pronounced drinking sprees in China or Eastern Europe or the after-work dinners in Asia taking up your free time.

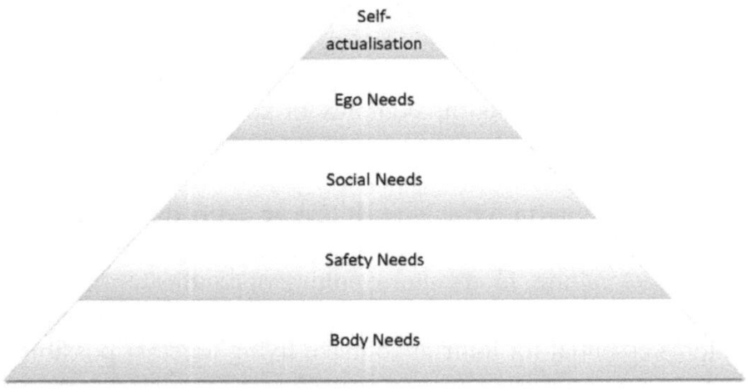

Fig. 2.1 Simplified illustration of Maslow's hierarchy of needs

– Your sense of security may also be affected because you simply do not understand the culture and its people. It may result in a feeling of being lost. This will influence your behavior, your real or perceived social integration as well as mutual acceptance.

2.2 A Generally Understandable Definition of Culture for Our Work

It is usually difficult to define a culture without falling back on stereotypes and clichés. However, to understand cultures in a direct and pragmatic way, we need a pragmatic understanding and a practice-oriented definition of culture.

The simplest and most pragmatic way may be to understand culture as the **intrinsic values of a society**, acquired through socialization and education.

They are the codes and rituals that govern our behavior and coexistence in a given society. They are applied intuitively and instinctively by the members of a cultural group and make living together possible in the first place.

Seen in the short and medium term, the **core or inner values of a culture remain unchanged and stable over decades, even centuries**. Changes take place over longer periods, often several generations or even centuries. Questioning or violating core values may result in adverse reactions.

2.2.1 Core Values and Lifestyles

When we speak of changing cultures, we ultimately refer only to the superficial layer of a culture, the outer, visible values, also called lifestyles.

An oft-heard comment is that cultures are changing. Americanization is often the buzzword to prove that cultures are becoming increasingly alike and aligning globally. That this is not the case is illustrated by the following examples of core values in China, Germany and Central and Eastern Europe:

– China has undergone rapid development within one generation. The lifestyles of many Chinese have changed and become westernized. From this we might conclude that the Chinese will adopt Western values. However, just the opposite is the case. China is returning to its Confucian roots, which the Cultural Revolution under Mao was not able to destroy. Confucian centers to teach this doctrine are being set up worldwide.
– The lifestyle in Germany has changed dramatically within two generations. Nonetheless, Germans recognize their fellow citizens immediately, for example, not only by their language but also by their behavior, the pursuit of perfection or directness of communication.
– We find similar examples in the countries of Central and Eastern Europe whose lifestyles have changed dramatically in the last 30 years after the fall of the Iron Curtain. The core values in Russia, Poland and Czech Republic, for example,

have not changed much for example, respect for elders, courtesy towards women, the respect for the boss, etc. (see Sect. 4.7.1 "*Culturally Defining Elements*").

Thus, we must differentiate between lifestyles on the one hand, and core values of a culture on the other. Lifestyles change extremely quickly, as shown in the examples above. Core values, i.e. the innermost values, on the other hand, do not change in the short term as they are what bind individual members into a community. If these cultural values are called into question or face external pressure, escalation or even civil wars may result.

2.3 Working with National Cultures to Reduce Complexity

In this manual, we work with national cultures. For example, we speak of the USA, Mexico, China, or Germans, Italians, Russians, etc.

It goes without saying this is a highly simplified view. There is no such thing per se as the British, the French in themselves. This simplified view is what allows us to delineate the differences between cultures, create conceptual models and thus reduce complexity. Social reality, however, is infinitely more multi-layered.

2.4 What Does Intercultural Competence Mean?

We will be working with a pragmatic, self-created definition which has proved to be successful. Intercultural competence is the ability to

- approach and deal positively with other cultures,
- respect differences
- act according to one's cultural standards in a given situation, be culturally appropriate without going contrary to one's own cultural beliefs
- recognize and understand one's own and the others' values, and manage the differences
- manage and resolve ambiguous situations,
- actively seek contact with other cultures
- avoid mental blocks and to maintain our ability to act.

Intercultural competence is founded on:

- an open value system, despite strong identification with one's own values,
- curiosity and openness for the new and the unknown,
- the ability to compare own attitudes with other cultures, to question, to look behind the scenes and to adjust the personal settings as needed.

To conclude, the success of one's intercultural competence is based on a high frustration tolerance and the ability to deal with ambivalent situations. These personal aptitudes and abilities are in high demand in an intercultural context.

Ultimately, intercultural competence is reflected on a daily basis in international activities—for example, in a culturally adapted style of leadership, a rethinking of one's own behavior and the appropriate use of language. The starting point is social competence in our own culture. A person without social competence in his/her national context will certainly have a very difficult time in cross cultural encounters.

2.5 The Effect of Intercultural Differences in Communication and Negotiation

When faced with an unfamiliar situation or action, our own values system is generally used as a yardstick. This often sets off snap judgements leading to valuations such as right and wrong, good or bad. Such stereotypes cause suspicion and prevent trustful relationships.

On the other hand, stereotyping can have a relieving and helpful function in intercultural encounters. When difficult situations arise, stereotyping help us to rationalize and account for a cultural situation or misunderstanding. The negative consequence of stereotyping is that the focus is on divergence of cultures, not convergence.

The question is, how do we deal with these stereotypes? There is a natural desire to have a cross-cultural checklist at hand that we can store in our memory. At the same time, this may be the first step to disaster as no two situations are exactly alike. It inhibits spontaneity and may end in a complete misinterpretation of the situation.

We would like to indicate a different path, that of accessing unknown cultures by using personal intercultural knowledge and experience. This is what we term affective learning.

2.6 From Knowledge-Based to Affective, Experience-Based Teaching and Learning

2.6.1 Two Teaching and Learning Methods

2.6.1.1 Knowledge Orientated Learning

Means acquiring knowledge that is related to relationships based on logic and causality. These include learning methods and systems based on structuring, objectivity, rationality, memorization and reproduction of the subject matter, as is customary in the Western world.

2.6.1.2 Affective, Experience-Orientated Learning

Focusses on knowledge acquired in socialization, the experiences in dealing with own values and the emotions associated with them. It relates to the rethinking of one's own and other value systems. It is social learning by means of emotional intelligence and intuition. It leads to changed attitudes towards one's own values. Experience-based learning goes beyond knowledge and understanding and involves the complex relationships of human personality development.

By analyzing these two teaching methods we will show that learning will always be a highly complex and holistic process which encompasses all aspects of learning. We believe that experiential learning is the key to our socialization as humans. We are convinced that this applies particularly to intercultural learning.

When seeking access to other countries, we must achieve a positive attitude towards their culture. Respect as an attitude toward difference is much more than primary acceptance and tolerance, which is rationally driven by the motto "*I accept you because I have to*". This attitude not only requires sufficient knowledge of the other culture, but first and foremost the ability and motivation to openly deal with difference.

2.6.2 What Does This Mean for the Structure of This Book?

Based on our experience we believe that learning processes are particularly effective when

- the contents are internalized and available for individual interpretation and adaptation.
- the information transmitted is perceived as authentic and worthy of imitation
- free choice exists
- one's own experiences can be integrated into it.

For all these reasons, the content and structure of this handbook are based on experiences. It exists from and through the experiences that we, the authors, can bring in from our intercultural background, professional and our personal experiences.

In principle, this manual is a juxtaposition of narratives of real stories from our experiences in international management, as facilitators and coaches—covering a broad intercultural diversity. It exemplifies how each culturally related way to think and act can be better understood and thus create a neutral and unbiased access to people from other cultures.

As a reader, you will review the content critically and test it for yourself. Only what you accept and assume for yourself can be effectively put into action later and implemented effectively when you meet other cultures.

2.6.3 Internal Attitude as Intuitive and Emotional Access to Other Cultures

2.6.3.1 Two Views of Africa

Our own perspective has consequences for access to another culture. As an illustration, let us take two examples: Reports on Africa from the journalist Peter Scholl-Latour and from a Project Manager who was in Tanzania:

View of Peter Scholl Latour

Peter Scholl-Latour,[1] one of the greatest authorities on other cultures among German journalists, wrote the following in the foreword—*Avant-Propos*—to his book "*African Dirge*" ("Afrikanische Totenklage"):

"*The question of globalization of course also arises in the Black Continent today. As far as technical and communicative processes go, the Africans of our day have almost the same number of mobile phones, internet and e-mail as we do. The triumphantly announced globalization of our Western ways of life, however, is not taking place. There are not even three states in Africa that match with our idea of democracy and freedom of expression.*"

The "Frankfurter Allgemeine Zeitung" is cited on the back cover of the book as saying: "*Genocide in Rwanda, famine in Ethiopia, diamond war in Sierra Leone—the whole of black Africa is in danger of drowning in violence and chaos. Peter Scholl-Latour draws a depressing picture of misery, murder and predatory capitalism relentlessly and forcefully, and investigates the causes of this devastating development on the ground*".

Experience Report by a Project Leader in Africa

A different view of Africa is projected by Peter Krötz'[2] of SES (Senior Expert Services) on the occasion of his farewell speech as manager of a project for the water supply of Iruwasa in Tanzania:

"*What experiences I gained here*:

1. *Time, having time, no stress, let time pass... what struck me first, later ... weeks later I found this behavior as relaxing. I appreciate it today.*
2. *Never experienced a company with so many people laughing. Especially laughing and working. I assume, you have the time—and not the clock as we do—you have time and freedom to laugh ... and when you laugh, then you touch ...*
3. *... you touch, touch with a lot of fun the other person. It's a gesture of friendship, in that moment of laughing, you are touching a friend. For me, each time you touched my soul.*

[1]Scholl-Latour (2003, p. 15).

[2]Peter Krötz, Trainer und Coach—Qualität durch Zusammenarbeit—Memmingerstr. 36. D-72762 Reutlingen, +49(0)7121 29 05 09, Email peterkroetz@t-online.de.

4. *Same . . . when you dance. Music—I like your wonderful music—takes you away . . .there is rhythm and singing, mostly by women.*
5. *There I am: women are your best treasures, African women. I have seen Chinese women, similarly treated in treated in centuries, I saw Vietnamese women, Russian and Cuban women, so I can assure you: the power of your women is overwhelming.*

   On the other hand they give to men, elders like mike, the feeling: I honor you. That exactly is the way men like to live . . .
6. *Altogether there is power on the way, there is passion, the elegance to play. You don't act or fulfill like we do. There is enough time to do, to go and time to let go . . . like "singing in the rain". That's life . . . light living.*
7. *Finally, I admire your "art of working": You discuss problems . . . knocking on the door . . . karibu . . . customer comes in . . . karibu . . . telephone rings . . . questions, answers, . . . taking notes ... talking to the customer . . . listening . . . calm and interested and so on. That's multitasking at its best. The best way to handle IT equipment, a mobile, a PC, a customer, a colleague, some problems . . . altogether in the same minute . . . I couldn't do that.*
8. *Those are my lessons learned here, with you . . . Thank you all".*

2.6.4 The Positive Way as the Key to Building Relationships

Both authors cited above see the same continent from different perspectives and both are right. The difference arises from the context in which these reports were created and the purpose they had to accomplish. Peter Scholl-Latour's analytical acuity provides a succinct view of the economic and political issues and is certainly helpful in understanding and addressing these issues.

The opposite approach of Peter Krötz and his affirmative perspective are the keys to coexistence in building relationships with people from other cultures. People in each country know their problems best, be they historical, political or economic. It is therefore unnecessary to rub it in. Because in most cases, they perceive this as a confirmation of their own prejudices and see in it the arrogance of Western cultures and societies.

To create a positive atmosphere in private as well as business contexts requires a positive view and acceptance of another person's life circumstances. This is based on a positive image of humanity and the belief that people want to live together in peace.

2.7 The First Step: Becoming Aware of the Impact of Your Own Culture on Others

To illustrate this awareness, the following paragraphs refer to the "*German*" perspective. People from German culture should be aware of the following:

In German culture, perfection is the foundation of both professional and private life. These include dimensions such as accuracy, detailed planning, punctuality. The aim is to eliminate risks and at the same time, accuracy and methodology provide a sense of security in the working world.

This pursuit of perfection can also become a barrier in international cooperation. Perfection often overtaxes others in their thinking and behavior, because they do not have the same opportunities and conditions available to them. This may even be perceived as an insult, because this perfect behavior is perceived as petty and as a vote of no confidence:

The Environmental Project in Tunisia

A project financed and controlled by Germany in Tunisia had to be stopped. The Tunisian team members refused to accept the German way of working and refused to give their allegiance to the two senior German engineers.

This was a project financed by the German government. The Tunisian reaction shows how deep the rifts, lack of understanding and therefore misunderstandings must have been on either side for the project to be discontinued.

Direct communication to build trust is part of the foundation of German culture. In most other cultures, this directness is often considered blunt and may even be offensive. Americans, for example, often find this style of communication unfriendly as they prefer to package facts more indirectly so as not to give offence. In one seminar with students from the US and Germany, an American student said, "*You are brutally direct*", after the German colleague did not understand or allow the argument of "*directness*".

The following two examples should again illustrate this perception of the German culture by two other cultures:

The French and German Perfection

A Frenchman in an intercultural seminar once told the German participants: "*Do not plan the projects down to the last detail, let us have some leeway!*" This message means that he had the feeling of being patronized and not being perceived as an equal with the Germans in his job.

German Directness and Chinese Indirectness in Communication

A Chinese client's high-ranking delegation, which had come specially from Beijing, stopped appearing at the negotiations during the multi-day negotiation process. The reason was that a German engineer, with the best of intentions, found that a suggestion for a change made by the Chinese side was not feasible and said so openly and directly during the negotiations. This resulted in an extreme loss of face on the Chinese side. The negotiations only continued after the German side presented the Chinese customer with a letter of apology for a minor contractual detail and signed by the President of Board. A direct reference to the incident and apology would have meant another loss of face for the Chinese.

2.8 Recognizing Stereotypes as a Basis for Self-awareness

Cultural conditioning is given to you in childhood and early youth through the socialization into the family and its milieu. These ingrained behaviors and values which are so essential for coexistence in the family and home country can become a barrier when encountering other cultures.

Every human being is programmed in terms of values, clichés and stereotypes about other cultures. He learns this over the years through his socialization and it shapes his way of thinking. In addition to the behaviors and rituals of our own culture, we absorb information about other cultures from early childhood on through direct contact, hearsay, social experience or through the media. This has intensified in our globalized and digitized information world.

Characterized by our own culture, we learn about other cultures and form opinions about them which are predicated on our assumptions. Due to lack of immediate interaction with the other culture, we automatically tend towards generalizations: "*The Chinese are like this* ...", "*The French do that* ...". "*I don't understand why this other culture thinks they are superior* ...".

This results in views of other cultures which often lead to almost insurmountable stereotypes. Certain pigeonholes are created into which one can put away the misunderstood culture and bring it out when deemed necessary.

Prejudices are formed and are activated in situations we don't understand and do not correspond to our own cultural experience. These prejudices and attributions can be very deeply rooted. They are often seen as absolute and in no need of justification, so they are not questioned and don't require evidence because they are doctrines. They are often vigorously defended because their debunking can, in extreme cases, lead to an existential disorientation. An aversion based on prejudice often leads to their being seen as arrogant. To see others as arrogant often means nothing other than "I do not understand these people".

Personal experiences when encountering other cultures may create an uneasy feeling of not being at home. An expatriate, for example, who has had the negative experience abroad of having been denied a promotion or having a dip in his career prospects is likely to attribute this to the foreign culture rather than to his own failure to work through his cross-cultural problems.

How Can we Overcome Communication Barriers?

The art of understanding an alien cultures means admitting different cultural perspectives and not always using one's own culture as standard in a direct comparison. At the same time, it is not advisable to abandon your own culture in an international collaboration for the following reasons:

A total assimilation into another culture would seem implausible to your counterparts and you may lose their respect.

Other cultures often demonstrate absolute loyalty to their own values and society. Betrayal of one's own values does not come across well in most countries. This is most extreme in Asian countries and Islamic civilizations, but it also begins already with our neighbors in France.

The most immediate access to other cultures is gained when you get to know them and constantly deepen your knowledge. This is an ongoing process of learning. Every culture is rich in knowledge and experience and people represent an endless source for learning. We can—and should—ask innumerable questions, thus demonstrating our interest and our curiosity. The required personal characteristics are:

- To be aware and able to reflect on your own stereotypes,
- Trusting other cultures
- Not only accepting the other culture but respecting it.
- Being aware of and dealing with your own vulnerability,

Trying to understand the other's perspective without denying one's own culture is the way to build trust. We see this as walking along a fine line associated with a continuous learning process.

Bibliography

Scholl-Latour, P. (2003). *Afrikanische Totenklage. Der Ausverkauf des schwarzen Kontinents.* München: Goldmann.

Access to Other Cultures: Means, Ways and Possibilities

3

Summary

In this chapter we show possible approaches to other cultures in the world. Respect is first and foremost the foundation of building trust in other cultures. Cultures are shaped by geographic, climatic and historical factors and correspondingly diverse. The chapter summarizes Hofstede's framework for classifying cultures as a tool to reduce complexity when examining different values and worldviews. The spectrum of approaches to communication and communicative behavior are the outcome of these worldviews. So far, we have come to the following conclusion:

It is not possible to grasp other cultures rationally, because it is often beyond our imagination and experience, particularly when it does not seem to correspond to our own learned values.

Experience-based and holistic approach is the key to understanding other cultures.

Understanding other cultures begins with how we view their otherness.

The constructive analysis of our own behavior and developing awareness for our (own) stereotypical thinking will broaden our horizons and give us new access to other cultures.

Respect is the foundation of building trust with other cultures and their members.

Learn to contain your gestures and read other people's body language. People from different worlds may pick up your signals rapidly and recognize whether they are being understood and respected or not.

P. M. Haller et al., *Bridging Cultural Barriers*, Management for Professionals,
https://doi.org/10.1007/978-3-030-17130-8_3

► The fundamental motto of intercultural interactions is Respect for diversity as the crucial basis for building trust and relationships across cultures! Tolerance alone is not enough, because in a certain sense it remains exclusionary, according to the principle: *"It's all right that you are the way you are—but leave me alone"*.

3.1 History, Geographic and Climatic Conditions

Geography and climate continue to influence the creation of values and shape the culture of a given society to this day. Climatically, a north-south disparity worldwide has shaped the indigenous populations of all continents. Due to distinct and prolonged cold spells, the people in northern climates had to continually plan better and provide for longer, which was not necessary in the milder climatic conditions of the south.

The availability of natural resources also shapes the values and foundations of living together. Understanding this enables us to comprehend the attitudes, behaviors and actions of other cultures.

History also has a decisive influence on cultural values as well as on the harmony within and between cultures. All cultures try to learn from historical experiences such as hazards and wars, but also from prosperous phases. They develop behaviors and norms that lead to more security in their commercial co-existence, as the following examples illustrate.

3.1.1 Conditioning Through Historical Experiences

3.1.1.1 Example, Germany: Recent History

The experience of the Second World War and the dictatorship of the Third Reich resulted in Germany's becoming a liberal society, which is enshrined in its Constitution, its basic principles and laws. Every citizen has the right to the free development of his personality.

The goal of German education is that everyone must earn to think and act independently. This shapes coexistence and communication and results in a critical analysis of all areas of life.

The capacity to critically engage is, however, not a new value. The Germans, who are often referred to as a nation of thinkers and poets, have regularly attempted to get to the bottom of things. However, this attribute has acquired a new meaning due to historical experience—it has led to an unprecedented degree of open and critical communication in all aspects of communal life.

3.1.1.2 Example: Belgium, and Switzerland: Foreign and Self-determination with Similar Demographic Structures

Belgium and Switzerland have similar demographic structures, namely Francophone and Germanic language groups that have been living together for centuries.

At the same time, both countries have a different historical experience regarding self-determination and external control.

3.1.1.3 Switzerland

Since its origin in 1291, Switzerland has seen itself as a community in a country that has no natural resources and whose only resources continue to be its people. From the beginning, the basic motivation of the Swiss community has been to rebel against any foreign determination. In the past this was achieved through armed conflicts, and in modern times through neutrality. An experienced political consensus system makes it possible to live peacefully in Europe's most multicultural society of German, French, Italian and Rhaeto-Romanic languages and cultures. This history has been mystified and exploited through the "*Saga of William Tell*" with the Rütli Oath in 1291 to strengthen and cultivate the sense of community and national identity.

3.1.1.4 Belgium

Belgium had a brilliant heyday in the early middle ages, during which Antwerp was the largest port in the world and Charlemagne ruled Europe in nearby Aachen. After its heyday, Belgium was constantly dominated by foreign powers. Spaniards, French, Austrians, and Germans were the politically dominant rulers. Today's Belgian was allocated to Holland at the Congress of Vienna in 1815. Only a military conflict with Holland in the mid-nineteenth century led to late independence.

Nations that are and have been dominated by foreign powers for centuries develop a survival strategy—the family and its network of relationships form the basis of existence. Everything that lies outside this network is, so to speak, enemy territory. The people of these cultures behave circumspectly to state and official agencies but are rather suspicious of it. Their own interest and well-being outweighs the common good and interest.

There is a lack of mutual recognition of the respective languages and cultures in Belgium. Francophone culture, economy and politics dominated Flanders and its population until the beginning of the twentieth century, all of which has left deep scars in mutual perceptions to the present day. As a result, Belgium has never grown into a state with a common identity and economic interests. The Francophone and Flemish cultures have maintained their distance from each other. Linguistic and economic differences between the language cultures lead to constant debates with economically negative consequences for the country as a whole.

Italy and Greece made similar experiences with identical consequences for the State and society. It is no coincidence that the formative term la famiglia arose in Italy; this becomes evident when we consider family clans such as the Agnellis, the Ferreros, the Berlusconis, Guccis, Versaces or in former times, the Medicis.

3.1.2 Topographical and Climatic Conditions

The influence of topographical and economic conditions on the development of cultures goes back even further than the history of a culture.

3.1.2.1 Japan: Extreme Climate and Environmental Conditions

Japan and its population live in an environment characterized by extreme climatic conditions—from the Siberian north to the subtropical islands of the south. The power of nature is omnipresent—typhoons, earthquakes, and landslides are daily dangers that can claim human lives. The recent 2011 earthquake and tsunami in the northern part of the main island, with Fukushima epitomizing the apocalypse, are the latest examples. Under these inhospitable conditions Japanese live in and rely on a strong, collective community and a faith that goes back to the mysticism of prehistoric times.

The third largest economic power in the world in 2018 rankings seeks its foundation in an animistic belief—Shintoism—which enabled it to survive successfully to this day.

The limited living space is another determining factor of Japanese civilization. Only 25% of the land surface is habitable. One hundred and forty million people live closely together on this area. This characterizes social life; privacy is maintained through personal distance–bowing instead of shaking hands. Conflicts are solved indirectly. The basis of communication is intuition, "*gut feeling*".

3.1.2.2 USA: The Vastness of Space and Its Consequences

The first Anglo-Saxon settlers reached the East Coast of America in the mid-sixteenth century. They were employees of English investors who wanted to make profit by selling products like tobacco in the old world. In the years of early US settlement, countless immigrants died of hunger, illness, and exhaustion (see Sect. 4.19.1 "*Culturally Influential Elements*")

The development of the West and of the vast spaces of the United States lasted until the middle of the nineteenth century. Even today, descendants of the first settlers, to whom these experiences and privations were passed on first-hand, live in California. This pioneering spirit lives on and influences the lifestyle and communication of Americans until today.

A pioneering spirit also shapes corporate life in the US. The emphasis on leadership qualities, and the assertiveness of individual competition—all these are core values in daily life and in American business.

The experiences of the pioneering era led to a pragmatism in the American economy; simple concepts, ideas, and presentations prevailed. The corporate time frame is not measured in terms of the next few years, but in terms of the next quarter.

Regarding communication, this leads to direct contact at the first meeting. With the greeting "*Hello, who are you and how are you doing?*" the American seeks to ascertain whether his counterpart is a friend or a foe. This was often necessary for survival in the pioneer era and has been preserved as the Modus Operandum to this day.

3.2 The Hofstede-Indices

Geert Hofstede,[1] a Dutch consultant and former professor at the University of Maastricht has been studying the impact of cultures on corporate life since the 1970s, first on behalf of IBM and then as a researcher.

He established the scientific basis for explaining and elucidating the cultural differences in business life through decades of direct, multi-level investigation. In recent years, these have been complemented by the collaboration with his son Gert Jan Hofstede. Hofstede has always been criticized for findings that were too one-sided, too compartmentalized, or too focused on IBM. In our view, Hofstede's research opens up a window into cultures, but we need to bear in mind that it is meant to be an illustrative framework. A one-sided black-and-white interpretation of the findings would be extremely dangerous. At the same time, we have repeatedly concluded that his research, in particular the topics of power distance, leadership style and individuality, has been very helpful in understanding intercultural settings.

3.2.1 Power Distance and Individuality

Two of Hofstede's dimensions play a particular role in Intercultural Management.

3.2.1.1 Power Distance

Reflects the style of leadership in a given culture and shows if people in a workplace accept hierarchical power or critically oppose it. A high index means that a direct use of power in organizational leadership is accepted, a lower index indicates the opposite.

3.2.1.2 Individuality

Reflects the style of cooperation in the workplace. It shows whether the cooperation in a business is characterized by individuality or by the collective. A high index indicates a strong individual orientation and a low index a strong collective orientation in collaboration.

German corporate culture, for example, is characterized by pronounced individuality and a minimal use of power. The table below shows a selection of countries for these two dimensions (Fig. 3.1):

3.2.1.3 Different Power Distance Indicators Using the Example of Germany and Russia

In German culture, power has a negative connotation. Germans often reject direct influences of power such as external control and interference in one's personal

[1]Geert Hofstede, Gert Jan Hofstede, Michael Minkov, "Cultures and Organizations, Software of the Mind", Third Revised Edition, McGrawHill 2010, ISBN 0-07-166418-1. ©Geert Hofstede B.V. quoted with permission.

Fig. 3.1 Selected power distance and individuality indices by Geert Hofstede (2010)

Country	Power Distance-Index	Individuality-Index
Malaysia / USA *(highest value)*	104	91
Russia	93	39
PR China	80	20
Arab Countries	80	38
Indonesia	78	14
India	77	48
West Africa	77	20
French-speaking Switzerland	70	64
France	68	71
Turkey	66	37
East Africa	64	27
Uruguay	61	36
Spain	57	51
Czech Republic	57	58
Japan	54	46
Italy	50	76
USA	40	91
Great Britain	35	89
Germany	35	67
German-speaking Switzerland	26	69
Austria	11	55
Austria / Guatemala *(Lowest value)*	11	6

sphere. This is related to the thorough examination of the history of the Third Reich and the Second World War.

But power can also be positive if it is applied constructively and for the wellbeing of a community. People in cultures with a high-power distance such as China, Russia or even France tend to perceive this.

Below you will find examples based on practical work with small groups carried out by one of the authors in the context of intercultural training for Germans and Russians with many years of work experience. In culturally mixed groups, participants described the ideal manager and ideal co-workers in each culture.

The idea for this work with small groups emerged from the publication of the article "*An Assessment Center of Russians for Russians*" in the trade journal "*Management Seminars*[2]". The article impressively demonstrates the very different approaches and requirements of executives in Russian and German corporate cultures.

[2]Harrs and Semidelichina (2006).

The Ideal Manager and Employee in Germany

The ideal German executive sees himself primarily as a coach and "*Primus inter pares*" (first among his/her peers). Above all, he/she bears the professional responsibility. He primarily assigns projects to his staff, sets technical goals, and helps with technical problems. He will only intervene in emergencies and relies fully on the professional competence of his employees.

The ideal German Employee is characterized by professional competence. His attitude is proactive, recognizable by accountability and cross-departmental thinking and action. This realization of professional individuality gives him security and acceptance in the professional community.

Communication between the involved parties is open and direct. Tasks are delegated in consensus meetings. Progress and possible problems are identified, discussed openly and solutions sought. An open exchange of information is a must.

The Ideal Executive and Employee in Russia

The ideal Russian manager sees himself as the boss with social responsibility for his staff. He will not assign projects to the employees, but rather, allocate precisely defined work areas for which they are responsible.

The ideal Russian employee is characterized by the correct fulfillment of his duties based on a precise objective for his area of work. The social involvement in the group and his network of relationships—particularly to his boss—give him security. His attitude is reactive, discreet, and modest.

The channels of communication of the participants are informal and indirect. Arrangements are made before the meetings. Reaching a consensus during meetings is not usual, joint meetings serve to announce decisions. Information is a collectable debt.

Summary: What Does All This Mean?

In cultures with high power distance the ideal manager is a kind of "*father*" who supports and protects his "*children*". He defines and sets the framework for his team, demanding unconditional respect at the same time. For this reason, Westerners need to adapt their style of leadership in cultures with a high-power distance, be it France, Spain, Poland, Russia or China, but also India, Brazil, and Arab countries.

Not adapting one's leadership style when conducting a seminar or workshop with people from high-power cultures will lead to failure. A trainer or facilitator will have to modify his role in responding to and meeting the expectations of his participants.

3.2.1.4 Behavior in Practice at Different Power Distances

How does power distances work in practice when people from different cultures meet? The key differences lie in the transmission, communication and review of goals.

Leadership Behavior at High Power Distance

An executive is more likely to assign employee goals for a clearly defined role. The employee is responsible for solving all tasks within his own area—and to prove his professionalism even in crises through unusual solutions.

Communication is verbal and informal, while prior coordination with superiors is essential. One would be ill advised to put forward a new idea at a meeting without prior coordination. The chances of implementation are minimal, unless the manager himself asks for ideas.

One of the authors found himself confronted with this situation at a Franco-German meeting with a French executive—"*Le Patron*". A project was discussed which he knew nothing about. As the discussions on the project went on, the "*Patron*" got increasingly irritated. As a result, he left the workshop in vehement protest and the project was canceled.

Meetings in cultures with a high-power distance serve the purpose of transmitting formal and official communication and decisions. First and foremost, it is personal relationships and oral agreements which are ultimately binding.

Leadership Behavior at Low Power Distance

In these cultures, the work is project-oriented. Supervisors assign projects and tasks with specific goals. Cooperation and thinking are across departmental lines. Hence meetings serve as platforms for the development and coordination of content, interfaces, and schedules. Communication takes place via the official channels, is strongly formalized and especially in Germany, also put down in writing. This form of communication is binding.

Comparing Individuality in Cultures with Different Power Distances; Example France and Germany

Individuality in cultures is experienced and acted out differently, especially in cultures where it is very distinct. According to Hofstede, Germany and France have a very high individuality index. However, there are great differences in the form individualism takes and how power distance and leadership culture are implemented and expressed at the individual level. This is due to different educational goals and systems in both countries.

Germans, for example, often perceive project crises as catastrophes because they had failed to eliminate risks at the outset by planning and countermeasures. For the French, crises in the project are often an opportunity to break out of a routine and to demonstrate professional commitment and competence through the originality of the solution (l'originalité).

In Germany, a crisis is a matter for the supervisor and the team, with the supervisor primarily contributing his technical competence. As a rule, crisis meetings are called, and solutions are sought as a group. Tasks are divided, and deadlines and responsibilities determined. Following the correct procedures in solving a crisis are an essential requirement for a manager.

In France, the onus is on the employee responsible for this sector to come up with a solution as he is professionally best suited for this. The supervisor will usually encourage his staff to do everything to solve the problem. As for the Patron, he will be informed, and will give his colleague a kind of "*carte blanche*" to take unconventional measures, if necessary.

This is illustrated by the case study below, which we were using in seminars:

Case Study: The German Production Manager in France

A German expert has been working as the production manager of a German subsidiary of a packaging manufacturer in Paris for 8 weeks. Shortly before closing time, an employee reports that an order for a major customer cannot be delivered on time.

The reason is that the cutting tool was calibrated incorrectly. The cardboard packaging cannot be put together to fit properly. The employee adds that he has already tried everything, but the supplier is unable to deliver a new cutting tool within the period in question. The customer is not willing to postpone the delivery date because it affects an important market launch and the media are already booked. During this discussion, the production head's office fills with employees who want to know how he will decide.

Question: How Should the German Production Manager in France Behave?

In the over 20 years that we have been doing this exercise, most German participants have suggested sending the curious employees out of the office and to call a meeting with only those involved to find a solution. At the same time, they wanted to be directly involved in the incident and the process by calling the supplier and the customer.

In French management culture, however, the functional responsibility for action remains with the employee. If the supervisor interferes, he will release the professional from his responsibility to some extent, which will be either a frustration or a relief, depending on the situation. As a rule, however, the employee himself will be fully committed to dealing with the crisis.

Solution

In this case the German production manager had asked his co-worker to do everything necessary to solve the problem. As a result, the employee put pressure on the supplier to make the cutting tool a priority. The employee then called his regular contact at the customer's office and described the situation to him. To put the product on the market in time, the deliveries were staggered and the delivery centers that were furthest from the production site were supplied first.

A German participant in one of our seminars, who was working on the above case study, related a similar story. One Friday afternoon, he received a call from a customer in nearby France. This call had been forwarded to him, a sales representative, because the spare parts warehouse had already closed. The German tried to put the Frenchman off until Monday so that everything could be handled procedurally. However, the French customer continued to insist until the German employee took the matter in hand, procured the spare part and immediately brought it to neighboring Alsace so that the weekend shift there could continue to work.

► **"Impossible n'est pas français"** The dictum "*Impossible is not French*"—is sometimes used as a joke and is an incentive to find creative solutions even in difficult situations. In the French business world there is always a solution even in the biggest crises, and he who masters this crisis is then the hero.

Here is another story within this context that occurred in France:

The New Delivery Service

A Frenchman had recently taken over as CEO of a large retail chain which had been left by his predecessor in a desolate state. The figures were in the red and the employees demotivated. The final catastrophe was at the end of the year where 25% of annual sales had to be achieved; the transportation companies went on strike. The solution? The CEO hired dozens of small trucks and sent his staff on tour to deliver the goods to the individual stores in time for the holiday season. The company not only met its sales objectives, but the results were also a motivational boost for the employees and led to a quantum leap in the approval of the new boss.

3.2.2 The Hofstede Indices: Masculinity and Avoidance of Uncertainty

3.2.2.1 Masculinity

This simplified representation of the masculinity index is intended primarily to describe the preference for assertiveness and material success in a given culture and less to address the question of the gender roles. For more information see "*Cultures and Organizations, Software of the Mind*" (Fig. 3.2).

A high masculinity index indicates an organizational form turned towards the outer world whose leaders and employees strive for revenue, recognition, career, and challenge.

A low masculinity index shows a feminine, inward-looking organizational form, whose members primarily strive for joint leadership, close cooperation and job security.

The Swedish Manager in France

A new Swedish manager takes over a plant in France and has all employees come to him for one on one interviews about their professional and personal situations so as to get a full picture of each one. The French employees are disturbed as they

Fig. 3.2 Selected masculinity indices by Geert Hofstede

Country	Masculinity Index
Slovakia *(highest value)*	110
Japan	95
Austria	79
German Switzerland	72
Italy	70
Germany	66
Great Britain	66
PR China	66.
USA	62
French Switzerland	58
Czech Republic	57
India	56
Arab Countries	53
Indonesia	46
West Africa	46
Turkey	45
France	43
Spain	42
East Africa	41
Uruguay	38
Russia	36
Sweden *(lowest value)*	5

perceive this to be too personal and intimate. The reaction from a senior French executive: "*That is not the way it's done over here!*"

In Sweden, on the other hand, the overall social well-being of an employee is a cornerstone of society and company life.

3.2.2.2 Avoidance of Uncertainty

In our simplified and practice-oriented presentation of Hofstede, we understand the avoidance of uncertainty as a benchmark for dealing with stress in unknown and uncertain situations. The causes of stress can be found in basic political and social conditions, but also in the way daily business life is perceived.

A selection of Hofstede's key figures (Fig. 3.3):

With a high uncertainty avoidance ranking stress is seen as a core problem in daily life and a disruptive factor. A low uncertainty avoidance factor implies that stress is accepted as a part of daily life and can be managed.

Fig. 3.3 Selected uncertainty avoidance indices by Geert Hofstede

Country	Uncertainty Avoidance Index
Greece *(highest value)*	112
Uruguay	100
Russia	95
Japan	92
France	86
Spain	86
Turkey	85
Italy	75
Czech Republic	74
Austria	70
French Switzerland	70
Arab Countries	68
Germany	65
German Switzerland	56
West Africa	54
East Africa	52
Indonesia	48
USA	46
India	40
Great Britain	35
PR China	30
Singapore *(lowest value)*	8

Singapore

The city-State is based on a multicultural society governed by an authoritarian regime. Total regulation of all areas of life by the political system leads to less stress.

Germany

The high stress factor is an expression of the working environment: Control by rules, previously agreed on processes, coordination meetings and written communication should add security, but increase the pressure of responsibility on the individual instead.

3.3 "*I*" and "*WE*": Two Opposing Worldviews

Worldviews, in our understanding, comprise the view of how cultures comprehend the world and the way it functions. Two strikingly opposed world views exist: The Western world view of the "I" and the collective world view of the "WE" that is very marked in Asia and in the Arab world, but also in African cultures and to a lesser extent in the Central and Eastern European ones.

The "*I*" and the "*WE*" Are Learning to Surf

This story is about a young Swiss man who gave surfing lessons in Hawaii and taught surfing to people from Western countries and Japan. Classes began with theory and then continued to practical dry exercises. This consisted of a surfboard that rested on springs to mimic the effect of waves and water. Classes were divided into separate cultural groups—Western and Japanese. During the dry exercise, one participant had to stand on the board and try to keep his balance. Almost everyone initially fell off the board several times. The groups reacted completely differently to this:

The **group from the Western cultures**, especially with participants from the USA, enjoyed itself enormously. If someone fell, everyone laughed and there was a lighthearted competition. They cheered one another on. With the "*I*" as the center of focus, everyone reacted spontaneously.

The **Japanese groups** acted as a "*WE*". Each one who stood on the practice board was supported by the others. At the slightest sign of weakness, every last man in the group jumped to his feet, hurried to the board and held on to their colleague until he regained his balance. The "*WE*" of the group always acted in the collective. There was no laughter, because that would have meant loss of face and shame.

This phenomenon was observed by the Swiss surfing instructor over a period of several years, i.e. throughout his professional life as an instructor.

Individualistic and collectivistic behavior grounded in diverging Worldviews are historically learned perspectives of our world whose influence and expression play a fundamental role in the daily coexistence of a community. Therefore, this fundamental perspective is also key to the basic understanding of another culture. In our regular seminars with coaches and participants from China and Eastern Europe, there is consistent agreement with the graph below (Fig. 3.4):

This chart depicts the following worldviews:

The holistic world of the "*WE*", which is very pronounced in Asian and in Islamic cultures, but also to some extent in Eastern and Central Europe.

The malleable and improvable world of the "*I*" especially prevalent in the Western Hemisphere.

3.3.1 The Western Worldview of the "*I*"

The Western perspective that the world is malleable and can be improved is the result of the Age of Enlightenment in the eighteenth century, the French Revolution and the development of the individual. We pursue the ideal of creating a perfect world

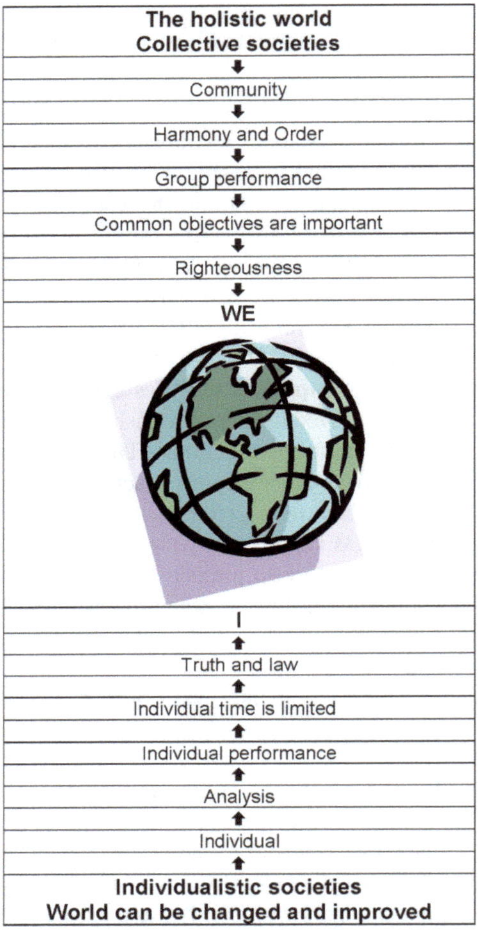

Fig. 3.4 Worldviews of collective and individualistic societies and cultures

one day. Scientific thinking originated in the Enlightenment and rapid industrial development and progress in business, technology, and education over the last 200 years is its consequence.

In the Western worldview, the individual works above all with analysis and tries to create an ideal synthesis from all the currently available knowledge. The individual works on his own, with a correspondingly finite capacity and time to work, and a set time frame. Truth and a detailed legal foundation are essential for cooperation to be possible.

3.3.2 The Holistic "*WE*" Approach in Asia and Islamic Cultures

In the Asian and Islamic perspective, as well as in parts of Eastern Europe, the world is seen holistically as unchangeable. It takes opposing but complementary forces to create a whole: day and night, man and woman, Yin and Yang, hot and cold, good and evil, etc.

These cultures do not believe in man's ability to dominate nature, because the forces of nature are seen as eternal and immutable. In such a world, the only community that can survive is the one that finds the foundations for a strong cohesion in faith (Islam, for instance) and/or a corresponding lifestyle (Shinto, Buddhism, Daoism, Confucianism). Living in close knit collective communities, often with lifelong bonds, forms the bedrock of this world. The pursuit of harmony is the goal both in personal and in professional life. The group is responsible for an achievement, with individuals integrating into it and contributing to the preservation of harmony. Since the group must constantly strive for a harmonious coexistence, it only requires a minimum of legal control. Framework conditions remain flexible, as circumstances may change. The time factor is subordinate to this societal goal.

3.3.3 Attitudes Towards Life in Japan and in the Western World

The following contribution is based on the work of Swiss journalist and author Lorenz Stucki (1922–1981).[3] In his book[4] on Japanese society he compares the Japanese attitude towards life to the Western view. The graph below is a synthesis of his observations. It shows a vertical line with a zero in the middle and positive or negative attitudes towards life in the West and in Japan at both ends. The horizontal line is a hypothetical lifeline starting in infancy and ending with old age (Fig. 3.5):

Western Attitude The core value, the development of the individual, is the gauge to evaluate success or failure in lives. The lifeline starts on the negative side: a newborn child is seen as helpless, needs to grow basically into the society all by itself. Self-determination is the key word even at the youngest age. Competition starts from the beginning with being best at school and thereafter striving for the highest possible leadership position. The higher the position, the more positive is the perceived vision which results in respect and financial well-being. With age, the view turns below the zero line, the individual is less and less needed for the economic process. He is seen as ineffective and unproductive, pitiable and even helpless.

---

[3]https://www.worldcat.org/identities/lccn-n50077810/. Last viewed 26.11.18.

[4]Stucki Lorenz, Japans Herzen denken anders—Die alternative Art modern zu sein: Was wir von der einzigen nicht-westlichen Industriegesellschaft lernen können, 1st edition 1978, Scherz.

English translation: "*Japanese hearts think differently—the alternative to be modern: What we may learn from the only non-Western industrial society*".

Stucki Lorenz, Die Kunst mit dem Herzen zu denken. Japan oder das Geheimnis der 'anderen Lebensart', 2nd edition 1990, Scherz, München.

English translation: "*The Art of thinking with the heart. Japan or the Secret of the Other way of Living*"

Author's note: The title had to be changed posthumously, because of an official Japanese intervention stating that "Japanese hearts would not think differently from western hearts", which is of course true. But I dare say that Lorenz Stucki meant it figuratively.

Fig. 3.5 Attitude towards life in Japan and the West (model)

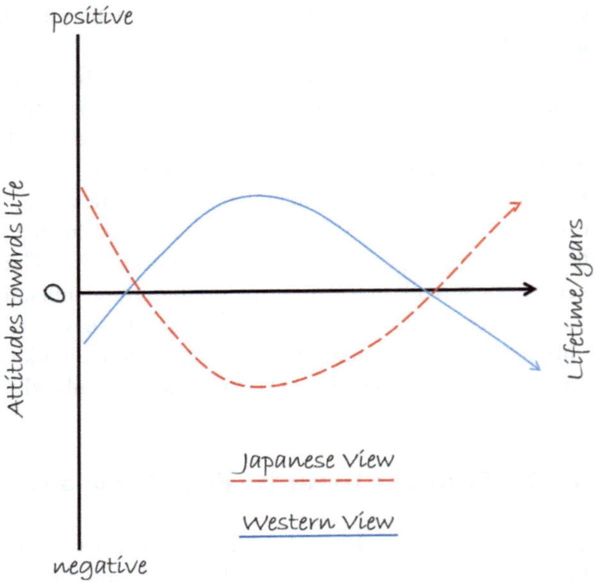

Japanese Attitude The core value is harmony, and the basic order in society is defined by the order of Confucius (see also Sect. 4.8.2, The Confucian Order): A child is born, welcomed as a continuation of the family line, the Japanese culture and nation and their values. Until the age of 6, he or she is considered young, with too little experience in life, and is permitted to enjoy freedom and indulgence. Soon after that, the reality of integrating into a collectivist society starts to kick in and the curve turns negative. A child has the obligation to demonstrate the highest filial respect towards his or her parents and to Japanese society. Parents aim to get their children admitted into the highest-ranked universities in Japan, e.g. "*Todai*" (Tokyo University) which guarantees a top job in industry or government, thus gaining respect for the whole family. After studies, the curve drops even lower with the pressures of working life. This means group pressure—the constant need to maintain harmony and to be an integrated part of a group, a company and society, and to earn respect. The higher the position, the higher the pressure becomes. With increasing age, the curve turns positive as age is accorded respect, honor and a social role as counselor to children and grandchildren.

Again, each of the societies has its advantages and disadvantages: The author's ideal would have been to be born into an individualistic society and finish life in a collectivistic society. However, it is virtually impossible for us Westerners to truly integrate into a collectivistic society or to understand and accept it.

A somewhat macabre way to show the differences between the two societies are suicides amongst teens.[5] A teen in the Western world may probably commit suicide because of isolation, missing love. A Japanese teen may most likely commit suicide because of failing at school and not fulfilling the expectations and obligation versus their parents. Teens committing suicide are one of the cruelest things in life. Yet it happens in both societies, but for different reasons.

3.3.4 The Influence of "WE" and "I" in Business

The differences between the worldviews of the "*WE*" and the "*I*" are often at the heart of intercultural conflicts. One typical example would be that of a trainer conducting a training in China or Japan who expects to receive immediate responses from participants. Contrary to expectation, he will probably be confronted with silence. If he is insistent and demands feedback, or even criticizes the behavior of the participants, he will suffer a loss of face that could cast doubts on the quality and success of the training. The same is often the case with projects. The persistence of a Western project manager if he has not yet received the expected feedback is a typical example. As he is unaware of the fact that his colleague needs the group's consent first, he may increase the pressure on him and thus make his counterpart in Asia or the Arab world withdraw from all further communication.

3.3.5 Which Worldview Is Better?

In our international activities as trainers, moderators and consultants, we continuously come across the world view collision of the "*I*" and the "*WE*". We would even go so far as to say that this conflict per se is often a major cause of intercultural misunderstandings. Our strongly individualistic conditioning through education and society in the West often thwarts the understanding and acceptance of the other world and its "*WE*" approach to life. In our view, neither world is better than the other. Each has its strengths and weaknesses in business contexts.

1. The Western worldview leads to technical innovations because an individual, the "*I*", can question things, and is able to test and prove feasibility on his own.
2. In "*WE*" cultures with a collectivist worldview, this approach would generally be unacceptable. The individual would run the risk of being marginalized or even expelled for disloyalty.

As the economic development of the East Asian countries shows us, their strength lies in group work, the "*WE*", and hence more in the user-oriented application of technical innovations. A group can deal with details more thoroughly than an

[5]https://www.ncbi.nlm.nih.gov/pmc/articles/PMC3367275/. Last viewed 14.11.18.

individual. This results in customer-oriented products of higher manufacturing quality; examples illustrating this are the adaptive services of Sony or Toyota, who achieved market leadership in their segments through improved and customer-oriented products in the 1970s and 1980s—products that struck fear into the hearts of their automotive and entertainment electronics rivals, not only in America, but also in Europe. China's rapid economic development is in itself a collective process of enormous proportions.

Interestingly, Japanese companies contribute their sense of "*WE*" and sense of solidarity with the local population when establishing branches abroad. The examples below of the Mission Statements from American Toyota and Ford from "*The Toyota Way*"[6]clearly reflect the two worldviews.

Mission: Toyota Motor Manufacturing North America

1. As an American company, Toyota Motor Manufacturing North America aims to contribute to the economic growth of the local community and the United States.
2. As an independent company, Toyota Motor Manufacturing North America aims to contribute to the stability and well-being of its employees.
3. As a Toyota Corporate Group company, Toyota Motor Manufacturing North America aims to contribute to Toyota's overall growth by generating customer value.

Mission: Ford Motor Company

1. Ford is the global leader in automobiles and related products and services, as well as in newer industries such as aerospace, communications and financial services.
2. Our mission is to continuously improve our products and services in order to meet the needs of our customers and to enable us to provide our shareholders—the owners of our company—with a reasonable return.

[6]Liker (2004).

3.3.6 True or Right?

Another barrier between the world of the "*I*" and the "*WE*" is the clear-cut notion of justice that we in the Western world deploy for virtually every situation.

In the world of "*I*", we only distinguish between what is right and its polar opposite, wrong. Our attitude to situations is "*either-or*".

"*WE*" cultures evaluate what is right in a given situation. In a community, a crisis must be borne by all and the solutions are sought jointly. The attitude is "*this as well as that*". The reasons for it are to be found in historical experiences that have shown that there may be pragmatic, and momentarily valid solutions.

No. 16 of the approximately 2000-year-old Chinese stratagems[7] "*If you want to catch something you have to first let it go*" is an impressive example in dealing with captured enemies. Mao used it during the civil war, during which he treated prisoners differently depending on whether their behavior was open or opposed to his policies. The former were retrained and then sent to enemy territory to promote Mao. From the Western point of view, prisoners usually remain enemies and are interned as such in a camp.

We will provide more detailed information and many examples in the chapters, Sect. 4.8 China and Sect. 4.13 Japan.

3.3.7 Communication and Cooperation in "*WE*" Cultures Using the Example of Asia

The one-to-one or face-to-face communication we know in Western business life is virtually impossible in a cooperation with "*WE*" cultures.

The "*WE*" of the holistic world can only give an answer once it has the approval of the group and the topic has been discussed until finally everyone agreed. No amount of Western insistence and urgency will help with that, because this is perceived as presumptuous and arrogant. It could even prompt a distressed response to save face, which we, in turn, perceive as a lie.

Adjusting our Western communication will help to prevent frustration and collaborative blunders. All available information should be provided in advance when collaborating with Japan, China, Korea or other Asian cultures, as well as with Arab and, to some degree, with Eastern European countries. This allows the group to discuss the subject in detail. Disclosing information in bits and pieces automatically leads to disappointment and an extension of the planning and project times. In addition, it indicates distrust. That is why more confidence should be shown in the partners from other cultures—admittedly difficult when transparency is lacking due to unfamiliarity with the language and with internal processes.

[7]http://de.wikipedia.org/wiki/36_Strategeme#Den_Tiger_vom_Berg_in_die_Ebene_locken. Last viewed 23.11.2012

Planning with East Asians is lengthier, not only because of the time difference, but primarily because of internal coordination processes. That explains why key milestones, such as start of production, product completion, market launch, etc. of a project, must be determined and planned in detail on site, for example in Japan.

The recipe for success is to wait for information to be delivered from Asia. Insisting does not help, and it is additionally viewed as immature or arrogant. Showing patience and trust indicates maturity. The Sect. 3.4.3 "*Showing a Face and Preserving it …*" gives further tips and an extreme example of the negative consequences of inappropriate pressure on the Japanese partner.

Meetings serve to get acquainted, announce, or exchange information and decisions. Every culture has its own specific rituals and processes for meetings. Knowing them and being prepared for them is one of the basic factors for success (see also Chap. 4 with the sector dealing with "*Communication and Cooperation*").

3.4 Relationship Quality and Relationship Networks

Relationships are essential across the globe. At the same time, there are marked differences in the significance of relationships in business as well as in private life.

In Germany, for example, the phrase "*Dienst ist Dienst und Schnaps ist Schnaps*" ("*work is work and schnaps is schnaps*") means that business and private life are kept separate. But even in a European environment, the French, the Czechs or even the Swiss are much more relational as can be seen in the following chart (Fig. 3.6).

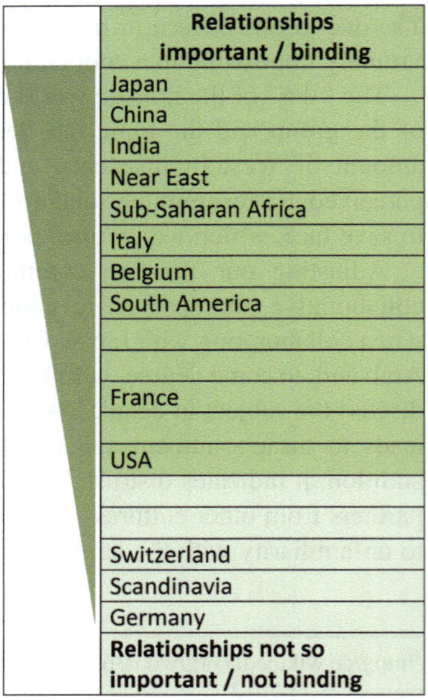

Fig. 3.6 Exemplary illustrations of significance of relationships in different cultures. How important are relations in your culture?

In individualistic cultures with low power distances worldwide, the relationship networks are relatively loose and based on personal affinity, whereas work and private life are kept more separate.

In collectivist cultures with high-power distance, relationships are an existential necessity, linking business to personal life and vice versa. In business life they form the basis for reputation and collective respect. Agreements are based on relationships, i.e. trust. In Asia, Western jurisprudence became necessary only when trade with the West was established. In Japan, for example, deals are still sealed with a handshake.

Swiss Business with Japan

A medium sized Swiss entrepreneur has two business relationships with Japan. In one case, he works without a contractual basis, that is the agreement has been made with a handshake and has resulted in a successful business relationship. In the second case, he began contract negotiations with the potential Japanese partner which has not led to a business relationship even after a year.

Relationship Networks in France and Japan

It is said that political and commercial France is controlled by 500 graduates of the major universities ("*Les Grandes Écoles*"). Obtaining a place in one of these universities requires total commitment and can be a substantial burden for students and their families. However, once students have been admitted to such an institution, they will become part of the country's future economic and political elite. As a rule, a student will receive an assistant position in a company or in public administration, with an alumnus as a supervisor. These relationships last a lifetime. For example, a ministerial official from a German Ministry of Economic Affairs visited Paris once and observed that his French colleague did not reach for the ministry's telephone list during a consultation, but rather to the telephone list of former alumni of the ENA ("*École Nationale de l'Administration*"). The ENA is the elite university for civil servants founded by Charles de Gaulle.

Japan's higher education system is similar to that of France. A "*Todai*", a graduate of Tokyo University, Japan's most prestigious elite academy, also has prospects for top jobs in industry and administration. The path to admission for study is at least as stony and difficult as it is in France.

Guanxi in China

Guanxi stands for networks of relationships and their importance for living successfully in China.

Figure 3.7 shows an overview of such a network in China as an existential platform for Chinese, a girl or woman by the name of Yan Chen also demonstrates the difficulty of gaining access to these networks, let alone of

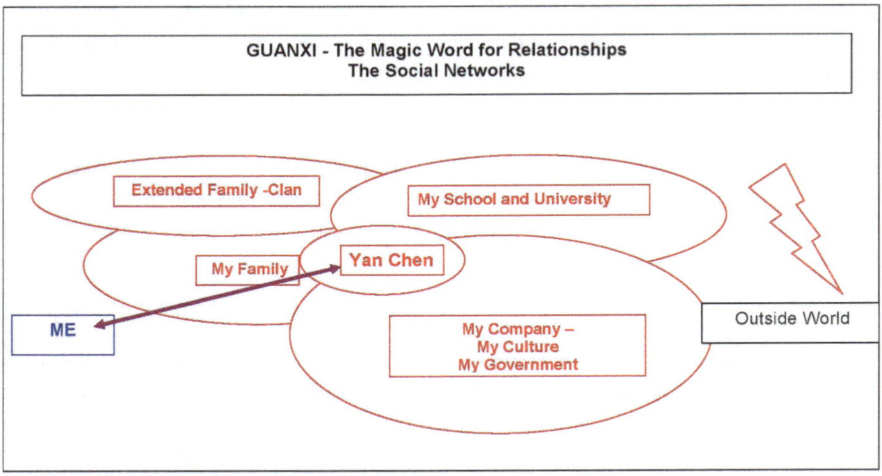

Fig. 3.7 Guanxi, the network of relationships as a basis for livelihood in China

feeling at home there. Everyone within this network of relationships abides by the appropriate forms and rituals to ensure harmony, today's version of the Confucian principle, according to which the family—the smallest cell in society—must be aware of members' rights and obligations.

The outside world, on the other hand, is perceived as hostile. The recent experiences of war, famine, and natural catastrophes in the second half of the twentieth century that killed 60 million people have painfully shown the Chinese that the family must struggle to survive.

3.4.1 The Concept of Time

In their heyday the ancient Greeks had two kings for time: Chronos and Kairos

1. Chronos is the god of timekeeping with the hourglass and the scythe, the hourglass for the quantitative handling of time and the scythe as a reminder of finiteness of life.
2. Kairos stands for the qualitative handling of time, the capture of the right moment. His head is shaved at the front and covered with a braid at the back to pull himself out of the clamp. In one hand he has a balance to weigh the right point in time, and in the other, a knife to cut unnecessary ties.

The Western cultures almost only do business on Chronos principles. The American saying "*Time is money*" is proverbial. Time is experienced as a limited commodity and leads to a race against time, with correspondingly negative consequences for the quality of the product and human health.

The Asian, Eastern European and Arab cultures still act on the principle of Kairos. It is still an integral part of life and of community with time to talk, exchange views, build and deepen relationships, and to strengthen cohesion in society.

This has an influence on the handling of time, i.e. private and business life are not isolated in these societies but experienced holistically. Establishing and maintaining relationships requires a more qualitative understanding of time.

3.4.2 Community Spirit and Common Good

What is community spirit and how is it lived and experienced in different cultures?

In Western cultures it is considered "*horse sense*" and stands for the common interests of a society, which are often positioned as the antithesis of individual or group interests. The common good in our social system depends on the interests and goals of those who invoke a particular interpretation. Community spirit and the greater good are based on ideals for which we constantly strive, but which are rarely realized. Conflicts in politics, economics and personal interaction are omnipresent.

In the Asian world, in China and Japan for example, public spirit is understood as a sense of family with its traditional value worlds and its identification with the state and culture of the country. Those who have experience in China are often amazed at the recklessness and assertiveness of Chinese people outside of the family and their home, in sharp contrast to the aspiration of harmony within the family and the circle of friends:

- Outside of his own home, a Chinese will often assert himself ruthlessly push his way to get to a counter or a buffet.
- Inside the house and in the context of his social environment, harmony and strict rituals are aspired to in dealings with others.
- Identification with the State and Chinese culture is consistent among the Chinese, unlike the image depicted by the Western media.

3.4.3 Showing a Face and Preserving It as the Basis of Relationships in WE Cultures

Living in "*WE*" communities (see Sect. 3.3 "*I*" *and* "*WE*") in which the individual moves in the same circles and within a set network of relationships throughout life is the foundation of harmonious coexistence.

Face is also important in the Western world. For us, Face stands for personal reputation. In the Western world we live within a mobile and loose network of relationships. We therefore find it hard to imagine that a loss of face in a "*WE*" society will have serious negative consequences for the psyche of the person concerned, especially if he is ostracized by the community. There are two well-known Asian terms that express what may happen with extreme loss of face in these cultures. One is the Japanese term Hara-kiri, i.e. suicide through slitting open the abdomen; the other is Amok (furious, raging) In Indonesia ostracism often leads to a short-circuit reaction with fatal consequences.

In business with collectivist societies the person concerned will do anything to avoid a loss of face because it is a loss of face for the group. This, in turn, is a core problem in the communication between "*I*" and "*We*" cultures. In direct conversations, members of a (Western) "*I*" culture often assume that the other person in the "*WE*" world can decide immediately on acknowledging a mistake.

People in "*WE*" cultures need time to coordinate. A decision must be borne by the entire team and the supervisor. Strategies for conflicts with Western partners:

(a) Taking the easiest way out, going silent and just not answering
(b) Moving the conflict on to a different managerial level or changing the topic.
(c) Simply smiling
(d) Ignoring the conflict.

More rarely a conflict will escalate when there is no way out. Once that has happened, it is difficult to retrieve the situation. It is therefore necessary to sense a possible loss of face in advance and prevent it.

Saving Face: The German Controller and His Japanese Colleague

The story of a controller in Germany, a member of the board, with his Japanese counterparts shows just how extreme such reactions can be. The German needed the budget figures for an IPO in Europe from his Japanese counterpart. He first wrote a few e-mails asking for the information, but only received evasive replies. After a few emails, the Japanese colleague made himself scarce and did not reply at all. As the deadline drew nearer, the German became nervous and called several times. The Japanese colleague confirmed that he and his team needed more time to go over the numbers. The German colleague ran out of patience and in an all-important phone call, he put massive pressure on his Japanese counterparts until he finally got the numbers he demanded.

The German controller got the numbers on the basis of which the stock exchange prospectus was created, and the IPO was carried out. A week after the phone call, his Japanese colleague called him and corrected the numbers downward by 50%.

What Happened?

The Japanese needed a white lie to get out of the situation. The solution would have been to exercise patience and trust the partner in the collectivist culture by giving time to accomplish his task.

3.4.4 Admit Guilt or Accept Shame?

Pinpointing and acknowledging a mistake or a lapse evokes different reactions in individualist and collectivist cultures.

3.4.4.1 Guilt in the Western World

In the Western world, an individual is accountable for a mistake. As a rule, this person will be careful to preserve his personal image, deny the mistake and defend himself. Personal behavior is measured primarily by one's own goals and ideals. Admitted misconduct results in feelings of guilt and the loss of self-worth, dignity and pride.

3.4.4.2 Shame in the Collective World

In collectivist "*WE*" cultures the group is accountable for a mistake. The group will decide situationally and relationally whether to admit the mistake or not.

The crucial point is whether the group member recognizes his mistake, has been loyal and identified with the group, or has "*dishonored*" the group. One possible consequence is that the group shares responsibility for the mistake as a collective. If this is not the case, the guilty group member is expelled.[8]

3.4.4.3 Self-determination and Influence of Outside Sources, Scope of Social Control

Something we struggle with in the Western world is accepting the concept of heteronomy (influence from an outside source) in hierarchical and collectivist cultures and organizations. It is diametrically opposed to our Western thinking and behavior. If we look at the newspaper, for example, we see reports of an increasing abuse of power in China. We do not want to question the truth of this. However, stereotypical discussions which automatically denigrate the entire culture in a certain political system are to be avoided. Abuse of power, for example human rights violations, exists in all political and economic systems, including our democracies.

The Western World's preconceived notion that cultures with centralized power structures and collectivist systems act unfairly per se or misuse power is one of the major obstacles to building value-free relationships.

Heteronomy is perceived differently across the world. It is omnipresent in all collectivist cultures. People in the Western world are partially traumatized by foreign determination and reject it. For people in collectivist cultures, heteronomy and thus the benevolence of a recognized power person is part of a secure life. It is usually only questioned or attacked when welfare is no longer provided, as the Arab Spring has shown.

8 Augsburger (1992).

Social Control Amongst Young People of Turkish and Arabic Descent in Germany

One of the authors conducted seminars in Berlin-Kreuzberg in 2011 and 2012 with city libraries' employees. His assignment was, among others, to give assistance to the librarians in dealing with young people of Turkish and Arabic descent. Social control systems emerged as both the central topic as well as the key to the problem.

In Germany a group is more likely to control itself. This means that the individual participants agree on what the group wants to achieve and how it wants to achieve this. External influence is usually rejected. In a German group, a core will always emerge which determines the topic and the process, and the rest take its lead by aligning themselves to this core. Anyone who does not appreciate this and/or doesn't participate is excluded.

In its cultural environment, a Turkish or Arab group is almost always externally controlled. At home it is the mother, then the father, older brothers and sisters. Outside, they are controlled by aunts and uncles, the Imam or other religious persons of respect, or the head or members of Turkish associations and organizations.

Young people with a Turkish background, for example in Berlin-Kreuzberg, have to navigate these collectivist and individualistic cultures every day. It is often a problem for these boys and girls to orient themselves in both cultures at the same time. An example from the library in an immigrant neighborhood:

During the training, the librarians complained that on school-free afternoons, the Turkish and Arab sixth graders in the reading room were boisterous, unruly and aggressive when called to order. The trainer—one of the authors—went to the library one afternoon to watch the proceedings:

- First, the girls with headscarves came in, sat down nicely at a table, and talked.
- Then the boys came, sat down at the computers, and started to play, argue, and fight.
- Then two boys stood in a corner and start shooting paper balls at the girls.
- The author—an obviously older person with graying hair at the temples
- looked at them until one of the boys looked back at him.
- The young Turk looked away for a few seconds and then checked so see whether the author was still looking. As this was the case, he had a brief discussion with his friend, both stopped and sat down.
- The reason: The coach, an obviously much older man, was to be respected. He also did not reprimand the young Turks but controlled them just by looking at them.

The librarians, on the other hand, tried to appeal to the German or Western control system by appealing to reason to get the situation under control. Young people who have not learned such a form of social control in their education and do not know the system of internal control are immune to it. In our example this led to escalation and mutual frustration.

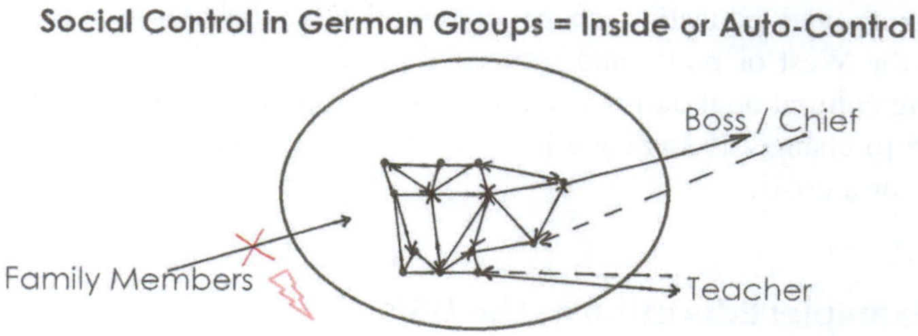

Fig. 3.8 Social control in German groups

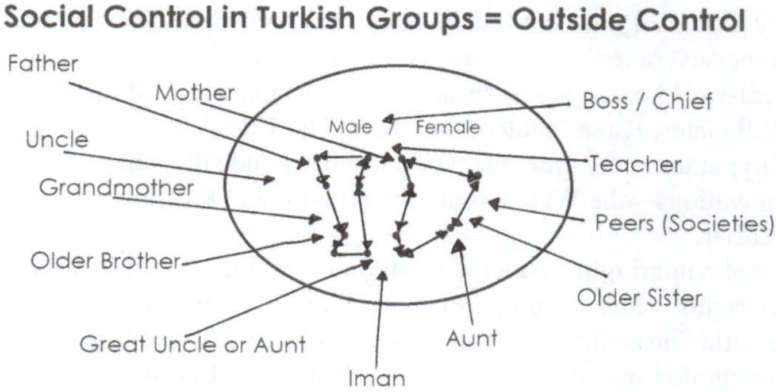

Fig. 3.9 Social control in Turkish groups

The trainer's suggestion was to hold a seminar for boys and girls with a Turkish male and female trainer. The goal would have been to guide the participants to work out the code of conduct for the library by themselves. These rules should be displayed on a large, white wall at the entrance. An additional effect of the seminar would have been to show the young people from Turkish backgrounds what was normally expected in Germany in terms of self-control, responsibility, and self-determination.

The following graphs make the difference between German and Turkish groups even clearer (Figs. 3.8 and 3.9).

3.5 Education and Communication Styles

Every culture has its goals and philosophies to educate and integrate people into its community. Anyone born into a culture will not want to or be able to reject or abandon his culture during his or her lifetime.

The goals pursued by each culture during the process of upbringing is a point of interest. As a rule, the aim in both democratic and hierarchical leadership systems is to create a national and cultural identity based on values.

Upbringing and education shape communicative behavior—either open and critical in the West or polite and respectful in Asia. This is a stumbling block to overcoming cultural boundaries as these learned communication patterns are almost impossible to change. If someone is forced to do so, it can end in a stalemate, an escalation, or a crisis.

3.5.1 Example: Education in the USA

In the US, children are treated as adults from an early age—a necessity in the pioneer days, when all hands were needed for survival. There is a belief in the land of opportunity that everyone can attain happiness, prosperity, and prestige through dedication, perseverance, and positive competition. The rags-to-riches dream is seen in many real-world examples such as John D. Rockefeller, Michael Dell, Hewlett Packard, Bill Gates, Estée Lauder and others. The US is repeatedly criticized for its superficiality; at the same time, the world has been and still is often reinvented there with IT innovations—the Web, e-mail, the GPS Global Positioning System—which make life easier.

During their upbringing American children are equated with adults. They also have equal rights when it comes to individual development. When families and friends are sitting around the table in the US, children usually sit at the table as well. They are integrated into the conversation. In Western Europe, children and adults often sit apart, at the same or at different tables.

Parents are proud when a child displays his or her individuality and character within the context of social manners and norms. Childish behavior is tolerated to an extent that would not be acceptable elsewhere.

For example, one of the authors has friends—a British husband with an American wife, who had a son late in life. At every visit the author noticed that the child almost never sat at the table for a meal. The mother sat down on the floor and fed the child while he was playing—his favorite pastime.

3.5.2 Example: Education in China

Up to the age of 6 years, a child in China is forgiven a great deal because he has not yet reached the age of reason. From the age of six, he is socialized not only by parents but also by grandparents, as both parents often work away from home and cannot devote themselves to him exclusively. However, other members of the family, such as uncles and aunts, nieces and nephews also contribute to his education. On the one hand, this education aims to teach Chinese culture, history, values and morals to children; at the same time, the best possible education also enables them to live a more prosperous life than the previous generations.

A child is therefore committed to obedience and respect towards his parents until the end of his life. The remark of a Chinese colleague, who spent her childhood in Southeast Asia and completed secondary schools in Singapore supports this. She was in her mid-40's and a very successful Chinese businesswoman when she said, "*My mother often irritates me, but I would never dare to contradict her*". A child whose demeanor reflects Chinese customs and morals is the pride of his parents.

3.5.3 Example: Education in Japan

To be a child in Japan means to belong to a children's world. It is a self-contained world that is clearly differentiated from that of adults.

Children have their own language, their own vocabulary. It is particularly interesting that there are Japanese numerals for objects and living things that Japanese children use, and which are clearly different from the language of adults.

The mother is the central figure in a child's upbringing. Fathers are only rarely present for children since the Japanese employee—the "*sarariman*", a Japanese form of the English word salaryman—leaves the house at 6 am and usually returns late in the evening, around 9 or 10 p.m. This is the norm on six, or in higher executive positions even 7, days a week. Regular contact with their children is therefore not viable. It is for this reason that the Confucian understanding of roles is still the basis of living together and probably will not change all that quickly due to economic conditions.

Japanese parents retain their children in their dependency, which, above all, gives children a sense of security and emotional closeness.[9] The inhospitable conditions in which the Japanese live may be the reason for this care. Firstly, only 25% of the territory is habitable and suitable for building. This means limited space in the apartments and houses. It is worth noting at this point that people in a 20 m^2 Japanese living room with one table in the middle and four people sitting in the lotus position have the same feeling of space as in a even larger Western living room filled with furniture. The constant natural hazards (earthquakes, tsunamis, typhoons and landslides) are also factors that explain this close parental care.

The consonants R and L do not exist in the Japanese language. Starting with their own language, it makes it difficult for Japanese to learn foreign languages later, especially English. Although today's foreign language education is often in Western hands in the higher education systems it is difficult for many Japanese to pronounce words with L and R's such as rice or the surname Serrille. The problem is overcome by assigning vowels to these consonants: L is pronounced as "*ERU*" and R as "*ARU*".

This was initially a huge communication hurdle for the surname Haller—the surname was pronounced Hara. The name was regularly misspelt in English as "Harrel" due to the confusion between R and L. This changed only when the author took over the Japanese way of spelling (see also Sect. 4.13.5 Japan communication and conflict resolution).

[9] Lin-Huber (1998, p. 52).

3.5.4 Education in France and Germany: A Comparison

Variances in education are not only between Asia and the West; remarkable differences also exist within the Western world. The following story originates from the experience of an author who was first an expatriate to Paris in France and thereafter to Hamburg in Germany.

His two sons, 2 and 6 years old, were enrolled in French schools, the younger one in kindergarten and the older one in the first grade. During the interview with the director of the primary school, he said, "*Nous allons leur apprendre la discipline française.*" ("We are going to teach them (the children) French discipline"). At the time, the saying surprised the father, because his own thinking—or his own preconceptions—contradicted this claim quite a lot.

In fact, children in France are closely supervised, disciplined and shown their social limits. At the end of a recess a bell rang followed by the class teacher blowing a whistle. Then the children hand to stand in orderly rows of twos, hold hands and go silently into class. The director stood at the entrance and supervised the process. This was in the early 1970s. Today, the children still march in rows of twos into the classroom. A documentary by France 2 TV network (formerly Antenne 2) broadcast in 2004 shows a scene in which a high school teacher remains standing in the doorway until the frolicking students calm down, sit down, and remain silent.

The Swiss executive was then transferred to Hamburg, where his sons were admitted to a German school. This school experience was a disaster. Both sons lost several years because they could not cope with the open educational landscape, were overwhelmed and could not discipline themselves. One of his children had an extremely hard time finishing high school and only graduated from a high school in Hamburg through second chance education, which then allowed him to enroll at University.

What Happened?

The sons lived in two cultures whose educational goals are opposite:

The educational goal in Germany is to educate children to become citizens capable of independent thinking and autonomous action because of the experience made prior to and during WW II. In principle, every thought is worth considering, discussing and evaluating. The ability to practice liberal thinking and to show a liberal attitude characterizes an educated and respected person in today's German society. Therefore, children must, from the very beginning of their schooling, take part in shaping and influencing their own development. Teachers are coaches providing guidance and instructions to help children to attain this goal. The bottom line is that the child must shape his own socialization.

The educational goal in France is to educate the children to become citizens of the French culture and the Francophonie, the French speaking world. The goal is to give them a general education based on French history, culture and the traditional values of French civilization. According to French pedagogics, this can only be achieved during schooling. Students may gain specific, technical knowledge later on in a job. Therefore, the education in schools centers around language, memorizing of poets such as Lafontaine, and good manners—"*la civileté*"—for polite personal interaction in the family and in public.

Classes in France are held in traditional teacher-centered teaching. In Germany, the individual student is given guidance on how to achieve his own development. This fact was confirmed to the authors in various seminars by participants who had studied in both cultures. German students were disturbed the frontal teaching in France, while French students were often overwhelmed by the open, participative system while studying in Germany.

3.5.5 Use of Language: Language Style and Communication Intensity—A Comparison Between Germany, France and Japan

Learned and instilled communication patterns have an impact throughout your entire life. In cross cultural practice, be it in private or business life, it can be the primary cause for misunderstandings that can escalate until it cumulates in active antipathy.

The graph below illustrates the differences in communication between Germany, France and Japan. The prime objective of communication in any culture is to build relationships and create trust. The graph below shows the extent of communication intensity in terms of content, form and emotion (see graphic legend) (Fig. 3.10).

3.5.5.1 Explanations

Germany

From the perspective of the authors, Germany has a unique position. Communication is direct and language intensity is very high. Content takes precedence over form. Someone in Germany who gives priority to form over content may be regarded as a spin doctor. Emotions are strongly controlled in conversations and when they do come up, someone is likely to intervene with "*Let us stick to the fact*". This communication style is necessary in Germany to build trust.

This directness, which is a necessary and almost integral part of German culture is often viewed negatively by many other cultures:

Even in German-speaking Switzerland the communication intensity is much lower. The multicultural Swiss society requires a restrained communication style according to the motto: "*Remaining silent is the best way to talk*" (in Swiss German: "*Gschwige isch am beschte gredet.*")

USA

In the US, directness of the Germans in business meetings is often perceived as rude and unfriendly. The conclusion of many Americans is "*These people do not like each other*".

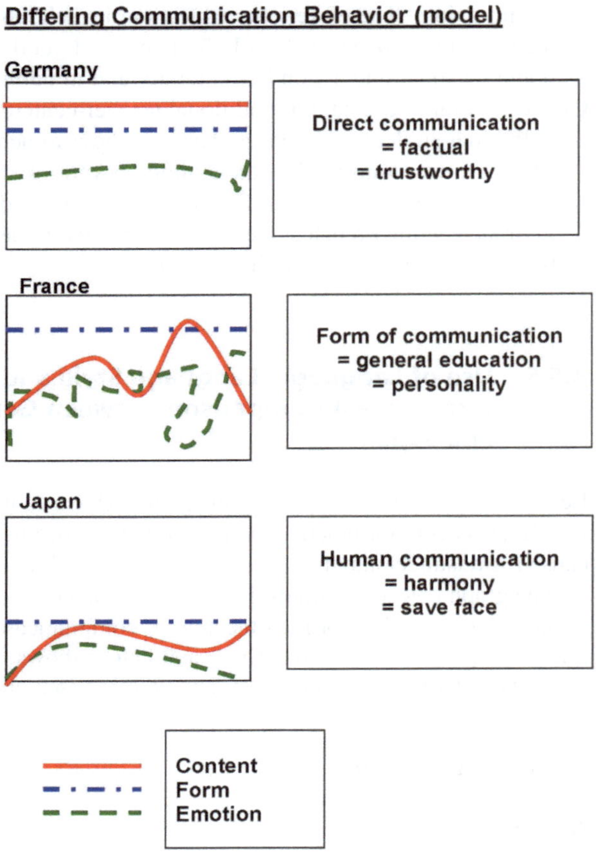

Fig. 3.10 Model of linguistic use in Germany, France and Japan

China, Japan and Asia in Arab Countries

In these cultures, the direct style of communication often leads to direct infractions, sometimes in very simple situations. For example, a seminar participant described a situation in Korea where he had built up a very good relationship with a somewhat older business partner. One evening, the Korean business associate proudly related that he had just started karate training. The much younger German responded spontaneously: "*I have been doing this sport for a long time and I have a black belt*". The conversation became difficult thereafter, and the mood was spoilt because his Korean friend, who felt unappreciated by the younger man, was hurt.

France

Like in Germany communication intensity in France is also very high. But form takes precedence over content and emotions can run high. For a Frenchman linguistic expression is a tool representing his personality, his educational background as well as his positioning in a social ranking, e.g. as a private person or as a leader in business. Since the French live in a high power distance business culture, see

Sect. 3.2.1 "*Power Distance and Individuality*", this approach is essential to gain acceptance and respect from subordinates.

A foreigner well-versed in French will be able to identify whether his French counterpart is from the working class, the bourgeoisie or the nobility from his choice of language. In the latter two groups of society, children may still address their parents, or even their spouses, by the formal honorific "*vous*", an example of which is former French President Mitterrand and his wife.

Normally, when meeting a foreigner speaking French a Frenchman will make sure that the language is used correctly and often corrects a mistake immediately. A French acquaintance from the fashionable Le Vésinet in the West of Paris once corrected one of the authors publicly on the street. The author said in passing, "*B'jour monsieur-dame*", which is what someone says when entering a pub. The French acquaintance stopped, turned to the author and said: "*One says: Bonjour Madame, Bonjour Monsieur*". Having said his piece, he continued on his way.

The educated Frenchman uses language like an instrument; it is a keyboard on which he can strike different notes and play melodies. And that becomes a problem for him when he must express himself in a foreign language, especially in English. A common preconception about the French is that they only speak French. The real reason for their dislike of speaking a foreign language lies in the importance of language to display personal identity. Firstly, the French are often not as fluent in English and secondly, the pronunciation based on the French alphabet is sometimes odd. A French accent can be perceived as charming, but from the point of view of French speakers it is just seen as ridiculous. That is why the authors have heard many French friends and acquaintances say: "*On n'aime pas parler l'anglais, parce que se sent ridicule*" (one doesn't like to speak English because one feels silly). French people sometimes complain that they speak "*no foreign languages!*"

Japan

Even if Germany and France are very different cultures, they are still Western cultures. Despite all their differences, they have a high degree of individuality and an intensive communication style. Japan is presented here as a contrast to the Western world.

1. The goal of communication in Japan is to preserve face and to show respect for the superior and the community. Therefore, silence and intuition are the essential means of communication. Anyone who has worked with Japanese may have been confronted with endless periods of silence which are hard to bear for Westerners. "*Hara gei*" (the art of belly language) or intuition is the basis for communication in Japanese culture.
2. As people have known each other and worked together for a long time, they are able to reflect on how their colleague or supervisor would react. They are thus able to preempt potential conflicts and the risk of loss of face. Couples married for a long time may know each other so well that no verbal exchange is necessary. There will be a silent compliance in given situations.

3. A Westerner will probably be tempted to break that silence to keep communication going. He will then probably confirm the bias among the Japanese partners that Westerners like to show off and are unable to listen.

3.5.6 China and the West: Differing Communication Styles Rooted in Education

The different communication styles between China and the West can be best illustrated by comparing educational systems between the Western world and China, whose written communication has influenced many other Asian cultures.

The graph below represents the schematic comparison between China and the West (Fig. 3.11).

3.5.6.1 Communication and Education in China

The Chinese character ("*Hanji*"—the spelling of the Han people) in the above graphic represents harmony. It originally showed a rice plant and an open mouth. This illustrative metaphor means, that if enough rice, meaning food, is available, then harmony prevails.

To be able to communicate in writing, the Chinese (including Koreans and Japanese) must master and memorize around 2000 characters. The learning process is holistic, i.e. pictograms are memorized as whole in the right side of the brain. Teaching is based on the historical experience of this culture and is conveyed "*ex cathedra*". The author has taught executives and lecturered in China and was amazed at how the material was received. As soon as the translator, spoke, the participants began to write down what was said.

In China, the benchmark for a good examination paper is therefore the exact reproduction of the teacher or professor's teachings. This educational style leads to holistic and inductive thinking. The script is central to communication because every character can be clearly assigned. The spoken word, on the other hand, allows for interpretations through the different tonal possibilities. Therefore, a character written in the air or on the palm often adds clarity. The communication ideal is that of calligraphy (handwriting in ink with a brush).

This correlation also exists in music education. Both in Chinese and Japanese music the experience of the master is passed on to the student. They teach the student to strike a note correctly on the harp. If this is mastered after many years, the student becomes a master himself.

Teaching in Asian Cultures Is a Serious Thing

An American language teacher, 22 years old, taught at an institute in China and was "guided" by an elderly Chinese colleague, as she felt responsible for his "*education*".

1. She once told him that he laughed too much in class.
2. He replied that the lessons were fun for him.

Learning in Asia and in the West

right side of the brain	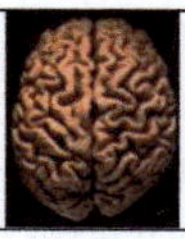	**left side of the brain**
Asia 和		**West** ABCDEFGHIJ KLMNOPQRST UVWXYZ
	Learning	
o visual perception		o logic
o holistic		o linear
	Teaching	
o experience		o analysis
o by heart		o method
	How to pass a test	
o exact replica of the teachings by the professor		o applying own thinking based on the methods taught
	Differing ways of thinking	
o inductively		o deductively
o general view		o synthesis
	The Ideal communication styles	
o calligraphy		o rhetoric
	Musical education	
o to strike and to keep a note on the instrument n		o to read music and to play scales on the instrument

Fig. 3.11 Education in Asia and in the West

3. She replied that it seemed a little strange to laugh at his own jokes.
4. The American replied that it relaxed the atmosphere, so why should he stop?
5. The Chinese professor's answer: "*Too much laughter makes one sick*".[10]

[10]Wenzhong and Grove (1999, pp. 85 and 86).

3.5.6.2 Communication and Education in the West

The Western learning style is diametrically opposed to the Chinese. In the West, we learn with the left side of the brain, which is logical and linear. Our written language is essentially based on 26 letters, with which we can create all the words in Western languages. The Cyrillic alphabet included.

We can write words in foreign languages, but we will not understand them if we have not learned the corresponding language. In contrast, the Chinese characters are basically understood in diverse cultures such as Korea and Japan.

Education in the West is based on systems and methods, and students are given guidance to develop their own analytical skills and creativity. Applying this ability to work out solutions and break new ground is rewarded with good grades. To simply repeat what the teacher said is, in our culture, an inability to develop one's own thinking.

Learned logical and analytical thinking leads us to derive solutions from an information base, i.e. to think linearly and deductively. Our ideal of communication is rhetoric, which often comes across as showing off to the Asian partner.

Even a musical instrument is normally learned linearly in the West. We learns the notes and scales first with the goal of technically mastering the instrument.

A Final Thought

Since people from Asia need to learn English, the "*lingua franca*" of world trade, they probably have better access to our culture as we to hers. There are comparatively few Westerners who learn such difficult languages as Mandarin, Japanese or Korean.

When people from Asia learn our language, it does not necessarily mean that it makes it easier for them to interact with us or that they are superior to us in intercultural cooperation. Intercultural competence depends on how the individual behaves in an intercultural situation.

3.6 Rituals

Rituals can be found in all cultures of this world. Rituals are regulatory processes to provide security. To observe, understand and respect rituals is the key to success in any intercultural context. In many cases, non-verbal rituals have as central a significance in communication as verbal expression.

In the Asian and Islamic world, rituals primarily serve the conflict-free pursuit of harmony. They create familiarity and trust. They give face or avoid the loss of face.

A very impressive and world-famous ritual is the Japanese tea ceremony, which has also been rediscovered in today's China. The ceremony is characterized by mutual respect between a tea master or mistress, the host and the guest. It shows the appreciation of nature based on the type of tea, the handcrafted utensils, especially the cup, and it ends with the incomparable enjoyment of this fine beverage.

Every culture has its rituals. Knowing and recognizing these is the basic condition for successful integration. It removes uncertainties on both sides and creates a bridge to understanding. Participating in rituals facilitates acceptance and integration.

3.6.1 Greeting Rituals

Culturally, greeting rituals vary greatly. They can be verbal or non-verbal. The spacing between the bodies, for example, is one of the key exercises in intercultural training with multicultural groups. A man and woman or man and man approach each other after placing them at a distance. The results are amazing. In man-woman situations, for example, people from Asian cultures remain at a distance, in Germany at arm's length and in Russia close to the body. In the latter situation, women take the initiative. To avoid embarrassing situations, it is best to wait and see what the host does. Such was the experience of a diplomat's wife in India who wanted to shake hands with a Brahmin, a holy ascetic, at a reception—and insisted for so long that she finally took her hand. With that, the atmosphere of warmth was gone.

3.6.2 Rituals for Apologizing

In many cultures and languages, a sentence or salutation very often begins with an apology. In German speaking areas, i.e. Germany and Switzerland, this is relatively rare. In many other cultures it is often the rule. An opening often starts with:

1. France : pardon or excusez-moi Madame, Monsieur
2. Italy: mi dispiace
3. Spain: perdona usted
4. Mexico: me disculpen
5. USA: I am sorry or please excuse me
6. Japan: shitsurei des or sumimasen

At the beginning of a contact or conversation, these words make the other person aware that "*something*" is coming, and that he can prepare himself. Apologies are expressed in many cultures at every opportunity, e.g. In France, for example, when a man helps a lady into a coat, opens the door for her, or keeps it open. As a rule, this action is then acknowledged with a "*merci Monsieur.*"

In her book "Chinesen verstehen lernen" (Learning to understand the Chinese),[11] Margaret Lin-Huber points to a ritual among colleagues. After an interesting exchange with a Chinese colleague, the visiting colleague will apologize with the words "*I wasted your precious time*". The host will answer him: "*Nonsense. I have learned a great deal. I should be thanking you*".

[11]Lin-Huber (2001, Seite 108).

3.6.2.1 Dealing with Rituals

There are countless rituals in every culture, even in our Western world. When we are unexpectedly faced with unfamiliar rituals in an unknown world, we are taken aback, dumbfounded, and unaware of how best to handle it.

For example:

1. Greetings: in Japan, should I bow? Or in Malaysia, fold the hands in front of my face?
2. Greeting in Poland: Do I have to kiss the lady's hand? And if so, how?
3. In Russia, at a dinner with business friends, do I have to do the same to the Russians ladies present and help my German boss, a lady, to put on her coat?
4. Seating arrangement in China; What is the order and ranking of the introductions and then the seating at the conference table? Is this fixed in advance?
5. Body language in France. How should I interpret the upright posture and the rather serious, even dismissive facial expression of the chairman? Rejection or just the ritual appropriate to his rank?
6. Sugar coating. Why does the Arabic business friend in his welcome speech only talk about the positive aspects of our business relationship knowing we have problems?
7. Chinese guests at a business dinner in Hamburg: Why are our Chinese guests suddenly disappearing at exactly 9:00 pm right after dinner?
8. Invitation to traditional meal in India. Can I also eat with my left hand as a left-hander or do I have to match the hosts who only eat with their right hands?
9. A Toast. The Russian host gets up, gives a five-minute speech, and praises me with a "Na Zdorowje". Do I have to drink the vodka and also give such a long speech? If so, when is the right time?

In an unknown culture and situation, rituals are often unfamiliar, difficult to assess and to understand. A ritual may not even be recognized, such as at a trade fair, when receiving a business card from a Japanese businessman we might make a note of the date on it. The Japanese will say a polite good-bye but probably thinks "*Another one of those from the West with no respect for anything!*" (In Japan, the business card is the face of the company and must not be written on. Incidentally, business cards are arranged not by family name but by company name.)

3.6.2.2 Ignore or Join in?

The solution is a balancing act between acceptance and absurdity. One who imitates may make himself look ridiculous or the local person has the feeling that the guest is making fun of his country.

It is therefore essential to restrain oneself, observe, and wait to see how to begin.

In addition, an attentive host of the receiving culture will also want to help his guest if he notices that he cannot cope with the cultural practices. It is best for the visitor to inquire beforehand from a culturally aware confidante about the meaning of the rituals and the behavior to expect.

The ideal route, of course, is intercultural training and preparation for a basic understanding of behaviors, so that the visitor can act more confidently in the foreign culture. Only then can he participate fully in the rituals and truly experience them with enjoyment.

3.7 Behavior in Case of Conflict: Carry Out or Avoid?

Conflicts in an intercultural context are often caused by misunderstandings and situations that originate in an overly direct Western style of communication.

The following graphic shows Western communication goals and styles compared to the Asian and Arab world (Fig. 3.12):

The communication goal in the West is conflict resolution. Problems are addressed directly, often in formal meetings in a larger circle, where consensus can be sought directly. The emerging results are usually recorded in the form of tasks, responsibilities and deadlines. However, there are no standard procedures in the Western world for conflict resolution. For example, in the Czech Republic, in Italy or in German speaking Switzerland, conflicts are pushed aside rather than addressed directly. Time will bring the solution.

Addressing conflicts openly is an absolute taboo in most intercultural and international settings. If conflicts are made public in the Arab or Asian world, then they are already in the process of escalation and run the risk of getting out of control. These results are loss of face and violation of honor with the corresponding negative consequences for relationships and even friendships.

The communication goal in the Asian and Arab world is conflict prevention through formal, ritual, and careful interaction with each other in daily life. When

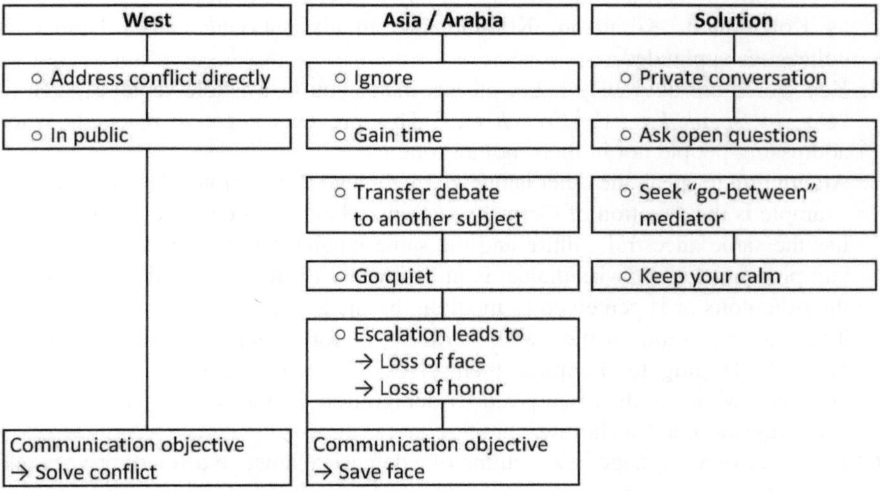

Fig. 3.12 Solving conflicts in the West, the Asian and Arabic world

conflicts arise, people in many cultures try to ignore, cover up, or turn away from them. Time does not play a central role in many Asian cultures, because patience and time alone can resolve a conflict. Saving face supersedes everything.

Conflicts in these worlds are almost always solved in private conversations, with respect for hierarchy and seniority as the thread leading to the solution. If an impasse is reached, a mediator who is generally a senior person, intervenes. A sound understanding of these cultures and stable relationships are necessary to find a credible, competent mediator who is accepted by both parties.

The qualities that a Western person needs in these situations are patience, the ability to remain calm, and not to exert undue pressure through interrogation. Leading questions with a "*why*" or "*what for*" and closed questions (yes or no) are not advisable.

One basic rule is to ask open questions. Rather than asking "*When can we set the next appointment?*" or "*Can you give us a date for next appointment?*" it would be helpful to say, "*We would like to arrange another meeting with you* (*Pause*...)."

3.8 Dealing with Languages in Business

Knowledge of a foreign language as a key to cultural integration is simultaneously overvalued and undervalued:

1. On the one hand, language skills facilitate access to a culture and building relationships with its people. Speaking only a few words—if used correctly—also shows respect and interest in the host country.
2. Advice: Try to learn a few words in the local language even if it can almost drive you to despair. One of the authors tried to pronounce the word for thank you Köszönöm for a project in Hungary for days. After days of botched attempts such as Kötzmönön, Kömözön, Kölömön he finally succeeded. His Hungarian colleagues applauded.
3. Key words are obviously hello, please, thank you or a whole sentence such as "*Do you speak English, French etc.*" This prevents negative reactions when addressing people not in their mother tongue.
4. Attempting to speak the other language might lead to rejection. The most extreme example is the situation of Germans in Switzerland, who come to a country that has the same ancestral culture and the same language root. However, imitating and pronouncing a Swiss dialect is unbelievably difficult and quickly slips into the ridiculous or is perceived as mocking by the Swiss.
5. The classic greeting of the Swiss "*Grüezi*", is, for example, pronounced with a broad E. Hoping to ingratiate themselves, Germans use it but pronounce it "*Grützi*", which is then perceived as denigration by the Swiss who react with silent rejection and withdraw.
6. Ignorance of a language is something of a defense against invasion of privacy and serves to preserve one's face. The authors have attended innumerable international meetings in which the participants suddenly switched to their own language

to discuss a critical point in the negotiation. The author's experience during a press conference of a Japanese organization in Berlin serves as an example. In the run-up to the press conference, the author spoke with the Japanese CEO, who was fluent in German. During the press conference, one of the journalists asked a critical question to which the managing director from Japan said: "*My German is not good enough for me to answer that question correctly. I will therefore reply in Japanese and Ms. Suzuki will translate for you.*"

7. Knowledge of the culture and the situation will reveal when it is opportune to use the language and when to hold back if one has not mastered a language perfectly.

3.8.1 Business Communication: Verbally or in Writing?

A distinguishing feature of communication in Germany is the preference for written communication. From experience Germans know that a response can always be expected in written communication. Written communication provides security amidst the uncertainty of professional life (see also Sect. 3.2.2.2 Avoidance of Uncertainty).

Most other cultures communicate more orally; this applies to cultures with a high power distance and also to collectivist cultures in which face saving and conflict avoidance determine communicative co-existence. Oral communication permits

1. Nuanced expression
2. Between the lines communication
3. Rewording and repackaging difficult messages,
4. Maneuvering round a potential conflict
5. Finding excuses
6. Remaining silent
7. Offering a credible white lie.

Written communication in Germany is based on facts. Germans tend to be very dissatisfied if this is not the case in other cultures. This is, however, one of the reasons other cultures prefer oral communication. Conflicts between German written culture and "*oral cultures*" may escalate if no answer arrives. A German colleague may follow up with a number of E-mails, irritating the other side. He thinks he is not being taken seriously or interprets it as a lack of confidence. Normally, oral communication is the key to building relationships and finding solutions between partners from different cultures, especially when there are misunderstandings or even conflicts.

The table below shows a comparison of the communication styles in European business cultures according to Maud Tixier[12] which exemplifies the dominance of oral communication (Fig. 3.13):

[12]Tixier (1994, p. 24).

Country Linguistic culture	Prefer written Communication	Prefer oral Communication
Belgium		●
Denmark		●
Germany	●	
German Switzerland	○	○
Great Britain		●
Finland		●
France		●
French Switzerland		●
Greece		●
Netherlands	●	
Ireland		●
Italy		●
Austria		●
Portugal	●	
Sweden		●
Spain		●

● normally applies / preference
○ applies only partially / not a clear preference

Fig. 3.13 Comparison of preferred communication styles in European business cultures

Primarily oral business communication is also found in many other countries of the world, such as China and Japan or Arab countries, where business is often successful without a contractual basis if there is a healthy level of trust.

3.9 Hospitality and Gifts

In German-speaking cultures, hospitality is restricted to the private sphere and is normally not intensively cultivated in business. Gifts also play a role, if at all, in personal relationships and are rarely, if at all, used in business. The idea that gifts might be construed as the gray area of bribery may also play a role here.

3.9.1 Hospitality

In most other business cultures, off-hours social networking is the only way to get to know each other personally and build a business based on trust. This applies to Eastern and Central Eastern Europe as well as to the Romanophone world, Asia, Africa, South America or Arab countries.

To refuse or fail to show hospitality is a personal insult in many cultures. The extent of the reaction varies greatly depending on the culture. Ultimately, however, the bottom line is always the same; there is no fundamental basis for cooperation in business.

Specifics of Hospitality in Germany

Relatively little attention is paid to hospitality in German business culture. Apart from the occasional working lunch and the invitation to dinner for a good customer, not much happens in terms of social contact. During meals, unless they are friends of long standing, business issues are discussed, with brief forays into personal life. Punctuality is important, and the meal times agreed upon are meant to be respected.

Specifics of Hospitality in France

France is representative of many Romance language—speaking cultures. Here, a meal is always a social occasion, be it for business or pleasure. Eating is also an opportunity to get away from the business and get to know each other better personally. At a business lunch, discussing business immediately is considered rude. Business is discussed almost casually at the end of the meal, "*entre la poire et le fromage*" (between dessert and cheese).

A seminar participant once described what had happened to her in Paris when she spoke about ongoing contract negotiations during the meal. She noticed that her French discussion partner showed disapproval and the atmosphere became increasingly cool and almost distant. The deal was not completed, as the French customer left the question open.

Back home in Germany, she told a colleague, an expert on France, about her perception. He pointed out that in France it is considered impolite, even a bad habit, to talk business during the meal. On her next visit, she took this advice and avoided discussing the contract throughout the meal. At the end of the meal, the French boss and customer said succinctly: "*Pour le contrat c'est d'accord*"—"*By the way, the contract has been approved.*"

In France, punctuality at meals, or even beyond, is not taken too seriously. Delays are common, especially in the big cities where traffic jams are commonplace and busy executives have time management issues. The meal is a break and that's why time is dealt with more generously.

In contrast, mention should be made here of the experience of a French director of a large international company in Tokyo, who reserved a table at lunchtime in the city's best restaurant several times and, being used to Paris, always came late. After the fourth or fifth time, the answer he received from the restaurant always was: "*Sorry sir, we do not have a table available for lunch*". He solved the problem by asking the Japanese boss of a service company he knew to book a table for him.

In France, one also never appears punctually, unless explicitly requested, to a personal invitation. One usually arrives 15 minutes after the specified time to give the hostess time to get ready. Apart from flowers, gifts are welcome. Flowers are delivered to the hostess from the shop prior to the invitation so that she has the time to arrange the bouquet in the right vase. Sending flowers after the event is almost an insult and could be misunderstood as a belated signal that one was satisfied with the invitation.

Specifics of Hospitality in Central and Eastern Europe

Hospitality is also carefully cultivated in Eastern and Central European countries such as Poland, Hungary, and Romania as well as in Russia, Belarus, or the Baltic States. Guests are carefully looked after, women in particular. Good manners are an expression of respect for the host. This ranges from appropriate clothing for the occasion to particularly courteous treatment of women. One is expected to help her with her coat or to hold the door open for her. In Eastern Europe it certainly happens that one is invited to a home as a business contact. There is an unvoiced expectation that the visitor behaves well and, for example, takes off his shoes on entering.

Specifics of Hospitality in China

Hospitality in China is mentioned here as an example because it has a much deeper meaning than we can imagine. Hospitality has a lot to do with respect and preservation of respect. The concern of a host is to make sure that the guest is comfortable, that he feels well and above all, that nothing unpleasant happens to him. Because this would be a disaster leading to loss of face.

One of the authors lectured in Nanjing and Shenyang in China in the 1990s on behalf of German educational institutions and in cooperation with the regional governments and educational organizations. He was very closely guided and looked after by the Chinese hosts during his entire stay, sometimes for several weeks at a time.

On arrival, he was picked up at the airport and taken to the hotel. In the morning he was brought to the university for the lecture and brought back to the hotel in the evening. He ate all his meals, even breakfast, in the company of the Chinese hosts or participants in the seminars. During his stay there was a festive reception dinner and a farewell dinner with Chinese officials. The times were always strictly observed. When the author once appeared five minutes late for breakfast, he was reprimanded by the head of the delegation.

Guest relations were a key issue during many of the author's China training sessions for multinational corporations. Western hosts assume that the Chinese will find their way over around by themselves when abroad. A participant put it bluntly in one seminar—"*our Chinese just wander around the company's site*". Unaccompanied and rather lost, the Chinese will conclude not only lack of interest, but also a sense that their visit was not of importance to the Western host. This was a central problem for Chinese visitors abroad, especially at the beginning of the 1990s at the beginning of closer business ties with the West. Unfamiliar with our lifestyle, they found it difficult to orient themselves, use Western appliances, whether fork and knife or the toilets. Although times have changed since the 1990s, it is imperative that the Western host be extremely attentive and remove any inconvenience to "*give face*" to the guest.

Jiang Zemin in Switzerland: A Far-Reaching Loss of Face

Two incidents occurred during the visit of former President, Jiang Zemin to Switzerland in March 1999, the first visit ever by a Chinese President. High security precautions during the visit meant that military honors had to be waived.

However, the authorities had forgotten to block access to the Federal Building and the square in front of the parliament. Loud protests from pro-Tibetan protesters in the central courtyard and on the roofs of neighboring buildings just before the official ceremony triggered a crisis.

The Chinese delegation arrived half an hour late, while the assembled Swiss government stood outside, waiting on the steps of the parliament building. President Jiang Zemin then criticized the unfriendly attitude of his hosts, the Federal Government, in his speech and complained about the reception which he received.

A flood of editorials on human rights in China appeared in the Swiss press, blaming the crisis solely on the Chinese president's claim to power. What Jiang Zemin was so furious about was not personal loss of face, but the insult to China and the loss of national face.

The second incident is based on an insider's report. At the reception dinner in Bern with every dignitary in Swiss politics and business present, Jiang Zemin was seated with his back to the door. He thereupon wanted to leave the room and it was only thanks to the courageous intervention of a popular minister that Jiang Zemin stayed. He appealed to him to stay and led Jiang Zemin to the seat that was his due.

Good preparation, close management and concern for the well-being of Chinese guests is half the success of a successful (business) relationship. This includes accompanying the guests on (almost) all their activities and arranging the appropriate food at restaurants. The Chinese believe that their food is the best in the world because they eat a variety of foods and take better care of their health than Westerners with their unbalanced diet do. In this context, it should also be mentioned that many older Chinese are not used to dairy products and can have problems because they lack an enzyme for digesting milk protein.

An essential aspect of relationship building is also life outside business hours. During the day, one meets under formal or rather ritual conditions, where personal access is hardly possible. During leisure time, however, relationships are built and maintained, i.e. while dining, but also on joint outings.

A Swiss company setting up a joint venture with China was to host a Chinese delegation of about 30 professionals in Switzerland for several weeks. In a preparatory seminar, tasks relating to the care of the guests were planned as a project. A "*food and beverage manager*" was given responsibility for understanding the guests' wishes regarding food, including selecting the right Chinese restaurants in the area and to do research on Chinese specialty shops, which were still rare at the time, so that guests from China could stock up on their own food. Then there was also an "*entertainment manager*" who was responsible for planning events, organizing the welcome and farewell dinners, and the weekend excursions, always accompanied by a rotation of persons from the Swiss company.

More information on these principles is described in Sect. 4.8.1 China, culturally defining elements. They are basically valid for many cultures in Asia and Southeast Asia.

3.9.2 Drinking Customs and Alcohol

One word about drinking habits. In many cultures, drinking alcohol is equated with sociability and is indulged in to an extent that seems excessive by our standards. Drinking at formal situations is often not tailored to individual needs as it is done in the group. But what if you want to avoid heavy drinking or abstain altogether?

▶ **Principle 1**

The first principle is that the guest does not have to drink, if he does not feel comfortable doing so. White lies are a tried and tested means of dealing diplomatically with the situation, such as: *"My health* (*or my liver*) *does not permit it"*. This does not offend the host and is recognized in all cultures.

Principle 2

Secondly, it is important to find the right way to deal with drinking. The following is a path that takes one's own needs into account and at the same time does not offend the host:

At a seminar in Shenyang, one of the authors was reminded by a participant, a professor, that there would be a party in the evening and it would be an occasion for hard drinking. Since the author had to lecture for 6 h the following day, intoxication would have had dire consequences.

He therefore turned to the Head of Delegation, who advised him to do it the way women do. This meant that when the men proposed a *"ganbei"*—the Chinese toast for draining the glass to react with "just one sip" in Chinese language. No sooner said than done. The evening was very lively, with karaoke singing, the hosts and guest in good spirits and the lecturer was fully operational the next morning.

How Much Should You Drink?

The author's second experience took place in Bin Hoa, the northern province of Vietnam, where, at the end of the lecturing assignment, the author was invited with a colleague to the wedding of the daughter of the province's finance minister. The celebration with several hundred guests took place in the guest house of the largest power plant in the province. After dinner, the guests came in groups to our table, filled their glasses with beer, made a toast, expecting us to follow their example. It was a tricky situation because we were to travel on the following day. We faked it, which was not to be overlooked and one of the professors, who had already drunk more than his fair share, remarked that if we did not want to drink, we should go home.

After the official ceremony, the authors were invited to the house of the Finance Director to continue celebrating in a small circle. First a glass of cognac made the rounds and was emptied in a toast to the bride and groom, a ritual in which they participated joyfully. After that, the group moved to the balcony, where they sat in lotus position around a clay pot of Schnapps with bamboo straws and everyone took a sip at the same time.

The question of drinking is not a question of the behavior of the host, but one of one's own attitude toward alcohol. In many cultures, drinking is an act of socialization in society. Excesses are rare, and one does not have to partake as the well-being of the guest has priority.

3.9.3 Favors

In the Western world, gifts are given primarily on a personal level, whether on birthdays or when invited. The gift is an offering in response to the personal preferences of the recipient. It is a favor with no strings attached. In fact, it is usually given in a way that there is no compulsion on the recipient to reciprocate.

In other cultures, a gift is part of a ritual that primarily deals with reciprocal relationships.

1. In Eastern and Central Europe, for example, gifts are usually brought along during a visit, and visitors are also expected to bring gifts. This is a mark of respect and appreciation for the host. An example would be the customary bouquet of flowers for the host's wife or a cognac for the host.
2. In Asia gifts are used to settle a debt or a favor. An example is the experience of German students in a graduate class at a university in southern Germany. The Chinese classmates were asked by the professor at the end of the lesson if they had understood everything. The Chinese smiled politely and nodded their heads. At the exit, they lined up to intercept their German colleagues, asking if they could borrow their notes. The German students handed over their notes, and each

Chinese student then said: "*And you will also get a gift!*" The German students then replied: "*I'm doing it gladly for you—no gifts necessary!*"

The following are some real stories of gift situations to illustrate the dimensions of ritual gift giving and its effects:

Russia: Immigration Aid

A German student studied in Moscow before Perestroika, the opening of Russia in the late 80s, and lived in a Russian family which seemed to be close friends with another family which frequently came to visit. This family often expressed the wish to emigrate to Germany. After this topic had been mentioned on several occasions, the student unexpectedly received a number of gifts from this family—expensive vodka, Crimean sparkling wine, and caviar, the cost of which obviously exceeded this family's means. The message was clear—they wanted assistance for immigration to Germany. The German student felt overwhelmed and pressurized. As a result, tensions developed between her and her host family. She did not return the gifts as that would be an insult in any culture but shared them with her friends.

China: Caring for the Daughter of a Chinese Colleague

This China story has parallels with the previous one but was solved immediately soon thereafter. One of the authors was a lecturer in Nanjing and was approached by a professor who wanted to visit him with his daughter. After several attempts, this visit also took place one evening. They had a very pleasant conversation, with the lecturer being showered with gifts that were modest from the Western point of view, but costly in the economic situation of the time. At the end, a photo was taken.

The next day, a German colleague—a China expert with several years of experience teaching in the country—asked about the conversation and how it went. The author's answer was, "*It was a very good conversation, and we talked mainly about the daughter's wish to study in Switzerland. I received a lot of gifts.*" The German colleague said, "*Then they want you to take on the daughter when she comes to Switzerland.*" The reaction of the author was the same as that of the German student in Russia. He did not know how to handle the situation and asked his friend "*What can I do about it?*" The China expert's answer was "*Return gifts, of course, not those you received, but the ones you have brought*". A few days later, the author gave the professor some souvenirs he had brought back from Switzerland and there was no further mention of the daughter after that.

Such requests are perceived as an invasion of privacy in the Western world and one feels out of one's depth. In the Asian and Arab worlds on the other hand, a relationship obliges one to fulfill requests. In retrospect, the professor's request could have been accommodated. Caring for the daughter does not necessarily involve sharing his house or apartment, but she would have had a contact in Switzerland that would have assisted her with integration and helped her out of difficult situations.

Arab World: The Beautiful Picture or the Beautiful Vase

The rituals and conditions of giving are particularly complex in the Arab world. Gifts correspond to the status of the recipient, show respect for his person, his culture and his religion. The special thing about it is that gifts are made public and reviewed by all those present at an event during which it is important to praise the gift lavishly.

Gifts in the Arab world are distributed very generously, as the story in Sect. 3.9.4 "*What is corruption?*" shows.

Japan: Breach of Contract by the Supplier

A particularly unusual practical example is that of a conflict between a German automotive subcontractor and a Japanese supplier. In seminar on Japan, a young Belgian purchasing agent returned enraged to the seminar after lunch and showed us an e-mail from the supplier in Japan. It bore the succinct text: As of next Monday, we will not deliver any spare parts X at price Y. Sincerely yours.

This practical case study was then used in a group session to offer the Belgian purchasing agent a solution. A board member, also a former buyer, who was also present in this group session related the following story:

He had had a similar dispute years ago with another Japanese supplier.

He had gone to his former head of the purchasing department for advice, who suggested that he call the supplier and arrange a visit in Japan. He also recommended buying him a music CD—the Japanese like classical music—, fly to Japan and hand over the gift.

No sooner said than done. The young buyer followed his manager's advice, stepped into supplier's office, handed him the gift and offered at that time his condolences on the death of Tenno, the Japanese Emperor, who had just passed away. The Japanese man was so touched that he showed the German around the company, sat down with him and they renewed their agreement.

In Western view, this procedure is unusual and even reprehensible—because the supplier had unilaterally breached the contract. In the West, we probably would have acted differently. We would not have made a long and expensive journey bearing gifts but rather summoned the supplier and threatened with legal action. In Japan, this would probably have ended in a stalemate because legal action leads to marginalization—Japan has only known the rule of law in the Western sense for a few years now.

From the perspective of both Japanese and Chinese, a contract is a policy document, the details of which are renegotiable at any time if circumstances require. In the present case, the relationship could be rebuilt through the journey, showing regard, and gifts.

Japan–Switzerland: "*Giri*" or Balancing a Debt or Favor

One of the authors once observed how a Japanese couple drove a rental car from Geneva to Zurich when traveling through Switzerland. He saw the couple at a rest stop, where they stood uncomprehending and a little lost in front of the of the restaurant's buffet, because they did not recognize the food nor understand the language. He met them again at the airport at the rental car return. Since they obviously did not know where to go, he helped them with their orientation. After the farewells, the author was already in the process of leaving, when the woman called him back with a "*chotto mate*" ("*a moment*") and presented him with a beautifully crafted pocket letter opener. The debt was repaid.

3.9.4 What Is Corruption?

Corruption is certainly not a cultural trait, but a personal view of behavior. Bribery can be a matter of survival such as the policeman in an emerging country who can no longer manage on his salary due to rapidly rising cost of living. Or it can be a matter of greed, or abuse of power to accumulate wealth when a well-paid senior official or politician makes corruption a personal source of revenue. Nevertheless, individual countries or cultures are stereotyped with these criteria, including in the media.

In principle, corruption is everywhere. Corruption is still used by Western companies to get contracts in certain countries in Asia or Africa. In Switzerland, it was possible to get tax deductions for corporate bribery until the mid-1990s.

Đổi mới: Economic Liberalization in Vietnam

Like China, Vietnam introduced free market reforms in 1986 since the command economy was no longer able to feed the population. The main staple rice, for example, was not produced in sufficient quantities and had to be imported from abroad. Within a few years after liberalization and opening-up, Vietnam became self-sufficient and could even export rice.

One of the government's main goals was to privatize the largest possible number of the approximately 12,000 Vietnamese state enterprises. Ten years later, less than 10 had been privatized and there were only about 6,000 state-owned enterprises left due to closures of the rest for various reasons.

To combat that, the government set up a commission in the mid-1990s to investigate the reasons. The core problem was corruption; the senior executives of the State-owned companies. They preferred the relative security of the state owned companies to the open competition and thus the insecurity of the private sector and made up the difference in income with bribes.

The problem of any state leadership is that corruption renders a state ungovernable and it is therefore imperative to combat bribery. The situation in Vietnam was so desperate that the government then decided to take drastic action and imposed the death penalty for large bribes.

Corruption in China

Corruption is a central issue in the Western world when talking about China, and a stereotype with which the country and its culture is categorized. Survival was a key issue in China because of the hardships of recent history. In the last 60 years some 60 million people died, not because of civil war but due to famine caused by Mao's drive to industrialize China. It's only too understandable that people want things to be better and do everything possible to have a good life. This is not an excuse for corruption but an explanation most people can understand if they ask themselves what they would have done.

In China too, it is a fact that with a population of 1.3 billion people bribery is a motive in the sense defined above. And here, too, the threat that corruption will make the state unmanageable is omnipresent. The central government fights this evil with all its might and uses the death penalty as a deterrent as well.[13]

63-year-old Zheng Xiaoyu, a senior official, was sentenced to death in 2007 for corruption and dereliction of his duties. The official news agency Xinhua reported that the execution took place after the Beijing Supreme Court upheld the death sentence. The background was a bribe totaling RMB 6.49 million (about EUR 650'000) for the approval of inadequately tested new medicines that killed at least ten people.

3.9.5 How Can Corruption Be Defined?

The answer: Corruption is when money flows, or assets are used as a means of bribery. However, there is a large gray area that shows that corruption is interpreted differently in given cultures:

1. The US probably has the narrowest interpretation of corruption. 30 years ago, General Motors already prohibited its employees from accepting any gifts. The only appropriate thing were invitations to working lunches in simple restaurants, but not in an upscale restaurant. Depending on the country, this can be a problem as the local business culture might require hospitality befitting the client.
2. In France, meal invitations—depending on customer status—in good restaurants or in one's home are commonplace. Important customers were sometimes even invited to an introduction of a new product as part of product training in an exclusive overseas tourist location.
3. In China, gifts and invitations are part and parcel of business life. They contribute to social cohesion, bind relationships and give face.
4. In Japan too, good customers are invited to the best restaurants and gifts are distributed, mostly of excellent craftsmanship.
5. In China and Japan, gifts often offset the moral debt of repaying a service that cannot be returned in kind.

[13] http://time.com/4298731/this-is-how-much-money-you-can-take-in-bribes-before-the-chinese-authorities-execute-you/. Last viewed August 15, 2018.

The Arab Sheikh and the Gifted Rolex

This story shows the conflict between American, Swiss and Arab gift culture. A Swiss was sent to Kenya as a technical consultant for an American company and was also responsible for Saudi Arabia during his 5-year stay. When he was to return to the company headquarters in Switzerland, the Arab trader, a sheikh, invited him to a farewell dinner and presented him with a Rolex as a gift.

This was a problem for the Swiss because it was considered bribery under American legal guidelines. He could not return the watch, as that would be a deadly insult in the Arab world. So, he accepted the gift with the idea of selling it for a few shillings at a garage sale in Nairobi before leaving Kenya. He kept the watch, however, and it accompanied him until his death, and is today the timepiece of one of the authors.

Summary of the Topic of Corruption

All these stories have one thing in common: they try to convey a differentiated view of this controversial topic and show that every single case must be considered individually. The motto is the Chinese proverb "*Before you criticize your neighbor, look in your own house three times.*" or the biblical verse: "*Let him who is without sin cast the first stone*". In other words, bribery and corruption are not cultural characteristics!

3.10 Open and Closed Societies

From the Western point of view, the individual is at the center of an open society, most typically in the USA.

We define societies that set themselves apart as closed societies. The reasons for this are diverse:

1. One reason may be geography. Island people tend to isolate themselves from other countries. Examples of this in Europe are Great Britain, Corsica, or Ireland, which express their independence even with their terminology: As they don't feel they belong to Europe they speak of the Continent.
2. Another reason for isolation is the fear of loss of identity, for example German-speaking Switzerland which is historically and linguistically closely related to Southern Germany, but nevertheless shields itself from these Germans to safeguard the autonomy of their culture. (see Sect. 4.16.2 "*Germans and Swiss Germans*").
3. Japan may be a special case, where isolation is based both on island life and on the fear of losing national identity. Portugal tried to Christianize and colonize the country in the fifteenth century. This was prevented and then led to isolationism in Japan until the nineteenth century.

3.11 Will Worldviews and Cultures Change?

Globalization often leads to the belief that cultures can and will change fundamentally. A Chinese coach and colleague once said, "*China is becoming more and more Americanized*". We advised this trainer not to use this statement in seminars, as it would be all too easy for the participants to accept. It would confirm their view that China would sooner or later become "*Western*". Similar viewpoints abound that this will happen to most other cultures.

Historical experiences, worldviews and a sense of what is right for a community will not change fundamentally. What changes are lifestyles, because it is what unites people in all cultures is the pursuit of material security, prosperity and a long and healthy life. The transformation in China from the austere lifestyle under Mao to today's Western lifestyle has been particularly dramatic; it has not even taken a generation in some parts of the country to change.

The best way to reflect on the question of whether worldviews and cultures will change is to compare it against the background of your own culture. Everyone has strong ties to his culture and its values acquired during socialization. We usually feel very strongly about it and change is often perceived as a threat. Although national culture is often made up of subcultures and lifestyles have become westernized or Americanized in many areas, the fundamental identity and values of a culture are the ingredients for a healthy society.

Gaining access to people from other cultures means to accept them and their values in their otherness, to meet them with respect and to express this through appropriate communication and body language.

The encounter with people of diametrically opposed worldviews and cultures often leads to polarization. Contrasting characteristics of cultures are instrumentalized negatively, particularly in the media. They are presented and perceived by each party as an attack on their world and their cultural values. Media users take up this view and spread it further.

The media play a key role in forming individual opinions about other cultures and the world view of public opinion. By simplifying facts, they often create and enhance prejudices about people living in different worlds. This is partly due to the fast-moving pace of today's news cycle which leads to superficial research and an undifferentiated proliferation of distorted images. It is also partly due to the fact the purveyors of information have little or no knowledge about foreign cultures. Media people often take their own beliefs and present it as facts, patronizing the reader or viewer instead of giving him the facts from which he may form his own opinion.

Media reporting on China is a prime example of this. Due to the lack of knowledge of Chinese culture, journalists copy from each other as Peter Achten,[14] longtime Asia correspondent for the Swiss TV and radio said in his farewell interview before retiring. From the Chinese perspective, the condemnation of their

[14]https://www.hiddenchina.net/web/deu/peter_achten.html. Last viewed 30.11.18.

culture by the West evokes memories of attempted colonization at the beginning of the last century, the Boxer Rebellion, and leads to counter-claims about the hegemony of the West. Simplistic reporting leads to polarization, a preliminary step to potential conflicts.

3.12 Taboos in the International Context

The following points have proved to be critical in our experience of dealing with other cultures:

1. Critical questions and intercultural debates: In the Asian and Arab world, but also in the American world, their own cultures enjoy absolute respect. Critical confrontation with these cultures leads to incomprehension and rejection. Only if there has been a longstanding basis of trust may such topics be addressed, preferably in private. Otherwise, resentments are created, and the relationship is doomed from the start.
2. Addressing human rights issues and corruption: Both issues have little to do with the cultural influences, and everything to do with political and economic scenarios. In other words, human rights violations and corruption are a reality in all cultures.
3. Religion, political system and gender roles: They do not lend themselves as topics for discussion, because they are strongly interwoven with the elementary value system of a culture. Religion, politics and gender roles are part of the cultural self-image of a community and their individuals.
4. Direct communication: In an international context, direct communication is a barrier that often leads directly to conflict and escalation. In some cultures, this may happen without us even noticing.

Summary

Viewing the world and its cultures from a different viewpoint—holistic and from a macro-perspective—is a pragmatic and direct way to overcome prejudices and stereotypes and to understand people who think and act differently. It helps us to maintain our natural spontaneity whilst our experience in dealing with the otherness will open new dimensions in discovering foreign worlds.

In conclusion we see that

1. Environmental conditions and the climate, as well as the historical experience of a society have shaped a community over centuries until the modern times. It gives us insights into understanding differing behaviors.

(continued)

From this starting-point we can proceed on how to approach and get access to people from other cultures successfully.

2. There are two different world views: the holistic in the Asiatic and Islamic world and the changeable of the Western world. Both perspectives have been cemented over centuries. Holding up the Western view of the changeable world is as an example to the Asian and Islamic world leads to conflicts. We brush it aside when a majority of people in a given culture tell us they do not identify with our view, i.e. as is the case with China and Russia.
3. Hierarchy and exercising power directly are a norm in collective societies. Hierarchy per se is not a negative, and abuse of power is not exclusive to collectivist societies. It also happens every day in democracies.
4. A collectivist society has learned over time to accept that survival is only granted within a collective. Social cohesion and preserving and giving face are essential for the mental health and well-being of its members.
5. Managing business may not only differ in Asia, but also within Europe. In Germany, the focus is on the challenges of the market while in Sweden, it is on the social well-being of the employee (see also Sect. 3.2.2.1 Masculinity).
6. High or low uncertainty, as defined by Gert Hofstede, cause varying reactions among individuals, resulting in differing behaviors. They high score in individualistic Germany characterizes stress in business life, which is managed by rules, documentation and assigned responsibilities. The very low uncertainty avoidance score in Singapore may be attributed to its strict laws, rules and regulations in the public sector. Therefore, uncertainty is not perceived as a problem by members of this society (see also Sect. 3.2.2.2 Avoidance of Uncertainty).
7. Establishing and nursing relationships is the basis for successful (business) life in many cultures—not only in Asia, but also in France, etc.
8. Education through socialization and schooling is related to communication behavior and style. As examples, empathy and eloquence are required in the US, whereas intuition, patience, and sitting out long periods of silence are the ingredients for acceptance in Japan
9. Rituals provide security and help to avoid conflicts: Togetherness in cultures is shaped by rituals in personal and business lives. Knowing what they are and how to deal with them is a key to gaining acceptance and building successful relationships.
10. Hospitality and gifts have a deep and binding meaning in many cultures and are ritualized in a broader sense. Corruption is not a culture-specific problem but has to do with the personal behaviors of people who act either from greed or need.

Bibliography

English

Augsburger, D. W. (1992). *Conflict mediation across cultures* (1st ed.). London: Westminster John Knox Press.

Hofstede, G., Hofstede, G. J., & Minkov, M. (2010). *Cultures and organizations—Software of the mind: intercultural cooperation and its importance for survival*. New York: McGraw-Hill.

Liker, J. K. (2004). *The Toyota way: Fourteen management principles from the world's greatest manufacturer: 14 management principles from the world's greatest manufacturer*. New York: McGraw-Hill.

Nägele, U. (2014). Lighthouses and warning buoys in the field of international project management. https://www.xing.com/profile/Ulrich_Naegele3?sc_o=mxb_p

Tixier, M. (1994). Management and communication styles in Europe: Can they be compared and matched. *Employee Relations, 16*(1), 8–26.

Wenzhong, H., & Grove, C. (1999). *Encountering the Chinese*. Boston: Intercultural Press Inc. (1991 und 1999).

German

Daniel, S., & Motak, H. (2005). *Kein Gemeinsinn in China?* Erstellt am 14.08.2005 in.

Harrs, C., & Semidelichina, O. (2006). Ein AC (Assessment Center) von Russen für Russen. *Fachzeitschrift ManagerSeminare*, Heft 97 vom April 2006 (see also www.managerseminare.de).

Lin-Huber, M. (1998). *Kulturspezifischer Spracherwerb* (1. Aufl.). Bern: Hans Huber.

Lin-Huber, M. (2001). *Chinesen verstehen lernen* (1. Aufl.). Bern: Hans Huber.

Nägele, U. (2011). *Führung in internationalen Projekten – Einflussfaktor Machtdistanz*. Ausgabe 07/2011 in www.projektmagazin.de

Cultures of Our World

4

Summary
In the following chapter we will attempt to transpose the findings from the previous chapter "*Access to other cultures*" in relation to individual countries. In this process, we—as authors—have primarily focused on the countries known to us from our business activities, project work and teaching. We believe that these countries will serve as examples for all those not described in detail and will serve the reader as a guide to develop his own approach to a culture of his interest.

However, in order to be able to report comprehensively on as many cultures in this world as possible, we have also employed third party authors to contribute on their cultures. The original book was based on a standard structure for each culture. Due to the addition of cultures by 3rd party authors, this basic structure will not be strictly adhered to in all the countries, i.e. Africa, Arabic and Islamic World, India, Canada, United Kingdom, which all have the individual touch of their authors.

Our main focus is on the people in these countries—their values, ways of life and how we can succeed in building successful relationships with them.

The individual chapters have the same basic structure, namely:

1. Culturally defining elements
2. Communication and conflict resolution
3. Cooperation in professional and business life

(continued)

P. M. Haller et al., *Bridging Cultural Barriers*, Management for Professionals,
https://doi.org/10.1007/978-3-030-17130-8_4

Some philosophical guidance on our concept and approach:

1. We differentiate between the individual country contributions in regard to scope and detailed structure in order to be fair to the uniqueness of every culture described hereafter, because every culture is different.
2. We write from real life experience as a journey through the cultures of the world.
3. Together with you, we want to illuminate the kaleidoscope of what constitutes the diversity of human existence, while we remain fully aware that it depicts only a cross section.
4. We will be creating images of different worlds, which may continue to work within you.
5. Collective work and communication with other cultures is not about doing everything right, but about interaction with people, developing a shared goodwill, and feeling at ease. Because all business is ultimately personal!
6. At the same time, we believe that we can create a deeper sense of understanding and a general broad sense of what various cultures represent, what it means to really engage with them, and how to accept what is different.
7. We want to touch you as well as be a little thought-provoking. We reveal what have experienced and are experiencing, which has deeply convinced us that positive emotions among people from different cultures can create something good, lasting and unifying.

4.1 National Cultures Versus Social Cultures

Modern intercultural teaching is moving away from the model of national cultures, because it is too loosely knit and cannot be sufficiently differentiated. There are undoubtedly any number of subcultures in every country, e.g. the regions Swabia and Bavaria in Germany; the Bretons, Corsicans and Occitanians in France; the East and West Coasts and cultural islands through immigration and slavery in the USA; the Han, Tibetans, Kyrgyz people, Kazakhs, Mongols etc. in China.

Everyone's world view is shaped by his own experiences, values, prejudices and clichés, and cultural affiliation is often recognizable at a glance. In cross-cultural situations, these are the actual barriers that prevent the creation of a common understanding and sustainable relationships. French friends and acquaintances used to say, "*When we first meet someone who comes from Germany, we first and foremost see the German or Germans*". We must first overcome this barrier to discover the human being and the personality behind his mother culture. This is pertinent to every human being and applies in and out of the cultural paradigm. Those who do not attempt to overcome their prejudices in intercultural contacts will inevitably communicate them through body language and thus prevent the building of trust.

Therefore, this book uses the discussion, analyses and understanding of stereotypes of "national cultures" as the basis for the building a personal and "*natural*" intercultural competence which gives us access to alien cultures. In taking this approach we are aware that this is a grossly simplified representation of a given culture. However, to get the grasp of the essential differences between cultures, this has been a proven way in our past experiences as facilitators and coaches to better understand, why people form alien cultures think and act so differently from what we are used to.

4.2 Africa

My name is Adiza Ujo, author of this contribution about the people and culture of Sub-Saharan Africa. I'm a graduate of English language and International Affairs and Diplomacy. I was born in Benue State, Nigeria in 1981 and live in Abuja, Nigeria. I am an entrepreneur and an environmental advocate, and the convener of an NGO called "Stewards of the Environment for Sustainable Change" Initiative best known as Stop Don't Drop. I love being in nature and enjoy travelling and experiencing different cultures especially through their music, fashion, dance, arts and food.

As third-party contributor to this amazing book on inter-culture, it is my honor to take you on journey to one of the most fascinating and most misunderstood continents in the world—the continent of Africa. The continent I fondly call the motherland. The continent of my birth. My focus however will be on the countries south of the Sahara Desert often referred to as sub-Saharan Africa or Black Africa, the reason being that north Africa has a shared Arab heritage which distinguishes it from other regions in Africa. However, there are social, physical, cultural, and historical connections which unite north Africa with the regions of Africa south of the Sahara.

4.2.1 Sub Sharan Africa

Sub Saharan Africa according to the United Nations is the term used to describe the area of the Africa continent which lies south of the Sahara Desert.[1]

In the post-colonial era many international organizations, foreign governments and academics divided Africa into two major regions: North Africa ('*Arab Africa*') and Sub-Saharan Africa ('*Black Africa*').

The rationale for this bifurcation of Africa into two regions was political and cultural. Many outsiders perceived sub-Saharan Africa as being socially and culturally distinct from north Africa. According to this regional and racialized

[1]https://en.wikipedia.org/wiki/Sub-Saharan_Africa. Last viewed 15.10.18.

classification, sub-Saharan Africa is comprised of traditional African cultures and societies and by the '*black race*'. North Africa, on the other hand is claimed to be dominated by the Arab culture, language, and '*non-black*' peoples, who '*physiologically*', culturally, and socially are not African, with their roots in western Asia (Middle East).[2]

4.2.2 At the Mention of Africa

At the mention of Africa, a lot of things come to the minds of people. When I asked a cross section of my friends, some well-travelled and others not, African and non-African alike, the first things that come to their minds when Africa is mentioned for a good number of them are clichés such a Black, Poverty, Crime, Corrupt dictators, Scammers, Violence, Pestilence, HIV/AIDS, Ebola, Famine and Hunger, Dying children with flies all over their faces, mud huts and half-clad people living on trees. On the brighter side, some thought Safaris, fantastic wildlife "*the big five*", the pyramids of Egypt, colorful tribes, hot sunny weather and exotic nature.

I was keen to find out what led to these clichés, so I asked my friends, why these clichés about Africa? To this they replied, information from the broadcast media through television, radio, newspapers, magazines and the internet. For some others, it was based on not just the media and internet but on interactions with some "*criminal*" African immigrants in different cities in Europe.

But do all these clichés depict the true picture of Africa?

- A proverb by renowned Nigerian writer Chinua Achebe says:

- *"Until the lion learns to tell his story, the tale of the hunt will always glorify the hunter"*. In other words, until Africans begin to tell their own story, the stories written about Africa will always glorify the writer of such stories.

4.2.3 Africa: A Country?

A few months ago, I visited Germany and I engaged some of my German friends in a brain picking session about Africa, I asked them how many countries there are in Africa and how many they could mention. The numbers varied from between 50 and 30 to 45. None of them knew the exact number but at least they knew that Africa is not a country. My African friends were shocked to be asked when abroad, especially in the USA, if they speak African, even though this has never happened to me personally.

---

[2]http://exploringafrica.matrix.msu.edu/curriculum/unit-four/module-eighteen/. Last viewed 15.10.18.

4.2.4 Do You Speak African?

The idea that African is seen as a language and Africa as a country is a jaw-dropping shocker to a lot of people from the continent of Africa. This is further reinforced by statements such as "*African children walk for hours from the village to educate themselves*" or "*African children walk seven to ten miles just to get to school for one hour*" or "*African families have no access to clean portable water*" or feeding programs making statements like "*for just one dollar, we can provide two nutritious hot meals for an African child*" or "*By donating a pound today, you, too, could save an African child.*" These statements have been made many times over and paints a picture of a "*needy*" Africa that is somehow engulfed in some kind of food, water, health care, economic or educational crisis, desperate to be saved by the western world. This picture suggests it could spell doom for entire Africa if nothing is done about it. While in some parts of Africa, this holds true, Africa in its entirety is not a hotbed of misery.

Over the years these stereotypes have formed the single story of Africa—the single story that Africa is a dark continent full of misery and wildlife. With this kind of mindset, it is difficult, if not impossible to truly grasp the essence of the people of the continent of Africa. It is this stereotypes that this work seeks to correct. In reality African is not a language and Africa is certainly not a country.

4.2.5 Meet Africa

There is no continent on the surface of planet earth quite like Africa, richly blessed with natural resources, wild life, striking beauty and cultural diversities. Africa is famous for its beautiful historical sites such as the City of Timbuktu in Mali, the Great Sphinx of Giza and pyramids of Egypt, the Isimila stone age site in Tanzania, and the Osun Oshogbo Shrine in Nigeria, just to mention a few. Its magnificent wildlife draws many people from around the world to Eastern and Southern Africa for the purpose of experiencing nature and watching these incredible animals in their natural habitat. Its unsurpassed natural wonders and coastlines, lush forest vegetation, unbelievable scenery, unforgettable cultures and the hospitality of its people.

Growing up on the continent of Africa, we were taught that Africa is the birthplace of the human species and there is literature to back up this claim. Of the seven continents in the world, Africa is the second largest continent, second only to Asia.

The continent of Africa is made up of 54 countries and well over 2000 languages.

Research from different online sources reveals that Africa sits on 30.3 million km^2 (11.7million square miles) including adjacent islands. It covers 6% of the Earth's total surface area and 20% of its total land area.[3] Geographically Africa is comprised of desert, savannas and rainforest. Some of the world's longest rivers are located on

[3]https://en.wikipedia.org/wiki/Africa. Last viewed 15.10.18.

the continent, including the Nile, Niger, Zaire and Zambezi. Mount Kilimanjaro is the highest mountain in Africa and the highest free-standing mountain in the world at 19,341 feet.[4]

Africa boasts of a vast majority of indigenous inhabitants. However, people from all over the world have migrated to Africa for hundreds of years. The Arabs began crossing into North Africa from the Middle East in the seventh century A.D., bringing with them the religion of Islam. Europeans began settling in the southern portion of the continent in the mid-seventeenth century as did South Asians, who settled in the areas of Uganda, Kenya, Tanzania and South Africa.

Over the centuries, African culture has meshed with cultures from around the world, although much of traditional African customs have remained intact.

The continent of Africa is rich with unique culture diversities which are found across different countries.[5] Nigeria, for example, has over 250 languages and over 300 different ethnic groups. Every culture has its own unique characteristics. People across the continent of Africa, are remarkably diverse by just about any measure; they speak a vast number of different languages and practice a number of distinct religions. The people of the continent of Africa are notoriously religious people. They live in a variety of different types of dwellings and engage in a wide range of economic activities. Even though African cultures are widely diverse, they are also seen to have many similarities such as respect for the elderly, religious and village heads, the communal way of life, hospitality etc.

African culture finds expression in a variety of ways, notably through language, arts, folklore religion, fashion, food and music. However, there are certain sad truths about Africa that must be told no matter how uncomfortable—the stories of colonialism, apartheid, corruption, civil wars, diseases and poverty which many countries in Africa are no stranger to. Several African countries have experienced oppressive military dictatorship regimes which saw gross violations of human rights and dignity, civils wars, ethnic cleansing, insurgency, and an institutionalized corruption which has also become a way of life for some people. In my country Nigeria, for example, corruption has eaten so deep into the fabric of the country that many Nigerians have become socio-culturally corrupt. Corrupt Nigerians in the corridors of power have become iconic role models and celebrities for many unemployed Nigerian youths who aspire to be like them by getting rich by any means. Many of them resort to advance fee fraud popularly known as 419 or seek greener pastures in Europe and other developed countries of the world. Many African leaders seek reelection into public offices which gives them unfettered access to the public coffers as well as immunity from prosecution.

Almost every aspect of national life in countries in Africa is affected by corrupt practices, which holds back development in other areas of social life. However, this is not the only story of African countries. There is more to Africa than what is

---

[4]http://www.moartdeland.org/wp-content/uploads/2013/04/Africa-Study-Guide-Museum-of-Art-DeLand 5. Last viewed 15.10.18.

[5]https://www.victoriafalls-guide.net/both-countries.html. Last viewed 18.10.18.

reported by the international media. Every country of the world has its fair share of problems, but those of countries in Africa are, more often than not, over-magnified.

4.2.6 Regions of Subsaharan Africa

Geographers, social scientists, economists, political scientists, and historians usually divide the African continent into four to six regions. Given the social, cultural and economic diversity within each of these regions, the rationale for constructing these regions is primarily spatial location.[6]

- Four regions: North Africa, West Africa, East Africa, Southern Africa
- Five regions: North Africa, West Africa, Central Africa, East Africa, Southern Africa
- Six regions: North Africa, West Africa, Central Africa, North East Africa, East Africa, Southern Africa.

This work will however concern itself with the five-region classification and will focus on four out of the five geographical regions of Africa. These include West Africa, East Africa, Southern Africa and Central Africa.

4.2.7 West Africa

Located in the western part of sub-Saharan Africa, the region defined as West Africa consists of 16 nations sharing various colonial heritages including British, French, Portuguese and even American. This makes West Africa the most culturally diverse region on the African continent. The 16 countries that make up West Africa include Benin, Burkina Faso, Ivory Coast, Cape Verde, Gambia, Ghana, Guinea, Guinea-Bissau, Mali, Mauritania, Niger, Nigeria, Senegal, Sierra Leone and Togo. Spanning over 5 million square miles, West Africa is bordered to the west by the Atlantic Ocean and in the north by the Sahara Desert.[7]

The nations of West Africa have vibrant cultures. Significant cultural and religious diversities exist among the countries of the West African region as well as different cultures within their boundaries. Despite the wide variety of cultures, similarities are apparent in dress, cuisine and musical genres. Musicians from the region are world-renowned and its musical traditions have influenced jazz, blues, rock and other music heard in the West and in Latin America. Traditional clothing ranges from the brightly colored and elegant Boubous worn by the women to the

[6] http://exploringafrica.matrix.msu.edu/curriculum/unit-four/module-eighteen/. Last viewed 15.10.18.

[7] https://en.wikipedia.org/wiki/West_Africa. Last viewed 15.10.18.

regal kente cloth robes with colors representing virtues such as peace, purity, healing, and renewal.

4.2.8 East Africa

East Africa is part of sub-Saharan Tanzania, Kenya, Uganda, Rwanda, Burundi, Eritrea, Ethiopia, Somalia, South Sudan, and Sudan. East Africa is home to Africa's tallest peaks, Mt. Kilimanjaro and Mt. Kenya. Lake Victoria, the second largest freshwater lake in the world, and Lake Tanganyika, the second deepest lake in the world, are both found here as well. The excellent weather, with moderate temperatures hovering around 25 °C/77 °F, has helped tourism thrive and plays a major role in certain economies. The Great Rift Valley and the surrounding savannas in Kenya and Tanzania are home to some of the largest game reserves in Africa, with a broad variety of big game animals. One of these large regions is the vast Serengeti Plain, located in northern Tanzania and southern Kenya. The Serengeti Plain is host to an extraordinary diversity of large mammals and fauna. The largest migration of land animals in the world occurs in the Serengeti. Every fall and spring, as many as two million wildebeests, antelope, and other grazing animals migrate from the northern hills to the southern plains in search of grass and food. The Ngorongoro Conservation Area, which is a UNESCO World Heritage Site, and the Ngorongoro Crater are located on the Tanzanian side of the border. The enormous crater is the basin of an extinct volcano that has been transformed into a protected national park for the animals that graze on its grassy plains.[8]

English is the official language in Kenya, Uganda and Tanzania while Kiswahili is the national language. There are hundreds of languages spoken throughout East Africa, ranging from those spoken by only a few thousand to those spoken by millions. With over 80% of the 130 million residents being Bantus, East African cuisine makes heavy use of grains and tubers, which are often processed into a mash, eaten with either bread or rice. Yams, millet, sorghum, beans, corn and teff[9](which belongs to the family of millets) are all widely prevalent. These dishes are generally accompanied by a meat dish and significant amounts of milk and butter. Pork is not widely seen in East Africa, because of the Islamic influence; most meat dishes consist of chicken, beef or buffalo.[10]

---

[8]https://saylordotorg.github.io/text_world-regional-geography-people-places-and-globalization/s10-05-east-africa.html. Last viewed 15.10.18.

[9]https://de.wikipedia.org/wiki/Teff. Last viewed 18.10.18.

[10]https://traveltips.usatoday.com/culture-east-africa. Last viewed 18.10.18.

4.2.9 Central Africa

Central Africa, defined by the UN sub-region, consists of the following countries: Cameroon, Central African Republic, Chad, Congo Republic-Brazzaville, Demo cratic Republic of Congo, Equatorial Guinea, Gabon, São Tomé & Principe. This region spans the Equator and contains the Congo Basin with the second largest rainforest in the world. Central Africa is also rich in mineral resources. Consequently, mining oil is a leading export of the region.

Africa has natural resources such as rivers, lakes and fertile soil that allow for farming and other agricultural activities. Central Africa covers a large physical area that can range from desert conditions to the north in Chad to tropical rain forests and mountains in the equatorial region of The Congo. The Equator runs through the middle of Central Africa. Tropical humid Type A climates are dominant in the region, complete with tropical rain forests and jungle environments. Lake Tanganyika and Lake Albert are two of the larger lakes in Central Africa along the western section of the Great Rift Valley. Lake Tanganyika is more than 418 miles long and runs the entire length of the boundary between the Congo and Tanzania. These are deep-water lakes. Lake Tanganyika is the world's second-deepest lake, with a depth of 4800 ft. Because of its depth, it is also the world's second-largest lake by volume after Lake Baikal in Russia, which has the record for both volume and depth.

Fish and fresh water from Lake Tanganyika support millions of people who make their living directly from the lake's resources or who live in the surrounding area.

Central Africa resonates with cultural and ethnic diversity. Hundreds of ethnic groups live and work together with a high degree of interaction. Traditional cuisine and beverages such as coffee, tea, or beer can be found throughout the region.[11]

4.2.10 Southern Africa

Southern Africa is the southernmost region of Africa consisting of the independent countries Angola, Botswana, Lesotho, Mozambique, Namibia, South Africa, Swaziland, Zambia, Zimbabwe. The region is rich in valuable mineral deposits. The discovery of gold and diamonds in the eighteenth century by colonial powers contributed to violent conflict and apartheid. Today the region is the most the developed one in Africa. The region has a wide diversity of eco-regions with significant numbers of wildlife species. Southern Africa is home to many cultures and people. It was initially populated by indigenous or native Africans. English is an official language in all the countries in the region except Mozambique, and most urban dwellers speak it fairly well. Afrikaans is widely spoken in South Africa and Namibia, and German is also spoken by some in Namibia. You may encounter

[11]https://saylordotorg.github.io/text_world-regional-geography-people-places-and-globalization

Portuguese in the region as well, especially in Mozambique where it is the official language. The Bantu languages dominate the area.

4.2.11 The African Woman and Her Role in Society

From our beautiful skin tones of caramel to mahogany and our curvaceous bodies, black women are the epitome of beauty. We have a long history of being devalued, ignored, ridiculed, stereotyped, called ugly, promiscuous, invisible to society—the list goes on—yet we are resilient and continue to rise and shine in our many talents and unique ways.[12]

Women the world over, especially on the continent of Africa, play very pivotal roles in upholding the cultures of their societies, especially in the areas of family and nation building. As mentioned earlier, Africa is not a single country or one cultural area, but a continent which is marked by great cultural and linguistic diversities. Generalizations about the role of women in sub-Saharan African will not paint a true picture, as the cultural roles women play in one tribe or ethnic group even in the same geographical sub-region may differ from others. A proper understanding therefore involves an appreciation of different cultural patterns and underlying similarities shared by many African societies. This segment will attempt to do just that, but before we dive into the roles African women play in different African countries south of the Sahara, it is important to know who the African woman is.

4.2.11.1 Who Is an African Woman?

As a woman of Nigerian descent, born and raised in different cities of Nigeria, I often get asked what country I am from whenever I get into conversations in the course of my travels to Europe, most especially Germany. After speaking with me for a few minutes, a few people ask me if I am from the USA or the United Kingdom. When I tell them that I am Nigerian, they ask me if I was born or live in Nigeria, to which I respond "*Yes!*" This is either closely followed by "*Really? Where did you learn to speak such good English?*" or "*you are so different*" or total silence, with looks of confusion or disbelief, maybe even embarrassment. To them, I am nothing like they imagined an African woman to be. Their expectation of me when I opened my mouth did not fit their picture of who they had in mind or had been conditioned to believe is a woman from Africa. But why not?

To better understand why, I asked a cross section of my friends once again from Germany, Italy and the United Kingdom, some well-travelled but not in Africa, to be brutally honest with me and tell me the first picture that pops into their heads when they are asked who an African woman is.

Here are the opinions of a few of my friends from Germany, Italy and the United Kingdom:

[12]Dr. Shanessa Fenner.

- “*Masai woman, with colored collars on her neck and a baby at her breast*”.
- “*Black, having different looks, and unknown behavior.*” I asked for further clarification and got this response: “*different people, different behavior, different ways of life*”.
- “*Migration to Europe, doing menial jobs and women of easy virtue (prostitutes on the streets of Europe)*”.
- “*Women in small villages away from big cities with mouth plates and rings around their necks*”
- “*Poor starving, illiterate woman with a lot of children to feed, an object of pity, walking for miles to get water for her livestock*”.

1. An Italian friend had this to say about the African woman
   (a) “*Friendly, smiley faces with sharp contrast between white teeth and dark skin*”
   (b) “*In terms of physical features* “*rounded hips and big lips and Rasta hair*””.
2. A Nigerian friend had this to say
   (a) “*A woman of African descent, a unique person with a lot of capacity to nurture*”.

When I asked why this picture of the African woman, a German friend said on a lighter note, “*Well, haven't you watched 'The White Masai?*'” Most of the responses my non-African friends gave were once again born out of what the media presented to them as the image of the African woman. These images were somehow burned into the memories so much that at the mention of African woman that is what pops up, not the image of me who is also an African of Nigerian descent or their female African counterparts from work or school from different African countries.

While it is true that traditional dresses and beads are a big part of African culture, a Masai woman with colorful beads around her neck in Kenya and a Mursi woman with a lip plate in Ethiopia do not represent the same image of the Yoruba, Hausa or Idoma woman in Nigeria or the Ashanti or Ewe woman in Ghana. Neither does it represent the Bamileke woman of Cameroon or the Forro woman in Sao Tome and Principe.

Pictures of women in drought-stricken rural villages in Somalia and Malawi walking for miles to get water for their children and livestock do not represent the pictures of rural women in Angola, Niger or Cote d'Ivoire, neither do women of African descent cleaning toilets or prostituting themselves on the streets of Europe represent the true image of the women from the continent of Africa. In terms of shapes and sizes, we are diverse; Fulani women of northern Nigeria and Masai women from Kenya are tall and slim compared to their counterparts from Zimbabwe and South Africa who are more rounded in the hips. So, who then is an African woman? African women according to Wikipedia are women who were born in, who live in, and who are from the continent of Africa. They are usually associated with darker skin and kinky or curly hair and who come in different shapes and sizes in terms of personality, too. Anna Njoroge, Founder-CEO of Ythera, describes the African woman best in the following lines: The African Woman is beautiful, powerful, unique, feminine and authentic. She is phenomenally resilient, passionate in the pursuit of her dreams and inspirational in her drive to succeed; she is multidimensional seamlessly moving between the traditional and modern, the village and the city, the, home and the office. . .she is Limitless. Her strength is remarkable, she holds the family together, she is a business woman, she is in the boardroom, she is a mom, and a wife, innovative and inspirational. She wears different hats effortlessly. She is amenable accommodating while still maintaining her independence and without being overbearing, which takes tremendous strength and confidence. She aspires to make a global change . . . She defies definition . . .She is limitless.

4.2.11.2 Roles of Women in Africa

Patriarchy, traditions, colonialism and religion all play a big part in the role of women in sub-Saharan Africa. With the exception of a few tribes where matriarchy is practiced, the traditional roles for a woman in most sub-Saharan African countries were to be homemaker, child bearer, water and firewood collector, farmer, and nurturer of children and the elderly subjected to repeated childbearing at short intervals to satisfy her husbands and societies´ quest for larger family size. Because of her role as a homemaker, she is often seen as a beast of burden as she's always seen carrying either a water pot balanced on her head or firewood, or farm produce in a basket on her head or shoulders or a baby or babies as they case may be. She comes from a background of not having as much independence, financially or otherwise. Women are supposed to take the back seat in traditional African settings. Limited by long standing traditional beliefs concerning gender roles and by patriarchal cultures, they are to be seen and not heard. Spending her youth under the authority of her father if not given out in early marriage and her adulthood under the control of her husband, she is sometimes left exposed to discrimination, exploitation and abuse in some African countries. Some cultural practices such as female genital mutilation, early marriages and a host of other traditions still hold sway.

In the last decades, however, social, economic, religious and cultural changes have dramatically altered the roles of African women in societies. Industrialization, urbanization, enlightenment, education and technological advancement have led to more women occupying more unique positions in society. The African woman is finding her voice and excelling in areas considered as male dominated and is able to uphold both family values and be efficient in society. Take Liberia, for example, that produced the first female elected president in the person of Ellen Johnson Sirleaf, and Agbani Darego from Nigeria who won Miss World, literature icon Chimamanda Adiachue, Kenya's Lupita Nyongo, Academy award winner, and so many too numerous to mention who have excelled in their chosen professions. However, one wonders why the image of helpless, oppressed and marginalized African women continues to be the first point of reference for a lot of people from the west. That answer can be found whenever the single story of the African woman is the only story about the African woman.

4.2.12 Getting Around Countries in Africa

No matter which region or countries of sub-Saharan Africa you go to, be it Southern, Western, Eastern or Central, they all have something unique to offer you, a rich experience that cannot be found anywhere else in the world apart from these countries.

Take for example my country Nigeria. My country Nigeria is the most populous country in Africa. A study done by the World Values Survey found Nigeria to be the world's happiest nation. Consecutive Gallup polls in 2010 and 2011 found Nigeria to be the world's most optimistic nation. Optimism has long been linked to happi ness in psychology, and Nigerians tend to believe that though things may be bad, they're looking up (*waitbutwhy.com* by Tim Urban[13]). The energy and positivism that one feels in Nigeria is contagious; the people of Nigeria will leave you inspired and energized. There's a spirit of hopefulness that shows in the way the people dance to any and everything, any and everywhere! Nigerians live as if tomorrow will be better and never ever give up. It is a coping mechanism in a country that has so much potential but has not yet harnessed enough of it.

Nigeria is Africa's largest economy, home to Nollywood and Africa's best musical industry, etc. Foreigners can walk the streets without fear of abduction and with a basic travel alertness and safety precautions, you can let down your guard and explore the wonders of the country.

Nigeria is hot–hot and humid! You're going to the right place if you're looking for sunshine because all through the year, Nigeria is generally warm. The weather varies from place to place. For instance, Jos (located in a plateau state in the middle belt zone of Nigeria) is typically cool while Borno in north-eastern Nigeria is typically hot. But it never snows, and it is often warm enough for kids to play in the rain. The high humidity also makes it feel much hotter than it actually is, and many people have air-conditioners in their cars, houses and offices to avoid the sticky sweatiness that comes with the weather. In Harmattan (the cooler, drier season that runs from late November till February or early March), the temperature drops slightly, especially in the evenings, and the trade winds bring along dryness and dust with them.

Everyone speaks English. Well, many people speak fluent English, but everyone speaks Pidgin English. Pidgin is a local variant—I would say it is a unique language on its own that combines local dialects, slang and some English words. No surprise, since English is the official language and most people speak it alongside one or two of 350+ local languages.

Nigerians are warm, friendly and loud. If you are lighter skinned or Caucasian, you might hear people call out '*oyinbo*' as you walk through the market or down more bustling areas. The term is often used in an endearing manner and should not be taken as an insult or rude reference to skin color. Nigerians are vocal and in areas where people rarely see white people, they may wave or say hello! In the same

[13]https://waitbutwhy.com. Last viewed 15.10.18.

markets and more bustling areas, personal space is a non-existent concept. Most people get right up to the next person when standing in line or tap shoulders/hands of strangers to draw their attention. With loud words and very dramatic gesticulations, Nigerians may also seem like they are arguing when describing an event to one another or passionately telling a story.

The country is chaotic. But relax, there's order in the chaos. In Nigeria, you might recognize aspects of the country that remind you of the roughness of Delhi, New York, London or Rio. In other areas, the roads are untarred, the buildings are simple, and the people lead quiet, agricultural lives. At first glance, there's no order; for instance, many people have their own generators to provide their own electricity as well as their own water supply. So, it looks like chaos when you see arbitrary police stops on roads, unclear instructions in government offices, loose security at borders, and unstable electricity. However, there's a formula to the chaos and with a local to explain a few things, you'll adapt to the system in no time.

Get ready for a meaty, spicy time. In major cities like Lagos and Abuja, you'll find every kind of food you are looking for in Nigeria—Indian, Japanese, American, French, Chinese—especially Chinese, and even Ethiopian. But what's the fun in coming to Nigerian without enjoying Nigerian food? Prepare for lots of meats, starches and spicy food. Pretty much everything in Nigeria is flavorful and often, spicy (hot). However, many places will gladly tame the pepper level of your meal if you give them a heads up. Nigerian food is a true representation of its people with an unlimited variety of options and a rich medley of flavors.

You are sure to completely win over the hearts of Nigerians if you say a word or sentence in a local language or Pidgin English. Nigerians appreciate it when others make an effort to learn their ways. You'll get even more points if you acknowledge a Nigerian legend: Fela, Agbani Darego, Jollof Rice. Want to take it further, sing '*African Queen*' by TuFace or dance 'Shoki' and watch people light up in glee. It is all about the effort. Public transportation might be a struggle. There is an availability of public transport, but they do not work with strict schedules and may be cramped. Your transportation will generally be taken care of.

Religion is part and parcel of everyday life. Nigeria is tolerant of all kinds of religion. However, do not expect people to separate their religious activities from those of their work lives. Even though the country is a secular state, almost half of the population identifies as Christian and a similar portion identifies as Muslim. The local traditional religions have managed to survive interspersed among Christianity and Islam. Do not be surprised to see people praying at the start of meetings or to see how proudly Nigerians wear their religious affiliations on their cars, door posts and popular culture. The country is also well decorated with churches and mosques.

Everything is a contradiction: there is so much wealth in the country—you'll find people living lifestyles that can rival that of British royalty or American tycoons, on legitimate wealth. In the same square mile, you'll find people living in penury. In Nigeria, everything exists side by side and in seeming harmony—wealth and poverty, corruption and religion. While these things exist simultaneously, the contrast is often stark and visible.

Nigerians are a flamboyant people. In Nigeria, big houses are big, parties are loud, and weddings are extravagant. Compared to other African countries, Nigerians often display their wealth in ostentatious ways. Nigerian weddings have a life of their own.

Funmi Oyatogun with her website *15 Things You Need to Know Before You Visit Nigeria* has some good advice to offer.[14]

4.2.13 Etiquette

Issues of etiquette are highly regarded in Nigeria. For example, age is greatly respected, and greeting of elders is a symbol of respect.

In most cultures, eating with the left or offering things with the left hand, is considered rude. It is also unacceptable to shake hands or pass things with the left hand.

Making eye contact with grown up is considered extremely disrespectful.

Calling elders by their first names is considered a sign of gross disrespect. You refer to them as aunty or uncle or ma, or sir.

4.2.14 Literature, Arts and Music

Nigerian has a long and incredibly rich literary history, Nigerians are traditionally story tellers. With colonialization and the introduction of reading and writing and the English language, Nigeria storytellers began sharing their talents with worldwide audience, notable among them Chinua Achebe, Nobel Laureate Wole Soyinka, Chimamanda Adiache, to name just a few.

In the area of graphic arts Nigeria is foremost for its sculpture, terracotta and bronze work of the ancient cities of Ife, Nok and Benin. These works are to be found in museums all around the world and these areas produce bronze castings, wood carvings and sculptures to this day. Nigerians are also expert weavers, dyers and tailors who also produce massive quantities of beautiful, rich colorful textiles.

In the area of performing arts, dance and music are perhaps the two most vibrant form of arts in Nigeria. Music is dependent on strong rhythms supplied by countless drums and percussion instruments ranging from highlife to Afro to beat Jazz, Juju etc.[15]

---

[14]https://twitter.com/funmioyatogun/status/988522284880154625

[15]https://www.everyculture.com/Ma-Ni/Nigeria.html. Last viewed 15.10.18.

4.2.15 Dealing with Cultural Differences: Background and Relevant Stories for Adaptation and Everyday Life

In his book "*Dealing with cultural differences: Contrasting the African and European Worldviews*" Orville Boyd Jenkins[16] draws up a summary from several years of experience in East Africa, particularly Kenya, where he lived for about 25 years. It is written in the hope that it will help people from a European cultural background to learn about the continent of Africa and also help those already living or planning to live in any part of Africa to adapt to that cultural background more easily.

Orville tried to briefly contrast of the African way of organizing reality and the European way of organizing reality. It is supposed to help foreigners in Africa to identify possible areas of conflict, to recognize such conflicts when they begin to arise, to accept the difficulties they have as foreigners as natural occurrences, to accept them in a positive manner and work through them, to try to develop a positive appreciation of the reasons in African culture for the differences, and finally to deal with differences, change enough to fit in with the African situation and to work within the terms of the existing differences. Though the book was essentially written for Europeans coming to Africa, it was also written to be helpful for Africans wanting to understand people from European backgrounds better and to understand why Europeans act in such strange ways and sometimes have such difficulties fitting into society.

Orville postulates that we are all products of the cultures in which we grew up. This is neither good nor bad—it is simply a basic component of being human. We have to learn how to be human in some way. The problem is in how we look at the other ways to also "*be human*". We can learn to deal with the differences if we try.

Orville's writing inspired me to begin to look around my immediate environment of Abuja and seek out foreigners who have lived and acclimatized and endeared their way into the hearts of so many locals to find out how they were able to adjust to a whole new culture other than theirs and embrace it with so much passion. They were all so willing to share their experiences and share how best people from other cultures like theirs can better adapt and avoid conflicts.

4.2.15.1 Africa Is How You Perceive and Live It!

A good friend and diplomat from the German Embassy in Abuja Nigeria recounted her story to me about her first posting to the continent of Africa, specifically to the country of Uganda. She told me that prior to her posting, she and her colleagues had to go through an integration course in Germany, where an elderly German lady who had lived many years in Uganda shared her experiences with them to prepare their minds on what to expect in Uganda. She came to Uganda armed with that information and of course what she read about the country from the internet. She was told during the integration course that Ugandan women are very conservative when it comes to dressing and she should mirror that in her dressing as a diplomat.

[16]http://orvillejenkins.com/langlearn/pdf/dealdiffbooklet.pdf.

On arrival at the city capital of Kampala, she saw that women were not dressed the way she had been informed but dressed very modern. She had a great experience and didn't feel like she stuck out being a white woman there. She integrated very well with the people.

4.2.15.2 What You Hear Is Not What They Mean

Greetings are an integral part of all cultures especially on the continent of Africa, either handshakes, palm touching, bowing or hand gestures, or just words to find out how someone's day is going. A friend of mine and first-time visitor to Nigeria expressed shock at being asked especially in the morning by Nigerians when exchanging pleasantries "How was your night?" The conversation usually goes something like this:

- Good Morning
- How are you?
- How is your family?
- ***How was your night?***
- Hope all is well with you?

So many other questions may be asked to which only the answer "*yes*" or "*We thank God*" or any short answer is required, but not extensive details.

The question "*How was your night?*" still does a number on my friend. As a German living only a few weeks in Abuja, she's gradually getting used to being asked this and responding accordingly.

The solution: When the question is asked, it means "*I hope you had a good and restful night*". Most Nigerian get that. Translated from Nigerian languages into English it doesn't literally mean "*tell me what you did in the course of your night*", which a lot of foreigners mistake it to mean.

4.2.15.3 An Extraordinary Way to Thank You

A friend was shocked while living in Zambia when she offered a lady a gift and the lady got on the ground rolling as a token of appreciation. She couldn't understand it at first but later got to understand that it was their cultural way of showing the highest level of gratitude or showing deep appreciation. There are still cultures around in the countries of Africa where people bow or prostrate themselves or kneel in appreciation even to greet elders. In the Yoruba culture of western Nigeria, till this day, during weddings the entire family of the groom must all lie face flat before the family of the bride before the wedding is consummated. It is not sign of slavery or superiority but a sign of total respect and a cultural practice.

4.2.15.4 African Time/Broken Clock

The concept of "*African time*", a term coined by Africans where they show up late for meetings or to events, was a great source of distress and anger to an Austrian/German business man I spoke to in Abuja. He told me when he first arrived in Nigeria that he was always the first to show up for business meetings while his Nigerian business partners would casually stroll in close to an hour later. He expressed anger at how he was kept waiting at government offices to see top government officials who never kept to time and appointments. This always ruined his day and left him disorganized and bitter towards the people he wanted to do business with. He abhorred meetings with them even for casual outings. Being German, he was accustomed to being punctual and planning ahead and could not understand why Nigerians never keep to time. As a result, his health and business were on the decline.

One day, however, he came to realize that he must walk with the timing and way of life of the people he wanted to do business with in order to succeed. He realized that he was coming from a privileged society where proper infrastructure was in place for things to work flawlessly. Today, he enjoys a successful business here in Nigeria and even though he still shows up early for appointments, he doesn't get as upset as he used to when he first arrived a few years ago and also when he travels and experiences similar delays in other African countries.

4.2.16 Culture Shock

Speaking on her cultural shock, a friend I spoke to had this to say: "*My culture shock was and probably always will be the fact that no artisan we have worked with so far has ever delivered on the date promised us. Usually, they would simply disappear for a few days, then later tell us a story why they couldn't deliver, promise a new date—with the same happening all over again. While I do understand there can be good reasons for a delay, I never quite wrapped my head around the way it was handled. This happened in Morocco, Zambia, and Nigeria, so I am almost inclined to call it an African phenomenon*".

Solution In dealing with people from the continent of Africa, it is important to never relate from the basis of European expectations in an African setting. Orville puts it clearly in his book when he writes "*The important thing is that standards for such values are not even: There are individuals in every society that fail to meet that society's expectations for politeness, planning, promptness, consideration, etc. The values themselves differ from one society to another. For example, societies have standards or responsibilities, but what is considered responsible behavior differs widely*".

► **Start from Zero When Going to Live in Another Culture**
A German diplomat advice's that coming to a country or embracing people of different culture entails coming with a mind as clean slate or a book. With no prior expectations and an understanding that people and cultures are different. He encourages engaging people of other cultures to better understand them before drawing conclusions. He gives an analogy of a European who is used to living in four-corner houses who comes to a culture where people live in round houses and expecting their maid to know how to clean the corners or getting infuriated when the maid is unable to cook and iron as it is done in his own culture, which he perceives to be the best way. Hanno Hille

4.2.17 What the West Can Learn from Africa[17]

The West is focused very much on individual success, individual rights, looking after yourself first. In Africa, there is a much stronger sense of community. Extended families are huge and often help each other. Sometimes, there is one breadwinner supporting up to 10 or 15 people. Caring for the elderly is up to the adult children. You don't leave your elderly parents in the lurch. Aunts and grannies help raise the kids, But the sense of community is strong. Life is not all about you.

Ubuntu
In South Africa, this is called Ubuntu[18]—human kindness, and human interdependence. The opposite of selfishness. We need each other, and we are there for each other. Hardship often brings people closer together. In Africa, you will find an amazing willingness to help strangers, to sacrifice for others, to think of others first. It's one of the most inspiring African values. We even have a popular Linux operating system named Ubuntu. This is definitely something the rest of the world can learn from us, especially Western, individualistic societies. African democracy is focused on including everyone, whereas Western democracy, with its basis in majority rule, divides people and nations.

Conclusion
To embrace people or culture without any stereotypes or expectations and be open to try out new experiences was the common thread I received from experts living and working in Nigeria. Culture shocks are to be expected but a thorough understanding of the cultural practices of the country one is in helps to prevent conflicts and strengthen relationships between people.

The African continent is home to 54 countries ranging from prosperous ones to countries that are plagued by violence and extreme poverty. Africa as a continent is probably one of the wealthiest in terms of mineral resources and natural beauty. It boasts of some of the world's most amazing wildlife destinations.

Despite all its wealth, it is the poorest and most misunderstood continent in the world, partly due to years of exploitation and colonization, empires taking from Africa without putting much back, raping and robbing the continent for their own gain, and partly due to years of mismanagement, poor government, corrupt leadership and bad education. In spite of this, the countries of Africa

(continued)

[17]https://www.quora.com/What-can-the-world-learn-from-Africa. Last viewed 15.10.18.

[18]Van Hooft L., (Author), King A., (Translator), Immaculee Uwanyiligira H.E. (Preface) The Power of African Thinking.: About Ubuntu, unifying leadership and a new world August 29, 2013.

are full of happy, beautiful, amazing and friendly people with a rich and vibrant culture.[19]

The culture of people is what marks them out distinctively from other human societies in the family of humanity—language, religion, arts, dressing, dance, norms, taboos and values. Getting beyond cultural stereotypes and seeing the individual is key to good cross-cultural negotiation preparation. Biased actions are the inevitable results of biased opinions. To understand people and their culture, to build profound relationships and to avoid potential conflicts it is pivotal to have many stories, not just a single story.

In the words of Chimamanda Adichie, "the problem with stereotypes is not that they are untrue, but they are incomplete."[20] To get along with other cultures a more balanced view is needed. All cultures must be respected and not impaired by color or geography or a single-story viewpoint. It is dangerous, if not oppressive, to hail one's culture as superior to another as all cultures are unique in themselves because '*universality can only be dreamed about when we have "slept" on truth based on specific cultural experiences*'.[21] Therefore, all cultures and the indigenous ways of knowing arising from them are to be respected and valued in their uniqueness.

4.3 The Arabic und Islamic World

Author's profile: *Raeid Meri, born in Bonn, is German with Palestinian roots.*

"People and encounters are my focal point." Motivation and proper communication have been the maxims that I've always been able to live by during my almost 15 years of management experience at various DAX companies and start-ups. After this valuable experience, I answered the call to work more closely and intensively for and with people. I have been following this vocation since 2012 and give coaching, training, and integration seminars or accompany action- and experience-oriented projects in corporate entities. I look forward to assisting and supporting people in the development of their intercultural competence and personality. raeid@walkthechange.de

[19]http://www.ipsnews.net/2008/09/development-africa-why-the-richest-continent-is-also-the-poorest/. Last viewed 15.10.18.

[20]https://www.ted.com/talks/chimamanda_adichie_the_danger_of_a_single_story. Last viewed Sept 21, 2018.

[21]https://www.ncbi.nlm.nih.gov/pmc/articles/PMC5442578/. Last viewed 18.11.18.

4.3.1 The Rules of Chaos: Driving a Car in the Orient

When you, as a Western person, take part in traffic in the Arab world, you will quickly realize that you have entered a different world. In the West road-users are accustomed to following the prevalent traffic rules such as right of way, traffic light signals, road markings and speed limits. In the Orient you find yourself in a different cosmos. The drivers look for suitable gaps in the traffic. Lanes do not seem to exist. Other vehicles drive unexpectedly from the left or the right onto other lanes. Even the capacity of a vehicle is not limited by the information in the vehicle's registration. This is regulated only by spatial capacity—eight or more passengers are not beyond the realm of possibility.

Even stronger than the strangeness of the rule-independent behavior of the "*others*" is the wonder that this chaos does not lead to constant accidents. The chaotic navigators master the traffic only because they orient themselves intensively—to the same extent as they set themselves above rules—by what is going on around them. They make their way in front of each other, look around, dare to shoot forward. But they stay in close contact with the others. They send signals and receive signals from the others. They know what may be possible, where to withdraw, and what they can dare to venture. The Westerner may perceive this as a violation of rules or even as a personal attack, but it is a finely balanced and tuned observation system focused on the surroundings without which nothing can work here.

One's first car rides in the Arab world can become an initiation into this other cultural space. Here, it is not the established (traffic) regulations that characterizes mutual interaction, but mutual attentiveness and near-physical contact. Not to mention the awareness that things work differently than what is "*planned*" or regulated.

Anyone who sticks to "*the rules*" or "*order*" in this process cannot expect to achieve his goals without further ado. Behavioral safety requires more active and communicative behavior than sticking to a codified regulatory framework.

4.3.2 Interculturality

Interculturality should be understood here as an encounter between people and institutions of the Western, European and Arab worlds. It takes place in three essential dimensions.

One dimension lies in the encounter of European oriented people with the Arab world and culture. The other, of course, is the encounter of Arab oriented people with European culture. Thirdly, however, one must be aware that the Arab oriented persons constantly encounter Western culture in their own world. This ranges from the products of Western technology and organization to the constitution of legal systems to the (Internet-based) presence of Western media and cultural products (sports, films, music, food, etc.). The Western/European mainstream often sees Arab cultural products as exotic exceptions. But for the Arab world Western/European cultural products are omnipresent, both as an orientation and as an aspiration.

While the Western oriented person enters Arab cultural space as a cultural illiterate, the people he encounters know and understand large areas of his Western culture, even if they themselves have a detached attitude toward it.

The basic experience of intercultural encounters is that anyone who moves through a new cultural space experiences the unsettling experience of strangeness. When I encounter strangers externally, I also encounter the stranger within myself. This unsettles and challenges.

In encounters with Arab culture, this risk takes place with a significant disparity. The Arab-enculturated person has the advantage that much of our culture is much more familiar to him than his culture is to us.

- *It is due to the character of the format that the explanations contained in this essay may occasionally be perceived as somewhat simplistic. However, they are not intended to deepen prejudice. Instead, the explanations are intended to show the range of benefits illuminating the existing structures and systems, creating thus an understanding of their significance.*

- *Firstly, we will convey the basic facts about Arab culture. After that, we will explore the fundamental characteristics of this culture to enable you understand its distinctive features. In the third part we will give you practical hints and tips for intercultural practice, the right attitude and competences for the Arab world.*

4.3.3 1. Part: Facts About the Arabic Cultural Area

4.3.3.1 From the Arabian Peninsula and Up to North Africa

When we talk about the Arab world, then we mean about 400 million people in 26 countries. These range from the Crescent (south of Turkey), across the Arabian Peninsula (Gulf States) and North Africa (Nile States) to the Maghreb countries. All these countries are united by the Arabic language, the Arab identity with remarkably similar cultural standards, and the Islamic religion.

The Arab League is a Federation of 22 of these 26 states and was founded in 1945. To work successfully in these countries, it is important to keep in mind that they are characterized by enormous differences in their economic development, economic and investment policies, and population structures.

Despite all the commonalities mentioned, large cultural differences between these countries and regions nonetheless exist and manifest themselves with great mutual animosity.

4.3.3.2 Islam and Its Importance to Society

The foundation of Islam (translated as peace) is the Koran. This is understood literally as the word of Allah delivered to the people in High Arabic by the Prophet

Muhammad. It is the guideline containing instructions for behavior and thoughts in daily life and towards which most of the almost 1.8 billion Muslims are oriented. Contrary to popular belief, Islam is not predominantly represented in the Arab cultural area. Although it originated here, it accounts for less than 25% of the world's Islamic population. Nearly half of the world's Islamic population lives in Indonesia, Pakistan, India and Bangladesh, probably spread through trade in the Indian Ocean.

The entire life of Muslims should be shaped in harmony with Islam. Because this faith is lived and practiced, it is also an attractive alternative to Christianity for Westerners seeking deeper religious affiliation. This is one of the main reasons that Islam is the world's fastest growing religion.[22]

The practices of Islam are essentially governed by five pillars:

1. **The Creed (Shahada)**—The speaking of the Shahada ("I testify that there is no God, but Allah and I testify that Muhammad is the Messenger of Allah"; "achadu ana la-ilaha-ill-allah wa achadu ana muhammadan rasulullah") is sufficient to be recognized as a Muslim.
2. **Prayer (Salâh)**—The daily ritual prayer (five prayers a day at three different times in the direction of Mecca) is the most valuable act in Islam.
3. **A Goods Tax (Zakât)**—is an asset-based donation.
4. **The fasting month Ramadan (Siyâm)**—is a form of abstinence and has the goal of self-control
5. **The Pilgrimage to Mecca (Hajj)**—which makes the global unity of Islam physically and socially experienceable

The end of the pilgrimage to Mecca is celebrated with a 4-day sacrificial festival (*Eid al-Adha*), the highest Islamic holiday. The festival of "*breaking the fast*" (*Eid al-Fitr or Sugar Festival*) takes place at the end of Ramadan, the month of fasting.

Unlike in Christian Europe, many Islamic-influenced countries know no separation of state and religion. The demarcation between legal and religious law is interpreted differently. The concept of value is closely tied to **Sharia law** (divine, indisputable law—a five-level religious-legal assessment) and includes not only the legal but also the moral aspects of coexistence.

[22] *Why Muslims are the world's fastest-growing religious group. In: Pew Research Center. 6. April 2017* (pewresearch.org).

4.3.4 Fundamental Insights

4.3.4.1 The Role of Women in the Arab World

An Introduction

A Swiss lady, intercultural facilitator and colleague of mine, married for 25 years to a Tunisian gentleman, said once: "*The biggest prejudice in the Western world is that we believe the Islamic world to be a macho world*".

We judge by outside appearances, but lack experience, as we have virtually no insight into the world of women in the Islamic world. We judge by our standards and take our beliefs and lifestyles as the sole acceptable way to organize a life. Media convey such a negative image of the women in the Islamic world, that it is hardly possible to represent an objective view. Those who try and wish to provide a more objective understanding in the internet are buried with loads of negative arguments and spitefulness.

How come that we measure the majority of the approximately 800 million of women in the Islamic world with the same yardstick? And what is wrong with the traditional role of women putting the interest of the family as a focus of their lifes?

Peter M. Haller

"*With Palestinian roots, I was born and raised in Germany, surrounded by a traditional family, almost the opposite to a modern western environment, I faced challenges to values and beliefs and questioned my way in life for almost a decade. Looking for orientation, I decided on a pilgrimage to Mecca, Saudi Arabia at the age of 20. As a third culture child.*[23] *a democrat and a Muslim believer I found my vocation in communicating with and caring for other people, constantly striving for a mutual understanding. My values are tolerance and equality.*

I have written this part after a visit to Jordan and Saudi Arabia and many discussions with very traditional women and men from the Muslim world".

Raeid Meri 18.11.18.

4.3.4.2 Gender Equality

The Quran is aspiration, benchmark and standard for all Muslims. Islamic scholars agree that it clearly states that women and men are not only equal before God. This is stated again and over again in unison by devout and faithful men and women. We all are considered to be the same dignified human beings with the same rights, religious and moral duties. Every human being is responsible for his actions and must stand up for the consequences.

[23]https://en.m.wikipedia.org/wiki/Third_culture_kid. Last viewed 18.11.2018.

▶ The Quran says:

▶ **"... The wives have rights similar to the obligations upon them, in accordance with honorable norms; and men have a degree above them (in responsibility), and Allah is all-mighty and all-wise." (Surah Al Baqarah 2:228)**

Purely as a result of the physiological and psychological differences and the differing strengths and weaknesses of man and woman created by God, individual tasks arise for both, with a special responsibility for the man.

The man is obliged to protect the family and provide for their maintenance. He must answer to God for his kindness and heart in securing the well-being of the family (Surah An-Nisa 4:19).

The woman, on the other hand, has the inborn responsibility for the well-being of her family and above all, for the education of the children. She is the main caregiver and reference person for their development and maturation. the Quran specifies that a mother should nurse her children when she physically capable of doing so.

▶ The supportive and responsible role of a husband serves to protect his wife and does not mean that one person is superior to the other.

▶ Justice in general is gender independent (Surah Al-Ma'idah 5:38 & 45, An-Nur 24: 2).

A Muslim woman must not only be supported, honored and protected in her role as a wife, but also as a sister, daughter and mother. Especially mothers gain a unique, lifelong status of respect and esteem.

The ownership of women is also clearly regulated in Islam. No woman is required to spend her funds for the family, if she owns or earns money. A woman is an independent legal entity from birth with the right to manage her property independently and on her own.

In a divorce, the spouse is entitled to financial compensation from her ex-husband—even permanent support for existing children (Surah At-Talaq 65: 6).

However, men and women are treated differently in the succession: A son will receive twice as much as a daughter. The reason is the man's role in supporting his relatives.

Starting over 1400 years ago the position of the woman has improved massively with the raise of Islam. Women were no longer seen as possessions and oppressed, but as free, equal, and dignified beings.

The Quran forbade inhuman practices of murdering girls who were executed before Islamic times:

... and when the girl buried alive is asked about crime or sin she had committed, she was killed? (Surah At-Taqwir 81: 8–9)

4.3.4.3 Respect

The Prophet Muhammad told the best among men is the one who cares best for his wife.

In my innumerable visits to Arab countries, I keep observing how courteous foreign women are also treated, whether it is the lowered gaze of men, the "*seating*" and "*right of way*" for women or keeping a door open during shopping or in elevators. Men go to the side in an elevator when a woman is approaching, and even stay out when it is too crowded. It happened to me last week in Jeddah that the elevator was empty, and I entered only after the single passenger, a veiled woman, gave me permission with a nod.

In the monorail of Dubai, I was kindly advised that I was in the "*woman's carriage*" and that I had to stay out or I might be subjected to a high fine. In fact, the women's section is physically separated only by large, clearly marked pink signs inside the coaches as well as on platforms. On my next ride I noticed the signs cautioning travelers: "*You are entering the women's cabin*". You cannot miss the signs in many buses. Under the "*No Smoking*" sign you can often find "*Reserved for Ladies & Elderly Passengers Only*".

4.3.4.4 Veiling

To set moral boundaries and protect the dignity of Muslims, there are dress codes for both sexes in Islam. Clothing should cover the believers so that the interest of the opposite sex is not attracted.

In the Quran, God asks believing men and women to look down and dress decently. God appeals especially to women when he says they should not display their jewelry except what is obvious, and they should pull their shawls over their bodies (Surah An-Nur 24:30–31).

These rules are also valid for visiting a mosque and whilst performing the prayer. The Islamic scholars agree that the woman's jewelry in this context means their hair, making the wearing of the "*hijab*" mandatory in the presence of men who are not close relatives, for the woman in everyday life.

I am not allowed to see my cousins or aunts without their "*hijab*". In visiting my family my entry is only granted once the veiling has taken place, even if male family members are already present.

Also challenging for me (with Arab roots): If I am invited to dinner with my partner it is not unusual that we spend the evening in separate rooms separated by gender and only see each other again after bidding farewell to the host.

The literal meaning of the term "*hijab*" is headscarf or cover or disguise. However, it goes beyond the act of covering the hair; it also includes the loose, long and opaque overdress that women should wear over their clothes. This "*veil*" resembles the traditional Christian clothing that nuns already clearly wore before Islam and still wear today as described in the Bible in Corinthians 11: 4–10.

The "*hijab*", however, is more than a veil: It shows awareness and consciousness in faith and his or her status as a believer Muslim women wear a "*hijab*" to obey God and to be recognized as honorable women. It gives dignity and stands for modesty, piety, responsibility and chastity (Surah Al-Ahzab 33: 59). As a very visible element of Islam, the "*hijab*" also stands for inner strength and power. It is not uncommon for women to defend their right to wear the hijab.

In Western cultures, the "*hijab*" is often viewed controversially and seen as a symbol of gender-specific oppression. However, most Muslim women wear the hijab by personal choice and consider it a privilege rather than a burden.

Women wearing a hijab often describe it as a "*liberating feeling*": Free from being reduced to a sexual object, to gender stereotypes, clichés or reduced to fashionable dresses expected by the society.

Various western friends who wanted to try the "*hijab*" on a visit to Jordan describe the experience as follows: "*No sooner had I put on the hijab, I felt a lot freer in the streets of modern Amman and more comfortable than before in my western clothes. It felt like being looked at and treated with respect—be it ordering a falafel, shopping in the souk or crossing the street*".

Practical and often to be seen—using the "*hijab*" as a "*cellphone holder*" on the ear. Not practical, as observed in Saudi Arabia only a few weeks ago—eating with facial veiling in public.

You can certainly argue whether concealing the face up to covering the eyes is in the spirit of the Quran. In my opinion, the writings refers only to the hair. Incidentally, in Mecca is not allowed to conceal or cover one's face whilst circling the Kaaba during the Hajj. This may give us a small hint.

4.3.4.5 A Few Facts About Marriage in Islam

In many Muslim families, the ultimate aim for a woman is still to make a good match in marrying as a virgin. However, women may not be forced to marry someone.

Unlike woman a man may marry several women. But he has to treat and support his women equally be it affectionately or financially.

The woman may marry only one man but can prevent her husband by contract from marrying several women.

A divorce, if founded and used for the protection of the wife, may equally emanate from husband and wife, assisted by a mediator (Surah Al-Baqarah 2: 227: "*And if they decide on divorce—then indeed, Allah is Hearing and Knowing*"). Islam teaches not only that the dignity of the family is inviolable, but also that this is the heart of the community.

4.3.4.6 Education and Work

The Prophet Muhammad said that gaining knowledge is a duty for every Muslim. Men and women are equally encouraged to educate themselves. There is no tenet in Islam that does not allow girls to go to school or work. In reality, especially in rural areas, limited financial resources or the family's fear of loss of control over the daughter are possible impediments to equal educational attainment.

4.3.4.7 Restraint or Freedom?

There is not a clear role model for women in Islam, just as there is no single role model for Western women. Families and individuals are shaped by country-specific and regional cultures, traditions and their social environment. The personality and its character should not be underestimated in this context.

The Quran's margin for interpretation of the is not inconsiderable: But it clearly states that there is no compulsion or oppression by faith (Surah Al-Baqarah 2: 256).

It is true that in some families and in some cultures, women are forced to wear "*hijab*" or to marry, but that is not the norm and, in my opinion, incompatible with Islam.

The circumcision of women, which is increasingly practiced in various African and Asian cultures, is not demanded by Islam, but rather a relict of a custom which is hard to overcome.

The foundation of Islam in the seventh century established an equal, just and dignified status for women on the basis of universal human principles. A Muslim woman is anything but oppressed. She is seen as a free and revered representative of God on earth.

For us in the Western world the most elementary question which we would like to have answered is therefore: "*Does the girl or the woman in the Islamic world act freely on her own and does she make her decisions out of free will?*".

The answer is not easy to find. However, it depends on how a Muslim woman in the African, Arab or Asian world has grown up and has been socialized. The way she has chosen to live is her sole responsibility.

Measuring and judging her by Western standards or even lecturing her about Western values being the only right ones to live with is a dead end. Respecting her path gives access to her as a person and to understanding her world and her values.

4.3.4.8 Governmental Regulations and Systems Versus Family and Clan Systems in the Arab World

In encounters with the Arab world, it soon becomes apparent how Western persons are accustomed to referring to and relying on state-mandated structures in almost all segments in life—from legal regulations and enforcement measures (e.g. fines for traffic offenses) to efficient insurance and social systems and up to state-enforced standardization and certification systems (TÜV, GS, ISO, DIN, Basel 2-X, etc.).

These institutions are of less overall importance in the Arab world and are often less pronounced. They are replaced by the family or the family group, an institution that pervades all areas of life.

Social security in the event of unemployment, illness or old age is not normally covered by insurance and the like. Instead, support is provided by the family—if at all possible. The elderly remain in the heart the family. Nursing homes would be almost unthinkable. The same applies to dealing with the disabled. If blood supplies are required for surgery, the family must provide a replacement to the blood bank.

Even in the case of credit rating checks for signing a contract, family involvement plays a fundamental role. Thus, in any larger deal, e.g. a car purchase, the question which family the buyer or seller comes from is asked. It is a means to establish how trustworthy the business partner is by referencing the soundness and decency of his/her family situation (Married? Divorced? Etc.). Every initial contact between strangers is shaped by these family connections.

The family is, however, more than the sum of its present members. It represents its accumulated history, its family behavior, its reputation, its dignity, its "*honor*". Therefore, in the ramp-up to a business deal—but also to a marriage—extensive research is frequently done within the network of families and clans. Europeans may still be familiar with these family networks from the nomadic patriarchal stories of the Old Testament (Abraham, Isaac, Jacob).[24] One might say that value of the family represents credit rating in the Arab world.

The people in the Arab world take pride in their own family, perhaps comparable to the national pride of earlier times in Europe. They cherish and foster this relationship continuously. Unlike in Europe, the family does not just represent (past) origins, but is a tangible, lived factor in daily life. Besides ranks and titles, it is the most important single indicator of the individual's standing.

The question of the cause and effect between weak state ties and strong family ties provides interesting insights. Are family structures (still) so strong because state-supported systems are so underdeveloped? That would correspond to the traditional wisdom in the (Western?) concept of developmental stages.

Or is it rather the other way around, that because the family systems are so pre-eminent, state systems cannot or need not be developed any further? Everyday experience with family dominance might lead one to favor the latter position.

It should not be kept secret at this point that such close family bonds can also have a flip side. For example, conflicts within or between families may be passed down through generations. Social mobility is also not necessarily promoted when most of an individual's attributes are pre-determined by his/her family history and family standing. In the Western world, the powerful effect of family bonds on an individual's attachments can be seen in the conceptual findings of systemic family constellations.[25]

The hierarchical order must also be mentioned in the context of an effective family system. It is considered only natural that older people in the family and their views carry much more weight than the views of the younger generation. The function of the experienced head of the clan, who virtually exercises judicial competence within his family, is most important for the system. He is the central point of contact for conflicts within and between families.

Knowing the internal family hierarchy and understanding its dynamics in negotiations or even conflicts can be extraordinarily productive. Taking them comprehensively into account can be a decisive factor for success in business projects or in difficult situations.

[24]https://en.wikipedia.org/wiki/Old_Testament

[25]Vgl. https://de.wikipedia.org/wiki/Bert_Hellinger. Last viewed 18.07.2018.

4.3.4.9 Negotiations in Meetings

Western-influenced culture (especially German-influenced) business encounters are dominated by factual perspectives. In Arab cultures, in contrast, the question of relationship is of fundamental importance. Accordingly, a much larger share of time spent together, especially in business negotiations, is devoted to forming and maintaining relationships.

While the particulars and details of the desired agreement are of great importance to Westerners, the Arab-influenced partner gains security in relating to his counterpart by intensive relational interweaving. Cultivated personal conversation, often about the little things in life, is therefore not "*small talk*" in the eyes of the Arab but "*big talk*"! It is not important whether the conversation revolves around a sporting event such as the Football Champions League, travel in general, cars, travel and accommodation, or a child's birthday.

As a result, Europeans may find it strange and disconcerting that so little time is assigned to contractual details. However, this does not mean that they are of less importance. These are often clarified rapidly at the end of a contractual negotiation.

Such encounters are about more than merely giving the Arab partner the "*feeling*" of having shared personal details with him. Business activities are primarily function-driven in the West. In contrast, they are conducted primarily through personal relationships in Arab culture. They are based on long-term personal friendships which may last a lifetime or even pass over into the next generation.

It is not uncommon to expect such a friend to help the family and work for its interests to the best of his/her ability. It means that the Arab business partner may even ask his European friend to take his son, who is studying in Europe, under his wing. These are the personal and temporal parameters along which Arab-influenced relationships are conducted.

4.3.4.10 Indirectness of Communication

Communication in Arab culture is likely to pose a challenge even for those in the West who are intimately familiar with the various levels of communication (object, relationship, appeal, self-expression; according to Schulz von Thun[26]). This is due to the fact that communication processes in Arab culture are often less direct and explicit. Thus, it is not uncommon for a direct question, statement or request from a Westerner to be understood in a completely different way by the Arab counterpart. For instance, a question may be answered with a story about an experience or something from the past, the meaning of which requires to be intuited.

Westerners cannot always expect to receive answers that are clear to them. Yes, an impression may even be created that questions or concerns are being ignored because they are not addressed directly in the interchange.

One reason for this may be that it is rather uncommon in Arab culture to engage in direct factual confrontation. An Arab is far too anxious to preserve his own

[26]https://en.wikipedia.org/wiki/Four-sides_model

reputation from being damaged, as also the reputation of the other or any third party involved as "*reputation*" is the basis of all relationships including those in business.

To insist on directness in such situations reveals a lack of empathy. It is seen as a sign of lack of refinement or even a lack of trust, thus casting doubts on the joint business proposition.

To articulate a clear "*no*" is culturally taboo and endangers the reputation of both partners. Instead, evasions are often used, such as the expression *Inshallah* ("*God willing*") or changing the level of conversation from the factual to the relational.

It is a fundamental cultural competence to be able to perceive these situations, to master the dance of a conversation, and to follow its twists and turns while at the same time figuring out the other's interests and potential. Throughout the movements mentioned, the partners show themselves to be culturally competent and personally connected people who are able to reciprocally include the other's context and situation. This competence is often learned the hard way by Westerners in Arab culture.

4.3.5 Encounters with the Arab World: Practical Hints and Tips

4.3.5.1 Invitations

For Arabs, it is a matter of politeness and respect to issue invitations. Invitations become more binding the minute they are issued with a specific date. To be issued an invitation for a meal (usually with the wife—not necessarily the partner) is to confer a great honor to the Western person, though this is often not realized. Be sure to accept this invitation. If you are unable to accept this invitation, explain the reasons for the refusal and, if possible, suggest a suitable alternative date that all parties can agree on. Acting recklessly or negligently in such a situation can severely affect the relationship.

When invited, do not ask if you should bring something. Of course, you are welcome to bring a present—for example a local dessert or sweets, which are then gladly served after the meal. Material gifts (avoid alcohol) are usually rejected at first, but then gladly accepted after several refusals. You will not get any acknowledgement; for the most part they are not opened in the presence of the gift giver. Asking about them is not recommended. And by the way, a return invitation is expected.

The meal: Not infrequently, men and women eat separately. Even if gender-separated, there is hardly any conversation during the meal. Eating is often done only with a spoon, avoiding food with the left (unclean) hand. Whoever finishes first leaves the table. Caution: The guest should not be the first one to leave the table, as the host would then be forced to follow. To signify abundance, the plate should not be emptied. Western people also need to get used to drinks being served only after the meal.

Spontaneous visits without notice are always to be expected in the Arab world. Loud and long laughter can be interpreted as undignified in Arab-influenced countries.

4.3.5.2 The Role of the Family

Always ask about the family in general at all meetings, but do not ask specifically about the wife or partner of the host under any circumstances. Asking about the family is seen as a sign of appreciation and promotes attachment and building of trust. Avoid any negative or critical talk about a family member. Even if the host does this, or if a family member behaves inappropriately, your expressed displeasure may very quickly be emotionally turned against you. A family member may relate his displeasure, but you as a non-family member may not.

In the event of a violation of family peace or in conflicts with the world at large, the entire family presents a united front to the outside world.

Children have top priority in the Arab world. They have the freedom to do whatever they want. No matter whether it is at home or in restaurants or cafes, children are given space and they are allowed to speak. Their urge to move around—unlike in Western-influenced culture—is not curtailed.

Contact, even physical contact, with other people's children is allowed. Playing with children, as also caressing, kissing or seating them on your lap is seen as a natural impulse and partially encouraged. Children afford an enormous relationship-building opportunity. For their part, children are very much as ease in the company of strangers.

As for the role of the seniority, there is an absolute authority-orientation and a strong hierarchy. Younger people always serve the elders, the oldest is always offered the hand first, the same applies to the serving of drinks or the distribution of food, or with prayer—the eldest is given the honor of reciting and leading the prayer.

4.3.5.3 Punctuality

Although punctuality is often seen as a matter of courtesy in Western culture, lateness or short-term cancellations of appointments are not taken personally in the Arab world, especially if there are family reasons; family ties have absolute priority.

4.3.5.4 Greeting and Proximity

Eye and body contact or initiating contact with the Arab woman should be strictly avoided. Cross-gender distance and waiting are recommended when greeting. Only when the woman holds out her hand may the greeting be reciprocated. Alternately, traditional Arabs put their hands on their heart. Basically, handshaking should be done only lightly and not firmly. A too firm handshake could be misunderstood as a test of power. Sometimes the hand is held longer, which is a sign of sympathy.

It is not unusual to see men hand in hand in the Arab world; hugs and kisses are also a sign of familiarity. If one is only greeted with reserve as a woman by a conservative group, it is by no means a sign of disrespect but rather a form of respect and reverence.

4.3.5.5 Arabic Idioms

The official language of the Arab League is Arabic. Show interest in the language. Your counterpart feels recognized and understood. It could be helpful if you know a few Arabic words:

1. Welcome	*Ahlan u sahlan*
2. Greeting (Peace be with you)	*Salaamu aleikum*
Response	*Wa aleikum as-salaam*
3. How are you?	*Kef halak?*
4. Thank you	*Schukran*
Response	*Afwan*

4.3.5.6 Clothing und Status Symbols

Clothes and status symbols are enormously important to Arabs and increase their standing. Great emphasis is placed on high-quality (brand) clothing, footwear, watches, jewelry and vehicles. Suits and ties are mandatory for men. Even at high temperatures, a summer look wearing sandals for example is considered disrespectful, as also showing the soles of shoes or feet. Women should dress discreetly and elegantly, but make sure that they do not show too much skin.

4.3.5.7 Women in Business

In the business world, but also in politics, women have become more and more present in recent decades. Western-style businesswomen move outside the social fabric and are accepted. The Western man should make sure that he does not sit next to a woman in a bus or a taxi. Women should not sit in the front of a taxi.

4.3.5.8 Work Procedure

Take your time when visiting your Arab partner; short appointments and visits are unimaginable. As already mentioned, there is no separation between work and private life in the Arab world. It may well happen that you receive "full service" treatment when visiting your business partner—from the airport pick-up to culinary hospitality to leisure and evening programs. "I have no time" is an insult, whereas a family matter is always met with understanding.

What a contract means for Europeans is what the relationship is for Arabs. After healthy relationship building, the Western conversation partner should not insist on memos or protocols, because this can be regarded as distrust. A tip: Repeat the content of the conversation at the end of the discussion and then try to work towards a contract when concluding the negotiations. A justification for this could be, e.g. the fixing of delivery and/or payment conditions. In the Arab world, contracts are still largely based on name, dignity and trust—the spoken word combined with a handshake outweighs any contract. Therefore, one should proceed with sensitivity here.

Private conversations during working hours or phoning and using the mobile phone in meetings are common. Family visits at work are commonplace and take precedence.

Decisions or appointments are difficult to implement in Islamic countries during the highest Islamic holidays (Sugar and Sacrificial Festivals) and during the entire month of Ramadan. External life comes to a halt, shops and restaurants open in the late afternoons and stay partly open all night. Professional and private life are completely aligned with these schedules.

Responsibility and hierarchical levels are enormously important in the Arab world. The location of meeting should take place at the same hierarchical level to avoid loss of face. When many attendees are present, opinions are expressed by the technical experts in charge, but the decision will only be made as a follow-up by the supervisor. In some Arab States, a local guarantor or sponsor who provides the foreigner with the standing and contacts necessary for for certain businesses may be required.

4.3.5.9 Trade and Haggling

Trade, exactly like bargaining, is part of Arab culture and history. After the long-winded process of developing a relationship, a business transaction can be completed quite quickly. For the Western partner it is essential to build a generous buffer in the price structure in advance and to remain flexible throughout the negotiation process. The Arab business partner expects to bargain. He can become quite emotional—and not only when he is deprived of this opportunity. Accept this customary emotionality in negotiations (Anything can happen, from outbursts of anger to the threat of stalling talks), but don't take it personally. Arabs tend to push the envelope to refine the price and avoid loss of face. Refusing to discount can harm the relationship and lead to the termination of negotiations.

4.3.5.10 Compatibility

Show genuine interest in Islam and the Arab culture. In this context, however, questioning or judging the meaningfulness of practices such as wearing a headscarf or not consuming pork and alcohol is to be strictly avoided. Avoid conversations about sexuality, Israel and Palestine, wars, rulers or kings and, as European knows from his own culture, conversations about politics. As I said earlier, the Arab conversationalist likes to talk about travel, food and sports, and especially about football.

Atheists can be perceived as unsuitable conversation or business partners in the eyes of devout Muslims. Much depends on the right wording. Christians who are not strict believers are accepted.

► Greetings for the Sugar or Sacrifice Holidays or good wishes for the month of fasting or a visit to Mecca (card or small gift) is considered a sign of empathy and promotes relationship-building immensely.

4.4 Austria

4.4.1 Culturally Defining Elements

4.4.1.1 From the Superpower to the Truncated State

The term East Realm ("Ostreich"), the root for the name Austria, appears in the year 996 for the first time and is the beginning of an ascent to a world power with spheres of influence in the old and new worlds. Through marriage with influential royal houses the Austrian empire's sphere of power was constantly extended until 1273, when Rudolf von Habsburg was elected German king.

In the following centuries, its possessions included large parts of the German-speaking realm with parts of today's Belgium and the Netherlands, the State of Burgundy in France, large parts of Central Europe and the Balkans. Its sphere of influence included Spain, Portugal and large parts of Central and South America. Austria was The World Power.

The French Revolution and the Napoleonic Wars were the beginning of its collapse. Its second heyday began in 1867 through marriage, with the dual kingdom of Austria-Hungary which, however, disintegrated into individual national parts after it lost the First World War.

Its role in World War II left behind a trauma that, along with its historical development, is the probable cause of the lowest of all measured power distances, according to Hofstede with the index 11 (see Sect. 3.2.1. Power distance and individuality).

Asked for the reason for this lowest power distance, a seminar participant from Austria said that was related to the three Austrian life questions:

1. Why me?
2. Anyone could say that!
3. It's always been like that!

But the deeper reason is likely to lie in history. Anyone who has ever had negative experience with power in the Western world will have a critical stance to it.

4.4.1.2 Communication and Conflict Resolution

A long history as a nation that ruled large parts of the world including many cultures, unable to solve all conflicts by war, allowed Austrians—and Vienna and eastern Austria are primarily meant—to develop a communication style that is shaped by respect and courtesy in dealings with one another, i.e. great diplomatic skill and talent.

The proverbial Austrian, i.e. Viennese, courtesy displayed in "*kiss your hand, gracious lady*," or in addressing contacts using every title, such as "*Mr. Director General, Doctor Magister Mayerhofer*" seems to speak for that. But perhaps this is also a way of cushioning the low power distance and not allowing the proverbial Viennese criticism to become a barrier to communication.

In the same vein, conflicts are usually not addressed directly, but are expressed in a well-packaged formulae with the aim of finding a compromise.

4.4.1.3 Cooperation in Professional and Business Life

Looking at Austria as a single entity is—as is the case with Switzerland—a difficult undertaking. The Vorarlberg culture is more closely related to German Switzerland than to those of Vienna or Tyrol. In Austria's economic center, the style of cooperation is shaped by respect and diplomacy to towards the hierarchy, which makes cooperation with other cultures very pleasant—very much the opposite of the direct communication style of neighboring Germany.

4.5 Belgium

4.5.1 Culturally Defining Elements

The Belgian soul is characterized by three elements: history, cultural diversity and the dispute about language, mainly between French and Flemish speakers.

Belgium has three official languages. About 60% of Belgians speak Flemish as their mother tongue and 40% speak French. A minority of approximately 75,000 people in the east of the country—in the region of Eupen-Malmedy—speaks German as their mother tongue and official language.

Belgium is a country steeped in history. In the early Middle Ages, under Charlemagne in Aachen, it was the center of Europe and Antwerp was the most important port of the so-called Old World. Until the thirteenth century, Belgium represented the economic center with the flourishing trading towns of Bruges and Ghent and thus also the most densely populated area in Europe. After that, an economic and social decline began which continued into the modern era. Belgium became a transit country which had to adapt to constantly changing foreign dominations; the French, the Germans, the Spaniards, the Austrians and finally the Dutch came and went.

In the Congress of Vienna in the year 1815, Belgium was not granted independence, but became a province of the Netherlands. Separation from the Netherlands and the official formation of the State as a parliamentary monarchy with King Leopold of Saxe-Coburg as its head followed only in 1831 after a 10-day war against Dutch supremacy.

Belgium was the first country in continental Europe to be industrialized, with rich deposits of coal and iron ore in Wallonia as its basis. In 1822, the industrial holding Société Générale was founded by the Dutch King William I and Wallonia became the center of heavy industry. A wealthy bourgeoisie was created which had a decisive influence on the cultural life of the country. French language and culture shaped public and cultural life politically and economically. Flanders, with its agriculture, became a poorhouse and many Flemings earned their money as workers in the mines of the South.

This is the actual origin of the division between the two cultural and language groups; the Flemings felt economically and culturally colonized and exploited by Francophone Belgians. It was to last until the first half and middle of the twentieth century, until Flemish was also introduced into the universities as a language of instruction and hearings in courtrooms could also be conducted in this language.

The wealth in Wallonia was further increased by the colonizing the Congo. The decline of Walloon industrial holdings began as early as the 1890s with a recession, while Flanders rose to a flourishing economic region through Flemish family businesses in emerging industries. After 1945, Flanders became the gateway to Europe, as numerous European branches of multinational companies from the United States were established there.

Now the North is rich and the South poor. Domestic economic and fiscal policy became the bone of contention between the cultural groups, with the result that the same amounts had to be invested, for example in improving transportation infrastructure, in the South as in the North whether it was necessary or not. This dispute, which has been an ongoing one for almost a century, led to a new constitution in 1993. Belgium became a Federal State with three regions (Flanders, Wallonia and Brussels), all with extensive autonomy in political and economic terms. Each region has its own government with a prime minister. Above the regions is the government of the whole country, but divisions run so deep that, for example, at the end of 2011 a new general government could only be formed after Belgium had been without a government for 535 days.

4.5.2 The Family as a Center and Basis of Existence

This evolving history of foreign determination over the centuries led to a perception of a hostile environment against which protection and defense is needed. The family became the save haven. Open conflict is not engaged in, but rather restraint to diplomacy. Reinforced by cultural and linguistic differences, this has led to a lack of identification with the state. An intercultural author once called the Belgians "*The Italians of northern Europe*" with the family as the basis of existence in the narrower and wider sense in both cultures.

The quality of life is determined by the here and now. Food and drink are of great importance. Belgium is the country with the greatest density of restaurants with Michelin stars. In the last century it was a significant purchaser of top wines; when the Bordeaux warehouses were empty in the 1980s, French vendors travelled to Belgium to buy their wines back.

The saying in Belgium "*Chaque belge a une brique dans le ventre*" means—literally translated—"*Every Belgian has a brick in his belly*". That means, that his goal is a house of his own, and Belgium has in fact one of the highest percentages of home ownership in Europe.

4.5.3 Communication and Conflict Resolution

Multilingualism is a basic requirement for doing business in this country—despite the language dispute. The goal of communication is not perfection, it is understanding. For example, an American corporation once appointed one of the authors to be Managing Director in Brussels. He was introduced to a very important client in the town of Leuwen with the remark "*He speaks very good French*", to which the client drily replied, "*We speak Flemish here*". The result was that the author received lessons in Flemish. English is also often used as the Lingua Franca between the cultures.

In his job in Brussels, the author had an employee who was a member of the Walloon Independence Party, but whose main clients were in Antwerp. He therefore learned Flemish, which he spoke with a French accent. He was a respected and esteemed consultant to the customer.

The interaction between and with each other is friendly, characterized by humor, even sprinkled with a dose of self-irony about one's own shortcomings. Understatement is the norm. Conflicts are seldom resolved openly, and the aim is to avoid them. A popular strategy is to say nothing; the Belgians retreat to a certain bunker mentality in critical situations.

4.5.4 Cooperation in Professional and Business Life

Belgians are usually successful business people because they speak several languages, are able to respond well to other mentalities and operate their businesses with a healthy dose of opportunism and pragmatism.

In Belgium, business is often based initially on pragmatic professional friendships from which networks of relationships develop, often lasting a lifetime. Since Belgium does not have the same human and financial resources as its large neighbors, for example 1:10 in relation to Germany, implementation in business looks for compromise rather than for an ideal solution. The aim is to maximize yield by minimizing costs and investments. Adaptability, flexibility and compromise are the ingredients of a successful Belgian businessman.

Projects and processes are implemented gradually. An example from the commercial sector: a German company had bought the market leader in Belgium and now wanted to start using the software in its entirety in all its branches 1:1. The Belgian colleague's response to this was "*One step at a time!*"

Belgium has two different management cultures, whereby the acceptance of hierarchy is similar in both parts of the country. According to Hofstede, the power distance score in Francophone culture is 67 and 61 in Flemish culture, both of which indicate a paternalistic leadership style.

However, Flemish management style is based much more on a consensus principle with a mixture of authority, a right to voice an opinion and a delegation of tasks. The leadership style is relaxed.

Walloons are based on the Francophone principle within clear and structured hierarchies with directives and the setting of goals.

The following case studies from Belgium are classic examples of Belgian pragmatism in business life. The intercultural experience in these practical examples derives from the historical experience of Belgium as a country that has been dominated by foreign powers for centuries. Only the retreat to the family and the total respect for self-interest guaranteed survival. This way of thinking and living is often alien to other cultures and is usually very difficult to deal with for outsiders in business life.

The International Project Report

A project manager from Germany worked with a mixed team of German and Belgian participants. His deputy was a Belgian. The German and Belgian team were in a joint kick-off meeting and had been working on the implementation for the past 2 months. The superiors in Paris had requested a weekly progress report.

Whilst the implementation in the German team was progressing well, the Belgian team seemed to have some problems. That is why the German project manager asked his Belgian number two to give him a project progress report. The Belgian did not respond. After several follow-up requests without a response, the German project manager asked if the level of achievement was in the region of 50 or 75%. Probably around 75%, was the somewhat vague reply from the Belgian. The German project manager then wrote this figure in his report filed to the management in Paris. A week later the Belgian deputy called back and said that the Belgian implementation had reached a mere 28%. The German manager was beside himself as he had to send a corrected report to the head office in Paris.

The solution: This concrete case from a seminar participant reveals the conflict between fact and personality orientation in German and Belgian business cultures. The problem was that the German manager did not have a personal relationship and trust of his Belgian colleague. Neither did he understand his work situation. The deputy may simply have said a number to get out of the pressure and uncertainty of the momentary situation. The reasons for this are the workload in the relatively small Belgian market, where less resources, i.e. manpower, are available for a project than in an economically more privileged market such as Germany.

Belgian Financial Accountants

A Swiss Managing Director of an American company was transferred to Belgium. He was inducted well by his predecessor, received a detailed briefing for several weeks and was introduced to the staff and clients before the predecessor took over as Regional Director in Asia.

The Swiss liked his new assignment, his relationships to employees and clients developed positively, with one exception—the financial accountant, who defended his territory. He provided only minimal information and only after some pressure, and then only the key figures, and no or little transparency.

Taken to task for this unsatisfactory situation, the Head of Finance said that the new managing director should deal primarily with business development and be relieved of detail work.

The solution? The new person coming in from the outside does not belong to the 'family' and is therefore kept out and given only minimal information. In business cultures with a high-power distance, only hierarchical enforcement or a dismissal remain the available options.

The Unorthodox Company Director

The chief financial officer of an American company discovers that the Belgian managing director bought a majority share in a small service company. He had never submitted a financing plan for this, let alone received permission. This was done although complete planning documents for every purchase had to be submitted and approved by the international headquarters in New York.

The Belgian managing director, who was very successful and well-respected, had circumvented these rules by financing the purchase with the hidden reserves in his own company.

A classic Belgian story—pragmatism in business in order to survive with clever business gambits. In this case, the parent company did nothing because the managing director was very successful, and the purchase made sense, even though company regulations had been flouted.

The same Belgian also made history in the company when he made a long speech at his retirement farewell party in the New York headquarters about the company's lack of new business development. The next day, instead of retiring, he turned up at HQ, sat down at his desk and created a new business development department.

4.6 Canada

I was brought up in Canada, worked all over the world and then returned to Chair a trans-Canadian advertising company. Surprisingly, other than the marked increase in immigrants from all over the world, basic Canadian attitudes were much as I remembered them. The overwhelming presence of their huge neighbor to the South. The language squabbles. The enormity of the land mass compared to the paucity of inhabitants. The comparatively low crime rate and neighborly civility. It was a good country to grow up in. A great country to work in. And a great country to visit—if you can handle the winters!

Mike Ferrier.[27]

[27] Mike Ferrier is also the author of "*Understanding the United Kingdom*".

4.6.1 How Different Is Canada from the United States?

Canada and the United States are both "*North American*" and they share more values than they both accept. Seen from Europe, or the rest of the globe, it's hard to know where the world's largest undefended border ends. Or starts. There are differences with the USA, of course. But arguably less than between Alaska and Kentucky.

4.6.1.1 Size

The USA is large. Canada is larger, but the entire population is smaller than California. Canada is a dynamic economy and has to provide the same business environment as its huge neighbor to the South. But because of the great distances and the sparse population, matching the US infrastructure (roads, communications, etc.) is more complex, making life, on average, more expensive for the Canadian.

4.6.1.2 "Flea on the Elephants Back"

Ninety percent of Canada's population lives within 150 miles of the US border. It is some 4000 miles from Vancouver to Newfoundland but only 100 miles from Vancouver to Seattle. About 230 miles from Toronto to Detroit. Montreal is no more than 80 miles from New York State.

This means that Canadians often relate more culturally North-South than they do East-West. The Maritime Provinces resemble New England. The Central Provinces of Saskatchewan and Manitoba follow life of Middle America. Ontario reminds you of Ohio or Michigan. British Columbia feels like Oregon or Washington State. (Exception: Victoria City, Vancouver Island, is more "British" than almost anywhere in Britain today!)

Add to this fact that Canada's economy is primarily resource-based—oil, mining, agriculture—and that 70% of their exports head South, the two countries might appear joined at the hip, and culturally and regionally almost identical.

4.6.2 Quebec and the "*Ethnic Mosaic*"

Yet . . . the country is rigidly bi-lingual. The USA is not. Quebec is French speaking, as are parts of New Brunswick and Nova Scotia. All road signs and all government regulations are issued in both languages. Although you will find very few French speakers west of Ottawa, every government published work everywhere is bi-lingual. And all company or product descriptions are mandatory in both French and English. French script has to be at least 3/4 the size of the English. Ironically, the one province that is most lax about enforcing these regulations tends to be Quebec.

At this stage it might seem appropriate to explain the origins of this "*Frenchness*". Canada was founded by the French explorers Jacques Cartier and Champlain. In fact, the name Canada stems from how the Indians described to Cartier their village (on Montreal Island) as "*Kanata*"—or collection of huts.

The French and British fur traders clashed and the new settlers of the 13 Colonies turned to the British Army to expel the French and remove their threat (the Seven

Years war). This finally led to the conclusive Battle of the Plains of Abraham (near Quebec City) where Commander Wolfe soundly defeated the Marquis de Montcalm in 1759. Some would argue that the origins of the American War of Independence could be traced to this event. Britain wanted American financial contribution to their military effort in the form of increased taxation. The Americans refused, and so the British taxed tea imports. The rest of the story is well-known.

After this defeat, and the eventual ceding of New France to Britain, French-Canadian leaders returned to France, but about 50,000 colonists remained. Britain magnanimously decided to let them retain French as their official language and maintain many of their French-based customs and laws. Had that decision been less liberal the French might have integrated more easily, and perhaps the "*Quebec Libre*" (Quebec independence) movement which very nearly ruptured Canadian unity, could have been avoided. (Happily, this nationalism has abated considerably lately as Quebec had absorbed many new English-speaking immigrants and the Federal Government has bent over backwards to address Quebec's "*grievances*").

Another cultural difference between the USA and Canada is a contrasting attitude to immigrants. America refers to the "*melting pot*" where those that arrive (legally) are expected to become "*American*" and slowly accept American norms. Also, there today is a growing resistance to new immigrants.

Canada desperately needs population growth and encourages immigrants to retain their ethnic identities. The "*melting pot*" is referred to as "*the mosaic*" as Italians, Greeks, Hong Kong Chinese or anyone else is urged to retain their ethnic values and let the whole country enjoy the variety. Today at least 20% of the Canadian population of 30 million is foreign-born.

4.6.3 Canadians Know America—America Does Not Know Canada

As already stated, most Canadians live within a short drive of the USA. Most Americans need a plane ride of many hours to visit their Northern cousins, Canadians visit the US regularly on business, to shop, or to vacation. Most Americans head South or to the main American tourist centers rather than freeze in the frigid North.

Canadians are bombarded with US media (even though by law 20% of all media content must be Canadian) and Canadians follow American affairs closely. Often a Canadian will be shocked to discover he knows more about US politics than his US visitor.

Americans like to joke about Canada, but the jokes are shallow—the use of "*eh*" at the end of a question. Saying "*aboot*" instead of "*about*". Wearing "*Tuques*" instead of woolen hats. Taking your shoes off to enter a house (of course you do—snow and sleet can ruin a rug or floor!). But in reality the average American finds significant cultural differences hard to find.

Canadians laugh about themselves but can be extremely critical of the USA. They point to the endless politics (Canadian elections are every 4–5 years normally), the gun culture ("*We use guns for sport—you for protection*"). The US resorts to violence to end a quarrel. We Canadians strive for compromise. You had to fight for independence from Britain. We just signed a paper (The British North America Act[28]).

Most of these frequent and often unfavorable comparisons are inspired less by a desire to be critical than by a wish to be compared on an equal footing with "*Big Brother*" down South.

Americans on the other hand, know next to nothing about their Northern neighbors and stereotypically regard Canada as essentially just a good friend. A politer and gentler version of themselves. Partly those attributes are true, as we will examine later.

Annoying to Canada is that the world knows and watches America closely. It is, after all, the world's premier economy and super power. The Canadian stock market, as an example, represents only about 3% of the global total. Canadians belief in their own significance in world events is somewhat at odds with reality—but that observation (if you agree with it) is best left unsaid.

4.6.4 Is Canada Just "*America Light*"?

The answer is yes and no. The way of life mirrors the USA in many aspects. But in other critical areas, there are substantive differences.

First of all, the history is different. Canada's initial formative years were created by the emigration of the "*Empire Loyalists*" who fled to "*Lower Canada*" (essentially Ontario) after the American War of Independence.

These "*Americans*" retained the British parliamentary system and the Queen is still today Head of State, represented in Ottawa by a Canadian appointed Governor.

Politics are not as strident nor is business life as aggressive. Canada retains a larger degree of "*British-style*" values of "*trying to see the other's point of view*".

The top four political parties are almost all left leaning. Life and politics are not as polarized.

The social model is mildly socialistic—taxes are high. Health care is free, if sometime fraught with endless delays. Education is subsidized, leading to a much higher University participation rate than the USA (55% versus 33%). University costs average (with board) only $15,000 a year against the US's average of three times that. Maternity leave can approach 15 weeks or 35 weeks for a couple.

Government, then, can be regarded as having a greater influence in community affairs than in America. That is not seen as positive in the more individualist USA—but it did mean that the closely regulated Canadian Banks withstood the 2008/2009 meltdown in far better shape.

So, you could call Canada a more middle class environment—wealth inequality is far less blatant than in the USA. Ambitious Canadians know they have to cross the border to "*make the big bucks*". And many do.

[28]https://www.britannica.com/event/British-North-America-Act. Last viewed 06.11.2018.

Potential business entrants to the country (especially from the USA) have to consider a few key factors.

Unionization is far higher in Canada than the USA, rising as high as 39% in Quebec, against an average 15% in the USA.

Employment laws are both Federal and Provincial. Most employees are covered by the latter (85%)

Employee rights are more liberal in Canada. All employees can claim overtime, against only wage earners in the USA. Holidays are mandated at 2 weeks for the first 5 years of employment and 3 weeks thereafter.

The Canadian worker leads a more balanced life. He works on average 36–40 h a week against the American executive's average of 47 h. Half hour breaks every 5 h are enforced as are at least a 24 h break each week. In Quebec workers have an absolute right to be addressed either orally or in written form in French.

Any good commercial lawyer can guide you through this labyrinth. Speaking of the law, be aware that the Canadian legal system follows the British precedent. Sue and lose and the winner's legal fees will be yours. Judges—not juries—set the financial awards which can be a fraction of a similar award in the USA.

4.6.5 What to Remember as You Enter Canada on Business

Canada might seem very North American to you, but do not voice this opinion. Canadians are proud of their nation. They are NOT American.

See a Canadian tourist abroad and be amazed how his bags and back packs are plastered with Canadian flags. Canadians will remind you that over 2000 words mean different things North or South of the border.

Remember too that Canada is metric and their dollar notes are mainly plastic and multi-colored. There is no one or two dollar bill. They are coins affectionately known as "*loonies*" because of the bird motif. US dollars are accepted almost everywhere but often at most disadvantageous rates. Take care !

The British heritage is still present—it is weak, but it is still influential. The parliamentary system. The Queen. The legal precedents.

Be on time for meetings and expect them to be more formal. Refer to everyone as Mr., Mrs., or Miss until first names are offered.

As in Britain, start with small talk and drift into your agenda when the Manager or "*Chair*" seems ready. Be factual and even-toned. Hyperbole is resisted. Reaction will be reserved and polite. But unlike Britain, a Canadian "*yes*" means "*yes*". A British "*yes*" means "*maybe*"!

Interruptions are considered rude unless the interrupter asks permission to respond or add a thought. Aggressive confrontation is resented, and the meeting Chairperson is expected to calm down overheating rhetoric and search for compromise.

Americans tend to be more blunt, direct and in a hurry. Canadians are more likely to seek group opinion and consensus before agreeing to further talks. Both take business very seriously—the tone is just more reserved North of the border.

A meeting in Quebec will be less "*Anglo Saxon*" and more energetic, with flowing speeches and flourishes. The Manager is more likely to take the ultimate decision. But still, the Quebecer is not as over-bearing as his Parisian counterpart. Most senior Executives know they must learn fluent English to succeed.

If you want to entertain, suggest breakfast or lunch. Canadians like to go home after work. Inviters pay, or increasingly a Canadian waiter will automatically deliver individual checks. If you want to pay, sweep these up.

Suggest Tim Horton's and not Starbucks for a coffee. Canadians love their own brands—even though many are American owned (Tim Horton's was purchased by Burger King, which in turn is owned by the Brazilians!). Tips are generally 15%. Don't confuse the normally not-included gratuity with GST (usually also 15%). This is the Government General Sales Tax.

4.6.6 Conclusion

Canada is a geographically beautiful country with hospitable and open-minded nationals. Ethics are high and corruption low (Canada scored 8th best position out of 180 countries in 2017). They are considerate of others and fair in business.

The climate may be harsh, but the welcome is always warm. Although overwhelmed economically by their Southern neighbors, Canada remains a very proud and independent nation caring of its population—which is increasingly diverse.

In international affairs they "*punch above their weight*" and are seen in a multitude of UN missions and policing initiatives.

To those looking in, they may seem as Americans by another name, but that observation (although defensible) is regarded as offensive and inaccurate by Canadians themselves.

So, our advice? Accept them as they see themselves. "*Vive la différence!*"

4.7 Central European Cultures

We use the term Central Europe here for all the former satellite countries of the Warsaw Pact plus the Baltic States. According to the latest geographical measurements, the center of Europe is located a few kilometers north of Vilnius, the capital of Lithuania. Central Europe includes the Baltic countries with Latvia, Lithuania and Estonia, then Poland, the Czech Republic, Slovakia, Hungary, Romania and Bulgaria.

Each of these countries has its own culture and values, which is why the following information can only outline some broad differences for this region when compared to Western Europe.

4.7.1 Culturally Defining Elements

4.7.1.1 Transit Countries and the Plaything of Foreign Powers

Since the ancient migration of peoples and until after the Second World War, these countries have been the scene of armed conflicts with conquests and resettlements. Periods of foreign domination alternated with periods of self-determination and sovereignty, but the uncertainty and danger of hostile intervention remained constantly present.

4.7.1.2 Commonalities in Central Europe

All the countries in Central Europe share a centuries-old European tradition and history. Sources traces these links far back into the Middle Ages, for example, when we think of the Christianization of German Knights' orders and the founding of Hanseatic cities like Riga or Reval and even beyond. Romania and Bulgaria have a verifiable ancient past predating Christ—consider Thracian culture or Greek and Roman colonization.

The forced occupation, Sovietization and integration into the system of Soviet satellite states as well as in the Warsaw Pact from 1944 until 1989/1990 are a common experience across Central Europe.

The fall of the Iron Curtain in 1989/1990 in these countries has led to the subsequent political and economic reorientation with the resurgence of their own history and the Renaissance of Church and religion.

4.7.1.3 Differences in Language

The countries of central Europe can be linguistically differentiated as follows:

- Hungarian and Estonian are Finnish-Ugric languages.
- Romanian has Romanesque roots and is related to Italian.
- Latvian and Lithuanian are the closest to Indo-European languages, Illyric languages. There are many words that are borrowed from the German language from the time of the German Teutons.

All other languages belong to the Slavic language group, i.e. Bulgarian, Polish, Czech and Slovak.

4.7.2 The Role of Religion

Religion plays an important role in all these countries. The Catholic Church dominates in Poland, Hungary, Lithuania and Slovakia. It is present in Lithuania as Lithuania formed a unit called the Polish-Lithuanian Commonwealth with the Kingdom of Poland in the late Middle Ages lasting for several hundred years. The Catholic faith is also strongly prevalent in Slovakia as well, which belonged to the Royal House of Hungary.

In Estonia and Latvia, the faith is based on Scandinavian Protestant-Lutheran denominations. Religious faith in these countries is even more pronounced than in the Catholic areas of Central Europe.

In Bulgaria and Romania approximately 80% of the population are Orthodox believers.

The Czech Republic is an exception. Non-affiliation to a particular religion, about 60% of the population, was widespread even before the First World War. This is attributed, among other things, to the Czech religious scholar and reformer Jan Hus, who taught in Prague and was burned at the stake at a council in Konstanz at the beginning of the fifteenth century. Incidentally, this remains a matter of concern for the Vatican and the Catholic Church to this day; Pope Benedict touched on this topic in 2009 on a visit to the Czech Republic.

4.7.3 Formation of Values and Cultures in the Soviet Era

The almost 50 years of dependence strongly influenced the people of these countries all the way up to East Germany. As the State and the Party exerted their influence on all areas of life, people retreated into the family, which was usually a safe haven and where everyone could behave more freely than in public.

Female emancipation: Since women were needed in the labor force for post-war reconstruction and industrial production, gender equality was enforced. Interestingly, this has not changed manners; men are courteous and polite to women, as if women were on a higher plane.

Passive behavior in the outside world: The social aspect of life was delegated to the State and the Party which was responsible for providing care for the comrades in the form of nursery schools, schools, secure jobs, vacations from the beginning to the end of their working lives. Communication in public was marked by caution and mistrust, partly expressed in silence or in gallows humor. A statement by a GDR official of the 1980s, when a West Berlin company proposed market research in East Berlin in connection with Berlin tourism: "*You can't do that, people will not tell you the truth*".

Through resettlements multicultural societies were created and kept changing. The displacement and deportation of Baltic Germans before and after the Second World War was followed by the settlement of Russians, who account for more than 20% of the population in Estonia and Latvia.

The acceptance of the Communist system, or at least the justification of the people who lived in these countries, was the social security system, a safe workplace and the lack of crime making the effects of the poor post war economy more bearable. Moreover, social relations were more pronounced, there was more mutual support, and people had more free time. This is still acknowledged by the majority as the good side of Socialism.

The protests against the System are legendary, from the riots in Hungary and Czechoslovakia during the Prague Spring to the peaceful revolution in Germany. This also includes thousands of individual destinies, people who were in prisons or even lost their lives because they did not agree with the supremacy of State and the

Party and sought freedom—something which finally became reality in the late 1980s.

4.7.4 The Turnaround and Its Direct Consequences

The restoration of parliamentary democracy and free market economy in Germany is called the turnaround ("*Wende*") because everything that was valid until that point was no longer applicable. Many people reacted with uncertainty and felt inferior to the West. They saw what Westerners had, what they could afford and the opportunities in the West. When groups of specialists and executives from Central Europe came to Germany for development programs the early 1990s, they were stunned by the luxuries available in what appeared to be paradise.

A generational conflict arose; the older members of society struggled to adapt to the new values, while younger people saw them as an opportunity. The authors experienced first-hand in these countries the conflict between known ideology and the younger generation's hunger for knowledge.

Younger people created careers in the west or founded companies in their own country. Elders remained passive and demanded the same social security and support from the new state or employer. The attempt to manage the expectations of the welfare state in the new world continue to the present day.

4.7.5 The Search for Values

The process of reworking national history, reactivating a national self-image and finding one's own roots was at the center of this development.

We experienced this impressively in Lithuania at the beginning of the 1990s, where the newly awakened national consciousness was a central point of discussion. We learned about the events leading to liberation from Soviet supremacy through personal narratives. On one of the first evenings, the President of the university led us to the moated castle Trakai—the symbol of the independence of Lithuania—which belonged to the national hero Grand Duke Gediminas in the fourteenth century. His statue and those of other heroes were placed at important places and streets named after them.

Another phenomenon was the revival of faith in the Catholic Church. With the turnaround, the desecrated churches which had been used as storage rooms in the Soviet era were renovated and consecrated. During several visits of the author Masses in Vilnius Cathedral, the church was filled to overflowing. The piety of the people was demonstrated impressively when looking up from the city gate of Dawn to the Black Madonna of Vilnius. Across from us stood a woman who suddenly crossed the street and struck the burning cigarette from the project leader's hand with a string of incomprehensible curses. Days later, the author climbed up the many steps to the chapel above the gate. The view into the chapel explained the violent reaction of the woman. Everyone was kneeling in front of the picture, while some lay stretched out on the ground. The author backed out. The Black Madonna of Czestochowa in Poland and its veneration as a relic and as a national symbol also speaks of the importance of church and religion in Central Europe.

4.7.6 Communication and Conflict Resolution

Communication in the countries of central Europe is more likely to be determined by the "*WE*". Monika Mochtarova[29] sums it up thus: "*We stick together. People are socialized not only in core families, but especially in large families... The family protects the individual, but it demands loyalty from him/her. Thus, the child learns to think in the WE form...*"

The identity of the individual in Eastern Central Europe is reflected in the social network. To ensure the functioning of this network, it is necessary for it to be enduring, and is safeguarded by avoiding disputes where possible.

Here we see parallels between the worldview of the "*WE*" with the examples of China, Japan or Arab countries in contrast to the "I" of the Western world (see also Sect. 3.3 "*I*" and "*WE*").

The following case study shows how one of the authors experienced the "*WE*" feeling in a Latvian group:

The Latvian Travel Group

In a training series for high-ranking Latvian executives from business and administration in the 1990s, a training session was completed in a very cordial communal form. On the last day of training there was a big festive dinner. After eating their fill, everyone met in the hall in front of the sauna in bathing suits.

Another cold buffet with Latvian delicacies was set in that hall, and Latvian music was playing. People went in and out of the sauna in between and chatted cheerfully in the hall until deep into the night.

On returning from the venue the following morning, the entire group sat in a large VW mini-bus. The Russian driver had the German singer Heino playing the song "*...so blau, blau, blau blüht der Enzian ... (...the gentian shines so blue, blue, blue...)*" at full volume.

All the occupants, except the driver, clapped to the music, smiling and bouncing to the beat with their feet. The Russian driver moved his head with the beat, needing his hands to drive.

In between songs, some participants unpacked sandwiches and shared them with the others.

[29]Mochtarova Monika.

4.7.7 Indirectness in Communication

Communication is rather indirect in central European cultures, and this is especially seen in a conflict. Criticism and disagreement are not expressed and dealt with overtly, but in private conversations behind closed doors. Elements of irony play especially an important role in the coding of messages. The following example with a Slovak tour group may illustrate that:

"Do you hear the silence?"

One of the authors accompanied a group of Slovak executives in an EU project. Their spokesman was a retired veteran Communist leader. Most of the other participants were resentful of this somewhat elderly gentleman, but at the same time they did not say so openly.

Even after one of the authors tried to find out what the group dynamics were by asking about it, he was given no direct response. At a group dinner, at which everyone was very quiet except for the leader, one of the participants suddenly said to the group: "*Do you hear the silence*?"

4.7.7.1 Private and Personal

Private, personal and professional matters are not as severely separated in these countries as it is in Germany, for example. People help each other or have time for a chat. The fact of taking time for one another or helping someone is certainly also a consequence of the Socialist past. In addition to the repression from outside, the lack of material goods was also an issue, especially when it came to malnutrition. We are personally acquainted with Central Europeans with diet-related growth disorders. In short, the family and the neighbors were essential for help and support.

4.7.8 Cooperation in Professional and Business Life

4.7.8.1 High Power Distance

All the cultures in Central Europe have high levels of power distance in their professional lives. Hofstede's studies clearly indicate far higher values for Romania, Slovakia and Poland than for France. Estonia still lies above Germany. This is similar to what people experience in France, Spain or Italy, where the chief is paternalistic, like a family father, leading and protecting his employees. In return, he expects respect and will crack down in an authoritarian manner if the "*children*" don't behave. This characteristic is still evident in dealing with service personnel such as chauffeurs.

The Romanian Driver and His Boss

In a project in the early 1990s in Romania, the German project team had a Romanian driver who was in the service of the Romanian client.

The driver was a highly educated man, spoke three foreign languages, had studied physics and drove his superiors for a low salary because there was simply no other work available.

At a festive dinner with the Romanian client, the driver sat by himself in a small corner at the back of the room. Noticing this, the German project manager felt an impulse to stand up and to bring the Romanian driver to the main table.

However, the consequences would have been disastrous. The relationship between the superior and the subordinates would have been disturbed, the supervisor would have lost face in front of the German guests, and the Romanian chauffeur might have lost his job because his boss would have assumed he had harassed the German guests in some way.

Luckily, the German project leader listened to his inner voice, which advised him not to follow his ideals and to stay in the role expected of him.

In work life, the participants generally see themselves as a community and look for a group feeling like in a family. Although it is sometimes even more competitive in many areas than it has long been the case with us in the West, the familial aspect is still significant.

Susanne Müller[30] writes regarding the Baltic States: "*What the economic landscape in all three young Baltic republics have in common is the following: Strong motivation up to enthusiasm for the development of the market economy... From the pace of development, the young manager generation practices a leadership style that identifies the following keywords: active, pro-active, pragmatic... In many respects, it corresponds to the Western leadership style more and more, is becoming more professional. However, with us (in the Baltics) the atmosphere is a bit more open, warmer and we want to keep it that way. Birute Kramer, head of the Baltic office of Karstadt Quelle in Vilnius, is not the only one to see the situation this way.*"

The following example shows the significance of personal contacts in professional life:

Problem Solving by Mixing Private with Professional Life

German engineers had the following problem with a German-Bulgarian industrial project. They usually travelled only for 1 day to Bulgaria, flew to Sofia early in the morning, completed all the meetings and other business matters in a 1-day marathon, to fly back exhausted in the evening.

Afterwards, the follow-up project supervision was largely virtual via e-mail. The Bulgarian partners were, however, unable to deal with this approach. They missed having a personal relationship with their German colleagues. The German side, on the other hand, said that they had so much to do, that there was no time for private meetings during their trips to Sofia.

[30]Müller, Susanne (2005), Management im Baltikum, Seite 6. https://www.een-bayern.de/een/inhalte/Anhaenge/Management-im-Baltikum.pdf. Last viewed September 09, 2018.

The solution was a compromise. On a follow-up date on-site in Sofia, the German colleagues added a vacation day to their trip, which they had to take privately. They asked the Bulgarian colleagues to show them around Sofia on a personal guided tour. The result was that Bulgarian and German colleagues came closer, and in some cases even created friendships. The positive effect was that business communication was improved, because they knew and trusted each other.

4.7.8.2 The Need for Improvisation in Order to Deal Pragmatically With Resource Scarcity

Their own hardships during the period after World War II and during Communism are still present in some of today's professionally active people. This has shaped people so strongly that they continue to have an improvisational and pragmatic approach to everyday life. This approach leads, for example, to making ad hoc decisions, even on quality standards.

The Art of Improvising

One of the authors was a project manager for several years for a continuing education project supported by a Foundation in the Baltic States. He always noticed that the seminar infrastructure taken for granted in many countries in the West was lacking, so project leaders often had to improvise. This also applied to an educational project for an organization in the Baltic States. The aim of this project was to support public administration with tools to increase productivity and effectiveness.

Various European training institutes that operated as sub-contractors had to create and establish procedures to assess the qualification of their facilitators and their ability to successfully achieve training goals without Western standards of technical equipment in the training locations.

It was always a major challenge for the facilitators and coaches to adapt to the modest infrastructure on the ground. Tables, for example, could not be set up in a classic U-form in the seminar rooms because they were bolted onto the floor. Projectors, projection screens and overhead projectors were sometimes not available at all. Some service providers struggled with it at the beginning and also made it very clear. It was critical for all project participants to adjust to these general conditions. Adaptability and improvisation skills were required and were in the end decisive for the selection of the providers.

The Western European training partners who were able to operate within these confinements had to adapt their seminar concepts to these conditions. The project manager of the foundation spent most of his time trying to change attitudes and to select the adequate training partners. All the partners involved had to be flexible, to improvise and to adapt training concepts and media support to these conditions.

Misunderstandings and conflicts caused by differing requirements could be cleared up. After the initial difficulties described above, the project could be successfully completed.

4.8 China and the Chinese Cultural Circle

4.8.1 Culturally Defining Elements

Natural disasters are omnipresent in China and shape the worldview of the Chinese (see also Sect. 4.8.1 culturally defining elements, China):-Earthquakes, typhoons and floods are commonplace and, thousands of Chinese repeatedly suffer the consequences of these catastrophes every year, including many deaths.

From the Chinese point of view, the family is the nucleus and basis of society, and the millennia-old commitment to Confucius, Laozi and Buddha, combined with the pursuit of harmony and identification with the State, ensures survival of society. With this attitude, China has made the quantum leap into modern times in record time. According to Martin Jacques *citing a research* 72% of all Chinese were satisfied with the situation in the country. With this, China is far ahead of all other Western nations (USA 39%, France 28%, Germany 25%).

The Chinese have created their own freedom: freedom from distress. President Hu Jintao told his citizens in 2010 that the worst times (since the founding of the PRC) were now over. The new freedoms are the freedom from uncertainty and the freedom to work.

From a Western point of view, however, we often assume that the Chinese are not doing well, and that China will eventually become like us and wants a Western democratic system, Western education and Western economic systems. This naïve view and arrogant Western ambition which projects our ideals on China and disregards the Chinese perspective is evident in the media. This attitude closes us off from access to and acceptance of the people in this culture for the mutual benefit. After attempted military and economic colonization, they perceive this as ideological and verbal neo-Colonialism.

Their explanations, desire for recognition and pride in their culture go unheard in Western media policies.

China is (still) the most populous country in the world. During its long history of self-perception as the Middle Kingdom it always had enough internal problems to maintain cohesion and therefore had little to do with the outside world. In his book "*China, a Superpower Returns*"[31] Konrad Seitz, a German diplomat, describes the history of China since its mystic origins in 450 pages. In this exciting narrative it becomes clear how difficult it is to govern the approximately 1.4 billion Chinese and how often China has narrowly missed disasters in the recent past.

[31]see Seitz (2002).

China already had contact with the Middle East and the eastern Mediterranean region in ancient times via the Silk Route. We know from travelers like Marco Polo that strangers were accepted when they recognized China as the Middle Kingdom. Throughout its history, China rarely tried to actively establish relations at diplomatic and economic levels. The sea voyages of Zheng He during the Ming dynasty from 1405 to 1431 are exceptional. He was a captured Mongolian Muslim who was made a Court Eunuch and had a brilliant career in the imperial administration. As Admiral of a huge imperial fleet he had the task of establishing diplomatic and economic relations with distant countries. The fleet included 317 ships and a 28,000 man crew and soldiers. The flagship was more than four times as large as Columbus' ship Santa Maria, which sailed in the same century. His travels led him to Southeast Asia, India, to the East African coast and to the Arabian Peninsula. He did not only bring goods from his travels, but also diplomats who were received at the Chinese court.

There was only one warlike confrontation, in Sri Lanka. After the fourth voyage, further journeys were then abandoned, because the costs for the fleet were too high and the funds were needed after natural disasters.

In contrast to Japan, which was a popular culture, China has always been an elite culture, where the officials—Mandarins—held the highest rank in society. The position, however, was not hereditary, but could only be reached by passing exams and audits during 12 consecutive years. In other words, even sons of peasants or non-native Chinese could attain this level if they had the aptitude.

The traditional, Laozi-assigned Chinese worldview of Universalism, which propagates unity between heaven, earth and man and the pursuit of harmony in society, is in stark contrast to the most recent developments in the country, which are marked by pragmatism and business efficiency, the pursuit of material happiness and wealth and a long life. This contrast makes it difficult for us to understand that these ideals still exist and that they are still adhered to. And yet we can assume that the majority of the 1.4 billion Chinese identify with these ideals.

4.8.2 The Confucian Order

The basis of relations in China is the Confucian order. Confucius (551 BCE to 479 BCE) worked as a teacher and advisor, sporadically also as a Minister of the then Chinese state. According to his philosophy, a society can only live in harmony in a holistic world if everyone knows his rights and duties. The smallest cell within a society is the family, in which everyone must know his/her rights and duties and live according to them. Over time, this became the national philosophy of China and remains so to this day.

The five fundamental roles in Confucianism are:

(i) The ruler or the prince protects his subjects.
(ii) The father bears the central responsibility in the family.
(iii) The wife or mother takes care of the family.
(iv) Friends support and help the family in distress.

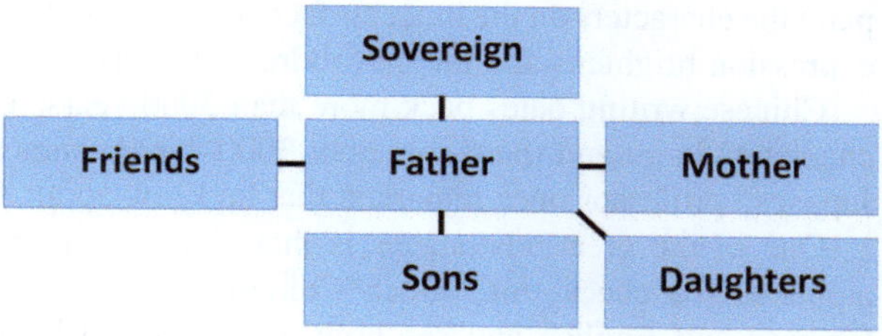

Fig. 4.1 Principle of the Confucian Order

(v) Among the sons, the eldest brother is responsible for the younger brothers.
(vi) Daughters go to a new family.

The graphic below reiterates that (Fig. 4.1):

The Confucian Order, by the way, also forms the basis of coexistence in many other countries in East and Southeast Asia, such as Korea, Japan or Vietnam. China actually tried to abolish the Confucian Order during the Cultural Revolution. However, from today's vantage point, it may be said that this 2500-year-old social order has emerged strengthened from it.

Today, China is increasingly refocusing on these fundamental values. Confucianism is even exported. Confucian Centers are emerging worldwide.

4.8.3 Communication and Conflict Resolution

4.8.3.1 Speaking in Pictures

The Chinese speak in pictures. Of all the world languages, Chinese is probably the most difficult for Europeans to master. Because of four different possibilities of intonation, even modern Mandarin lacks clarity in the spoken language, as shown by the syllable "*Ma*" below:

(a) mā (constant tone) = Mother
(b) mà (falling sound) = Scolding
(c) má (rising tone) = Hemp
(d) mǎ (falling, then rising tone) = Horse

To understand the meaning and the context of the sentence, it is often necessary to know the context and situation speakers are confronted with and referring to during the conversation. Living in a stable environment with a network of relationships therefore facilitates communication.

In contrast, the characters are clear. Each character and combination of characters can be assigned to a fixed term. If the Chinese do not understand each other, they will paint the characters on the inner surface of the hand or in the air, and then the puzzled expression brightens and the one addressed, nods.

Chinese writing dates back more than 3000 years. There are more than 100,000 characters in all and there are about 3000–5000 characters needed for daily life. A Japanese professor once remarked that he knew about 8000 characters.

One of the great advantages is that Chinese can be read faster than the Latin alphabet. To check this, watch Chinese TV, such as CNTV4 with subtitles in Chinese and English and see how fast the English (and the Chinese) disappear. You barely have the time to read it.

Another advantage is that quite a few words are expressed by two or more characters. "Crisis", shown below, includes both danger and opportunity (Fig. 4.2).

Chinese are very lively and interested communicators and their sensibilities can usually be read very well from body language and facial expression. One of the authors, for example, was frequently addressed on the street during his stays in the mid-1990s in Nanjing and Shenyang and was also invited to have a chat.

In business life, the atmosphere during discussions is calm. Differences are addressed privately and outside a meeting. An escalation rarely takes place. Because a group strives for a consensus, it can take a long time for a decision to be reached. One of the authors spent an entire afternoon with professors and lecturers in Nanjing discussing who would give the introductory speech on Monday. The Chinese colleagues discussed it quietly among themselves, came to a decision and then brought in the Dean to endorse it. He introduced some new aspects and so the discussion was resumed. After several rounds of the process and three hours later, a decision was finally reached.

Fig. 4.2 The Chinese character for "crisis"

4.8.3.2 The Interpreter as Alter Ego

Simultaneous interpretation from a Western language into Mandarin Chinese are particularly difficult. One of our experiences may serve as an illustration here:

The Professor as a Translator in a Marketing Seminar

In a weekly seminar in Shenyang with approximately 40 professors, lecturers and industry executives in the mid-1990s, Mrs. Chang, a university professor of German, was employed as an interpreter. The restlessness started during the first lectures; there were concerns which were communicated through the class spokeswoman, Mrs. Yang. She protested unusually loudly. At the lecturer's inquiry, Mrs. Chang said that Mrs. Yang had not understood something, but that she had corrected it in the meantime.

The lecturer was accompanied to lunch and dinner. At the very first meal he was told by a colleague of Mrs. Chang's that she was not able to translate properly. The question of changing the interpreter was negated, but an interim solution was found for particularly difficult passages with an experienced interpreter who filled in these passages. At the end of the seminar, the lecturer received a rating from the participants stating that his teachings had been very "*simplistic*".

Back in Germany the lecturer reported his difficulties with the interpreter. Consequently, a Chinese linguist in Germany was sent to China to prepare the interpreter for the delegation's next visit. In this seminar Mrs. Chang translated for about ten minutes but was constantly corrected by her Chinese colleague from Germany. In the end she sat down, and he then took over her role as interpreter.

In his response to the question of how Mrs. Chang's translation had been, he said, "*A third was correct, a third was wrong and a third was mere fiction*".

Although Mrs. Chang was perfectly proficient in the German language, she was not at all familiar with the subject. She lacked the technical background, terminology, an understanding of the Western marketing concept as well as the business environment involved.

As in every other culture, an interpreter is the alter ego of a traveler in China. He/she should be familiar with the economic climate. the living conditions, the business culture, the products and the market, as well as with the specific vocabulary. Preparing him/her in-depth is the key to success, especially if he/she is an outsider, i.e. not an employee of the organization.

4.8.3.3 Saving Face and Face Saving Actions

Below are some classic examples as case studies. The first two deal with the special status of the client in China. As the author would say in his seminars: "*In the Western Europe, the customer is a disruption of the daily routine, in the USA, a king and in Asia, he is a God*". This is certainly exaggerated, but in essence, it is the truth, as the following two case studies show.

The Visit of a Chinese Delegation to Germany

This story dates to the end of the 1990s. A delegation of Chinese clients arrived for a first visit in Germany to discuss a national IT project at the proposal of a German company.

Considerable problems arose in the meetings due to communication failures. In this case, a German engineer said "*It's not a good idea*" in the first meeting with one of China's then largest companies in telecommunications. "*It is not a good idea*" was perceived as a *no,* which led to the breaking off of negotiations. Afterwards, the German head of the delegation asked the Chinese colleague what the cause had been, and he confirmed the faux pas. The hurdle was finally overcome with a letter from the German company to the Chinese company, apologizing for a minor detail in the contract. This letter was signed by the then Chairman of the Board of Directors in Germany.

The apology was not precisely directed at the incident, because this would have exacerbated the problem; in Asian conflict avoidance and conflict resolution the problem is often shifted to another area.

This Chinese visit proved to be extremely difficult in other respects as well. Although an exact time was agreed on for meals and a map was distributed in advance, the visitors always appeared individually and too late.

A possible explanation: The visitors from China arrived late because they thought that they were unimportant and/or that time didn't matter. However, tardiness can also cause disharmony in China.

To show respect and give face to Chinese guests, they would have to be picked up at their hotel and driven to the restaurant. After dinner, they would either have to be dropped back or asked if they want to be driven elsewhere. If they wanted to go out on their own, they would usually say so.

As a rule, Chinese feel responsible for their guests and want to make sure that they are well cared for. This may change with time, but hospitality is inextricably connected to giving face (showing respect). Western hosts would do well to go along with this and offer more than less.

Postscript: Over the following years, this client developed into an important key account for the German company.

Christmas at Home

Shortly before Christmas, a 29-year-old Swiss engineer was sent to a client in China who had a software problem. The production plant was immobilized. The Chinese engineers were unable to rectify the problem and therefore requested support from the Swiss supplier at short notice—three days before Christmas—to initialize test runs with the software and repair the system.

The Swiss engineer had recently got married and wanted to be at home for Christmas. In one of the first conversations with the client, he announced his intention, and was then amazed by the indignation of the Chinese. During a break, a Chinese colleague came to him and said that they would call the police and he would go to prison if he continued to insist on his wish.

It was incomprehensible and inadmissible to the Chinese that an individual can put his personal wishes as above those of the collective. They were so appalled by his statement that it came to: "*If you leave tomorrow, we will call the police and put you in jail!*"

The Chinese then tried to solve the problem themselves. The tests ended in a crash, and in fact the system could not be repaired before Christmas. The Swiss engineer then called his boss, who made it possible to order him back home.

The incident certainly reinforced the Chinese prejudice that we Westerners are all egomaniacs who only think of ourselves. And it is indeed the case, that we Westerners often live in a kind of service wasteland where clients frequently have the feeling that they are disturbing our daily routine.

In contrast the customer is king in the USA and in Asia he is "*God*". We would do well to treat the clients accordingly.

A similar story happened to another Western supplier. Because the Chinese client feared that the supplier could leave early, his passport was taken away claiming his visa needed to be checked. It was returned to him after the repair had been done.

The following story is a classic on how a conflict between Chinese and Western executives may arise and can be solved:

The Shared Secretary

A Swiss CEO was transferred to a Shanghai subsidiary, which up to then had been managed by the Chinese Managing Director. The two developed a very good relationship from the beginning. As a mark of respect, the Chinese colleague offered the Swiss CEO his office and insisted that he use it to send clear message to the employees about his role in the company. The secretary was to support both.

From the first day, she tried to fulfill her duties. One day she unmistakably gave the Swiss executive to understand that she was unable to carry the entire burden. He then called a meeting with all three parties, summed up the situation briefly and told her she could choose for whom she would like to work. To his amazement, she asked for a raise and left the meeting outraged.

In this genuine case, the new executive from the West wanted to introduce Western management methods by which the employees are involved in decision-making. However, he was thereby putting his secretary in a predicament that could only end in conflict and a loss of face for all, since she would have to hurt the feelings of one her superiors. So, she shifted the conflict to another level by asking for a higher salary and delegated the problem back to her superior. In this case, the Swiss executive decided to take her over as his assistant. She was a loyal and committed employee after that.

The following two examples show how a loss of face can occur in conversation and how a hidden request can be refused without loss of face:

The Political Discussion on Tiananmen Square

A German engineer walked Tiananmen Square with a Chinese colleague whom he knew well, liked, and with whom he had established a relationship of trust.

The German engineer talked about the student revolution and the massacre at that place. His Chinese partner first ignored the subject, and then said that the State would have been endangered. The German insisted that a serious injustice had occurred there. The Chinese denied it again, referring to the subversive behavior of the students. The discussion continued in this vein until the Chinese suddenly agreed with his German colleague.

From this, the German concluded that Chinese had agreed that an injustice had been done. But later the German sensed that the relationship of mutual trust had been impaired.

From a Western point of view, democracy is the only correct system of government. We forget that this system also has its strengths and weaknesses and that it is experienced and implemented differently in every country. We also forget that there are other forms of government—each with their own strengths and weaknesses—that have helped cultures and people to live and survive successfully for millennia.

From the point of view of the Chinese, the German had strained his loyalty to his country with his insistence that it had been unjust. To keep the conversation from escalating, he backed away from his position, but felt that there had been an infringement on his loyalty. It would have been correct not to get into the issue at all. Both sides knew that the views were different and that there was no basis for a comparative discussion. The relationship could thus have been maintained.

Gifts from Chinese Colleagues

A Swiss had a lecturing assignment in an institute at Nanjing University at the beginning of the new millennium. One day, a Chinese Professor mentioned that he would like to visit him with his daughter and after arranging the dates, the meeting took place.

The conversation centered on the family, the beauty of Switzerland and the warm working relationship they have with China. The father brought small gifts. Occasionally, the father mentioned that his daughter had just completed her studies in economics and would like to study for a postgraduate degree in Switzerland. After a photo was taken, they departed.

The message, although not explicitly expressed, was clear. The father wanted help and support for his daughter to study in Switzerland. The Swiss lecturer was overwhelmed and asked his German colleague what he should do, as he was unable to provide any support because of a critical situation in his family.

The German colleague advised return gifts—not the ones he was given, but the ones he took with him to China.

As explained in Sect. 3.9 "Hospitality and Gifts" every gift has a meaning—it serves to balance the "*debtor's account*" to balance the relationship. In the present case, it was clear that the Chinese professor wanted the visitor from the West to accept the mentoring of the daughter. After settlement of the gift account, the request for help was never mentioned again.

The unequal treatment of two Western guests in China led to a conflict for the host:

Room Reservation in Nanjing

Two lecturers from Germany were accommodated on the campus of an institution at Nanjing University. Since it was a 4-week stay, they received written confirmation that they would be housed in small apartments.

Both arrived at different times. Upon the early arrival of the one lecturer, the receptionist revealed that, unfortunately, only a normal room was available for them. The first arrival accepted the offer.

His colleague who arrived later, looked at the single room, refused it and insisted on the apartment, to which he was then assigned.

This difference in treatment led to a dilemma for the Chinese host. The result was that one of the Chinese professors appeared in the room of the disadvantaged lecturer several days in a row in the mornings. He was constantly apologizing and at the same time complaining about the other colleague's behavior.

From a Chinese perspective, it would have been good not to insist on complying with the agreement, as it led to escalation and conflict. Doing what is right in a certain situation takes precedence over the right to do it.

4.8.4 Cooperation in Professional and Business Life

4.8.4.1 China and the West: Two Diametrically Opposed Approaches to Life and Business

Few Westerners have a profound, in-depth insight into the Chinese soul. We judge China by our standards and values and look at this millennia-old culture in a generalized way. This is particularly true for nearly all mass media, particularly the electronic media. In 90% of the reporting on China, well-researched background and nuances of context are generally absent. Broadcasts are mainly negative, lecturing the Chinese on what is wrong with their country and on how they should be governed. Chinese dissenters are becoming heroes in the Western world. We forget that a majority of the 1.3 billion Chinese are loyal to and support their country's policies. In bicultural marriages between Chinese and Westerners, the Chinese partner is often confronted with prejudices within the family.

François Jullien,[32] a French philosopher described the differences between the Western and Chinese culture in his lecture at Hawaii University in 2003. The chart below is a synopsis of his lecture (Fig. 4.3):

[32]Jullien François and Lloyd Janet, Treatise on Efficacy: Between Western and Chinese Thinking, University Hawaii PR, July 1, 2004.

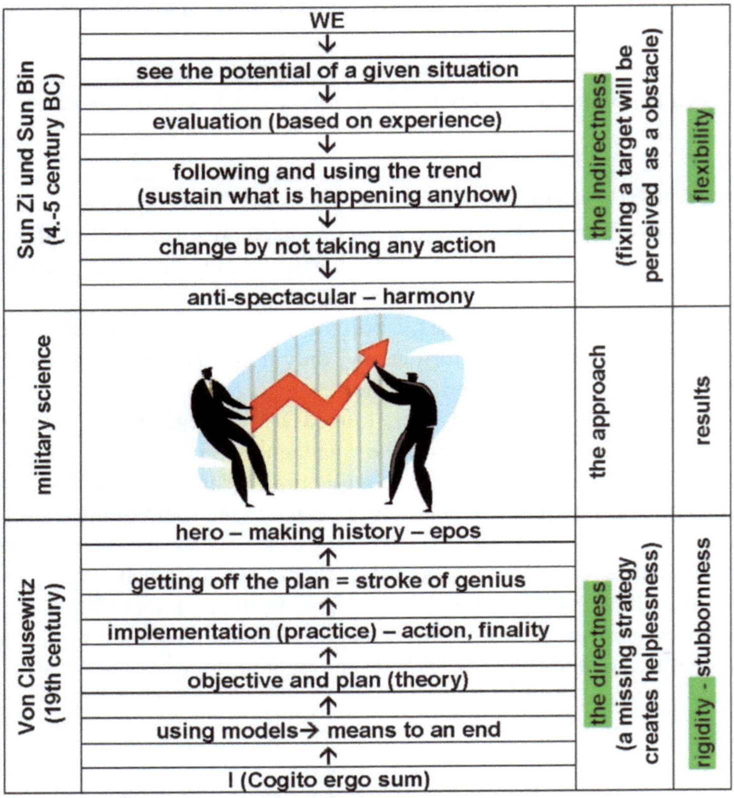

Fig. 4.3 Efficiency and effectiveness in China and the West

Once again, this is our world view based on the "*I*" not the "*WE*" when trying to achieve efficiency.

The Western approach is based on models, a plan, and action-oriented implementation. The most direct way is judged to be the most efficient. This leads to inflexibility. Any unplanned incident is a catastrophe. Those who are nevertheless able to achieve the goal become heroes and make history.

The Chinese approach is the complete opposite: the "*WE*" look for the potential of a given situation and proceed from there on by following trends, sustaining what is naturally happening, without any abrupt changes to achieve harmony. It is an approach guided by total flexibility.

It is interesting to note the age of teachings in military strategy: In China they date from fourth to fifth century B.C., in the West from the nineteenth century.

This philosophical approach will help us to understand the fundamental differences between China and the West better. There are, of course, many nuances to these approaches in real life in both cultures!

4.8.4.2 A Business Culture of Families and Networks

The Chinese ideal is to live and work on a life-long basis of stable networks and to go through good and bad times with mutual loyalty. For example, a Chinese restaurant owner in Baden-Württemberg said: "*If we do well, everyone benefits. If we do badly, we all tighten our belts.*"

With their sense of family and cohesion, the approximately 60 million Chinese living in foreign countries with estimated total assets of $1.5 trillion, are an economic power and the most important investor in the People's Republic of China. According to the Asia Times from December 10, 2002, economists ranked Chinese living abroad as the world's third-largest economic power behind the United States and Japan. Today, the national economy of China, based on GDP (gross domestic product), is the world's 2nd largest economic power and is expected to overtake the USA by the year 2030.[33]

The relationship networks, Guanxi, decide on the well-being and career of the individual and of his family. The same applies to foreign companies (see also Sect. 3.4 "*Relationship quality and relationship networks*").

The high-power distance in China—index 80, according to Hofstede—confirms what we all know, i.e. that Chinese business is managed hierarchically. The CEO of a Chinese company serves both as a role model and an integrating figure. His prime responsibility is to care for his employees. In reverse, their loyalty and tireless joint efforts lead to steadily improving their performance and thus that of the company.

4.8.4.3 Social Relationships and Social Events in Business Life

One of the authors taught in Shenyang and Nanjing in the 1990sby where he experienced Chinese hospitality. He was accompanied throughout his stay, picked up at the airport, driven to the university and back every day, and had company for lunch and dinner. Formal banquets at the beginning and end of his stay were held, with all the executives and lecturers involved present.

Personal involvement during leisure time outside the work environment is just as essential to success as the time that Western businesspeople spend in meetings and conversations. Personal conversation between colleagues goes deeper, so they get to know each other better and build trust. The following describes a well-established ritual in Chinese business:

Seating arrangement: Seated at a round table the Western guest usually faces the door and to the right of the Chinese host. The interpreter usually sits on the right of the guest.

The host proposes an opening toast, and the guest is expected to do the same after a while. Drinking means socializing, and as a rule, there will be more drinking after a short toast. This aspect, i.e. drinking habits and alcohol, has been explained in more detail in Sect. 3.9.2 "*Drinking customs and alcohol*".

Each new dish will be set on a swiveling stand or "*Lazy Susie*" on the round table and served directly in front of the guest. The host has a special set of chopsticks with

[33]https://en.wikipedia.org/wiki/List_of_countries_by_GDP_(nominal). Last viewed Sept 9, 2018.

which he picks out the best pieces and then places on the guest's bowl or plate. Food has a fundamental role in human well-being in Chinese eating culture, which is why an incredibly wide variety of food is served, including specialties that are sometimes strange for Western palates and eyes. Usually, the guest will try every dish unless he has an aversion to it or an allergy. In this case, this item should just be passed over. If you have a problem with certain foods, you should let the host know beforehand.

The event is officially ended by the host after approximately two hours if no more festivities, such as Karaoke singing, are scheduled.

If ever a Chinese host has a request, you can forget about your Western approach to business. The following story happened to one of the authors is an example:

The Company Visit in China

One of the authors visited a textile company as part of a teaching assignment. He was led through the weaving mill and then through the tailoring and sewing shop for men's underwear for the Chinese and Japanese markets. These were simple products, such as pink long-johns with a drawstring.

At the subsequent meeting with the company management, the author was asked for addresses of possible distribution partners in Europe. From what the author had just seen, it was obvious that these products would have no chance on the European market. He therefore tried to repeatedly persuade the management to first work on the design, to no avail.

We were all sitting in a large room with fauteuils along the walls. Suddenly all the lights went out due to a power cut, which was not unusual in the early nineties in China. It was like a sign from above to demonstrate what the Chinese probably thought of the author's intervention.

One lesson learnt: The author should have acceded to the request and helped with the contacts. Since opening-up, China has proven that it is capable of quickly adapting to Western techniques and implementing them successfully.

And lastly, yet another detail... but an important one.

An Encounter in an Elevator or Physical Integrity in China

In the early nineties one of the authors put up at a government guesthouse in Nanjing took the elevator down to the main floor the very first morning. There was a housekeeper standing right next to the control panel when he entered. He stretched out his arm, index finger extended, to push the button for the lobby, whereupon the maid withdrew in obvious alarm to the back of the elevator.

In China, pointing a finger at someone may be perceived as an aggression. Be cautious with your body language. Restraint is always a good advice, i.e. apologize, smile, and then approach the panel slowly to press the button, instead of stretching out your hand as people would do in the West.

4.9 France and French Speaking Cultures in the World

4.9.1 Culturally Defining Elements

4.9.1.1 Population and Population Density

The population of France has always been—and still is—low in comparison to other large European countries. After the French Revolution and during industrialization in the nineteenth century, the population density of France, with approximately 100 inhabitants per square kilometer, corresponded to about half of Germany's. This ratio has remained roughly the same to this day.

France did not have enough manpower to carry out industrialization on its own, because the French were mainly engaged in agriculture and food production at that time. As a result, France's industrialization began late—only at the end of the nineteenth century. It had to fall back on foreign workers; first on Germans and Swiss, then, in the twentieth century, to people from southern Europe, afterwards to the regions of North Africa, the Maghreb, and still later from the former colonies of black Africa such as Senegal or the Ivory Coast.

In contrast to Germany, France has therefore always been a country of migrants, which—from the French point of view—could have become a burden, or posed a threat, to French culture. Therefore, everyone who has mastered the French language and identifies himself with Francophone culture is considered a Frenchman. Former President Sarkozy (2007–2012) gave always the impression that he was a French leader, which made one forget his Hungarian origins.

4.9.1.2 France and Its Languages

Seen from the outside, French is the only language in France. Viewed historically, foreign languages and cultures were constantly perceived as a threat to France. The French language map shows the following language and cultural groups within the current national borders:

1. Alemannic and Frankish dialects In the east, in Alsatia and Lorraine
2. Flemish in the north
3. a Celtic language with various dialects spoken by Bretons in Brittany
4. the Basque language in the southwest,
5. the Catalan language in the French Pyrenees
6. Occitan in the south, a large language group that goes all the way to Piedmont. The Provençal language also belongs to it.
7. Corsican, which is more closely related to Italian than to French, in Corsica.

The now standard French language has its roots in the fourteenth century, when the common northern dialect called *"la langue d'oeil"* matured to become the national language under the Royal House of the Carpathians. In the course of its history, cultural diversity was perceived as a threat to the French language and culture due to outside pressure, both from other nations and also from the many sub-cultures within France. This may have led to French centralism in culture, politics and economics which extends to the present day in spite of various presidents, i.e. de Gaulle and Mitterrand, trying to promote regionalism.

This perceived cultural threat has lasted to the present day. It is well- known everywhere in Europe that Corsica aspires to independence and does so even by means of terrorism. Less well-known are the efforts of the Bretons to restore their language against resistance from Paris by reintroducing Breton as a language in primary schools.

Being Germanic, the Alsatian language exists on the margins. It is closely connected with the Second World War after which the German language became taboo. Today there are efforts to revive Alsace in the form of cultural associations and societies. The regional channel France 3 broadcasts regularly in the Alemannic language. Older Alsatians, however, believe that the language will die out after their lifetime.

On the other hand, there is also a desire by young people to return to these linguistic roots. A French woman in our seminar in Germany, who was Alsatian, used to be a member of a society for the preservation of the Alsatian language. She gave up this membership because she worked for a national French organization and was concerned that this membership might not do her career any good!

An antithesis to centralism is created by the fact that in the EU, more and more culturally similar regions across borders are coming together. In the region where Northern Switzerland, the French Alsace and German Baden-Württemberg meet, Alemannic is being revived through the use of this language in daily human interaction across borders.

4.9.1.3 The Académie Française : A French Language Institution

The Académie française[34] was founded in the year 1635 under Louis XIII with the help of French minister Cardinal Richelieu. The 40 lifetime members are called "*Les Immortels*" (the Immortals). The Chairman, the "*Secrétaire Perpétuel*", is chosen for life. The responsibility and the primary objective of the Académie française is the preservation of the purity of the French language by setting very strict standards, the effects of which are noticeable in the media, advertising and daily linguistic usage.

The following examples are taken from the IT industry. English idioms have been adopted in the German language, but French has its own expressions (Fig. 4.4):

There is a television authority that examines the correct use of French in TV commercials.[35] Back in the 1970s, one of the authors experienced how this board at first rejected the expression, "*aquastable*" for a car tire TV commercial, even though this was a branded term based on Latin roots. Only after lengthy discussions was the term accepted for television broadcast.

There is a strong sense of the purity of language in every Frenchman. Especially educated French people will correct others' mistakes immediately, or if expressions

[34]http://www.academie-francaise.fr/. Last viewed Sept. 09, 2018.

[35]https://fr.wikipedia.org/wiki/Conseil_sup%C3%A9rieur_de_l%27audiovisuel_(France). Last viewed September 14, 2018.

English Original	German	French
computer	Computer	ordinateur
software	Software	logiciél
website	Webseite	site
email	*E-Mail*	courrier éléctronique
internet user	Internetanwender	internautes

Fig. 4.4 Avoiding "Anglicisms" in the French language by the IT Industry

from an Anglo-Saxon language are used, they will point them out as "*Franglais*", a combination of "*Français*" and "*Anglais*", to indicate that this is poor style. Mostly an alternative will be offered in pure French.

4.9.1.4 The International Organization of La Francophonie

"*La Francophonie*",[36] the International Organization of the Francophone world is committed to the political and cultural heritage of France and has broad worldwide support.

Although there are only 70 million native-language French speakers around the world, 230 million people speak French as their official language.

In comparison, there are 120 million people in German-speaking countries who use German as their native and official language.

Under the auspices of this international organization and the aegis of France, French cultural heritage and international relations with other Francophone regions are maintained worldwide. This includes the French overseas provinces, Haiti, the Francophone parts of Belgium and Switzerland, Francophone Canada and countries in North and West Africa, as well as Asia, e.g. Vietnam.

4.9.1.5 The French and Their History

The French have a strong sense of history; historical events enter into social conversation in daily life. This is also a way of showing education, cleverness, wit and humor. French people have an absolutely unapologetic relationship with their own history and are proud of it.

This differs completely from their eastern neighbors in Germany where recent history of the Nazi era is constantly addressed and "*Vergangenheitsbewältigung*" (coping with the past) is an ongoing issue in politics, the media and amongst people in general. This was always a central theme in every single one of the hundreds of cross-cultural seminars with German participants held by the authors.

In Switzerland, history is idealized, glorified and the country represented as a unity since 1291—despite the fact that modern Switzerland only became united in 1848. Prior to the foundation of modern Switzerland, individual parts of the country, such as the present cantons of Aargau and of Vaud were colonies of the ancient Swiss Confederation, where serfdom existed practically up to liberation by Napoleon.[37]

---

[36]https://www.francophonie.org/. Last viewed September 14. 2018.

[37]http://history-switzerland.geschichte-schweiz.ch/swiss-revolution-helvetic-republic-1798.html. Last viewed September 14, 2018.

Historically, the relationship between France and its big neighbor Germany is still strained by the trauma of German perfection and dominance. Politically, this belongs to the past. However, the older perspective still plays a role in the economy, as the following case study shows:

Launch of a French Credit Card in Germany

The subsidiary of a French bank in Paris hired a consulting company in Germany with the mandate to investigate the German credit card market, with the aim of introducing a successful French product there.

After a quantitative study and a survey with German experts, the consultants recommended launching the card in Germany because the French had an edge in terms of technology and marketing.

Before the decisive presentation to the bank's board of directors in Paris, the French managing director and project manager told the German consultants that the management would most likely decide against launching in Germany. The well-founded German research showed that the product would stand a good chance of success. To the German consultant's astonished question about why the Board would not continue the project, the French managing director reasoned: "*Parcequ'ils craignent éfficacité allemande*". (Because they are afraid of German perfection)

To the great surprise of the consultants, that is exactly what happened. It is probably the most extreme intercultural example of a cliché serving as justification for a largely emotional decision.

4.9.1.6 Food and the Quality of Life

The French have always spent more money on food than the Germans because there is a tradition of quality in lifestyle and food in France. Weekly food markets have not disappeared because of the large food chains to the same extent, as for example in Germany or Switzerland. In France they continue to be held. Every Parisian can buy food directly from the producer or dealer on seven days a week.

Since the advent of the organic trend in the 1980s, weekly markets in the German-speaking regions have become more popular. At the same time, as early as the mid-1960s, France was the first country in Europe to have a "*Hypermarché*", a wholesale distributor of food and other goods. This was a necessity because disposable income for daily needs was much lower than in neighboring Germany or Switzerland. The demand for high quality food products means that a higher proportion of the total budget and disposable income is being spent on it in France.

The following touching example was experienced by the author with a French friend visiting Germany:

The Perfect Strawberry Tart

The author's French friend showed his food expertise impressively during his visit to Hamburg. As he was a reputed cook, the author's family was looking forward to him cooking a delicious dinner. He had promised a strawberry tart for dessert.

As strawberries were needed, the first stop was at a delicatessen. Our friend checked all the punnets on the shelf and rejected every single one.

The second stop was a supermarket, with the same result.

Fortunately, it was harvesting season and a farm north of Hamburg had a stand which sold large baskets of strawberries. Our friend reviewed dozens of baskets on the counter, but none of them were acceptable. Then, to the bemusement of the sales staff, he went behind the counter and began to look through all the baskets. Halfway through the pile of dozens of baskets he called out "*This is it!*"

They were the best strawberries the author has ever eaten. Whether it was the ritual of choosing or the fruit, is hard to say. The secret was that our French friend was able to determine the ripeness of the fruit from the color of the seeds and was thus able to make the right choice. This kind of specialized knowledge is something he shares with many of his countrymen.

In the mid-90s, the French government discovered that the traditional knowledge about the quality of food was slowly being lost. They introduced the subject "*Le goût français*" (the French Taste) into primary schools where children were again taught basic knowledge on the quality of food and nutrition. Every year a theme week supported by the Ministry of Education is held[38] in which the results of these efforts are commended.

Meals are a social event for the French, be it in the family, with friends, acquaintances or even in business life. "*La convivialité*" (convivial social interaction) is as vital as food intake. The French talk about everything under the sun at mealtimes, but (almost) never about business.

4.9.2 Communication and Conflict Resolution

Style and form of communication characterize the French personality. These include courtesy and linguistically refined interaction with one another. One of the most significant differences in the communication style between Germans and the French lies in the German directness, i.e. the comprehensibility and clarity of what is being said.

Directness in communication serves as a key to solving a conflict in Germany. In contrast, the French language describes, even circumscribes issues and problems in an elegant way. This may be the reason why French is often regarded as one of the most beautiful languages in the world.

The French normally use form and style diplomatically to criticize and will not address points of criticism directly. They have learned to reconcile differing viewpoints and are in a position to represent both conservative and progressive

[38]http://www.gqnpc.com/semaine-du-gout/. Last viewed September 14, 2018.

values. And they are proud of their francophone cultural heritage, "*Le patrimoine français*". At the same time, they are also citizens of this world and politically interested and committed.

Even if they seldom speak out directly, they are very disciplined in achieving goals. "*Savoir Vivre*" is not something that is only cultivated at home, it is an all-pervasive attitude and philosophy in life, also in business.

Conflicts are usually not discussed openly. Should this be the case, the conflict has already escalated. Men must maintain a particularly attentive and polite approach to women if they don't want to be considered uncouth. Criticism is carefully packaged, even in private conversation, which are the panacea for conflict resolution. Observing linguistic conventions and rituals will prevent conflicts from the outset.

For example, the statement "*C'est n'est pas la meilleure des idées*" (It is not the best of ideas) means in plain language "*This idea is useless*".

A classic use of diplomatic French for whitewashing is shown in the following case study.

A French Managing Director Reports to His HQ in London

An American Regional CEO for Europe in an international advertising agency received the following report from the French managing director:

"Meeting Report:

Last Thursday we had our half-yearly meeting with our key client. The client's sales during the first quarter were unsatisfactory, which he attributes to the overall market situation. Although the biggest competitor increased its sales volume by 10 percent, others in the market all have stagnating sales volume.

As for our performance, the client was not entirely satisfied with our order processing and the accounting. In addition, some qualitative deficiencies have occurred in recent ad campaigns, but this has been corrected.

Lunch took place in an excellent atmosphere. The client particularly emphasized his satisfaction with the dedication of our employee Monsieur Henchoz".

This translation into English is from memory. The French original would have been even more elegant. The euphemistic style, however, sent the American managing director into a rage. He saw this as a manipulation of the truth. This cost the French manager his job.

From a French perspective, this type of communication serves to gloss over conflicts; in French "*noyer un poisson*" (literally meaning: "*drowning a fish*"). When you receive a report in the French, you had better read between the lines. The above report clearly shows that the situation is out of control.

4.9.3 *"The Patron"*: Cooperation in Business and Professional Life

The very high-power distance with an index of 68 is, according to Hofstede, significant. "*Le patron*" is above everyone else. A French superior will use his education and thus the French language as an instrument, a keyboard on which he can play different melodies. His language will be nuanced depending on whether it is a meeting with the back-office staff, with an employee in the workshop, or with a client.

Even the salutation is nuanced. While first names and informal salutations are often applied through the hierarchies in marketing and advertising, the salutation "*Vous*" the formal "*You*", is often retained in traditional companies, even if the addressee is addressed by his first name.

Here are some examples of variations when the imaginary boss Guy Durand addresses his employee Bernard Dupont:

1. "*Dupont*", the salutation in daily use.
2. "*Monsieur Dupont*", used formally or if stressed, as the beginning of an admonition or criticism.
3. "*Bernard*" is used if they have known each other for a long time, although the boss normally uses "*Tu*" or "*Vous*", whereas the employee will often call his superior "*Monsieur*", and sometimes even add the boss's last name, i.e. "*Monsieur Durand*". Often the title is also used, as in "*Monsieur le Directeur*". Addressing a Chairman of the Board as "*Mon Président*" is quite usual.
4. "*Mon cher Bernard*" or "*Mon cher Dupont*" (my dear Bernhard or Dupont) may be used affectionately, paternally, caringly or jovially. Referring to a particular situation and assuming that the employee has had a mishap, the boss might say something like: "*Mon cher Dupont, je vous demanderai de faire plus attention la prochaine fois*" (my dear Dupont, please be more careful next time)" This sounds very mild to us but is a rather strict admonition and criticism for an employee.

In Germany, a German project manager with a new assignment will usually convene a meeting with the entire team to discuss the project plan and its implementation, to agree on details that will then be reported to the hierarchy.

A French project leader will try to get a formal or may be even informal contact with his superior. He/She may walk as if by chance past the open office door of his/her *patron*, knock and ask if he/she has two minutes to spare. He/she will lay out briefly the main points of his/her approach, to get a nod or an agreement. He/she will then go to the most important project members, do the same there, and subsequently convene a meeting at which the procedure is announced. Having been pre-approved by the *patron*, it can no longer be questioned. It is actually very efficient in terms of time management! personal relationships and informal contacts providing personal access across all hierarchies lubricate the smooth cooperation.

The development of relationships is the basis for success in business relationships in France. This includes, first and foremost, the acceptance of the *patron* in his role.

France's schools and universities may teach American business methods, but "*patronage*" and "*patron-like*" behavior remain the cornerstones of this society. Those who doubt it should study the deportment of French presidents from de Gaulle to Macron. They all had different personalities, but their conduct as *patron* is very similar.

What Relationships Really Mean in France

One of the authors learned early how special relationships are in France. An employee of a longtime client was ill with cancer and did not have much longer to live. The client's superior suggested to the author that it would be a good idea to visit this employee and wish him goodbye. It was the author's first experience of a person marked by death. The subsequent funeral was a crucial experience; emotions were shown openly by all his colleagues, not only sadness but also shedding of tears.

For those who wish to know more about French educational and business culture, we recommend the book in French "*Citizen Du Monde*" or in English "Inside Nissan's Historic Revival".[39] It is the success story of Renault CEO Carlos Ghosn, who became the "*savior*" of Nissan in the 1990s. His unique Japanese experience can serve as a model for intercultural management. His core statement about his experience at French universities is also revealing: "*We were never taught teamwork, only analytical thinking*".

4.9.3.1 "Patronage" and Power Distance in the German: French Context

Dealings between French and Germans with regard to management attitudes and practices are a particularly sensitive issue. France having a high and Germany a low Power Distance carries the seed of a conflict in itself. French people usually accept the *patronage* of a leader, Germans resent it. The latter will often compare it with Louis XIV and his statement "*L'Etat c'est moi*" ("I am the State").

The following story of a German company, which was bought by a French group, is particularly illuminating:

The Initial Meeting in with the New Owner

The German company had a much larger revenue than the French parent company. They had a key client, for whom they had exclusively developed software. They were reputed for their excellent R&D capabilities. Their importance in the German market outweighed by far the potential of the new French owner.

The first meeting after the purchase started with a confrontation between the new French *patron* and the German CEO. As a result, the German CEO pulled out of the meeting followed by a board member with an Italian background who said to him: "*You can't do that, they are our new bosses*". The German CEO

[39] Ghosn Carlos, Riès Philippe, Shift: Inside Nissan's Historic Revival, Crown Business, March 21, 2006.

replied with an analogous saying by "*Old Fritz*"[40] the former Prussian King, the gist of which was: "*We will mind our own business*"*!*

From that moment on, a long decline of the German company began, with thousands of jobs lost, although part of the breakdown was certainly also market-driven. International key positions in R&D were gradually filled with executives from other countries such as Belgium, who had more affinities with the francophone world. The entire process took place without loud words or public confrontations. Here too, French courtesy applied. The disaster on the German side was a gradual one, noticed only in hindsight.

German executives were only sent to and accepted in the French headquarters more than a decade later.

One of the authors used to hold intercultural management seminars for the "*Young Tigers*", the future generation of executives of this company for several years. On the first evening of this program, a German Board Member would talk about company strategies and other factual issues. After the presentation there was usually a lively debate on the topic.

In one of the last seminars, the guest speaker was a woman, the first German executive ever at the head office in France. She did not address any factual subjects but told the young listeners in an impressive lecture to build relationships as the foundation for success!

Another example illustrates what can happen if the manager from France is not adequately involved in decision-making.

The Forgotten Patron

The German subsidiary of a French corporation initiated a project to optimize business processes in Germany. The project leader was German and had got approval for the project from his German supervisor. The implementation of the new organization and business processes was entrusted to an external service provider, who was to train all the specialists and executives concerned in Germany.

One of these training sessions was attended by the French executive responsible, who had been transferred to Germany from the parent company in France. Shortly after the training started, this *Patron* went into contradiction mode. After an hour he exclaimed angrily, "*Je ne suis pas d'accord! Pas avec moi!*" ("*I disagree! Without me!*") and left the room angrily. He complained to his network of executives in Germany and France, ultimately leading to the project being canceled and the restructuring abandoned.

The reason: The *Patron* was upset because the project leader had not involved him at the start of the decision process. He felt ignored and disrespected in his role, causing a loss of face for him with his employees and senior management.

[40]Friedrich II. or Friedrich the Great (* January 24, 1712 in Berlin; † August 17, 1786 in Potsdam).

As a rule, senior management in France should always be involved at an early stage to get support for a project or decision. After the first exchange, management should be regularly kept up to date. This may often happen through informal encounters in the corridor, at the coffee machine or in the canteen.

In Germany, on the other hand, only formal proceedings are recognized and accepted as a rule. Decisions are only made with the immediate supervisor. There is no informal consultation or settlement of company issues.

4.10 Germany

4.10.1 Culturally Defining Elements

4.10.1.1 German Characteristics: A View From Inside and Outside

This information is based on the author's experience as an international executive in multinational companies, as an intercultural corporate trainer for mainly German participants, as well as on his intercultural seminars at universities and colleges.

The participants were divided into small groups. After a short introduction, the question "*What are the characteristics of*. . .*e.g. Germans, Russians, Chinese?*" was to be answered and returned in writing on flip charts. The participants were encouraged to start this exercise by brainstorming and to discuss the findings only after a few minutes, when no more spontaneous responses to the cultural characteristics were generated.

The knowledge gained from this group work helped the seminar leader to assess the knowledge and cultural imprint—positively or negatively—of a group, and to focus the seminar on that. The following entries were mostly made by Germans, but also by participants from all over the world. The characteristics listed here for Germans are based on feedback from various working groups over the course of two decades. The ranking corresponds to the frequency of the entries:

1. Punctuality:
   Was most often cited as the salient feature for cooperation with Germans.
2. Perfection:
   Was the second most common feature. The pursuit of perfection can be assigned to the following oft-mentioned characteristics:
   (a) Order and cleanliness
   (b) Reliability, honesty
   (c) Structured thinking
   (d) Methodical planning
   (e) Application of rules and standards
   (f) High need for security
3. Directness:
   This third-party characteristic is mentioned by German participants with international experience in other cultures. Further comments on directness:
   (a) Critical

(b) Conflict Resolution
(c) Decisive

4. Industrious:
was the fourth common characteristic assigned to the German business world.

Anyone who has had business dealings with Germany or knows a lot about the German business world will probably be able to understand these characteristics. However, this representation is a "*robot image*" of a German business partner or employee. In reality, no German business partner is identical to another. Yet these stereotypical cultural characteristics exist in various forms.

This listing of these typical German characteristics intended to serve as a yardstick to compare with your own cultural thinking. With this, you can deduce your personal attitude and behavior in future contacts with German businesspeople.

How German Perfection Is Received in Hungary

A German project manager once had a bilateral project in Budapest. After the project had been running for some time, he flew to Budapest for group and individual meetings. To clarify some issues, he phoned before he left about what exactly had to be discussed. He prepared very well for the meeting and drew up a detailed agenda which he printed out for the participants.

Upon arrival in Hungary, the project manager was invited to a festive coffee buffet. After expressing his warm, appreciative thanks he said that there would now be time before the meeting to clarify some of the project's unresolved points. He requested that everyone be seated, distributed the agenda and wanted to implement the meeting quickly and efficiently.

To his astonishment, the Hungarian colleagues quickly became relatively restless and avoided all concrete questions with general answers. The more the project leader insisted, the more evasive they became.

Finally, he said "*Good, let's just go to the coffee buffet and discuss something else*". The mood immediately became more relaxed. All unresolved issues could then be informally addressed while drinking coffee and eating cake, even if not as perfectly as the project manager had planned.

The project management had simply overwhelmed the Hungarians with its perfect preparation and efficient implementation. When he let go, things worked out better. In addition to dialing down the perfectionist requirements of project management, it was also an occasion to build up relationships in an informal atmosphere.

4.10.2 Intercultural Management in German Practice

When dealing with the German business world, you are confronted by values, communication and working styles that may be contrary to your own business experience. The solution is to manage otherness.

An in-depth study of the history and values of this country from practice-oriented books helps to clarify and understand the differences. The key to the other culture lies in recognizing, understanding and acknowledging the otherness, as well as your personal ability to cope with it. Your own culture has shaped your personality and has made communal living possible. It influences your thoughts and actions. Intercultural cooperation does not mean abandoning or even denying your culture, but it requires a constant attempt to adapt to the other without falling into the trap of stereotyping or prejudice.

4.10.2.1 Relationship Building

In our view, Germany is a special case for the development of relationships in business life. The authors do not know of any other culture in which trust is gained primarily through factual content. This rational behavior is alien to most other cultures and can often lead to conflicts. The building of trust and then the relationship in the German business culture takes place primarily through the exchange of facts. Personal and social issues are usually excluded.

▶ **Reminder**

Remember that the private domain can be a taboo in a business relationship with Germans. In Germany, business and private life are strictly separated. An oft- heard saying is: *"Work is work and schnapps is schnapps"*. A German will want to discuss objective facts and problems during business hours. In Germany, a business lunch with business partners is called a *"working lunch (Arbeitsessen),"* which it is!

The following case study clearly shows the difference to another culture:

A Working Lunch During a German-French Negotiation

An example of a conflict was described by a German participant in a seminar: After contract negotiations with the French, the German continued to discuss business during lunch in Paris. Gradually she became aware that her behavior was depressing the mood of the French partners.

Back in Germany, she shared the situation with a colleague. He explained that the French find such behavior extremely rude. As in many other cultures, eating together is a social occasion for getting to know each other at a personal level and as an expression of respect for the guest.

During her next visit, the German businesswoman adapted and made just social conversation during lunch. It was a success. At the end of the meal, the

French manager said: "*pour le contract nous sommes d'accord*"—"we are in agreement about the contact".

► Avoid current conflict issues in politics or in business if you don't want a heated discussion.

4.10.2.2 Gifts/Corruption

The term corruption is interpreted very narrowly in Germany. To avoid embarrassment, avoid generous gifts and invitations, as they will be rejected. A small gift for the company, such as a typical handicraft from your country, is acceptable.

4.10.2.3 Communication and Conflict Resolution

Directness in communication and the direct pursuit of conflict solutions are often the main barriers for Germans in international collaboration, because this directness can be perceived as hurtful and hostile. In Germany, in principle, all problems must be disclosed and all solutions critically scrutinized. To the best of our knowledge, the German culture and language is perhaps the only one in which there are several words for differentiating a question. They are actively used in conversation to reinforce a question:

- "*Ich habe eine Frage*" ("I have a question")
- "*Da muss ich doch nochmals nachfragen*" ("Now I have to, insist, inquire again")
- "*Lassen sie mich nochmal hinterfragen*" ("Let me scrutinize it, get to the bottom of it again")

It is very rare for a German to use the above in translation, but a question can be repeated several times. The above explanations will hopefully make it easier for you to take it in the right spirit. It might prevent hurt feelings or being turned off completely.

In other Western cultures—for example in the English and Romance language speaking world—communication is more cohesive. Facts are made more palatable. The proverbial courtesy of the diplomatic languages, French and English, expresses their educational and linguistic culture and is the foundation for social acceptance in these countries.

For such cultures, dealing with German directness could therefore be a difficult aspect in business. But from a German perspective, the directness only serves the search for truth. The German language does not only contain the word ask, but also the words "*inquire*" and "*question*". If you hear the words, "*I would like to inquire about this point again*", then be prepared for an intense and critical conversation.

Bear in mind that this is the cultural trait that sets Germans apart from the others. It is not for no reason that Germany is called the land of poets and thinkers; without this communicative quality of seeking the truth, it would not have gained this reputation.

4.10.2.4 Negotiation

In Germany, the facts and only the facts are usually at the center of the discussion. As a rule, a German negotiator will arrive well informed and well documented to a negotiation. If any information is missing, negotiations are likely to stall. From the German point of view, this may be seen as inefficiency or disinterest, both of which can have a negative impact on the negotiation.

4.10.2.5 Teamwork

Teamwork is the basis of German business culture. Every individual is expected to get involved and contribute. Anyone who does not is suspected of hiding something, pursuing a personal agenda or being incapable of contributing.

4.10.2.6 Meetings

Meetings in Germany have preset agendas with subjects and timelines set in advance. They end with a road map and a future schedule with individual responsibilities listed. Meetings are held at the beginning of a project but also during the intermediate stages or whenever snags come up.

The results of these team meetings help the supervisors with their own decisions. They will intervene directly in the team process only in times of crisis. This is to avoid the risk of triggering frustration and defensiveness and of absolving the team of responsibility.

When Germans refer to their "*meeting culture*" they mean the regular meetings focused on facts and critical issues. They are about managing a project, supervising project progress and addressing critical points to come to a joint decision. Other business cultures e.g. the Americans, find this a mere waste of time. You can achieve all this informally in minutes, and a meeting is more a brainstorming than a detailed review.

English CEO Meets Germany

The following is a story of one of the author's closest friends, an extremely successful international manager with worldwide experience and numerous assignments to different parts of the world.

He was sent to Germany some years ago as the head of an international service organization, the unit being Number 1 in in the market and representing the 4th largest worldwide within the company.

Having spent nearly 10 years in a managerial function in Germany, the author received frequent calls from his friend, centering around just one topic: German meetings.

He complained constantly: "*Why do they have all these meetings? It is a waste of time. Business is so simple! You just sit down and do it!*" All the author's explanations were of no help. The frustration went on and on. Finally, his friend was happy to depart from Germany after 2½ years as Regional CEO to the Far East.

4.10.3 Project Work with Germans

German employees are convinced that the detailed planning leads to the best quality, functionality, operational safety, punctual delivery—in short, to success.

Projects are prepared exclusively in meetings with the goal of detailed planning with as many milestones and measures as possible. Once the details in the team are coordinated, the project plan is submitted to the decision-maker for approval.

This attitude to project management is unique to German business culture. Others, even in the West, do not plan in such detail. And in many cultures, decisions and policies are taken by the supervisor before even a meeting with the project team takes place.

For this reason, problems arise in international collaboration if the Germans demand the same qualities from others. Partners from other cultures often feel overwhelmed, either because their approach is more pragmatic or they do not have the same time and resources at their disposal as the world's fourth largest economic power.

4.10.4 Preparing for Contact with Partners in Germany

4.10.4.1 Preparation

A German business partner will expect the foreign partner to come very well prepared to negotiations. The precondition for success in negotiations is clearly formulated goals and factually supported documentation with arguments and evidence.

► In most cultures—even in the Western world—a concept is an idea that can be verbally recited or perhaps written down in a brief note. In Germany, a concept is a written document that has already been substantiated by research and facts and appears feasible.

If your employees are going to be in direct contact with German business partners, be it verbally, in writing or in meetings, they should be trained, fully integrated and well-informed during the preparation. Business partners from abroad who are able give competent answers, gain trust fairly quickly.

4.10.4.2 Initiating a Business Relationship

As a rule, every potential German business partner will be receptive to interesting offers. Initial contacts are usually made by e-mail or by letter, where courtesies are omitted, factual issues are central and addressed directly. Make sure that the spelling in written documents is correct. Besides the native language, English is also the predominant business language in Germany.

4.10.4.3 Paying a Visit

In contrast to your own culture and experience, in which visitors and guests are often well cared for and guided, you will probably receive no special care or guidance in Germany. It is expected that the visitor will find his own way and make all the necessary arrangements for his stay.

4.10.4.4 Your Introduction to the Company

Appear on time for the meeting and plan enough time, so as not to be late due to traffic jams. If this should once be the case, then do as the Germans do. Apologize for the delay, because Germans don't like it when their time is at someone else's disposal.

Your personal introduction on arrival at the company will be done with a handshake, with a quick look in the eye and an informal presentation of the business card. After two or three general sentences about your trip, accommodation, etc., you will be led straight to the meeting.

Leave the initiative to the German business partner and try not to make small talk, because this is perceived as a waste of time and your German counterpart could become impatient.

4.10.4.5 Your Introduction and Presentation

As a rule, meetings will last no more than two hours, unless you are at an advanced stage of the negotiations and the timing has been agreed upon in beforehand.

The preferred business communication in Germany is the written form. Therefore, prepare a presentation detailing your goal so that your business idea and intention become clear. In the preparation process, think of all sorts of questions that may be asked, and prepare evidence-based and supporting arguments and facts so that you can present them at the meeting. The better prepared you are, the greater the chance that a deal will be made. If necessary, bring in an expert on the German market for preparation.

4.10.4.6 Negotiations and the Contract

During negotiations, the German partner will start with the key issues or the main differences as there is no point in going into details without agreement on fundamental issues.

1. A successful deal always ends with a written document, letter or contract. A handshake instead of a contract, which is still common in many cultures, is not accepted in Germany. Once the contract has been negotiated and signed, it cannot be changed and is considered absolutely binding.
2. Social Contacts: Do not expect the German business partner to pick you up from the airport and to spend time with you after business hours. Lunch is usually in the canteen or in restaurant where employees usually have their midday meal. You will usually have to spend the evenings alone, perhaps with some suggestions from your host.

3. Follow-up: This is also done in the written form. An email is the usual format for confirming a visit, agreements, dates, the next step, or for staying in touch. Keep thanks and personal messages as short as possible—in a sentence or two—and focus on the issues and facts.

In Germany, for example, emphasizing or over-emphasizing a relationship in business can harm the reputation of an employee due for a promotion, based on the assumption "*He is only getting ahead because he knows the boss well*".

► **Be Mindful of the Difference in Available Resources**
In Germany, a company usually has greater financial and human resources than a comparatively smaller country, for instance, compared to Belgium resources both human and financially may be 10 times greater. If this is an issue, make it known to the German partner.

4.10.5 Cooperation in Business and Professional Life

It may seem a contradiction, but group consensus is fundamental in Germany's individualistic society as well as reporting along the line of command.

1. Group consensus is reached in joint meetings at which problems are presented, discussed, and a common basis for objectives is achieved. These, sometimes critical, debates are, as explained above, a peculiarity of German business life and are often perceived by people from other cultures as very aggressive and unfriendly ('*These people don't like each other!*'). The Germans, on the other hand, say that they miss this kind of cooperation with people from other cultures. German professionals classify such countries as lacking a *meeting culture*.
2. Following the line of command is the formal communication channel in business life, i.e., strict adherence to the hierarchy for procedure in the search for solutions. Skipping over hierarchical levels is seen as uncooperative and creates distrust. In most other cultures, handling conflicts and making decisions are done pragmatically through informal channels, either among the protagonists or by means of intermediaries.

Communication in Belgium and Germany

A Belgian company had just been acquired by a large German retail group. A seminar was held for the Belgians to introduce them to the German way of doing business.

The fact that Germans deal differently with each other in a hierarchical structure came as a shock to the Belgian group. For the Belgian side discussing conflicts and decisions with every hierarchical level were not only normal but a fundamental value. Since this was their first international experience, the participants had never been confronted with such a situation. The group discussed this issue for an entire evening, then finally accepted this new situation. To them, reporting along the hierarchy automatically meant that Germans were very hierarchical in their decision making. It was a prejudice which took time to abandon.

The differences become more pronounced when it comes to how both cultures approach the same project:

How Belgians and Germans Handle Decision Making in Projects

To establish this, the trainer in a seminar with Germans and Belgians put together three working groups. There was one group of each, Germans and Belgians, and one mixed group. They were given the following assignment:

"*The workforce in the offices in Brussels and Frankfurt am Main has to be cut by total of 20%. Frankfurt has 100 employees and Brussels has 10. The French parent company has asked for a workable solution*".

Each of the groups was given a process observer. The mixed group got stuck in the process and failed to find a solution. The German group sought consensus and proposed to cut 20% each in Brussels and Frankfurt. The Belgian group proceeded as follows:

- We will send a *spy* to Frankfurt to determine what the Germans have in mind.
- We will send someone to Paris to find out which solution the top management prefers.
- We will work out a solution based on these findings
- We will again send a *spy* to Frankfurt to determine the solution that the German side plans to suggest in Paris.
- We will finalize our solution and go to Paris to lobby for it with our top management.

As we already mentioned, Belgium is a country with limited financial and human resources. Therefore, from the Belgian point of view, this pragmatic and compromise-oriented approach is also the most efficient, and it guarantees the greatest success with the minimum of means.

Needless to say, that the Belgian approach was perceived as dishonest and as a betrayal by the Germans!

4.10.6 Don't Mix Business with Pleasure

A strict separation of private and business life is another characteristic of working in Germany. Business and leisure are two strictly separate areas. In most other cultures, the transitions are fluid, i.e., the employee is expected to place business concerns and goals above his own. This is, for example, a frequent stumbling block for German expatriates in Asian countries. If, for example, a young professional with a wife and child is sent abroad, he will probably try to live as he would at home and devote enough time to his family. In Asia this is likely to lead to a conflict between work and family life, which may lead to a premature return to Germany or even the couple separating.

4.11 India

Vinita Balasubramanian, the author of this article, was born and raised in India where she earned a master's degree in English. After moving to Germany, she started out as a language consultant and court-appointed translator, but for the last two decades her main field has been intercultural training, coaching and consulting for international companies worldwide. She is a therapy interpreter, lectures at universities and is currently doing research on communication gaps in global remote teams.

4.11.1 Many Indias

The legendary wartime British Prime Minister Sir Winston Churchill, who was not noted for being favorably disposed towards self-government for Indians, once remarked in 1931 that:

"*India is no more a political personality than Europe. India is a geographical term. It is no more a united nation than the Equator*".[41]

Though India 70 years after its independence from Great Britain has certainly developed its own political personality, there is more than a kernel of truth to this comparison between India and Europe. In size India is comparable to Europe, roughly extending from Norway to the southern tip of Italy in a north-south direction, and from Great Britain to Russia from west to east. The primary resemblance lies in the wealth of languages, ethnicities, creeds and cultural practices in India, a convergence of influences that is welcomed and sheltered under the umbrella of '*unity in diversity*'. Despite sporadic lapses, this is a motto which is taken seriously, frequently evoked, and on which every Indian schoolchild is required to write an essay.

The ancient Indian parable of the blind men and an elephant is often cited as an example of this principle. A group of blind men who have never come across an elephant before try to conceptualize what the elephant is like through touch. As each blind man feels a different part of the elephant's body, each one describes the elephant from his partial experience as looking like a snake (the trunk), like a tree trunk (the leg), like a rope (the tail), a fan (the ear), a wall (the side) and a spear (the tusk). The moral of the parable concerns the evasive nature of absolute truth, but it is often used as a symbol of the country itself—dissimilar in its details and only to be understood as a sum of its many parts.

[41] "Churchill: In His Own Words" Richard Langworth 2008.

4.11.1.1 Statistical Overview (Source: CIA the World Factbook, April 2018)

Population	1,281,935,911 (July 2017 est.)
Birth rate	19 births/1000 population.
Area	ca. 2,973,193 km^2
Languages	15–24 languages, ca. 544 dialects
Government	federal parliamentary republic with 29 states and 7 union territories

4.11.2 History

The concept of India has existed for millennia, but it has been a more or less unified political entity only very rarely in its long history.[42] However, modern Indians have a strong sense of history based on philosophy and scholarship going back thousands of years and this has provided an unbroken narrative and diffuse sense of self despite innumerable waves of invasions. Ancient Indian contributions to science are a source of great pride: the scholar Aryabhata defined pi and postulated that the earth revolves around its own axis as early as 500 CE.

The city of Delhi was ransacked in waves innumerable times, but many invaders settled down in the territories they vanquished and added yet another layer to the palimpsest of Indian culture. The Europeans, namely the British, the French and the Portuguese, remained outsiders and left the country when their power waned. The British managed to establish control over almost the entire territory[43] of modern-day India and Pakistan before dividing it into India and Pakistan in 1947. This partition of India left deep scars in the Indian psyche which are evident in the political tensions between the two countries up to the present day.

There is something of a North-South divide not only in linguistic terms but also historically, as invaders from the North such as the founders of the Mughal dynasty did not consolidate their influence south of the traditional North-South boundary of the Vindhya ranges. The South had non-invasive influences from the outside world. The southwestern state of Kerala, for instance, is a microcosm of every major religion, as traders and travelers to the fabled Spice Coast brought along Islam, early Christianity and Judaism. Today not only Kerala but the whole of India may be seen as having been enriched by layers of cultural artefacts—splendid Islamic architecture, a variety of culinary influences and the English language, to name just a few.

[42]The third century BCE under the Maurya Emperor Ashoka was one instance, but the furthermost southern tip of India did not belong to his empire.

[43]A few small pockets remained in French and Portuguese hands, in Pondicherry (Puduchery) and Goa respectively.

4.11.3 India as a World Power

For over a decade now India has been touted as a future superpower which is likely to overtake the current dominant economies by 2050 to become the second largest economy in the world after China.[44]

It is already the world's fifth largest economy and even if some of the more extravagant projections might not come to pass, there is no denying the economic potential of a nation which is expected to be home to the largest population on earth within a decade. It is the world's largest free-market democracy by population (1.32 billion people) and the decline in poverty has created a burgeoning middle class which is already a magnet for products from all over the world.[45]

Quite apart from the demographic factor, India is likely to emerge as a major player in the global arena when economic indicators are taken into consideration. In 2016 and 2017 India's GDP shot up to over 8%, and despite some downturns, an 8% growth is seen as a realistic prospect for the coming years. While India remains a diverse, contradictory and labyrinthine market, many global companies have been spectacularly successful in overcoming its challenges by tapping into its undeniable potential—the size of its aspirational middle class, a well-educated, young talent base and a keen interest in leveraging new technologies.

Less obviously, there is the additional factor of what may be termed '*soft power*': a nation's ability to influence others by virtue of its immaterial sources, such as its culture and institutions.[46] 'Soft power' is reflected in the influence wielded by Bollywood, yoga, Ayurveda, vegetarianism and meditation, to name just a few. Though difficult to define and measure, it may be (and often is) both capitalized on for monetary gain and it also contributes to the standing of India in the eyes of the world.

4.11.4 Languages

For those unfamiliar with India, the sight of Indians conversing with each other in English is sometimes mystifying. It is simply to be attributed to the fact that with 24 official state-based languages and 544 dialects, the likelihood of a larger group sharing exactly the same mother tongue is low. Many Indians speak three languages, but as the alphabet varies, most are only conversant with reading and writing in two.

As it is impolite to speak a language even one other person does not understand, Indians take recourse to either Hindi or English in a group conversation or with strangers. Hindi being the national language, it is relatively widespread, especially

[44]https://hbr.org/2018/02/3-reasons-global-firms-should-keep-investing-in-india

[45]https://www.gpidnetwork.org/wp-content/uploads/2017/09/Country_2.pdf. Last viewed September 14, 2018.

[46]http://eprints.lse.ac.uk/43445/1/India_India%27s%20soft%20power%28lsero%2. Last viewed April 14, 2019.

due to the burgeoning popularity of Bollywood films which are made in Hindi. Nonetheless, Hindi is much more prevalent in the North of India than in the South, where states such as Tamil Nadu take great linguistic pride in their own regional languages.

As India was a British colony until 1947, English continues to be the lingua franca in many fields—bureaucracy, higher education and business communication. It is a convenience for travelers from abroad as they are able to read street signs, business contracts and daily newspapers along with the locals. However, a conversation in Indian English can pose something of an initial hurdle, especially on the telephone. Firstly, the accent, intonation and speed are based on the Indian mother tongue, and secondly, semantic mother tongue influences may cause some confusion. Hindi (or any other Indian language for that matter) and English are often interspersed with each other to varying degrees in everyday conversation—a language sometimes described as "*Hinglish*", a portmanteau word combining Hindi and English.

Besides, there are certain words or phrases specific to Indian English:

Indian English	Standard English
Lakh	A hundred thousand
Crore	Ten millions
Pooja	Ritual of worship, prayer
I have a doubt	I have a question
To revert	To respond, to reply
To prepone	Opposite of postpone
Out of station	Out of town

4.11.5 Religion

As a multi-faith country, the Indian constitution does not mandate religious observances in any form, leaving religious public holidays to be regulated at the state, company or even individual level. In practical terms, this means that the '*weekend*' may be on any day of the week, not just Sunday, and that every company compiles its own list of holidays for the year, often including a couple of '*flexible*' public holidays to suit individual religious inclinations. Certain matters such as marriage and divorce are viewed less from a legal standpoint than as religion-based customs. Muslim customs such as polygamy and instant divorce ('*triple talaq*') enjoyed a tentative legality in the past; these are now being energetically questioned for their repercussions on the status of women and the Indian Supreme Court ruled instant divorce unconstitutional in 2017.

Religion is a highly visible element in both public and private life, not only in terms of temples, mosques and churches, but often also integrated into the workplace with altars and '*poojas*' (prayers) on occasions such as inaugurating a new building or a piece of machinery. The majority of Indians are Hindu (over 80%), with Islam as the largest minority (around 13%). Christians (2.4%) and Sikhs (1.9%) follow, with Jains, Zoroastrians, Buddhists and others making up the rest. It is a largely Hindu-based society, but the influence of even the smallest minorities may not be underestimated.

4.11.5.1 Hinduism

Hinduism is considered the oldest extant religion in the world.

"*Unlike other religions in the World, the Hindu religion does not claim any one Prophet, it does not worship any one God, it does not believe in any one philosophic concept, it does not follow any one act of religious rites or performances; in fact, it does not satisfy the traditional features of a religion or creed. It is a way of life and nothing more*".[47]

It encompasses a wide spectrum of philosophies and beliefs which are not governed by a central authority or institution. It is nonetheless predicated on a cumulative tradition of shared concepts and textual resources, the most important of them being a belief in reincarnation, certain ritual practices, and the pursuit of '*Dharma*', which is often translated as '*duty*' or as a code of conduct, precepts of righteousness and social behavior.[48] The panoply of gods in Hindu cosmology appears bewildering, but they are all structurally interlinked in the cosmological landscape in some way and regarded as manifestations of the one Supreme Being ("*Nirguna Brahman*"), Eternal Spirit, or God. The unknowability of the Supreme Being, which is an abstract, all-pervading divine consciousness, is a recurrent theme in Hindu scripts. It manifests itself in various personal forms ("*Saguna Brahman*") or gods, thus enabling people to worship it in any conceptualization of their choosing.

Unlike most other world religions, the female "*Devi*" principle is a powerful element, represented by goddesses such as Lakshmi and Kali. Being amorphous and multi-faceted, Hinduism is practiced at an individual or family-based level. Family traditions indicate preferences for a deity, or deities, which are termed "*kuladevata*" (family deity). Besides, certain deities preside over certain occasions; "*Ganesha*", for instance, is invoked for overcoming obstacles or before starting a new venture. Rotund and cheerful, this pan-Indian deity is an unfailing presence in every Hindu home (Fig. 4.5). Alongside these everyday religious traditions and beliefs, there is a vast body of profound religious philosophy (such as the Upanishads) which deliberate on the nature of the Infinite.

4.11.5.2 Communities and Castes

A combination of markers such as ethnicity, geographical origin, caste, language and religion combines to produce what are termed '*communities*' in India. As with many other aspects of the subcontinent, the definition is diffuse. Self-categorization is often clearly delineated; most Indians are in a position to define themselves as belonging to a community.

[47]The Supreme Court of India.

[48]Walker (1968) in Rao A. (2004).

Fig. 4.5 Ganesha

"*We are Marwadis, but we've lived in Bangalore for generations*".

There are innumerable stereotypes attached to each—Baniyas and Marwadis are supposed to have a head for business, Sikhs are considered suitable for military professions, in much the same way as Italian, German or French stereotypes are prevalent within Europe. Whether every community actually possesses a cultural DNA or not is a moot point; community affiliation is of relevance to self-identity and in social life.

The caste system in India is one of the last surviving systems of social classification still extant in today's world. Originally based on a profession-based stratification of communities, it divided society into four hierarchical levels, with the intellectuals at the top, followed successively by warriors, traders and workers. The so-called '*untouchables*' (now termed Dalits) who worked with human waste and dead animals were below the pyramid as they were considered outcasts. These broad classifications are further sub-divided into innumerable castes and sub-castes (Fig. 4.6).

For centuries caste was a hereditary system which determined profession, status and every other aspect of social and religious life. It has been suggested[49] that the caste system was much more diffuse and fluid prior to British rule, and that the British oversimplified its features rigidly into clearly-marked boxes.

Though the awareness of caste affiliation continues to be passed on through the generations, its influence is on the wane. It is no longer an indicator of the actual profession or status of the person concerned and has gradually developed into one of many markers of self-identity, one which is of considerably more importance in rural than in urban areas. The caste system retains much of its official relevance for two main reasons: its political manipulation as a vote-bank, and the affirmative action plan introduced to redress its iniquities. The well-intentioned affirmative action plan includes quotas for the traditionally underprivileged castes in educational institutions and in government jobs, but it has at the same time cemented caste divisions in a bureaucratic sense. In a social context caste continues to be a factor when marriages are arranged—a widespread practice even in modern India.

[49]Cohn (1987) in Tharoor (2016).

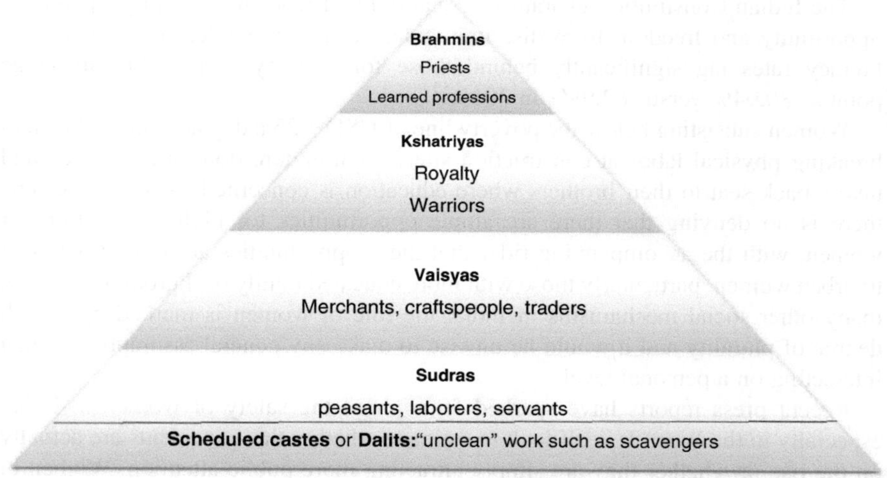

Fig. 4.6 The caste system: a simplified overview

4.11.6 The Role of Women in India

The Vedas, a large body of ancient scriptures and knowledge texts originating during the second millennium BCE, provide some interesting insights into the social mores of the times. These scriptures indicate that women enjoyed equal status with men in ancient India. With the Laws of Manu (around 100 CE), an influential religious and juridical textual code attributed to the lawgiver Manu, these rights were in decline and women were gradually relegated to a position of inferiority. In today's India there is an unexpected juxtaposition of both positions. Certain communities, such as the Nairs of Kerala and the Khasi of Meghalaya still have matrilineal traditions. Powerful goddesses in the Hindu pantheon such as Kali have created a symbolic resource for Hindus to accept and accommodate strong female figures. Heroines of the past include Razia Sultana (1205–1240) who ruled Delhi competently until her throne was usurped by her half-brother, and the warrior queen Laxmi Bai of Jhansi (1835–1858) who died on the battlefield fighting the British. Former Prime Minister Indira Gandhi and the bandit queen Phoolan Devi (1963–2001), who started her career as a bandit and went on to become a Member of Parliament, continue this tradition of feisty Indian women up to the present day. A cursory look at the internet reveals the remarkable fact that 11% of CEOs at 240 large companies in India are female.[50] They are to be found not only in typically "*female*" professions, but in every imaginable sector—in banking, the hospitality industry, construction, medicine, equipment, and in information technology. The glass ceiling is very permeable for advantaged women in India.

[50]http://www.indiamarks.com/indias-top-women-executives-their-academic-qualification/. Last viewed April 14, 2019.

The Indian Constitution guarantees equality to all women, including equality of opportunity and freedom from discrimination. Seen as a whole, however, female literacy rates lag significantly behind those for men by almost 20 percentage points—80.94% versus 62.98% in 2015.[51]

Women subsisting below the poverty line of USD 1.25 a day are forced do back-breaking physical labor at construction sites, often endure domestic violence and take a back seat to their brothers where education is concerned. At the same time there is no denying that there are ample opportunities for higher education for women, with the accompanying rider that these opportunities are more accessible to urban women, particularly those with more educated family backgrounds. As with many other social mechanisms in India, the role of women is marked by a high degree of plurality and it would be unwise to make any general assumptions when interacting on a personal level.

Recent press reports have sparked fears about the safety of women in India, especially in the West. It is difficult to estimate whether these incidents are actually on the rise or whether they are simply attracting more public attention. Women in India have always been cautious about being out alone after dark. A young woman would rather address an unknown woman rather than an unknown man if she is in need of information. Concerns about safety have led to company regulations which ensure that women do not work late in deserted offices or are provided reliable transport home.

While a healthy level of caution is advisable while travelling alone, India is by no means off limits for female travelers. Women are sheltered through ladies' compartments in trains, reserved seats on public transport and separate queues. The American journalist Margot Bigg goes so far as to say that, in her experience, "*India's one of the safest and most accommodating countries for solo women travelers*".[52] Women are an integral part of every regular street scene, not shut away in seclusion. They are friendly to strangers and no traveler, male or female, can hope to spend time on a bus or train without being drawn into a conversation. Most restrictions apply to young, unmarried women; with age Indian women gain respect, confidence[53] and a greater measure of freedom.

4.11.7 Socialization and Education

As in most parts of the world, the role of homemaker is generally assigned to the women in the family. At a glance one might assume that these women are in a

[51]https://www.statista.com/statistics/271335/literacy-rate-in-india/. Last viewed June 29, 2019.

[52]https://www.nationalgeographic.com/travel/destinations/asia/india/should-women-travel-solo-india-tips/. Last viewed June 29, 2019.

[53]Alice, a character in a Paul Theroux book, describes a fellow traveler as a *'typically bossy Indian woman'* (Theroux 'The Elephanta Suite' Penguin Books 2011).

position of complete subservience in India, particularly if they are traditionally dressed and remain in the background when male guests from abroad are present.

What is less evident is the status of the woman of the house in family relations. She is revered as the initial driving factor in the socialization process and as the transmitter of cultural heritage. The number of nuclear families is on the rise, particularly in cities, but at the same time the cohesion of the extended family has endured as a key factor in raising children and as a lifelong source of emotional and often financial support.

Free schooling is constitutionally mandated for children between the ages of 6 and 14, even if regular school attendance is difficult to enforce consistently in every part of India. Nonetheless, literacy rates have risen tremendously, from 12% in 1947 when the British left India to 72% in 2016.[54] A wide range of schools, state-run, charitable and private, provide education based on various teaching philosophies and in various languages. Higher education is becoming much more accessible due to the increasing number of universities and colleges, even if not all of them conform to the desired standards of quality. There are a number of highly ranked institutions for engineering, medicine or business studies (such as the Indian Institutes of Technology, abbreviated to IIT) which select candidates based on their performance in entrance examinations. Competition to these select institutions is fierce, with high school students spending every spare moment after school hours cramming at preparatory coaching classes for the entrance exam. As physical labor is valued less highly in India, formal vocational training used to be neglected, but with the rise of manufacturing in the last decade, there has been a surge of interest in establishing vocational schools.

Most Indians value education highly as a passport to a financially stable future, especially in the fields of engineering, medicine or management. Parents are willing to endure untold hardships for the sake of their children's education, and the corresponding family pressure to excel academically is high. The threat of failure can also prove overwhelming for some students, with a spate of attempted suicides reported every year during the exam season.

The USA is an attractive destination for a graduate degree and despite some of the weaknesses of the Indian educational system, such as its focus on theoretical knowledge, many Indian students have gone on to become extremely successful in their adopted country. Recently, the most notable examples of Indian-born CEOs in the USA are the heads of Google, Microsoft and Pepsi Cola, all of whom initially went to the US for higher studies.

4.11.8 Political System

India is proud to call itself the world's largest parliamentary democracy. Considering the country's size and potential for fragmentation, it is indeed remarkable that the system of a multiparty democracy has continued to survive since 1947. It is a

[54]https://www.statista.com/statistics/271335/literacy-rate-in-india/. Last viewed June 29, 2019.

quasi-federal system based on North American experience, with India's lower house, the Lok Sabha, modelled on the British House of Commons. The head of state is the President, who is elected for a 5-year period, but the actual reins of governmental power are in the hands of the Prime Minister.

The political climate is more turbulent than in Western democracies, with tensions running high during elections and the use of colorful language in political discourse. The press contributes significantly towards maintaining democratic standards by reporting candidly on political misdemeanors. The last few years have witnessed a political shift towards a more hardline nationalistic approach. Cases of political interference in dissenting editorial content have been reported, and it is to be hoped that the freedom of India's rambunctious press will not be compromised.

Summary

The diversity within India makes it difficult to create a manageable profile of the Indian subcontinent. An even greater challenge is posed by the contrasts in matched and unmatched pairs: conspicuous consumption and subsistence living, high-tech and nineteenth century implements, dynamic women in positions of power and abortions of female fetuses, rationalists and devout believers. Modernity is irregularly distributed—India's aerospace engineers successfully launched 20 satellites in a single flight in 2016 while the degree of literacy was around 72%.

This diversity represents both an opportunity and a challenge. It promotes the accommodation, flexibility and easy-going tolerance of the Indian mindset, but there are also instances of communal tensions leading to hate crimes. In the business sector it provides a vibrant palette to mix and match ventures, but on the other hand it limits the predictability of outcomes. Problem-solving in India is often based less on standardization than on stand-alone solutions tailored to each situation and context—an approach which is situational and flexible, but which can also impede transparency for non-Indians.

Case Study: An Invitation to Dinner

Situation

A German company was to set up a joint venture with an Indian company based in Mumbai. The preliminary talks held in India were a success and the German delegation, which included two Frenchmen, were wined and dined[55] by their Indian hosts in Mumbai at the best restaurants.

[55]The consumption of alcohol is not always regarded favorably in India, but there is a strong belief in serving food and drink to suit guest preferences. It is generally assumed that the "Westerner" is accustomed to consuming alcohol.

A month later, the Indian delegation visited Germany and the Europeans were glad to be able to return their hospitality. The three Indians arrived and despite some jet lag, they seemed to be enjoying themselves. It was only when dinner was served that the Europeans began to feel disconcerted. One of the Indians ate everything with apparent enjoyment, Mahesh ate just the French fries which was the side dish with his fingers, and Praveen did not eat anything at all. Nonetheless, the mood was cheerful and there were no complaints or remarks about the evening the next day.

Explanation

This incident is symbolic both of the diversity of India and the importance of hospitality in business. Finding the right food options poses something of a challenge in a country made up entirely of minorities[56]—even for other Indians. A large number of Indians are vegetarians to some degree—ranging from those who avoid even root vegetables to those who only eat poultry. Additionally, fasting on certain days is not uncommon. At the same time, none of these are hard and fast rules and include numerous individual exceptions.

In this case study, Atul had been a student in Sweden and was familiar with European cuisine and manners, Mahesh ate just the French fries because everything else was unidentifiable (and might have included unacceptable forms of meat), and Praveen did not eat at all as it was his day for fasting. No mention was made of all this as it would have been impolite to embarrass the hosts.

As hospitality is an essential element in both social and professional life, it is advisable to check out food preferences in advance or offer a wider range of options to choose from, such as a buffet. Fingers are commonly used for eating in India.

4.11.9 Professional Cooperation

Both work and personal life in India are governed by a similar set of assumptions and attitudes; there is no clear demarcation between these two areas in terms of values. Indian philosophy is based on the interconnectedness of all things and on the belief that everything—animate and inanimate—is an expression of the one Supreme Being ("*eko aham bahusvaami*") and hence constitutes one ordered and interconnected cosmos.[57] This cosmic collectivism (*ibid*) contributes to two significant elements in the Indian value system—relationality and a cyclical view of time.

4.11.9.1 Collectivism and Relationality

Indians tend to be perceived as collectivist.[58] but as seen in Hofstede's research, Indian society also has certain individualist traits. Individualism is most evident in

[56]Shashi Tharoor (1998).

[57]Sinha, Jai B.P (2014) "Psycho-Social Analysis of the Indian Mindset". Springer.

[58]Marriot (1976) in Nair-Venugopal (2012).

spiritual practice, which focuses on the quest for one's own path to enlightenment. The concept of '*Karma*' is in itself based on a personal fate which is carried across several lives and is shaped by individual action in the cosmic scheme of things.

In everyday life, however, Indian society is socially collectivist with identity based on family lineage and community/caste membership. Family ties are at the core of everyday life—it is significant that the Sanskrit word for family and the world are identical—"*samsar*". In a country without a social security system, the family network provides a stable fallback option for those in need.

The topic of family is a standard conversation starter, which can verge on the intrusive; the question "*Are you married?*" often crops up too early in a conversation for a Western visitor's taste. Indians cannot relate entirely to the Western value of privacy. In a country where crowds are the norm, people often live in extended families and children do not get their own rooms, there is an expressed belief in furthering social cohesion rather than individual development. According to Indian folk wisdom, character development is best served by learning flexibility, accommodation and compromise—traits which are essential for maintaining harmonious co-existence.

Rather than a broad-based collectivism, which puts the interests of the group before those of the individual, Indians tend to favor in-group collectivism, which is relationship based. As a result, outcomes are often directly connected to the persons involved and their relationships to each other. Building up relationships and trust through personal contact, hospitality, small talk and networking is a make-or-break factor for success in India. As a result, business deals can appear unfocused and time-consuming until the desired degree of personal rapport and understanding of the wider context has been reached.

4.11.9.2 Attitude to Time and Structure

Indians like to joke self-deprecatingly that IST (Indian Standard Time) actually stands for Indian Stretchable Time. The pace and bustle of Indian cities indicates a sense of urgency, but punctuality in the Western sense—of time as a finite resource with a linear sequence of deadlines—is not generally prevalent in India. This can lead to innumerable misunderstandings, including concerns about the work ethic, reliability and even honesty.

Some commentators attribute the casual approach for deadlines to a cyclical rather than a linear perception of time arising from the Hindu belief in reincarnation. The fact that the very same Hindi word is used both for yesterday and tomorrow[59] ('*kal*') might lead one to suppose this is indeed the case. The eminent historian Romila Thapar postulates that both approaches existed in ancient India—a cyclical approach for cosmology and a linear approach for manageable, everyday human concerns.[60]

[59]This does not apply to the South Indian languages such as Tamil or Kannada.

[60]http://www.thehindu.com/todays-paper/tp-national/Ancient-India-had-both-cyclic-and-linear-time-concepts-says-Romila-Thapar/article15958152.ece. Last viewed April 14, 2018.

In actual fact, punctuality is a flexible concept in India. Deadlines for their own sake appear unreasonable, not to mention arbitrary. A high degree of punctuality can be expected, but only when the reasoning behind it appears plausible from an Indian perspective. Airport drops and pickups, immediate pressure from the supervisor, and emergencies involving family or friends belong to this category. However, as these are singular occasions rather than a systemic approach, it is difficult to maintain a sustained adherence to schedules in India. In social life it would even be considered rude to insist on punctuality; invitations are often accompanied by a cheerful instruction to '*come anytime*'.

Indians consider it unrealistic to expect that long-term planning can be implemented in any detail. The work approach tends to be polychronic, multiple tasks and deadlines are juggled simultaneously while giving relationships and situation due consideration. This can lead to unforeseen developments when any of the balls in the air either falls or is dropped at any given moment. On the other hand, it is an agile approach with a high tolerance for ambiguity, spontaneous solutions and a willingness to adapt to changing circumstances without missing a beat—an approach Indians term "*jugaad*". Constantly shifting goalposts are accepted with equanimity. Not only are all things in the universe in a state of flux, but changes might providentially also ring in opportunities. At the same time, planning for the children's future is not left to chance, with savings plans for education and marriage initiated straight after birth.

4.11.9.3 Hierarchy

To start with, it must be emphasized that the pursuit of worldly gain ("*artha*") is a legitimate personal goal in Hindu tradition, represented by the goddess Lakshmi. In today's terms, the young generation's aspirational mindset is to be seen in the quest to climb the corporate ladder and job-hopping for more lucrative positions. Hofstede's study indicates the high power-distance in India, where people in positions of power and authority wield considerably more influence in all spheres of life—family, society, politics and organizations. This respect accorded to seniority is multi-dimensional, spanning age, social status, caste affiliation, role, expertise and many other factors. Demographics play a significant role in this setup; as the median age in India is around 27,[61] age and expertise are rarer commodities and correspondingly valued in professional life.

In organizational terms the importance of the superior is not overtly questioned, and leadership tends to be paternalistic rather than participative. Family orientation, in-group collectivism, and relationality are all reflected in the humanistic leadership paradigm. Professional qualifications are by no means irrelevant, but leadership in India requires a higher degree of people and emotion management than is usual in the West. Managers are looked to for direction and guidance, experience is valued, and a high degree of employee self-agency is not to be expected. In private

[61] https://www.indexmundi.com/india/demographics_profile.html. Last viewed June 29, 2019.

businesses it is routine to employ those who are related to the management and/or other employees, as the degree of loyalty is enhanced by family connections.

Case Study: Starting a Project

Dieter Schneider is starting a new project with his Indian counterpart Ashok. The project lead is on the Indian side, but the person has not been nominated yet. However, the basic parameters of the solar power project are already clear when Dieter Schneider meets Ashok for the first time. After exchanging the usual pleasantries, they get down to business.

1. Dieter: Ashok, what do you think of the technical specifications? What do we need to modify to suit the Indian market?
2. Ashok: They look quite good, I don't think we need to make any major changes. Anyway, let's find out who is going to head our project.
3. Dieter: Well, we don't know yet, do we? We can work on the technical details, otherwise a lot of time will be wasted.
4. Ashok: Yes, exactly. We don't want any time to be wasted. It would be better to find out who the project head is likely to be. I'll do some asking around—it could be either Sanjay, or Roopika, or Harish. . .

Explanation

Decisions belong to the domain of the superior and work strategies are based on the subjective approach of the person in charge. Hard facts and data are often superseded by consideration for people's feelings and acknowledging the intuition of superiors. Consequently, Indian employees' primary concern is accommodating the boss rather than evaluating task-based strategies. Loyalties are to individuals rather than to organizations, as the superior is in a position to offer support, perks and favors. While this attitude inhibits employee self-agency, it also provides management with unparalleled opportunities for creating tailor-made work philosophies and approaches, not to mention molding young employees.

4.11.10 Communication and Conflict Solving

4.11.10.1 Role and Relationship-Based Communication

Communication patterns in India are supple, adaptive and in a constant process of evolution during an interchange. The initial approach is based on the roles and relationships between interlocutors, in keeping with the ancient philosophy of dharma, a code of conduct and social behavior. Dharma provides guidelines for interaction, one of them being the consideration of the relative status and roles of the interlocutors. As a result, the very same individual can express a wide range of communicative behaviors depending on the role and the context. A colleague known for his diplomacy and tact can unexpectedly metamorphose into a blunt, authoritarian communicator when interacting with a slow subordinate.

The relationship factor adds additional flavors to the interaction: Indian employees are quiet and withdrawn in the presence of unknown/authoritarian bosses, but open and expressive when hierarchy is known and supportive. As the foreigner to India is usually a guest and business partner/ contractor/client, the values of hospitality and respect for the business role make it imperative for the Indian host to create an environment of warmth and trust. Reciprocity is expected, both by responding gracefully and in kind during a return visit. Whatever the situation, the appropriate tone and degree of communication is the key to managing every facet of life in India.

4.11.10.2 Emotions

Establishing personal rapport and credibility is crucial to business interaction and emotions are displayed to achieve this end. Emotions in communication are not merely a manipulative tool, though it is not unknown during hardball business negotiations. Indians devote a great deal of thought to the emotional impact of a message on the listener and calibrate their communication to suit the situation and the individuals addressed. It is an ongoing process which is focused less on the content of the message than on the anticipated reaction of the listener.

Consequently, giving and saving face are primary drivers in interaction. Giving face can be in the form of compliments, hospitality, gifts and showing deference to elders and superiors. Not giving enough face can cause a cascade of unintended and unwanted reactions. Saving face implies avoiding situations in which there is the potential for loss of face, and communication strategies are handled accordingly. As India becomes increasingly egalitarian, face is considered important even when dealing with subordinates or vendors, unless the power asymmetry is markedly in one's own favor. This is often evident in the offhand behavior of public officials such as policemen or airport security staff. As the general public does not belong to their in-group and they wield immediate, if reflected, power, most of them tend to be impersonal and cursory in interaction. Those in service-provider roles, on the other hand, are obliging and accommodating to a high degree, as also those who are within any kind of personal or business network.

4.11.10.3 Degree of (In)directness

It would be simplistic to maintain that Indian communication is consistently indirect. The degree of directness is contextual and role-oriented. Direct communication is the norm between those who with close-knit relationships; in fact, Indians can come up with unadorned personal feedback or direct requests if they feel a sense of familiarity and trust. Hierarchy also permits direct communication which is, however, usually a top-down, one-way street. The 'junior' interlocutor may be permitted a certain degree of openness, but objections have to be couched in temperate and packaged language.

The importance of pleasing the superior and face-saving in general leads to a greater prevalence of indirect communication patterns than in the West. Driven by the need to avoid conflict, Indians have no issues with conveying good news but are hesitant to express criticism or refusal. Starting from childhood, Indians are brought up to not judge their elders (and '*betters*') critically, or to say '*no*' to a request.

4.11.10.4 Indirect Communication Strategies

The tendency to avoid conflict within the in-group gives rise to a range of communicative behaviors which can be baffling to people from the West. One strategy is to circumvent the problem by either remaining silent or changing the topic completely. A lack of response, most commonly experienced in digital, asynchronous communication is generally a sign of trouble. No news is generally bad news in India, signaling embarrassment, offence, unwillingness or helplessness.

A refusal can be couched in vague, formulaic language such as "*maybe*" or "*I'll try my best*". Circularity is sometimes deployed when conveying bad news, by elaborating on the background and circumstances from which the listener can elicit the core message. In keeping with the polychronic work approach, discussions and meetings in India have a tendency to wander. Contentious issues and polarizing viewpoints are avoided, particularly when hierarchy or outsiders are present. Critical issues are addressed later in a less public, one-on-one forum, such as during the tea-break.

4.11.10.5 Conflict Solving

As Indian communication is prone to be conflict avoidant, it is only very rarely that an overt conflict with a foreigner is in need of solving. Usually a conflict comes out into the open only when all the preceding hints and signals have been ignored or brushed aside over a period of time. It is therefore essential to develop an awareness for the communication patterns mentioned above and react accordingly.

The Indian reluctance to say '*no*' or disagree openly is more likely to annoy the interlocutor from the West than the other way around. Unless in a virtual setting, non-verbal signals are a good indicator of the implications of a message. Awkwardness, hesitancy and embarrassment are generally easy to detect once the interlocutor develops a corresponding sensitivity and, more importantly, is also willing to act upon intuition.

In most cases, the lack of transparent messaging from the Indian side can be preempted by building up a personal relationship which encourages open communication. Until this stage has been reached it is advisable to learn the art of asking the right questions to elicit an informative reply. '*Pull*' communication in India is a constant and time-consuming process in which the assigner of a task is communicatively involved with the assignee on a regular basis. Checking status, monitoring deadlines and offering guidance are customary, whether in management or when dealing with the handyman hired to fix the plumbing. A mobile phone is a vital item in the survival kit for India.

Critical feedback continues to be a delicate issue, even for modern Indians. Making a mistake public, especially if it is personally attributable, leads to loss of face and can even result in resignations. A cautious one-on-one approach is advisable—starting with a friendly overture, then delineating the actual issue clearly, and finally concluding on a supportive, upbeat note. This classic 'sandwich' works in email communication, face-to face feedback requires a '*lasagna*' in which the layers of reassuring communication alternate with the points of criticism depending on the reaction of the individual involved.

In cases of obvious conflict, mediation with the help of a third party trusted by both sides is a common strategy, once again indicating that in India, calibrated personal interaction is far more effective than facts, figures and contracts.

Case Study: Communication

Herr Bauer is sent to India for the final approval of the supplier's facilities. All the preliminary work has been done by his eager young Indian counterpart Rajesh, who has been the interface between Herr Bauer and the Indian supplier. Herr Bauer is met by Rajesh at the airport and the very next day they travel to the supplier on the outskirts of the city. They are warmly welcomed by a large group, provided with refreshments and shown around the premises. Exhausted by the flight, the long drive and the traffic, Herr Bauer asks to be shown the production line as soon as possible. Except for a few minor details all the requirements have been met to Herr Bauer's satisfaction. Rajesh has done an excellent job. On the drive back to the hotel Herr Bauer explains the minor modifications needed and Rajesh assures him that they will be taken care of. However, he does not seem as cheerful and enthusiastic as before—in fact, he sounds quite subdued.

Explanation

Relationship-building being an invaluable part of business interaction, Herr Bauer has erred on two fronts through his lack of communicativeness. First of all, he has not properly acknowledged the hospitality shown to him by his supplier by cutting short the preliminary pleasantries. Secondly, he has neglected to acknowledge Rajesh's contribution to achieving results. This task-focused approach often leads to misunderstandings with peers and lack of motivation with subordinates. Expressed appreciation of hospitality, hard work, and even of India as a whole is an emollient both in business and personal life. Rajesh is disappointed by Herr Bauer's taciturnity both on his own and on his suppliers' behalf. Given that India can be physically strenuous for the Western traveler, it is generally advisable not to visit on a tight schedule.

4.12 Italy

4.12.1 Culturally Influential Elements

In its almost three-thousand-year history, Italy has always been under foreign domination and foreign control. East Goths, Vandals, Turks, Vikings, and in the not so distant past the French, Austrians, and Germans.

Cultures that have centuries of experience with a foreign dominance tend to have a distant to hostile relationship with authorities and retreat into the family. We have described similar attitudes in Belgium. In order to avoid conflicts with the authorities, everyone is polite and diplomatic. Luigi Barzini[62] has this to say on the life goals of an Italian in his cultural classic: "*He wants to make as many friends and as few enemies as possible and be part of a family with a strong patriarch, a Padrone –who assures him a lifelong basis for his existence*".

Examples of these personalities are:

1. Business: Armani, Agnelli, Berlusconi, Ferrari, Gucci, Versace, Ferrero, Benetton.
2. Politics: Machiavelli, Garibaldi, Mussolini, Moro, Berlusconi.
3. Explorers and Researchers: Galileo, da Vinci, Polo, Columbus, Vespucci, Volta.
4. Artists: Da Vinci, Michelangelo, Titian, Verdi.

It is easy for outsiders to make contact with Italian citizens, but it is difficult to be accepted into "*la famiglia*", i.e.to become an accepted member of the family. In an intercultural seminar we once held for young German executives, a participating Italian responded to the question if a stranger could be accepted into the family with "*in the best case scenario, as a satellite*".

One of the authors had a similar experience in his time as National Manager of a large advertising company with an Italian as his European boss.

It never turned into a successful business relationship because the author never sought to establish a firm relationship with the Italian boss, relying on his own expertise instead. A French female colleague and manager had, after intensive contact with Italian colleague executives, attributed her apparent non-acceptance to "*machismo*". Her attitude led automatically to a lack of support and a fading relationship.

For an Italian, life is a drama that takes place on the public stage, with everyone taking part, playing his role and trying—in compliance with the hierarchy—to look good, if not brilliant. For an illustration, watch TV extravaganzas on the Italian station Rai 1 which many non-Italians may find it difficult to relate to.

A marked illustration is the film "*General Della Rovere*" by Roberto Rossellini produced in 1959.[63] The film takes place in a Roman prison at the time of German occupation and shows a good-for-nothing played by Vittorio de Sica incarcerated there. He looks confusingly similar to General von Rovere, an anti-Fascist hero and resistance fighter who is wanted by the Gestapo, and for whom the other inmates mistake him. They show him their adoration at every meeting, kiss his hands—all of which he fiercely resists at the beginning as he suspects what would be in store for him if the Gestapo also mistook him for Rovere.

[62]see Barzini (1996).

[63]https://en.wikipedia.org/wiki/General_Della_Rovere. Last viewed September 15, 2018.

At the end of the film, he is taken for General Rovere, submits to his assigned role and his fate, refuses the blindfold in front of the firing squad and dies shouting "*Viva Italia*". This is Italy—comedy and drama as destiny with the fitting motto: "*Finire in Bellezza*" (To end in beauty)!

La Mamma is the center of the family. She is a calming influence and also the absolute supervisory authority who is obeyed by all. Even in modern Italy, a wife and mother gains this status in the family at the latest at a mature age.

From the viewpoint of many non-Italians, Italians lack community and public spirit, because Italians regard the State as an adversary. But this does not prevent Italians from being proud of their culture, their "*Italianità*".

4.12.2 Cooperation in Professional and Business Life

4.12.2.1 Why Are Italians so Successful?[64]

History, social and economic experience and living conditions have made Italians inventive. It has led to a society that has survived difficult situations over the centuries and is also very successful internationally.

The weak State means that Italians, in the broadest sense of the word, see themselves as self-sufficient and that essentially only personal power and authority count. The power base is the family, kin, the clan; the clan is also in politics and the economy, including the Mafia. They are the source of strength, they provide security, and are the basis for the successful existence of an individual. That is why it is important to belong to the most successful family, to have a "*Padrone*" who is respected by everyone. The limit to his power is the interface to another family. Public power is also shared, i.e. there are two police forces: "*La Policia*" and "*Gli Carabinieri*".

The ultimate goal in life for an Italian is "*un posto fisso*", a job for life, be it in a family business or as a civil servant. That's why in combination with a strong "Padrone" there are so many family businesses in Italy that have worldwide success.

Every Italian must continuously prove his loyalty to the clan and take part in this great public live show to make a good impression, "*fare una bella figura*". This makes life bearable. White lies and glorification which everyone can see through are frequently used colloquially and without reserve amongst equals:

1. "*Dottore*" for a clerical employee
2. "*Inginiere*" for a craftsman
3. "*Consigliere*" for an elderly figure of respect
4. "*Commendatore*" for a public person.

[64]see Barzini (1996).

My Italian Shoemaker in Switzerland

He was at that time a young immigrant from Italy building his own business in Zurich. From the beginning we had a confiding relationship as I speak some Italian. He used to greet me with "*Buongiorno Dottore*". After a while I said to him, that I was by no means a "*Dottore*". He raised his eyebrows and did not call me any longer by this title. But somehow our relationship changed, the closeness disappeared, and I felt that I had taken something away from him.

These forms of address should never be used with higher ranking persons, because they could backfire. The correct address required here is "*Signore*", "*Signora*", "*Professore*", "*Capitano*" (Police), etc.

White lies prevent conflicts, at least for the moment. It may happen that a person agreeing to a deadline, knows already that she or he will not be able meet it. Instead of getting into a clinch straight away, Italians believe it will be early enough when the client discovers the missing delivery on the promised day. At least he may have had a good weekend in the meantime.

Barzini compares international economies with a naval unit. The US economy is an aircraft carrier, the German a battleship, the French a frigate and the Italian a raft. The advantage: A raft cannot be torpedoed!

4.12.2.2 Communication and Conflict Resolution

An Italian in general perceives the world, its ideologies and people to be equal and not worth a discussion. There is little directness in the language, everything is well packaged and relayed the same way. Conflicts are obscured. When things get difficult, an Italian may "*take cover*", will be cautious, but will then try to show a daring attitude to create sympathy within his social milieu and above all will cultivate relationships.

Italians have one of the richest body languages of all cultures. The show is not only performed verbally but supported by expressive gestures to clarify and emphasize what is being said.

4.12.3 Italianità: The Italian Lifestyle

Italians have emigrated by tens of thousands to find a better livelihood in other countries and continents: North and South America in the nineteenth century, Australia, and Northern Europe in the twentieth century. They have brought their way of life everywhere, their food and drinks which have become an integral part of worldwide cuisine. Italian wines, mineral water and Italian food are considered to be of high quality, and it is not difficult to find a good Italian restaurant anywhere which serves good meals.

The export of Italianità, however, dates further back in European history: Italian lifestyle was already brought to France in the sixteenth century with the marriage of Caterina de Medici to Henry II, King of France. The Tuscan chefs who followed in her train greatly influenced today's classic French cuisine, which is still a worldwide standard for fine dining and hospitality.

4.12.3.1 Italian Words of Wisdoms and Proverbs

To conclude, here are a few words of wisdom in Italian that express their attitude to life:

1. Se non e vero, è ben trovato—Even if it is not true, it is well invented.
2. Fidarsi è bene, non fidarsi è meglio—Trusting is good, distrusting is even better.
3. Che sarà, sarà—What will be, will be.
4. Finire in Bellezza—Finish in beauty.
5. A fundamental life motto in Italy is: Be pragmatic about life's contradictions.

4.13 Japan

Japan is perhaps the culture that is the least accessible to people from the West. There is hardly any open and explicit communication or critical discussion, unless one is connected by a long friendship with a Japanese. In daily life, however, communication is ritualized with the aim of achieving harmony among all participants and saving face.

Since Japan is still the number three economic power in 2018 behind the People's Republic of China and the USA, people in the West allow themselves to be misled to think of Japan as being increasingly westernized. Geography, environmental conditions and history are such strong defining elements that they also influence Japan's culture to this very day.

4.13.1 Cultural Formative Elements

4.13.1.1 The Omnipresence of Nature and its Catastrophes

Japan being situated in the middle of Continental Plates,[65] the country is shaken by tremors every single day. The stronger quakes of seven and above on the Richter scale caused the great disaster such as the Great Kanto earthquake in 1923 with 140,000 dead, the Great Hanshin earthquake in 1995 with 5000 dead and the 2011 Tohoku earthquake, with a magnitude of 9 on the Richter scale and nearly 20,000 dead or missing. This most recent earthquake was a disaster with immense consequential damage. The quake was followed by a devastating tsunami, which in turn was responsible for the damage to the nuclear power plants with the danger of a total meltdown in Fukushima. Another threat to nature are the typhoons, whose season lasts from June to October and causes landslides.

[65]https://en.wikipedia.org/wiki/Geography_of_Japan. Last viewed September 14, 2018.

The Japanese would never dream of dominating nature. Experience has taught them that only a community based on mutual support and collective values can mitigate the consequences of natural disasters. And that has indeed been the case. The authorities were at first overwhelmed in 1995 and 2011. It took a while for first responders to arrive, which at first came only from the local community. This was due to the missing or damaged communication channels and the time it takes all governments to become aware of a catastrophe and to react. The subsequent assistance was efficient because Japan is used to disasters and has advance planning and preparedness in place based on centuries of experience.

4.13.2 Japan's Roots

The historical origins of today's Japan are mystifying. According to the Japanese, they migrated from the Pacific in prehistoric times and displaced the aborigines, the Ainus, who still live on the northern island of Hokkaido—some of them in a reserve-like environment. The Ainu were originally immigrants from the Ural region, i.e. White Caucasians. They only received political recognition as an indigenous people by a Parliamentary decision in June 2008.

According to Japanese history, the founding of the Japanese Empire took place on 11th February 660 BCE. The Japanese Emperor, the Tenno, was the divine descendant and earthly representative of the Goddess of Sun Amatseru until Japan's unconditional surrender to the USA in 1945, the end of the Second World War.

According to Japanese tradition, the imperial dynasty is directly descended from Amaterasu, a central deity in Shinto faith. Continuing this almost 2600-year-old dynasty, Emperor Akihito became the 125th Tenno in 1989. He gave his reign the name "*Heisei*", which means "*Era of Peace*". That is what he will be known for in history.

Japan uses two calendars: The Western Gregorian and a Japanese calendar which always begins with the reign of a new emperor. In other words, 2018 corresponds to Heisei 30.

4.13.2.1 The Shinto Religion and the Sacred Shrine on Ise

Since capitulation in 1945, the divine status of the Emperor, as well as his military and political power, have been abolished at the urging of the USA. De facto, however, he is still the highest, revered authority and representation in terms of the Shinto faith. His insignia—the saddlery, sword and the holy mirror, the symbol of his descent from Amatseru, the goddess of the sun and the light—are kept at the sacred shrine in the city of Ise on the Shima Peninsula.

According to Shintoism, no one other than the Emperor is allowed to look into the Imperial mirror. To ensure this, the mirror is always packed in brocade bags. When it begins to wear out, the mirror, including the previous bags, are packed into a new one.

The Temple complex in Ise, built in the fifth century, is surrounded by four high fences, so that only the thatched roofs with gilded wooden gables of a building in the complex are to be seen.

Until the nineteenth century the innermost part of the complex could only be visited by the emperor; today priests are also allowed to enter.

Japanese believers are allowed to cross the first fence accompanied by a priest and are then blessed with salt. Gajins—non-Japanese—are not allowed to enter individual parts of the building.

Every 20 years, after one generation, the temple complex is dismantled, the old square is covered with stones, and next to the complex a mirror image is rebuilt out of cedar wood from sacred groves.

Most Japanese have two beliefs serving as a basis to organize their lives. Over 80% are believers in Shintoism. Most Japanese are married in a Shinto ritual. About the same percentage of Japanese also believe in Buddhism and will be buried according to this ritual. Only 1% or 2% of Japanese are Christians.

4.13.2.2 Periods of Japanese History

Japanese history does not define itself by years, but by names given to the different periods of history. According to historical tradition, the following periods were decisive for the country and have remained so in Japanese memory to this day:

1. Nara (600–784) is named after the former capital in the south of the main island and is associated with the arrival of Buddhism from China.
2. Heian (794–1192), when the Emperor establishes himself in the new capital Kyoto; a time of peace follows.
3. Kamakura period (1192–1333) is named after a city of the same name southeast of Tokyo, in which the mighty warlords—Shoguns—were established and the power of the emperor was weakened This was followed by warlike conflicts between the warlords, two of whom remained victorious.
4. Muromachi and Azuchi-Muroyama (1336–1598) were two castles inhabited by the most powerful warlords of the country. At that time the arts developed, but also armed conflicts between the two shoguns. During this period the arrival of the Portuguese and the attempt to christianize Japan occurred.
5. Edo or Tokugawa (1603–1867), named after the former name of today's Tokyo or the victorious and most powerful Shogun Tokugawa, whose former residence is the current Imperial Palace in Tokyo. The Portuguese had bet on the loser and were therefore expelled with all the other foreigners. The Japanese who had converted to Christianity had to renounce this belief by making a double oath to their Christian and Buddhist beliefs. The country was sealed off for 200 years, foreigners were not allowed in. Trade was conducted with the Dutch East India Company, whereby the Dutch were only allowed to make their calls on a small artificial island in the bay of Nagasaki on the southern island of Kyushu.
6. Meiji (1868–1912), named after Emperor Meiji, considered a great reformer and the father of modern Japan. The opening was made under pressure from the United States, when on March 31, 1854, Commodore Matthew Perry forced the

Japanese ports of Shimoda and Hakodate to open for trade with the United States. Emperor Meiji left the capital, Kyoto, saying he was making a trip to Edo, and settled in the Tokugawa Castle, now the Imperial Palace, thus making Tokyo the new capital. What followed was a rapid modernization of Japan but not comparable with China today due to different means of communication and transportation. German scientists, professors and specialists made a decisive contribution to the creation of modern Japan. The Japanese view of Western cultures, teaching and the working world are therefore strongly influenced by German values.

7. Taisho (1912–1926), *Era of Justice*: This is the period during which the Japan fought on the side of the Allies in the First World War and occupied Manchuria and Korea.
8. Showa (1926–1989), *The Era of luminous Peace and Harmony*: Japan entered the Second World War with the attack on Pearl Harbor combined with the conquest of large parts of Southeast Asia. After the success of the US and its allies and the atomic bombs on Hiroshima and Nagasaki, Japan had to surrender unconditionally. Under General McArthur as Commander in Chief of the Occupation Forces, the democratization and demystification of the Tenno began. In particular, the changes to the Emperor's role caused difficulties for the Japanese. A work group McArthur had employed came back with minimal amendments, so the general lost patience, sat down at the typewriter, put the principles down on paper and handed them over to the working group for implementation. This was followed by a rapid economic upswing; Japan made the leap from the Middle Ages, from being an economy with farmers and craftsmen, to the world's second largest economy by the second half of the twentieth century. Today it is the third largest economy in the world after China.
9. Heisei (1989 up to date), *Era of Peace*: Japan is expanding abroad. Its dependence on the global economy led to its hitherto biggest economic crisis with a pronounced deflation in the 1990s, i.e. a shrinking economy with falling price levels. The country only recovered from it with difficulty and today[66] the Japanese economy has returned to its pre-crisis level.

4.13.3 The Interwoven Society

There is probably no modern society as interwoven as the Japanese. It is a society where each and every one has his or her own assigned place to fulfill his or her duty towards the society. The Japanese mafia, the Yakuza, is also a part of society, with its own assigned role. Among other things, the high level of crime detection in Japan is attributed to the cooperation between the Yakuza and the police.

An interesting event happened at the beginning of the 1980s, when the most powerful Yakuza in the country in the city of Kobe showed their desire for expansion to the north, rented a plane and flew to Sapporo. The police learned of these intentions. To prevent a gang war, the Kobe Yakuza were met by the police as

[66]https://www.nippon.com/en/currents/d00375/. Last viewed September 14, 2018.

they disembarked from the plane, escorted to a hotel where their local opponents were already waiting at the conference table. The negotiations took place in the presence of the police with the result that the Yakuza from Kobe withdrew from extending their claims to the north. This story is not based on an insider's view, but on a Japan Times article.

One of the strangest Yakuza stories comes from a friend of the author's in Kobe:

The Kobe Yakuza

My Japanese friend was sent by his father to the Jesuit school because it was known and valued for its strict upbringing. The son of the Yakuza chief of Kobe was at the same school, a class below him.

My friend was charged with overseeing this class because he was older. He once punished the son of the Yakuza boss for insubordination with a few extra laps on the racetrack. The son and the bodyguards accompanying him every day to the school gates were so angry that the frightened friend went to the school Principal. The Principal, a priest, said, "*Don't worry, I'll talk to his father.*"

Sometime later, the friend received an invitation to have dinner at the Yakuza Chief's villa. He was very worried when he went there, was received at the stairs by a line of Yakuza members in black suits and then escorted to the father. Not only did he receive an excellent meal, he also received many gifts, and the father said, "*You did well to punish my son because I want him to be treated like everyone else. I don't want him to become a Yakuza.*"

The two students then became friends, and the elder mentored the younger, who asked him for advice on where to study. My Japanese friend advised him to go to the US where his Yakuza reputation would be unknown, and he could decide on his own future. The Yakuza's son, however, remained in Japan and worked in traditional Yakuza businesses with sex and gambling. When the young Yakuza married, our friend was invited to the best hotel in Tokyo for the wedding. When entering the ceremonial room, he was astounded to see the number of people renowned in business and politics.

From a Western point of view, we find this story objectionable because it does not conform to our views of ethics and morality. In Asia, the holistic view of the world applies, e.g. the world is unchangeable and is to be taken as it is. In order to be able to live together in harmony, the only question that remains is the role one plays in society and how to deal with it (see also Sect. 3.3.2 The holistic world view in Asia and in Islamic cultures).

The Yakuza is certainly perceived as a dark point—as shameful—in Japan, Therefore, the Japanese government has recently tried to enforce stricter laws to control their Mafia. But implementation is difficult because the Yakuza argue that they are being discriminated against.

4.13.4 The Role of the Woman in Japanese Society

The role of women in Japan is often underestimated or misinterpreted by the West. The authors used the following cultural exercise at the beginning of their intercultural seminars:

Cultural Riddle

Please fill in the blanks with "Japan" or "Europe" or the corresponding variation:

"The women of... cannot not leave the house without the permission of their men".

"... women have the freedom to go where they please without the knowledge of their husbands".

"In ... it is not common for women to be able to write. The women in ... find it a humiliation that they cannot write". (Portuguese Jesuit Father 1585)

In 80% of the cases, the participants allocated the first section, "*not being allowed to leave the house without the permission of their husbands*" to Japan. Western participants fell into the cliché trap in their belief that Japan is a sexist society where woman have fewer rights. Westerners have this image because it is constantly conveyed and projected through the mass media.

Those who noticed the small print about it being from a Portuguese priest dating back to 1585 were doubtful and correctly concluded that at that time Japanese women had the freedom to go to wherever they wanted. It is true that even in ancient times, with their responsibility for home and children, Japanese women were able to move around freely while they could not do so in Europe, especially not in southern Europe.

Later, Japanese women and men had to adhere to classical gender roles through the centuries until today. The Japanese man dedicates his life to the company, with hardly any free time, and little time for his family. A "*sarary man*" gets up at 5 or 6 a.m. to arrive at the workplace at 9 o'clock after 1–2 h of traveling by public transport. At 5 p.m. he works for one or two additional hours, goes out to eat or drink something with his colleagues and gets home around 11 o'clock at night. The wife has to stay at home to take care of the house and the children. This traditional understanding of roles is still in force today, and the division of labor is still the same as in former times.

The following example of the role of women in Japanese society is from the author's personal experience:

Where is my Money?

The author has a Japanese friend, who tragically lost his wife at a very young age during childbirth. As a widower with a 6-year-old son, his biggest problem, apart from this personal blow, was that he did not know anything about his financial affairs because his wife's death came so suddenly.

During their marriage, his wife played the classic Japanese role in the family as "*Finance Minister*". Her husband brought the paycheck home, received an allowance for his daily expenses, and the wife handled all the finances.

This couple behaved in a traditional Japanese way with the man bringing in the income and the wife as homemaker, despite the fact that they had been exposed to a Western lifestyle—the man having studied in the US and worked for an American company, and the wife having worked as a flight attendant prior to her marriage.

The Western prejudice about traditional gender roles in Japan is so strong, that Westerners are having a hard time to admit this. In a seminar a student with German-American roots who had studied in Japan, said that during her studies in Tokyo she was bothered by the fact that her fellow female students did not care about their careers and only saw their futures as wives and mothers.

Contrary to the Western view, Japanese women do not think that they are disadvantaged in their society. Despite traditional gender role, they have always enjoyed the same rights as men, e.g. in education. This leads us to the second part of the above riddle regarding the ability to read and write. In the fifteenth century, most women in Europe were unable to read and write whereas Japanese women were sent as girls to Buddhist temple schools, where they were taught to read and write in classes with the boys.

This intercultural exercise is an example to demonstrate that our Western culture cannot be compared with the one in Japan. Japan is different: Attempting to project our points of view into this world will probably result in silent rejection from the Japanese side.

Japanese Saying

Men never grow up, from cradle to grave they are accompanied by and cared for by women.

4.13.5 Communication und Conflict Resolution

Before one of the authors went to Japan, he took lessons in Japanese. On their first meeting the language teacher said: "*There is some good news and some bad news. The good news is that Japanese is not as difficult to learn as Chinese. The bad news is that you have no idea how difficult it is to learn Japanese because all your language knowledge will not do you any good*".

And that is how it was. With time, the author learned basic Japanese and was able to communicate colloquially for some daily necessities, but he never got far enough to conduct a reasonably intelligent conversation.

Japanese is a language of words unlike Chinese, which is a language of syllables with different intonations. The disadvantage in Japanese is that the vocabulary changes depending on the speaker, the receiver and the occasion. Men in business, women and children all use different words, for example, even the word "*we*" varies:

1. 'We' for women: *watachitachiwa*
2. 'We' for men: *bukotachiwa*
3. 'We' for supervisor: *wareware*
4. 'We' for priests: *warera*

This makes the learning of this language as an adult almost impossible. Western men who marry Japanese women often learn polite women's language, which is misinterpreted by the parents-in-law in Japan. In fact, only the Japanese, having learned it from childhood, can speak this language properly and intelligently.

The second difficulty is that the Japanese struggle to speak accurate English because their language lacks the distinction between the letters *R* and *L*. As a result, they often shy away from speaking English, although they might know English from school or university. In the 1970s, the author found that older employees came to him and presented their case in writing in flawless English. They had learned English from Japanese teachers, made mistakes in pronunciation and were therefore hesitant to speak English.

The situation today has changed as many of the teachers and professors come from English speaking countries. However, the basic problem remains: when I spelt the name "Haller" in English, the name was regularly written "Harrel". It was not until the author assumed the Japanese way of spelling that the name was written correctly—turning the *L* into "*eru*" and the *R* into "*aru.*"

Since Japanese is a word language, many words have been taken directly from English, and there are a whole range of adaptations, some of which are easy to understand, others more difficult. For example:

- *marketingo = marketing*
- *shigareto = cigarette*
- *nighto curabu = nightclub*
- *hoteru = hotel*
- *teeshatsu = T-shirt*
- *sripu = slip*

The Japanese's ideal of communication is intuition, i.e. as little talk as possible, avoiding conflicts and sensing what the other thinks.

When dealing with Western people, they tend to retreat into the Japanese language because of a dislike of speaking English, feeling ridiculous or finding oneself in an awkward situation.

The Difference Between Speaking and Understanding English

A Japanese creative director never spoke a word of English to his Western superior in 2 years.

At a presentation to a client with 20 Japanese staff members from each side sitting at a long conference table, a Japanese interpreter translated in a low voice into English for two Westerners.

The creative director was presenting at a quite a distance from the interpreter. Suddenly, he interrupted her to ask for a correction of the English translation.

His Western superior asked him about it after the presentation: "*Sabatasan*" *(Mr. Sabata), I thought you didn't speak English!* He replied: "*Hai (Yes) I do not speak English, but I understand English!*"

Japanese writing is as complex as oral communication. Its basis are the Chinese characters that were adopted at the beginning of our calendar. Every Japanese has to learn about 2000 Kanji characters so that he can read and write. As Japanese is a word language, two 48-character phonetic alphabets called Hiragana and Katakana were created as early as the eighth and ninth centuries. They enable the Japanese to write words that are not covered by Chinese characters, such as phrases or place names adopted from foreign languages. Incidentally, the first Japanese book to be published was written in Hiragana by a tenth century Japanese princess.

4.13.6 Japan's Economic System

As far as the Japanese economy is concerned, the West is often convinced of state interference and that international competition is obstructed.

Japan's history of success begins with its forced opening to the Western world at the end of the nineteenth century and a learning process based primarily on American and German science and technology. Since Japan is a resource-poor country and only the human resource could make the difference in competitiveness, Japan started trading overseas at a very early stage by importing raw materials, refining them in Japan, and then selling them on export markets. The large Japanese trading houses were either led by Samurai families such as Tokagawa, or established by merchant families such as Itoh, Mitsui, Sumitomo and Marubeni. Japanese diligence and industriousness led to the rapid industrialization of Japan and its ever-increasing importance on the world market. Initially the Japanese textile industry became a worldwide leader, but it collapsed with the crash of the 1930s.

Before the Second World War, the economy consisted of the Zaibutsu, the Clan of the Giants, which included 352 large companies. The victorious powers of the Second World War viewed the dominant industries and their need for raw materials as a major reason for Japan's entering the war. In consequence, they demanded that the companies be dissolved (similarly in Germany after 1945).

In reality, only 18 of the 352 large Japanese corporations were dissolved. After the war, companies like Mitsubishi diversified into other industries and services and bought licenses from successful Western companies, such as Coca Cola or the fast food chain Kentucky Fried Chicken.

Post-war start-up companies, now global corporations like Sony, Panasonic, Canon, Sanyo, Bridgestone, Toshiba, Toyota, Honda, Nissan, etc., form the backbone of the Japanese economy. The car and entertainment industries drove Japan's economic recovery and made Japan the world's second and now the third largest economy.

Japan's economy is fully connected and interrelated through politics and the Ministry of Economic Affairs. Companies are externally financed. Other economies, especially the US, accuse Japan of unfair competition, since Japanese companies generally have a very low equity base of 10%, which would make Western entrepreneurs break out into a cold sweat. To restructure the Japanese economy with Western standards would probably mean its collapse, which would probably have devastating consequences on the entire world economy. From the Japanese point of view, every business is part of the nation's socio-economic fabric and has the common goal to work for the good of the country. For large companies, profit is not the primary goal but rather turnover and full employment. The motivation of university graduates is to work for one of these companies because it still means a lifetime job. Dismissal and unemployment primarily affect suppliers. An employee of a large corporation can generally be relocated to another company or subsidiary of the corporation.

However, the decisive turning point came in the early 1990s, when the real estate bubble collapsed due to the economic crisis and drove the country into deflation. Public debt in 2010 amounted to 215% of the gross national product, 60% more than that of Greece.[67] On the other hand, there were foreign exchange reserves amounting to two-thirds of the national product in Japan. In the West, this situation would have been alarming. In Japan's networked society, it was a momentary blip, because they believe that their commitment and devotion to their society and culture will enable them to master and recover from any crisis. Today, the Japanese economy is back to normal cruising speed!

4.13.7 Working Together in Business and Professional Life

The Japanese motto for a successful career is called "*Nihonteki*", meaning "*to behave like a Japanese*". Basic conditions are

1. Honesty
2. Commitment to the team
3. Sense of duty.

This sounds easier than it is. The following example shows the conflict between self-determination in the West and foreign determination in Asia:

[67]http://de.statista.com/statistik/daten/studie/152666/umfrage/staatsverschuldung-japans-in-relation-zum-bruttoinlandsprodukt-bip/. Last viewed September 16, 2018.

The Internship at Toyota

A seminar participant, a German engineer, spent 1year in the Toyota factory to learn about Japan and its working methods.

Since he was the youngest there, he had to serve his boss and team of about ten colleagues lunch in the canteen. But everyone only ate as long as the Head of the Group. When he put down his chopsticks or spoon, everyone stopped eating. Most of the time when the German engineer was done with the serving of the dessert, the boss had usually already laid down his cutlery.

He said that he had almost never been able to eat dessert the whole year. Asked if he would go back to this Toyota factory he clearly said "*no*".

Westerners have extreme difficulty integrating into a collective society, because external control is not permissible in the majority of situations.

Niall Murtagh narrates a typical story in his book "*The Blue-Eyed Salaryman: From World Traveler to Life at Mitsubishi*"[68] He was the first Westerner ever to get a regular contract Mitsubishi. He planned to go to work by bicycle but received a phone call from the Personnel Manager right at the beginning who told him that this was not possible. Murtagh's argument that it was faster, more economical and more environmentally friendly did not help. All these logical reasons were rejected by the hiring manager. To put an end to the discussion, the Personnel Manager finally said: "*We have no parking spaces for bicycles*".

The authors' department head at an advertising agency in Tokyo observed another unusual situation. His Japanese team always scheduled appointments with a Japanese automotive customer for 5 p.m. The team usually had to wait for one to two hours in the anteroom of the Advertising Manager. and were able to leave work only after 8 p.m. at the earliest, in many cases even later. From the Western point of view, this is a degree of self-sacrifice and heteronomy that is difficult to accept. In this case, the stress on the Japanese team was so great that even they asked to change the client after a few years.

What drives the Japanese to accept this way of life? It is the reciprocal loyalty and the sense of duty that governs the cooperation between the company and its employees:

1. The company looks after the employee right after university, trains him, always gives him a job and an assignment, takes care of his family, insures him, and sends him and his family on vacation to company owned resorts. The Japanese "*sararyman*" put up with this lifestyle during his entire working life until he retires. Senior executives may get a position as a consultant to the company. They can play an important role as go-between for Western businessmen entering the Japanese market.

---

[68]Murtagh, Niall (Feb. 1, 2009) Profile Books; The Blue-eyed Salaryman – From World Traveler to Life at Mitsubishi.

2. In return, the employee devotes his career and professional life to his company. Total loyalty and commitment are required, which means putting in a large part of his free time.
3. Back in the early 1980s, the author's Japanese supervisor used to say that a Mitsubishi employee whose factory or business closed, could just go home and wait there for a new job opportunity for which the company would call him back.

This changed with the onset of deflation in the 1990s, as there were unemployed people in Japan for the first time. The rate fluctuated between 4% and 5%, depending upon the sources. It is now again at its lowest in the past 25 years.[69] The majority of jobless were not from the "*Keiretsu*", the large corporations, but employees of suppliers to the large companies. These employees were the first to be laid off.

As of the late 1980s Japan experienced homeless people for the first time after WW II. Visitors to Tokyo's Shinshuku Park could marvel at the neat tents with blue tarpaulins and neatly lined shoes in front of them. All this came as a shock to the Japanese.

The basic conditions may change, but the basic philosophy of a closed society and its rituals remains. Japan has transferred their company rituals to Southeast Asia and China with similar success. At the beginning of China's opening up, Japanese keiretsu not only brought their technical know-how, but also their corporate rituals, from clothing, singing the company anthem at the beginning of work, to afterwork socializing with karaoke.

4.13.8 Rituals in Corporate Life

The Japanese have business terms expressing certain rituals that are familiar to everyone.

4.13.8.1 The Role of the Company Principal

The Japanese Head of a company is often perceived in the West as an absolute ruler. From a Japanese point of view, total respect is due to him, not as a person, but as the official representative of the company. This is reflected in the formal behavior of his employees, who bow especially deeply before superiors such as the "*syachō*"(General Manager).

In contrast to the West, few top managers earn more than $1 million because they find excessive salaries embarrassing. It would disturb the harmony.[70]

In fact, the head of any company or department knows that he is entirely dependent his employees. They are the specialists, they have the latest know-how.

---

[69]https://tradingeconomics.com/japan/unemployment-rate. Last viewed Sept. 16, 2018.

[70]https://www.emolument.com/salary-reports/jobs/executive-management/38357. Last viewed Sept. 16, 2018.

Due to his often advanced age his knowledge is outdated. His role is to look after his people, because disharmony could produce just average results in his team.

If a company makes a serious mistake and this becomes public, the Japanese CEO is required to stand up to it and take the blame. He will often resign as a consequence.

The following example shows how serious the consequence can be for a Western company if the expatriate CEO is not familiar with Japanese business practices and disregards the essentials:

The Deadly Accident

A Swiss elevator and escalator manufacturer had been active in Japan since 1985.

In June 2006, a company elevator in an apartment building in Tokyo started moving while the door was still open, killing a 16-year-old teenager. The incident made media headlines throughout Japan. A Japanese friend of the author's, who visited with him in Switzerland shortly, thereafter, told him the story and was horrified by the behavior of the CEO of company in Japan.

In a TV interview broadcast nationwide, the Swiss CEO did not accept the blame, but said—in a typically Swiss manner—that the causes and question of responsibility had to be clarified first.

As a result, the Swiss company was immediately pilloried in the media.

The nationwide indignation over this behavior led Japanese companies to remove these Swiss products and to replace them with other brands. Thereafter, no Japanese company ever bought these products again. Sales collapsed completely, and the Swiss company was forced to sell its business to a Japanese competitor on April 5, 2016.

In a newspaper article, one Swiss journalist actually claimed that this would not have happened to a Japanese company! He may not have meant it literally, but the fact remains that a Japanese CEO would have behaved responsibly and taken the blame. He might not have resigned immediately but would have promised assistance and compensation for the damage.

There was also the legal issue of guilt. On September 29, 2015 the lawsuit ended with an acquittal of the Swiss company,[71] because the court declared that the problem was not the elevator's design but inadequate servicing by a 3rd party company.

This case study also shows the crux of transfers abroad. The manager behaved the way he would have in Switzerland. Like so many expats, he had not "*arrived*" in Japan, culturally speaking. If he had behaved like a Japanese, he may have taken the blame and stood up to the consequences. However, the Swiss manager would probably have had trouble with his headquarters in Switzerland, who would not have understood why its representative would take the blame when the question of guilt was still wide open!

[71]https://www.nzz.ch/wirtschaft/unternehmen/freispruch-fuer-schindler-in-japan-1.18621740. Last viewed June 27, 2019.

4.13.8.2 Above All, Harmony

The main responsibility of a company or department head is to take care of the wellbeing of his staff and ensure equitable, harmonious interrelationships. One of the authors noticed that his Japanese client's personnel policies were in stark contrast to those of his own company. The clients hired their Japanese employees on the basis of a Western model, with English language skills and personality as the deciding factors.

The following case study from the author's experience shows the principles on which Japanese companies hire their employees:

Hiring a Japanese Specialist

The author was Director for the Client Services of an advertising agency in Tokyo and reported directly to the Japanese General Manager.

An important American client commissioned us to launch a first credit card in Japan. The core problem was that there was virtually no direct marketing know-how in the entire Japanese market at that time. For that reason, an American specialist was flown in with the task of building a direct marketing team within an year to assist the client with his product.

During this time the author was to hire a Japanese specialist who could be trained to become Head of the Department to replace the American expert. It was extremely difficult to find someone who was both technically qualified and who was able to speak English, as there was virtually no direct marketing knowhow in Japan at that time. After an exhaustive search, the ideal candidate was found. He was a young man with pleasant manners who spoke good English and had direct marketing experience. The author then met with the Human Resources Manager, a slightly older Japanese man who had previously served Mitsubishi in the same capacity, to discuss the hiring formalities.

The following dialogue ensued:

1. Author: How long will it take for the documents to be issued for employment?
2. Personnel Manager: Three weeks.
3. Author: Why so long?
4. Personnel Manager: We have to make inquiries.
5. Author: But those are a few phone calls or are you asking everywhere where he has worked?
6. Personnel Manager: Yes everywhere!

Two weeks later, the Personnel Manager came back and opened the following dialogue:

1. Personnel Manager: You cannot hire him!
2. Author: What! Why not?
3. Personnel manager: He took part in the student riots.
4. Author: That was 15 years ago! Was he ever arrested?

5. Personnel Manager: No!
6. Author: He made a very good impression on everyone who met him. After 15 years he may have changed and besides, we have a probationary period.
7. Personnel Manager: You cannot hire him. Ask the Shachō, the Japanese manager, he will also say no.

And that is how it was. We had to initiate a new search where Japanese principles applied. Not technical knowledge but character and the ability to integrate were the deciding factors for selection. In this case, the candidate had once committed a transgression which made his adaptability questionable. He will never find employment at a larger Japanese company, and he will always have to work for smaller companies and/or suppliers all his life.

This case shows the severe consequences in a collective society when someone is seen as guilty of a transgression. A company will always first try to support and integrate the person in question, but once they have contravened against social norms, there is no turning back—an attitude that is difficult to understand for Western people.

A leading Western headhunter once told the author that he had numerous profiles of excellent Japanese executives on his files, none of whom could be placed with Japanese companies because of a mishap during their careers!

Only much later did the author understand why his Japanese General Manager was so strict about choosing his staff. Most Western companies hired their Japanese employees on the basis of professional and language skills.

As a direct consequence, they experienced frequent social unrest. Conflicts were the order of the day in Western companies in Japan and a topic which came up whenever the author met with the heads of such companies.

On one occasion, the author came to a meeting of a Western company, where he had to beat a path through the reception area, as the entire lobby was occupied with sitting strikers and their banners. During the meeting, loudspeaker trucks drove around the block and a delegation even drove to the CEO's home to complain loudly to his wife.

In our company we only had symbolic strikes that started with headbands and ended with overtime strikes. Whenever there was urgent work for a client, staff members would go back to work. Japanese strikes are a way to show displeasure but should never harm the business of the company. Once again, loyalty above all!

4.13.8.3 *"Honne"* and *"Tatemae"*

This means literally translated: "*the truth and the formality*". It is the philosophy of working life. "*Tatemae*" describes ritualized work during the day, when everyone strives for harmony and tries not to provoke conflicts or arguments by avoiding critical issues. The principle of harmony reigns.

You have to bear in mind that Japanese are like everyone else. They have same emotions and frustrations, but their tolerance limit is, in most cases, higher than that of the Western business partner. Besides, they are expected to contain their emotions during the working day.

"*Honne*" or the "*truth*" is the context in which they may release pent up tensions and frustrations. These are occasions after work, when the team gets together at a bar or a restaurant. This may happen on several evenings during the week. A "*misurari*" (a whiskey with water) or a beer helps to loosen tongues and to create a more relaxed atmosphere where diplomatically packaged problems and conflicts can be addressed more directly. Like many other Asians, the Japanese lack the enzyme to metabolize alcohol efficiently. They become tipsy more quickly, leading to a relaxed and convivial atmosphere. Since critical subjects are broached with intoxicated jollity, they don't carry the same weight as at work.

Singing karaoke helps also loosen inhibitions and to strengthen the ties within the group or company, just as our ancestors did, dancing and singing around the campfire to strengthen the sense of community. Readers with experience of military service may also remember singing to overcome stressful situations.

Western expatriates often believe all business matters can be handled during office hours. Their professional lives are limited to formal workday business encounters, which is why the entire scale of a problem is rarely recognized. A fundamental precondition for successful leadership in Japan is attendance at "*honne*" events, where problems are brought into the open or even tackled openly. However, this is time-consuming and—from the Western point of view—interferes with private life. It is hardly surprising that the marriages of expatriates to Japan are subjected to considerable strain. Expatriate wives who have difficulties adapting to Japan often return home for a long-distance marriage or even file for divorce.

When a Japanese wants to get over his individual frustrations, he visits a "*Pachinko Parlor*", a games arcade equipped with several hundred pinball slot machines, where steel balls fall through intricate grids of brass nails and plastic flaps with a deafening noise. Points can be collected and then exchanged for prizes or cash.[72]

Japan's economy works perfectly. With their teamwork, working methods, philosophy and principles there is no need for coaches and team developers. This is quite unlike the Western world, where external consultants are constantly being hired to get rid of spanners in the works.

4.13.8.4 *"Nemawashi"*

Translated literally, this means "*planting a tree*". This is a well-established term and a ritual to establish relationships or to resolve conflicts. One of the authors heard this term for the first time from a senior colleague at his advertising agency in Tokyo:

[72]http://www.youtube.com/watch?v=b2q9eDvpN-o. Last viewed Sept. 16, 2018.

How to Renew a Terminated Contract!

One of the authors experienced how the CEO of a licensed American company belonging to Mitsubishi wanted to terminate his contract with the ad agency by every means.

The author talked to the client several times, urging him to stay. He invited him home for dinner where the client confirmed that he wanted to look for a new agency. There was a final conversation with the client in the presence of the Japanese CEO and another employee.

The author tried his usual approach—coming up with new solutions for the client. This insistence made the Japanese client so angry that stopped the author short and said: "*ima nihongo de ikiamashoo!*" ("As of now we will only speak Japanese".)

After that, the client turned to the CEO and addressed him furiously. This was evident from the CEO's body language—his face became flushed and his reactions clearly signaled discomfort. The upshot was that the client insisted on leaving.

While departing, another Japanese ritual became apparent. As the client had been offensive towards the CEO, Japanese custom demanded that he bow lower to signal apology. The Japanese client was quite tall whereas the CEO of the agency was quite short even by Japanese standards. So, we had the pleasure of seeing the client contorting himself to bow low enough, whereas our CEO just nodded his beetroot head.

Because of this conversation, the agency got a second chance to present a new concept to the client. The presentation took place at 5 p.m. in the client's classrooms for the staff training with the author the only foreigner present. When the presentation started, the Head of the client company put his head down on the table as if he were sleeping. When the presentation ended an hour and a half later, the client seemed to wake up and said something terse to those present. When asked, our interpreter said, "*He said our work does not meet his expectations*"*!*

In the West this would probably have been the end of the matter. However, the Japanese agency CEO did not give up. The CEO managed to successfully convince the client to remain at our agency by putting together a new team headed by a Japanese. As he was the author's friend, he explained how he would go about handling the client with "*nemawashi*" (tree-planting). This was described as follows: "*I will drive to the client's home, knock on the door, say that I happen to be in the neighborhood and if I may have a word with him. Tradition then demands that I will be invited inside, and I can say what I came for, i.e.to ask the client what he now expected from the new team. After a cup of tea or a beer and in about ten minutes, he will then wish me goodbye. This is what "Nemawashi" is all about*".

The tree evidently thrived, because 40 years later, even after retirement, the Japanese friend and the former client are still friends and working together. Once everything had been settled, the author also had the pleasure of socializing and playing tennis with the client at the Tokyo Lawn Tennis Club.

4.14 Jordan: Homeland of the Refugees

This contribution was written by Raeid Meri, a German with Palestinian roots, and author of "*The Arabic und Islamic World*" in Sect. 4.3.

For the past 25 years, I have witnessed the changes and contrasts that have taken place in Jordan. Anyone traveling around in Jordan will quickly realize that this is a country in transition.

In its diversity, with its ancient sites, castles, the desert Wadi Rum, the world wonder the rock city of Petra, the healing Dead Sea and the busy Red Sea, it still remains an insider's tip for tourism. Despite its geographical and strategic location, Jordan embodies a remarkable degree of peace, stability and balance.

This may be because of its population. Jordan has a total of nearly 10 million people[73] in 2018. That's 20 times as many as there were in the 1950s. This is, above all, due to the refugees admitted from Iraq, Kuwait, Syria and Palestine. Almost two-thirds of the population are refugees from neighboring countries.

Far more than 50% of the total population is of Palestinian descent and has been largely naturalized. Jordan is still the only Arab state to offer full citizenship to Palestinian refugees.

Another 1.5 million Palestinians who have fled live in the Arab States outside Jordan; another 0.5 million in the EU and the Americas. Only about 5 million of a total of about 9.5 million Palestinians[74] live in the West Bank and Gaza.

Ethnic conflicts within Jordan are hard to imagine. The majority of people have a history of immigration—whether Iraqis, Syrians, Palestinians, Armenians or people from the Caucasus. People meet with tolerance and respect. Even religious conflicts are hardly conceivable due to the very homogeneous composition. 97% of the people are Sunni Muslim, 3% Christian or belong to other religious denominations.

Jordan has one of the highest birth rates in the Arab world. Accordingly, two-thirds of the population is younger than 30 years old. More than 80% of the people live in the three big cities in the north of the country.

The prosperity in Jordan is unevenly distributed. The unemployment rate is just under 20%. The income gap is growing.

In Jordan, compulsory education is required until the age of 16. There are a variety of free State elementary and secondary schools. Accordingly, the literacy rate of young people is over 98%.

A maxim of Jordanian families is to provide the best available education for their offspring. A variety of private schools and universities are trying to meet this demand.

Eating in Jordan could be a big challenge for vegetarians. The bulk of the very versatile Jordanian food is very meat-based. However, there are more and more good alternatives such as vegetarian falafel (chick-pea balls) and hummus.

---

[73]https://www.auswaertiges-amt.de/de/aussenpolitik/laender/jordanien-node/jordanien/218006. Last viewed June 27, 2019.

[74]https://en.wikipedia.org/wiki/Palestinians. Last viewed June 27, 2019.

▶ Watch out! Refusing food on an invitation is an insult. Inform your host about your eating habits in advance.

Jordanians have an extremely high affinity for smoking. There are hardly any places where smoking is prohibited. Thus, it can happen to a visitor already on his very first taxi ride, that the driver smokes without reservation during the entire journey. Hookahs[75] in all flavors can be found on every street corner.

Not only because of its moderate and very Western capital, Amman, but also because of the mild summer weather, Jordan is a popular holiday spot for Arabs from the Gulf.

4.15 Russia

4.15.1 Culturally Formative Elements

4.15.1.1 The Great Russian Soul

The phrase "*The Great Russian Soul*" was used a great deal by Russian participants in our seminars to describe their endurance and stoicism in their struggle for survival in the harsh climate and under the oligarchy of tsars and landlords over centuries. Russia was the last country in Europe to abolish serfdom in 1861. In this climate, it was only the family and the community which guaranteed survival. Emblematic for this is the word MIR, which we know as the name of the Soviet space capsule, but its original meaning is "*village*" or "*peace*".

4.15.2 Communication and Conflict Resolution

4.15.2.1 The Bridge Between Occident and Orient

This vast country of 12 time zones, stretching from Western Europe to East Asia, sees itself as spanning these two worlds. Oriental traits show in communication and conflict resolution.

Initial contact is made with a cautious, wait-and-see attitude verging on mistrust. However, with personal involvement and sympathy one quickly discovers that Russians in general are very accessible, modest and reserved.

The authors led and lectured at many training projects with Russian participants between the ages of 30 and 50 and always noticed this watchful attitude. After a short while it dissolved, and both authors were often received and accepted with a warmth that made these group experiences memorable in a way that is no longer experienced in the West.

The respect for age was also striking. A lecturer, even at retirement age, was always treated with extreme respect. Participants spontaneously offered to take over

[75]https://en.wikipedia.org/wiki/Hookah. Last viewed June 27, 2019.

work, make photocopies, or to help set up the equipment in the room. Ladies sometimes picked up a dropped item, assuming that a lecturer over a certain age could not bend over so well. Although many attendees were of a mature age with a lot of life and work experience, trainers and project managers always noticed their modesty and restraint, especially in mixed courses with German students.

4.15.3 Working Together in Business and Professional Life

Russian managerial culture became apparent to one of the authors in a seminar for modern management methods at a Moscow university in the mid-1990s. After the 2-day seminar, one of the 40, head of a steel plant in the Volga region stood up and said in Russian, "*This method is for Western Europe, but not for Russia.*" When asked why, his brief reply needed no translation—"*traditie*" (tradition)!

Russia is a classic example of high power distance in terms of leadership, with employees feeling and acting collectively (see also Sect. 3.2.1.1 "Power Distance")

In this regard, Russia is also underestimated by Western politics, the media and public opinion. In the West, Putin is often considered a nefarious power-hungry despot, but 80% of the Russians support him and see him as the country's father, who prevented chaos and led them out of the political crisis of the 1990s.

Incidentally, the same applies also to China. Collective cultures have evolved successfully over centuries or even thousands of years with strong leaders. They do not want to be and do not have to be transformed into a Western style democratic system, as is repeatedly demanded by politicians and media in the West. The success of these leaders for their people determines the degree of approval they enjoy, and ultimately whether they will survive and stay in power.

4.15.3.1 Pragmatism as a Livelihood

When asked about the essence of their culture in cross cultural seminars, Russians often said: "*We need a long time to begin working and we finish quickly*". History has taught Russians to survive with modest demands and with little to live on. The here and now is important, thinking of tomorrow is unnecessary, because the climate or even a shift in power might question or overturn everything.

A seminar participant from the former German Democratic Republic who spent a summer vacation at the dacha of a Russian friend, vividly illustrated this with an anecdote. Sitting outside in the sun he got bored after a while and started to look around. As the grass was high, he searched for a scythe, found it in the barn, sharpened it and mowed the grass. Villagers passing by stopped at the gate and asked: "*Why are you doing this, German? You have no cattle!*" The next day he saw that some slats were missing from the fence in front. There was also a fence behind the dacha. He removed the posts from the fence behind the dacha and began to insert them in front. Again, the passing villagers stopped and asked: "*Why are you doing this, German, you have no chickens!*"

Another story was contributed by a German seminar participant who studied in Russia and worked as an assistant and interpreter for a Swiss managing director in

Moscow. This involved the expansion of a new office wing in a joint venture for which the plans were made in Switzerland.

One day, the Swiss manager discovered that the electrical wiring was not routed as planned along the wall and across the ceiling, but instead led directly from the power supply switch across the ceiling to the lighting. All the arguments to reroute it were in vain; the Russians were not to be persuaded. Their argument was: "*It is easier, and we save meters of cables*".

4.15.4 How to Make Successful Deals with Russians

For Russians, the focus is on people and relationships. Western businesspeople should schedule time and patience and use every available social opportunity for get-togethers. They should accept invitations to eat (and drink) and not, as is often the case, excuse themselves to work on emails at the hotel!

A Russian business partner wants to be convinced and to hear about all the arguments and discussions that led to a decision. An illustrative example emerged in a Russia seminar with a Swiss participant married to a Russian, who had also lived and worked in this country. What annoyed him in daily routine work were the long discussions after decisions had been taken and which he confirmed by a brief email. Long telephone conversations then ensued, where he had to go into all the details all over again. Based on what he learnt during the seminar, he changed his style of communication and sent a detailed account of why a decision had been taken. In the follow-up phone call, he expected to get asked about all the usual details, but this time his Russian colleague interrupted him with: "*No need, I know all that.*"

When the great Russian soul opens up, it becomes emotional and warm, as the following story shows:

The Group Photo

One of the authors once worked with a group of Russian managers. It was a networking project of several weeks with German companies who shared their business interests. Various excursions to export-oriented companies were made. Group photos were taken of the visiting Russian managers with their German counterparts and distributed to the participants and the author.

On the last Friday before the Russian delegation departed, a farewell party was held for the Russian managers. Many guests were invited, and the mood was excellent. At around 10:00 p.m., the author briefly went to the office to write an e-mail. Suddenly, one of the Russian managers and a few colleagues entered his office and the following dialogue ensued:

1. Russian Manager: "Please call company XYZ right now. I've lost my photo. It's impossible to fly back to Russia without the photo."
2. The Author: "Nobody will be there, it's Friday night. This is Germany! I'll send you the photo later, no problem."

The Russian manager was not interested in this logical explanation. In principle, he expected the author to go to the company in question on Friday night and to somehow get hold of the photo. He would not be appeased and went on persisting. Since the author did not know what else to do, he gave him his own photo at which point the situation became very emotional.

The Russian manager, who was a head taller than the author, embraced him warmly with tears of emotion running down his cheeks. "*Thank you, thank you, thank you*" he said repeatedly, while his colleagues stood around and applauded.

4.16 Switzerland

4.16.1 Culturally Influenced Elements

Switzerland is a multicultural society in several ways:

1. Basically, there are four language cultures with affinities and values to the neighboring countries with corresponding cultural origins: Germany, France, Italy, and the Romansh speaking minority of a language derived directly from Latin and spoken in Switzerland, Eastern Austria and Northern Italy.
2. Switzerland has the highest percentage of first to third generation immigrants and naturalized foreigners in Western Europe. About 35–40% of the total population are citizens with an immigrant background.
3. In 2017, 45% of the highest ranked executives were foreigners.
4. In addition, there is a high number of border crossers, i.e. employees from neighboring countries who work in Switzerland without living there.

The question about the cultural values of Switzerland is difficult to answer:

1. There are no culturally overlapping values, except perhaps the cultural diversity. The only true value is that Switzerland has achieved the creation of a multicultural society where people live together in peace and where there are no ghettos or fundamental problems.
2. Foreigners are required to learn Swiss culture and language. But which culture? Which language? High German, the official language, or Swiss German, the vernacular in everyday communication?

In principle, someone is considered integrated in Switzerland if he or she fits in with the Swiss system. In other words, if he or she behaves in accordance with the prevailing rules of order, cleanliness, punctuality, restraint, modesty and care in dealing with resources. In spite of sporadic cultural tensions and even racism, Switzerland's sound economic base may also contribute to the relative lack of conflict.

4.16.2 Germans and Swiss Germans: A Common Language Separated by History

Historically speaking, the Alemanni, the ancestors of the Swiss Germans and the Swabians of Southern Germany have the same roots. They belonged to a tribe originating from the Ural, migrating in the early Medieval Ages to Northern Germany and from there to the Northern edge of the Alps.

The cultural separation of the Swiss Alemanni began with the revolt of the Central Swiss Cantons in the late thirteenth century striving for independence from the Habsburgs and the consecutive wars between the Habsburgians and the first Swiss cantons.

In 1515, after losing the battle of Marignano in northern Italy in which the Swiss lost a war against France to gain supremacy in Lombardy, the Council of Cantons decided to renounce expansion plans abroad for all times and to concentrate on the homeland.

Modern Switzerland with its constitution of 1848 is a creation of the Congress of Vienna in 1815. The currently valid demarcation and the emphasis on independence originated from the end of the nineteenth century, when the economic power of Germany and German capital increasingly threatened the independence of Switzerland. External pressure from World wars I and II emphasized the sense of a Swiss identity distinct from that of its Northern neighbor.

Today, German speaking Switzerland sees itself as a "*closed society*", especially towards Germans, although the German-speaking Swiss have more in common culturally with the Alemanni of South Germany than with their Swiss compatriots speaking French, Italian or the Romansh language.

4.16.3 Communication and Conflict Management in German Speaking Switzerland

The communication behavior of the German-speaking Swiss is the main reason for the successful coexistence of this multicultural society. Swiss Germans—in contrast to their northern neighbors, the Germans—don't normally communicate directly. If they did, living in a multicultural society like Switzerland would be difficult, if not impossible. Therefore, in many cases conflicts remain in a sort of gray area and brushed under the carpet in the hope that time might solve them. Solutions are sought in a lengthy process of reaching consensus. If Swiss Germans bring a conflict out into the open, then it has already escalated.

For German citizens working in Switzerland, this is often the first stumbling block and cause of interpersonal difficulties with the Swiss, because they are used to openly discussing conflicts. In Switzerland conflicts are usually resolved on the sidelines, in one-on-one talks which sometimes skip hierarchical levels. The publicizing of a conflict usually leads to an escalation because criticism may be perceived as a personal attack.

4.16.4 Working Together in Professional and Business Life

Swiss have two basic values: pragmatism and diligence in dealing with resources, including human resources. Swiss small to medium-sized enterprises account for more than 60% of the gross national product. They see themselves as responsible social employers for the local community. Creating jobs and increasing turnover is often still more important than making big profits.

As for the employee, the prerequisite for professional success is lifelong continuing education, without which there is no professional advancement. Anyone successful in business has had a number of training programs either behind or ahead of him, some of which take years.

4.16.5 Pragmatism of a Small Country

Critical issues are resolved before meetings in private conversations. There is usually no open criticism in meetings. The supervisor stays in the background and only intervenes when a conflict arises. Personal relationships are fundamental to be successful in business. Colleagues eat and drink together. Business relationships often develop into personal relationships and may last a lifetime.

4.17 Spain and Other Cultures Speaking Romance Languages

With 460 million people who are Spanish native speakers and another 90 million who speak Spanish as an official language, this is the fourth most widely spoken language in the world after Chinese, English and Hindi. From the end of the Middle Ages until recently Spain was orientated towards the West rather than to northern Europe, which is due to their conquests in Central and South America.

A common feature and ideal of all Spaniards are the nobility and dignity of man and pride in descent, which always require respect. Hurting pride can lead to fierce conflicts.

As in many Southern countries, extended families and friends form networks of mutual loyalty. This is the foundation of Spanish society.

4.17.1 Culturally Formative Elements

From the outside, Spain seems to be one entity. In reality, there are a number of different cultures that make up today's Spain:

1. In the geographical center are the Castilians, epitome of the proud Spaniards whose conquests in South America have contributed to spread the Spanish language and culture across the world.

2. There are other cultures with their own languages: Andalusians, Basques, Catalans, Aragonites and Asturians with differing historical backgrounds. They are self-contained and insist on their independence.
3. Catalans and Basques are against the influence of the Castilian center. Catalan, which is not an official national language, has the world's largest literature in an unofficial language.
4. The bloody clashes and attacks of the Basque independence organization, the ETA (“*Euskadi Ta Askatasunabaskisch*” (*For a Basque State and Freedom*),[76] are hopefully a thing of the past after the separatist organization and the central government came to an agreement on October 20, 2011.
5. However, the outcome of the regional Catalan parliament's vigorous push for independence which started in Barcelona in 2017 is still uncertain.

Based on this overall understanding of Spain, it is important to immerse oneself in the cultures of the regions because “*mañana por la mañana*” (postponing until tomorrow) or bullfighting may be a way of life in the South or in Castile, but not in northern Spain. The Catalans, for example, are considered to be the Southern Germans. Getting to know the regional cultures and historical background are the prerequisites for building trust and successful business throughout Spain. It is the surest way to avoid possible conflicts in the form of generalized clichés about entire Spain. Spaniards are proud of their history, the story of a world power on which the sun never sets. To know this and to point these out in conversations is a possible expression of respect for Spaniards.

There are two attitudes that are reflected in the world-famous chivalry novel “*Don Quixote de la Mancha*” by Miguel de Cervantes. They are embodied in the two main characters, Don Quixote, the idealist seeking unattainable ideals, and Sancho Panza who goes through life with healthy common sense and pragmatism. Seen historically, these are the two dimensions, the extremes, that have shaped Spain, especially in Castile and the South:

1. The contrasts of nature, cold winters and extremely hot summers.
2. The landscape: Green in spring and parched in summer.
3. The religiosity: belief in fate and pre-determination.

Machismo may be a thing of the past: After the fall of Franco's dictatorship the role of women has changed dramatically. Their presence and contribution to politics and economy[77] has advanced in a short time to levels of Northern European countries.[78] Education is based on a European, as well as the US-American model.

[76]https://en.wikipedia.org/wiki/Basque_nationalism. Last viewed on Sept. 17, 2018.

[77]https://en.wikipedia.org/wiki/Women_in_Spain
https://www.thespanishblog.com/2012/03/the-changing-role-of-women-in-spain/. Last viewed on Sept. 17, 2018.

[78]https://en.wikipedia.org/wiki/Women_in_Europe. Last viewed on Sept. 17, 2018.

The romantic "*el paseso*", the evening walk in Castile and in the South is a thing of the past, when unmarried girls, usually accompanied by a mother or a grandmother, would walk along the main street to throw stolen glances at the young men passing by. The father of one of the authors, who used to work in the region of La Mancha in central Castile before the Spanish Civil War, enjoyed these evening walks very much because he stood out as "*el rubio*" (the tall blond from Northern Europe).

The seemingly subordinate position of the woman in the past was certainly attributable to the strict Catholic education in schools as well as and the traditional gender roles during Franco's regime, when women were not allowed to work. In addition, it may also have been an Arab heritage in the south of Spain. The powerful Moorish kingdom reigned for 800 years in the Middle Ages. The impressive buildings and cultural monuments from its heyday, such as the Alhambra in Granada, testify to its past grandeur.

► **Don't Mistake Spanish Dignity for Machismo**

The author's daughter-in-law has Spanish roots, her Spanish father having been a very successful joint surgeon for more than 20 years in Northern Germany.

At the very first contact by phone the author suggested that they address each other by the German "*Du*", the informal version of 'you'.

Later on, the author learned from his daughter-in-law, that her father was surprised and only accepted it because the author was 2 years older than he was!

Afterwards I wondered how a women might have reacted to tis story?

4.17.1.1 Communication and Conflict Management

Close body and eye contact are a means of communication, starting with the "*abrazo*", the embrace among men, which is only done in private and with good friends. An "*abrazo*" is unacceptable with and between ladies. If old friends meet in business life and a lady is with them, then the men will hug, and the wife will politely nod or perhaps shake hands. Ladies expect the man to behave very politely and courteously towards them.

The goal of communication is preventing of loss of face and avoiding conflict. Conflicts are always resolved in private conversations. Oral communication is preferred because difficult issues can be expressed and discussed in nuanced ways. Written communication has always been of secondary importance. This means that letters are often left unanswered. Dealing with officialdom is referred to as "*silencio administrativo*"—the silence of the administration—by the Spaniards, which is then taken as consent.

The attitude to written communication has changed little with modern e-mail. Multiple e-mails on the same topic, such as a follow up for an appointment, usually go unanswered because the recipient considers it unnecessary, or even believes that it is not worth considering.

4.17.1.2 Working Together in Business and Professional Life

"*El Jefe*", the boss is decisive, much like the *Patron* in France. Although "*El Jefe*" is humane, he expects absolute respect. According to Hofstede, Spain has a high power distance with an index of 57. Spanish pride and dignity will reinforce this paternalistic attitude and appearance. This is also evident in clothing: A suit and tie are compulsory for business people even in summer temperatures. The same principles for interaction between superior and subordinate in business life apply also to cultures mentioned in Sect. 3.2.1.1 "Power Distance".

4.17.2 Other Spanish-speaking Cultural Regions

Although the Castilian language and culture had a great influence on the countries conquered by Spain in the Middle Ages, they did not—unlike the French language and culture—dominate the original native cultures. Instead, there has always been a coexistence, leading to very diverse and sometimes contradictory national and regional cultures.

4.17.2.1 Formative Cultural Influences in Latin America

Central and South America show a great cultural diversity, which is the result of different native cultures and differing historical experiences:

1. Geography and the environment shape people, their desire for freedom and their optimism so that they can master life despite adverse circumstances.
2. All the countries, with the exception of Chile, have a penchant for isolationism, because they are lacking in international contacts and practices.
3. The mentalities of the Indian, the indigenous, native populations influence all cultures to differing degrees. This embraces their attachment to their land and their traditional lifestyles. Their historical experience under foreign rule and heteronomy are reflected in their belief in predestination, insight into human nature, resentment against exploitation and suppression by the government and the authorities.
4. Public recognition and mañana come with the Moorish heritage: social standing of people and circumstances are more important than rules and laws, the moment determines the behavior.
5. Ultimately, there is the Spanish heritage, which includes pride, a feeling of superiority towards North Americans, the central importance of status, the art of conversation and the Catholic heritage.
6. Every single Central and South American country has its own distinct culture, of which it is proud of and which sets it apart.
7. As in Spain the same principles apply in business life and communication.

The following are the main differences between two South American rural cultures:

4.17.3 Argentina

Argentina is a proud country, full of contrasts and with varying historical experiences. In 1936 it was one of the richest countries in the world, and in 2001 it was bankrupt. Although Argentina is located in southern South America, it still feels like the most European of all countries in South America. Buenos Aires looks like a European city, somewhat like Paris, Rome or Madrid.

Also, worth mentioning is the elegance of the Spanish diction of Argentinians, which is much softer and stands in stark contrast to the harder pronunciation of Spanish in its home country.

Gaining independence in 1816, Argentina experienced a turbulent history of democracies and military dictatorships, combined with coups and civil wars. The last coup and the military dictatorship from 1976 to 1983 became known worldwide because of the "*desaparecidos*," political dissidents, often students, who were abducted and vanished without a trace, often thrown from planes over the ocean. Their mothers demonstrated in front of public buildings despite threats and danger to themselves[79] until January 2006 when the movement ended.

4.17.4 Chile

Chile's history is comparable to that of other Latin American countries, marked by dictatorships and social unrest. Its culture is, however, very different from that of its neighbors. Chileans are often called "*the Prussians of South America*" because they are said to be like the Germans. In addition to English, the German language and culture has always had a great influence on Chile. Chileans like things to be punctual and precise, to get straight to the point, have formal meetings and are more reserved than people from other Latin American cultures.

Chile sees itself as an American hub between Europe and Asia and has therefore traditionally had its place in international trade. In the recent past, this position has been reinforced by farming and export of agricultural goods, such as wines, fruits and vegetables.

4.18 Understanding the United Kingdom

I have many family and friends in Europe and I have lived in at least six European countries and learnt five European languages. I like Europe and it saddens me to encounter so often bafflement at the attitudes and perceived hostility of my countrymen to "the Continent". The man in the plane quietly reading his book is not necessarily hostile—he just wants to be left alone. It's that simple.

[79]https://en.wikipedia.org/wiki/Mothers_of_the_Plaza_de_Mayo. Last viewed Sept. 17, 2018.

Less easy to explain is maybe the British attitude to business and cultural professional idiosyncrasies. The German says "Nein" loud and clear. The Frenchman will scoff "Ooof". But what is the English prospect really saying? Or thinking? Or not saying? I will try and open up that box of mysteries for you. The more you know the better you'll comprehend. The positive side of that equation is that once you do understand—once you break through that legendary British reserve—you will likely have a friend or colleague forever.

Mike Ferrier.[80]

4.18.1 Who Are You Doing Business With?

France is France. Germany is Germany. Britain is ... what exactly? England ? The United Kingdom? To start to converse effectively with what the American's colloquially call a "*Brit*", it does help taking a little time just to understand what "*Brits*" are. And are not.

The country is called officially "*The United Kingdom*" and that is the sign you will see on a United Nations desk or Brussels membership. Most of the country is comprised of two large islands 20 miles west of the French coast—Britain and Ireland. But in fact, the entire area consists of 6000 islands of varying political make up and independence.

Together these Islands are known as the "*The British Isles*". Britain, or Great Britain, technically, refers to the country created by the Act of Union (1706) which joined the thrones of Scotland and England/Wales after many centuries of conflict.

Britain became "*The United Kingdom*" when Ireland joined the Union in 1801. In the 1940s Ireland (or Eire) left the United Kingdom, although the Northern provinces (populated mainly by Scottish Protestant immigrants) stayed within the "*Union*". The famous flag—the Union Jack—seals that confluence of nations and combines the flags of St George of England (the red cross on white) the Scottish flag of St Andrew (white Saltire on blue field) and the Irish Saltire of St Patrick (red cross on white field).

So today the United Kingdom consists not of one culture, but of many. English, Scottish, Welsh, Northern Irish, and the "*Crown Dependencies*" i.e. the Channel Islands (Jersey, Guernsey, Alderney, Sark etc) and the Isle of Man. It is not necessary to know the varying degrees of autonomy for each unit of the U.K. in detail, but it is important to remember that they are different and often operate to their own rules and codes of conduct.

Most have their own parliaments. In fact, the Isle of Man "*Keys*"[81]are probably the earliest parliament known to man. Your hosts will expect you to understand that

[80]A personal note from the author: When I started in international advertising in 1967 Mike Ferrier became my first boss and thereafter mentor, coach and friend. I owe my international career to him and therefore also this book. Peter M Haller.

[81]https://en.wikipedia.org/wiki/House_of_Keys. Last viewed 30.10.2018.

the "*locals*" often feel more "*Local*" than "British", even though the UK Parliament in London remains the ultimate authority in most vital areas. But a Scot is a Scot first, British second, and maybe European third.

If you need any further proof of this cultural division, consider this: The United Kingdom does not have a national soccer or rugby team. The Islands have English, Scottish, Welsh, Irish and Northern Irish "national" teams—unique in Europe.

A word on London. As Paris is not France, London is not the UK. It is a world financial center and political and social apex. At the time of writing, London was Europe's fourth largest French speaking city. Most infrastructure investment is foreign, usually Middle Eastern. Joking about British food is outdated. London is today probably the culinary capital of Europe. And the city is expensive.

You will not get to understand British culture without leaving the capital. Take a trip out of the city on week-ends.

A word on the Commonwealth. These are countries of the old British Empire who have agreed to retain the Queen as head of state. Some 21 counties are "*Overseas Territories*" (read '*Colonies*') which are still ultimately controlled from London. Some 16 more (including Canada, Australia and New Zealand) are entirely self-governing but retain the Monarch as titular head of state.

4.18.2 Pragmatism and the Non Constitution

Although the United Kingdom is an amalgam of "*nations*" and cultures, it does share a number of attributes which color many of their attitudes to life.

First of all, they are immensely proud of their past—they look back fondly on the days of "*Empire*" when the Union Jack fluttered over 25% of the world's surface and British factories were the industrial envy of everyone.

Secondly, they have never been invaded since the Norman Conquest of 1066. And not since King John was challenged on the meadows of Runnymede and forced to sign the Magna Carta in June 1215 has the country faced any major political upheavals. (For purposes of this report we can ignore the War of the Roses (1455–1485) or Oliver Cromwell's "*republic*" (1599–1658) which were essentially more episodic than permanent. In both cases the British status quo was restored.)

Thus, there never appeared to be a need to re-think the "*constitution*" or re-invent the political system. For the last 600 years it has been tinkered with but never abolished, No third Reich. No French revolution. No Code Napoleon. No King Charlemagne and his Holy Roman Empire. This historical fact of continuum is often at the root of British attitudes towards life.

They adapt, they improve, or they "*modernize*". They look back for solutions and respect tradition—because tradition and the loyalties they imbibed seem to have served the nation well. Evolution, not revolution, is deeply instilled in the British DNA.

What does that mean for the foreign businessman? His hosts will expect his presentation to show progression in easily handled stages, walking before you run. Extravagant and flamboyant claims will be mentally resisted, especially if those changes seem to challenge well-loved traditions. Referring to one's own "*foreign*" culture or experience will have little impact. The average Brit has little interest in other cultures and has even less exposure. As he travels, he takes his own culture with him. Concentrate, therefore, on Britain and the application of your project to the British arena and local customs.

A recent example illustrates this ingrained resistance to pressure. As an experiment, some well-meaning but rash officials in the Office of Overseas territories appointed a non-English Governor to a very British island in the Caribbean. He wanted to change everything in a few weeks. His ideas were good but his "*knee-jerk*" method was anathema to the British Overseas Territory. His constant referral to "*what we did elsewhere*" was highly provocative, even taken as insulting. He was removed in 3 months.

Similarly, remember that the British (as Germans and most of North Western Europeans) demonstrate a literal attitude to business. They expect you to show up on time, be fully prepared, present a logical agenda, and follow it, speak slowly and clearly (200 words a minute as opposed to the Frenchman's normal 350) and keep calm.

The British adapt slowly and resist change for its own sake. Pragmatism at its most obvious was the decision in 1917 of the very German British Royal Family (origin Saxe-Coburg) to change their name to "*Windsor*" as the First World War ground to stalemate.

The negative side to this constant looking backward for forward inspiration has had the dangerous effect of ill-preparing British management to cope with the pace of modern business change. Almost all major British enterprises are now either foreign owned or foreign managed. Even their many cherished and famous football clubs have "continental" managers.

Napoleon's quip that Britain was a nation of shop keepers was not totally inappropriate. British work well individually or in small teams, less well trying to manage the complexities of large scale modern production.

They invent. They create. They master the arts. They teach. But they do not enjoy walking the factory floor.

4.18.3 British Social Norms

Visitors often complain that they do not understand British working culture or social behavior. And it can be confusing.

Not only—as we have seen—is the country a collection of semi-autonomous regions, but the slow pace of change has left a social structure that is both hierarchical and very local.

Let's start off with language. Basically, French is French, and German is German. There may be a Bavarian accent or an Austrian lilt, but the accents are relatively mild. In Britain accents are both regional and social. It is almost impossible for the untrained ear to understand deep Cockney rhyming slang (South London): "*ow's yer sugar and spice*"?[82] or deep West country, or Glaswegian (Glasgow). Wales has its own national language.

But you also have to contend with the still active "*Upper Crust*" language of the higher classes (the so- called "*Oxford English*"). As Professor Higgins stated so vividly in "*My Fair Lady*", utter one phrase and an Englishman can usually tell the origin within a few miles of the speaker.

The English upper classes are dying out slowly—but their life style is still very active and distinct and needs to be appreciated. They shoot, hunt, play rugby and polo, go to "*public*" (actually meaning "*private*" schools) and come from what Americans would call "*Ivy League Universities*". But they also retain a very strict set of values of fairness, politeness, and business ethics.

And, it has to be said, an often deep suspicion of foreigners. This is the Englishman (mainly) characterized by foreigners of "*the stiff upper lip*", well-tailored, and sporting a hat and umbrella.

Flippancy, arrogance, or aggressive selling will definitively be resisted by this breed. They admire the gifted amateur rather than the enlightened professional. The famous Shell Hong Kong telex sent to London HQ as sales slumped is anecdotal and true: "*Sales down—please send a Cambridge Blue!*" (Graduate of Cambridge University).

Class distinction is fading, but it is not dead. Its traditions hang around in the board room manners of many companies.

Even if the modern Board appoints few or no "*upper class*" members, the legacy lives on. Social cohesion and politeness reigns. The head of the company is usually the "*Chairman*" and that's his job—to "*chair*" the meeting, set the agenda, make sure everyone is heard and—no matter how contentious the issues might have been—to ensure the group shares a friendly "*gin and tonic*" or even lunch together before going back to their respective duties.

It is best to engage a British board of this composition in a round of firm handshakes looking each participant eye-to-eye and start with a few exchanges of a general or even moderately humorous nature. "*Air France was late again, as usual. Probably should have taken Ryan Air*" "*But I did bring the sunshine with me.* "*At home we we're worrying about the upcoming elections. By the way, Peter sends his regards.*" Ending up with the under-stated and modest introduction: "*Well, since we are here together you may want to take a look at why I asked you for this meeting.*"

Then tend to stick to the facts, deliver your pitch in an even voice (no exaggerated sales pressure) and be prepared to ask a few questions to get the discussion started. "*Did I explain the delivery schedule adequately? Is the product performance as you had imagined it?*" British need prompting to arouse a meaningful reaction.

Do not emulate one Texas presenter who ended his pitch with: "*OK, you guys, tell me, do I have a deal? Who'll be the first to shake my hand?*" To which the chairman answered coolly: "*I will, sir. I wish you a good return trip and thank you for coming. You will hear from us.*"

[82]Translation: How's your wife?

A British businessman's reaction is very hard to fathom. The board members will avoid being rude or even honest at all costs. The usual reaction is a polite "*That was very interesting—allow us some time to consider your very well argued points*".

Three warnings here:

1. A seemingly warm reaction means nothing. It is just politeness. It takes on average four meetings to convince any British group (quote from Richard Branson) to trust you or want to do business with you. Being known as "*the masters of the understatement*" means a direct question will rarely score a direct answer. Expect a practiced waffle "*My dear chap, I need time to take a deeper look at that.*" Nor will any facial or emotive response like "*Oh—I love it!*" be expressed on an initial encounter.
2. Make sure you leave behind an exact copy of your presentation for the board to discuss openly in your absence. They will not want to be critical to your face. Nor wish to expose "*all their cards*" before deep consideration.

   A New Jersey drug cartel felt sure they had a three-million-pound investment from a UK bank "*in the bag*". The board had repeatedly thanked the presenters for their visits and expressed great interest. The NJ group hired staff and London premises on this hopeful outcome. Two weeks later came the apologetic refusal on some technicality.

   "*But you said you were so interested*" wailed the presenter. "*We were*" replied the Chairman. "*But being interested does not mean we were about to commit.*"

   Another telling anecdote. A German author asked for technical contributions from four British experts. All agreed, but none actually contributed. They did not like the rigid guidelines for the contributions but were too "*polite*" to be honest.
3. Follow up your meeting with the points you believe were agreed on, thus giving your counterpart the opportunity to re-engage in your presentation. The British have a literary side to them. They express themselves better in writing that on their feet. Opening a written dialogue may prove more productive.

A Harley Street mainly corporate doctor we interviewed admitted almost 20% of his patients came to him asking for help in controlling their nervousness for an upcoming speech or presentation. He explained "*In Italy, everyone is out in the sunshine and gabbling all night in the nearest café. Here the rain and the clouds keep us isolated and indoors. Café cultures can address a crowd at 5 minutes notice and enjoy it. An Englishman either writes his speech or carries detailed notes. And hates it!*"

To conclude, the most often misunderstood reaction to a presentation to a UK group is the difficulty is gauging true interest over courtesy. Thus, it is wise advice to assume the worst until you have the contract signed in front of you.

4.18.4 Social Business Behavior

The Swiss and the Germans go to work on time and to work. "*Arbeit ist Arbeit und Schnapps ist Schnapps*" (Work is work and play is play). The British executive obviously goes to work to work, but also to cement team understanding and with the objective of "*getting to know them better*".

Hence the long Friday pub lunch, the Executive dinner, and group social events, all of which play an important role in working life. The writer watched two Swiss with the same name (Herr Huber) sit opposite each other for over 20 years without ever using a first name or dropping the formal "*Sie*" for the more informal "*Du*". Such a scenario would be impossible in the UK business environment.

Similarly, guests who are invited to a social event find it hard to understand why it is so difficult to connect at, say, a cocktail party. It appears no one will automatically invite you into a conversation. British are naturally socially shy and are probably wondering what to say to you. As already noted, they have no innate curiosity as to your background or culture.

It is best to enter such a function with one of the hosts and stick with him/her. Being shy by nature, the drinking of alcohol to aid social intercourse can often lead to excess. Excess can expose prejudice. Be careful.

Similarly, make sure you understand the culture and tradition of the event you are invited to. Go to Ascot in jeans and a T-shirt and you will win few friends. Go to a formal society dinner without your tuxedo (dinner jacket) and you will equally show your cultural ignorance. Always check the dress and tradition of the event you are invited to.

"*London is the only city where I was invited to a Black Tie (Tux) boxing match.*" (Quote John Coombs, Racing Driver)

Remember that in all social or other interactions, the British like to maintain "*their space*". They abhor the closeness of the Mediterranean embrace, or the back-slapping bonhomie of the American.

► Keep your distance at all times.

Regarding the attitude to women, acceptance is usually universal these days. Male-dominated groups will still expect the woman to be "*one of the boys*" and join the pub crawl. They will also call a woman "*dearie, ducky, or love*". Don't take umbrage—it has no suggestive connotations. A tip for women: cross your legs at the ankles, not the knees. The latter is seen as defensive. And don't smile too much—the British find it irritating if women smile too often while presenting.

For socializing, the inviter is usually expected to pay. Don't be too eager to invite your counterparts out until they feel comfortable with you, or they may feel that accepting the invitation could be construed as compromising.

The usual courtesies apply. Do not start eating until everyone has been served. Try and accept your hosts suggestions on the menu, especially with regard to the wine selected. British pride themselves or their wine knowledge—a merit badge they probably do not deserve, but just play along.

Gifts are unnecessary, except maybe flowers if invited to someone's house. But do remember that "*An Englishman's home is his castle*". Be appreciative of the venue.

Subjects to avoid are jokes about the Queen and the Royal Family, religion, and politics, especially the current debate on Brexit (Britain's exit from the EU).

Business cards are expected, but the exchange is not ritualized as in the East. If you are not asked for your card, that is probably not a good sign.

European visitors would be well advised to remember that the British are not particularly comfortable in their presence. They remain a proud and independent island nation which, in many ways, sees itself as a world leader without a world following. Without ever quite understanding how to interact effectively with Europeans, they tend to favor mixing with those of Anglo-Saxon heritage, viz. the Americans, Irish, Canadians, Australians, etc. Their news focuses mainly on the English-speaking world.

They generally do not consider themselves "*Europeans*". Europe is the continent. And the continent stops at Calais.

4.19 USA: The United States of America

4.19.1 Culturally influential Elements

4.19.1.1 The Spirit of American Pioneer

Our fundamental idea about the USA is the pioneering spirit that runs like a thread throughout its history to the present day.

1. The early colonization of the East Coast occurred in the mid-sixteenth century, first by the Spaniards, who took away the best land from the indigenous people. As a consequence, they were driven out or killed and could only settle afterwards in southern Florida.
2. The next settlers were English. They arrived in Chesapeake Bay[83] at the beginning of the seventeenth century. Their passage and activities were paid for by English investors who were looking for profits from the tobacco boom and other farmed produce. The settlers committed themselves to staying for four to 7 years and in return received 50 acres of land if they survived.
3. The newcomers did not settle on the best land, but rather on the less fertile and unhealthy riverbanks, so that every year almost the entire crew of a fort died of illness due to the summer heat, icy cold or starvation in winter. These settlers did not bother the Native Americans because they believed that nature would provide a solution as all the settlers would die anyhow. The English investors

[83] National Geographic Magazine (2007): map in issue May 2007.

continued sending a constant stream of new settlers to replace those who had died. By the time the native populations realized this, it was already too late; the settlers had become firmly anchored and banished the natives.

4. Other European settlers, mainly from the Netherlands and Sweden, followed. Pioneering history shaped the United States until the second half of the nineteenth century; 250,000 to 650,000 settlers moved westward to Oregon, California, Utah, Colorado, and Montana in wagon trains in the 25 years between 1841 and 1866. In the twentieth century there were still eyewitnesses who were part of these trains. Even today, there are family members of the first or second generation. who have heard of these difficult times, the dangers and challenges of crossing the plains and the Rocky Mountains with the Wagon Trains.
5. This experience as pioneers has had a strong influence on American culture and way of life to this day.
6. For instance, the pragmatic fast decisions in business or simplistic black and white views of an economic or political situation are shaped by the pioneering experience. A look back at the pioneering era shows the pattern for such behavior: if a settler had staked his claim to land during the rush westward and tried in vain to grow grain, he had to decide quickly for the survival of his family whether to switch to livestock or simply move on and look for a better piece of land. Hunger was a constant threat and led to the overstocking and overconsumption of food now common in the US.
7. The conviction of living in the best country in the world –"*God's own country*".
8. The belief in the inexhaustible bounty of the country and its nature, where each and every person can build and safeguard his existence.
9. The vastness, the limitless freedom where everyone can safeguard his place and defend his belongings by carrying firearms. The country of the "*good old boys*". One of the authors had an apartment in Florida, where most of the neighbors were from the Midwest. When one spoke about his home town, he said that the neighborhood had changed so much for the worse that he sat on the porch, armed with a rifle when his wife took the dog for a walk. Quote: "*I always sit on the porch with my gun when my wife walks the dog in the evening*".[84]
10. This also applies to possessions. An American saying is "*If you have it, you own it*" meaning if you have something, it belongs to you. The sheriff was and is the law. Laws were previously made by lawyers who left enough room for interpretation. American court judgments with their very high claims for damages are legendary.
11. Competition and belief that anyone in life can achieve anything they want, and that state intervention is presumptuous and a waste. The intense and bitter dispute between Republicans and Democrats on health, "*Obamacare*" , is a good example[85]

[84]https://www.gunstocarry.com/gun-laws-state/. Last viewed Sept. 17, 2108.

[85]https://en.wikipedia.org/wiki/Health_care_in_the_United_States. Last viewed Sept. 17, 2018.

12. The USA is the land of political extremes: From neo-conservatives like G W. Bush or the Tea Party to decidedly left-leaning Mike Moore, from Obama to Trump. From the DINKS generation (double income no kids) to the Pennsylvania Dutch, the Amish People or the Anabaptists. The latter were expelled from the German Palatinate and from the Swiss Emmental at the beginning of the nineteenth century, first settled in Alsace to later find a new home in the USA. Today they still speak their German dialect and live in large family communities with the model of conservative Christian ethics and morality, largely without the goods of modern American civilization, such as cars or tractors.
13. With industrialization, the US was the first country in the world to develop a broad middle class whose high disposable income and consumerism formed the basis of the successful American economy even before World War II. Western Europe did not complete this development until the 1960s and 1970s.
14. American lifestyle is an expression of class and at the same time loyalty to American ideals. The simplest expression of this is clothing in business life, but also on social occasions. Especially on the East Coast, the classic dark suit with a plain shirt and tie is required in formal business situations.
15. Part of that lifestyle is that members of the middle-class live in the same area, own the same home and car, and meet in the same country club for golf or social events.
16. An American's political outlook will be apparent fairly quickly, and he will also voice his opinion on politics and social issues. These are therefore taboo issues in the contact between foreigners and Americans, who generally do not tolerate the critical debate that Germans sometimes love. The majority of Americans belong to one of the two major parties, whose members are convinced of the correctness of their party's politics, as well as the belief that the other party is driving the US to ruin. This also includes the saying that became known worldwide by George W. Bush: "*He who is not with us, is against us!*" (From the Book of Matthew in the Bible)

The following cultural riddle illustrates this:

Background

The scene took place at noon in a restaurant in the Florida Keys, the senior citizens' oasis in the United States. A white-haired woman using a walker enters a restaurant. An old man on crutches comes toward her. He looks at her and says a few words to her that make her laugh!

What could this gentleman have said?

Solution

This is an example used in the introduction to seminars on the USA. It demonstrates a key value in US American culture as opposed to European cultures. European responses might have expressed sympathy, regret or offers of help.

What the American actually said was: "*Shall we have a race?*".

With that, he touched on a central value in his culture, the winner mentality and competitiveness that has always been part of his life.

4.19.1.2 The American Dream

America sees itself as the cradle of the Enlightenment and democracy. It has over 200 years of a successful history in developing the individual as the pillar of a modern society in which everyone can find fulfillment and happiness through his own efforts.

The first amendment in the US Constitution states that "*all men are created equal*". Striving for and believing in equality is the thread running through American history.

1. Slavery was abolished in the nineteenth century
2. Racial segregation was lifted in the South in the mid-twentieth century
3. The Civil Rights Act of 1964[86] outlawed discrimination based on race, color, religion, sex, or national origin. It bans unequal application of voter registration requirements, racial segregation in schools, employment, and public accommodation.
4. Efforts to install equal opportunities for employment and acts against hate crimes[87]
5. In 2008 and 2012 America chose Obama as the first president of African-American descent, whose father was Kenyan. Previously, two foreign ministers, Colin Powell and Condoleezza Rice in George W. Bushs neoconservative government were the first African Americans in this second-highest US office of Secretary of State. Colin Powell is the son of immigrants from Jamaica and Condoleezza Rice was born in Birmingham, Alabama as a child of African-American parents. Her grandparents were still cotton pickers.

Nevertheless, like everywhere else in the world, there is still racism. The number of lawsuits in American courts for race-related violations are countless. One example: African Americans started a lawsuit based on the Civil Rights Act against the Coca-Cola Management in Atlanta in April 1999 because the company's share of African American employees and their pay were below average. The verdict came in November 2000. In addition to high fines of about 200 million US dollars, the damage to Coca-Cola's image among African Americans was considerable, since they represent an important share of their consumers. Today, the Coca-Cola Company is an Equal Opportunities Employer, committed to diversity and announcing it in every publication.

[86]https://en.wikipedia.org/wiki/Civil_Rights_Act_of_1964. Last viewed Sept. 17, 2018.

[87]https://en.wikipedia.org/wiki/Hate_crime#United_States. Last viewed Sept 17, 2018.

Nowadays, the USA is no longer seen as a melting pot of cultures, as was originally envisioned, but is now known as a salad bowl. People from different cultures live together side by side in this salad bowl. Some are closed, self-contained societies such as neighborhoods in New York's Little Italy or San Francisco's China Town, or the Amish settlements in Pennsylvania.

Political correctness is very pronounced in the US. It demands the correct terminology for the coexisting cultures both officially and colloquially:

1. Native Americans = Native (Indian) Americans
2. African-Americans = Americans of African descent
3. Caucasians = Americans of European descent
4. Asian-Americans = Americans of Asian descent
5. Hispanics = Americans with Spanish and Latin American roots

Due to the mobility of US Americans and the fact that the US is still an immigration country, the demographics are constantly changing. An extreme example is the South:

1. Florida, where Hispanics now make up a fifth of the population, has increasingly bilingual street signs. Everything was written in English until the 1990s.
2. According to the 2010 census, 50.5 million US residents are Hispanics.[88] In the last 10 years, this part of the population grew four times faster than any other population group.

The central symbol of American values is the American flag—the "*Star Spangled Banner*", *the* "*Stars and Stripes*".

The credo is that anyone can become American if he or she identifies with the ideals of the country and the constitution.

The pioneering spirit also shapes the style of day-to-day communication up to the present day. The curiosity of a US-American who welcomes a stranger with a "*Hello, where are you from?*" is the impulse to classify someone immediately and determine through dialogue and empathy whether he is a friend or an enemy.

It is for a good reason that modern communication research has its origins in the USA. Mention should be made here of the psychologist, Marshall B. Rosenberg, whose work on nonviolent communication (NVC) significantly influenced interpersonal communication internationally.[89]

Critical aspects or criticism are packaged so as not to be hurtful. The pioneering times demanded that one get along with everyone, because mutual help could save lives.

[88] https://en.wikipedia.org/wiki/Spanish_language_in_the_United_. Last viewed Sept 17, 2018.

[89] https://en.wikipedia.org/wiki/Marshall_Rosenberg. Last viewed Sept. 17, 2018.

Packaging a message

One of the authors witnessed an impressive example when ocean-fishing in Florida. The skipper put a very expensive fishing rod with an equally expensive reel in his hands, looked at him and said succinctly:

"*Peter, if you drop it, you own it!*"

The message was understood, because it meant that in case of loss, the fishing rod had to be paid for, but it was said in a way that did not hurt.

In German and German-speaking cultures, the guide would probably have said, "*This rod is very expensive. If you drop it, you will have to pay for it*".

An example of the conversational tone in politics is an excerpt from the hearing on the role of then Defense Secretary Donald Rumsfeld in the Iraq war and the demand for his resignation in 2005.[90] The head of this commission, Ted Kennedy, summarizes the message with a baseball metaphor: "*In baseball it's three strikes and you are out*". As you may see from the You Tube excerpt Donald Rumsfeld was visibly shocked despite the well packed metaphor.

Communication between adults and children in the US is also characterized by the pioneering era. Children are treated as adults. In social settings, for example in conversations with the family, children are always included.

Conflicts are usually resolved in private conversations—there is no exposure in public. When this happens, the dispute has already escalated.

To avoid conflicts, communication is set to the recipient. The central motto is from one of the author's American directors. He used to say: "*Communication is with the receiver*" meaning you may talk as long as you want, but if it is not understood, it is your problem. And you had better adjust your communication until the person's response indicates that the message has been understood.

Alongside courtesy there is also an urge for sincerity. An American who suspects a falsehood will usually keep inquiring until the truth is out. World-famous examples from politics are Richard Nixon with the Watergate scandal or Bill Clinton and the Lewinsky affair.

Politicians and businesspeople in Switzerland experienced this with the "*Holocaust Fund*", which were the unclaimed assets of Jewish victims in Swiss banks. When the first suspicions emerged and the pressure from the US began, a high-ranking Swiss banker described the amount of "*Holocaust money*" involved as "*peanuts*". He should have held his tongue. This statement cost Switzerland $1.25 billion in 1998. If the Swiss and the Swiss authorities had instead admitted to having money in their banks and apologized, the penalties may not have been so severe and, above all, the image loss to Swiss banks among the American public could have been contained.

A less known story in Europe is the scandal over Martha Stewart. Born in 1941 as a child of Polish immigrants, she had a successful television career as a presenter of

[90] https://www.youtube.com/watch?v=PX2KJkIR7s0. Last viewed on Sept. 17, 2018.

cooking shows, programs on house and garden, and as editor-in-chief of her own magazines in the 1990s. Her name was a brand, a symbol of good housekeeping and used on many products of the K-Mart department store chain. In the late 1990s, she had made a fortune of several hundred million dollars. As a former stockbroker, she continued to speculate on the stock market, including the pharmaceutical company ImClone Systems, which wanted to launch a new drug that was later rejected by the FDA (Federal Drug Administration). The highly traded share price plummeted. Martha Stewart cashed out her stake in time and was charged with insider trading. She initially denied having got inside information but was accused by a secretary to the investment broker and convicted. The sentence was 5 months' imprisonment, 5 months' house arrest, a $30,000 fine and a 2-year ban—all this for a small profit or loss of a few hundred thousand US dollars compared to her net worth. Martha Stewart is back in business today and is still wealthy by US standards. However, the damage to her public reputation and the ridicule on late night shows has remained for quite some time.

4.19.2 Social Togetherness

Social interaction is common in the private and business sector. This includes showing interest in social life. A European CEO who does not meet and care for his or her employees on a social level is likely to be negatively judged by a US company's management for lack of social skills and can affect his or her career.

4.19.3 Belonging to the Right Social Class

Growing up in the right neighborhood and attending the right universities will open society's doors. As an adult, one joins a local country club—a mix of social venue and sports facility which includes tennis, golf, gym, pool etc. It also includes an upscale restaurant with dedicated halls for various occasions. In a big city like New York, for example, it is advisable to join one of the well-known sports clubs and a Chamber of Commerce or an association representing one's own professional group. It is customary to host dinner parties or cocktail parties for neighbors, friends, customers and employees at home.

The '*old boys*' *network* of friends, acquaintances, business personalities—a network of relationships often forms the basis for social and business success.

4.19.4 Small Talk

In German-speaking countries, we sometimes find small talk difficult because we often find it superficial and even dishonest. However, in the US and other Anglo-Saxon cultures, it is the lubricant for social coexistence. It is advisable to get involved immediately in a social event, e.g. a party, and to mix with those present, listen, or start a conversation with anyone using common interests. Engaging in such a way not only displays self-confidence, but also interest in people and a commitment to society.

4.19.5 Cooperation in Business and Professional Life

Some of the pragmatism and short-term business strategies stem from the pioneering days. To make a profit in the here and now is more desirable than to think long and hard about a future strategy. Business concepts are simple; an idea has to sound convincing and be reasonably explained in just a few sentences. The advice of a successful America businessman for presenting a business idea: If it is complex, ask yourself how you would simplify it for a friend in a few words and a maximum of two sentences. One of the authors who spent 20 years with American companies was always amazed by how his American superiors, colleagues, and customers could condense complex business situations to provide clarity for decision-making.

The US American focus on the customer and on service clearly sets it apart from many other business cultures. For example, a shopkeeper will say "*Thank you for passing by*" to a customer who leaves without a purchase or "*Thank you for giving us your business*" if something has been bought.

In his exciting bestseller "*Closing*", one of the best-ever training manuals for salespeople, James W. Pickens[91] sums up the essence of US service-orientation with the motto "*Sum Tertius*"—Latin for "*I'm third*", i.e.

1. God is first
2. My fellow man (client) is second
3. I am third

US American values include the belief that anyone can "*make it*". Those who make it then become role models, heroes. Some notable examples are John D. Rockefeller, Michael Dell, Bill Gates, or Steve Jobs, all of whom represent the American dream—from the mail office boy to the millionaire.

4.19.6 Meeting with US Americans

There are no consensus meetings like in Germany. As a rule, the most important points are discussed informally in advance. Regardless of whether it is about information or the exchange of detailed arrangements, meetings are conducted by the boss or the person responsible on the basis of an agenda and with a fixed time for the beginning and the end. This procedure ensures that everyone is involved, and at

---

[91] Pickens, James W. (1991): CLOSING – Erfolgsstrategien für offensive Verkäufer, 1. Ausgabe, Wiesbaden.

the end, the result is briefly summarized. Responsibilities and timing are laid down in an action plan.

4.19.7 USA: The Cradle of Modern Marketing and Advertising

Marketing, i.e. extolling the virtues of a product, and advertising have a long history dating back to antiquity. What we call marketing and advertising today originated in the USA and spread worldwide after WWII. The author worked for over 20 years for US advertising agencies with international blue- chip accounts.

As marketing and advertising were in their infancy in the 1960s, it was an American on-the-job-learning style. Over the years, as both sectors became more complex, divisions for Marketing and Advertising were created worldwide and both were fragmented into further subdivisions, mainly due to digitalization and economic constraints.

It is interesting to note that every culture has taken the US principles in these fields and adapted them culturally.

A simple comparison of marketing theory and its practical application in the USA and Germany is demonstrated by the illustration below (Fig. 4.7):

Pragmatism primes the US approach, perfectionism the German one. As described above and in Sect. 4.10.1.1 "German characteristics" cultural characteristics are the guidelines on which business practices are based, even in the global world of today. To the best of the author's knowledge, this hold good for virtually every culture in the world.

4.19.7.1 The Presentation

A preacher was once asked why his sermons were so successful in his parish. He answered: "*Because first I tell them what I am going to tell them, then I tell them, and then I tell them what I told them*".

The criteria for a successful presentation for American business partners are:

1. <u>Introduction:</u>
   Attract attention by outlining the content of the presentation and positioning the subject as well as possible. Right at the beginning, the speaker will usually try to engage the audience with a personal remark picked up from the preceding talks or the small talk before the presentation.
2. <u>The main message</u>
   will focus primarily on the idea, on its uniqueness and its potential. German presentations are often provided with a lot of background information and technical or strategic considerations. This may bore the US audience, ruin a good idea, and encourage participants in their prejudice that Europeans give lectures.
3. <u>Conclusion:</u>
   Summarize why the idea will succeed.

Marketing in USA and Germany

Cultural Influences in Marketing Practice and Teachings

USA Prof. Philip Kotler	Deutschland Prof. Heribert Meffert Prof. Klaus Backhaus
Goal	
Profit	Perfection
Approach	
Pragmatic ideas and concepts	Structured and well thought through strategies and processes
Time to market	Avoid failures
Result	
Shorter planning cycles	Longer planning cycles
Draft planning with major milestones	Detail planning with many milestones
Informal contacts and meetings	Formal meetings
Errors corrected on the spot	Several meetings to correct errors
Effect on the Teachings in Marketing	
One learning method for both consumer goods and investment goods	Separate learning methods: for consumer goods: Prof. Heribert Meffert for investment goods: Prof. Klaus Backhaus

Fig. 4.7 Marketing in the US and Germany

Americans prefer short presentations of 20–30 min with few charts and a minimum of figures.

4.19.7.2 Negotiations

Americans are among the most skilled negotiators in the Western world; it's a tough, but fair competition. But once the conclusion has been reached, then it is also valid. The motto: A deal is a deal.

Harvard University explored the foundations for successful international negotiating in business and governmental and non-governmental organizations (GOs and NGOs) back in the 1970s. In recent years, this classic has been reissued in English.

The graph below briefly summarizes the Harvard principles (Fig. 4.8):

The pragmatic standards for assessing and entering into a business partnership from the US point of view are:

1. What's in it for me?
2. Why should I do business with him or her?

Negotiations based on the Harvard Principles

Deal with factual issues and people separately	
o	Do not draw conclusions based on your own apprehensions as to the intentions of the other party involved
o	Do not attribute problems to the other party
o	Explain your ideas in detail
o	Get to know the other value-system and respect it
o	Save face ⇒ for everybody!
o	Identify emotions and search for their origins
o	Articulate your emotions + and show understanding for the others
o	Listen attentively + and give feedback
o	Avoid unclear wording – speak simply and clearly
o	Think first ⇒ then talk
o	Get feedback on the understanding of the adverse party
o	Build an active relationship ⇒ relax
o	Go after the facts – not after the people

Concentrate on interests not on positions	
o	Avoid too much pressure – find a balance between both interests
o	Find out about the interests behind positions + try to harmonize both interests and positions
o	Lay the groundwork for the future

Develop alternatives	
o	Do not get nervous, if an agreement cannot be reached quickly
o	Solutions are never the result of a linear negotiation-process
o	Develop as many alternative solutions as possible
o	Take your time – plan intermediate steps
o	Figure out your solutions in detail

Fig. 4.8 Harvard Principles for negotiating

4.19.8 It's a Great Country!

The US is a beautiful and diverse country that captivates people. At the same time, the US is going through the hardest period since its founding over 200 years ago. The previously unlimited natural resources need to be conserved if they are not to dry up. As a world power, the US and the Western world will have to redefine their roles.

As Kishore Mahbubani says in the final paragraph of his book, "The New Asian Hemisphere":

"At the beginning of the twenty-first century, as we enter into one of the most intense periods of change experienced by humanity, America is abandoning its pragmatist streak when it needs it most. We are moving into very uncertain political and economic terrains. It would be foolish to assume that the Western ideological assumptions of the nineteenth and twentieth century will necessarily work in the new century. It would be wiser to keep an open mind and to challenge every ideological assumption embedded in our minds. Pragmatism is the best guiding spirit we can have as we venture into the new century."

Summary and Outlook

This chapter shows you how to find an entry into other cultures. You will see, that there is no standard approach, because each culture has its unique social structures developed over centuries with its own, specifique values and rituals. Its historical experience and social interaction is distinctly different from each other. They are all unique and comparing can only lead to an impasse.

Through the previous four chapters, we wanted to give you ideas on how to stimulate your own creativity and thus be able to rediscover, implement and share your own experiences in another culture for yourself or with others for an open and free access at par to alien worlds.

Bibliography

General Intercultural Literature[92]

Axtell, R. E. (2007). *Essential do's and taboos: The complete guide to international business and leisure travel*. Hoboken: Wiley.

Cavalli-Sforza, L. L. (2001). *Genes, people and languages*. London: Penguin Books.

Fisher, R., & Ury, W. (2012). *Getting to yes: Negotiating an agreement without giving in*. London: Random House.

Hofstede, G., & Hofstede, G. J. (2010). *Cultures and organizations—Software of the mind: Intercultural cooperation and its importance for survival* (3rd rev. ed.). London: McGraw-Hill Education.

Hofstede, G., Hofstede, G. J., & Minkov, M. (2010). *Cultures and organizations: Software of the mind*. New York: McGraw-Hill.

Lewis, R. D. (2005). *When cultures collide: Managing successfully across cultures* (rev. ed.). Boston: Nicholas Brealey Publishing.

[92]The books listed in Bibliography, both in English and German, are sources of information on general cultural issues, specific countries, and tips for *savoir-faire* and the codes of conduct in social behavior in some cultures.

Mole, J. (2003). *Mind your manners: Managing business cultures in the new global Europe: Managing business culture in a global Europe* (3rd ed.). London: Nicholas Brealey International.

Thomas, A., Kinast, E.-U., & Schroll-Machl, S. (2010). *Handbook of intercultural communication and cooperation: Basics and areas of application*. Göttingen: Vandenhoek & Ruprecht.

Urech, E. (2004). *Speaking globally: Effective presentations across international and cultural boundaries* (completely rev. ed.). Rollinsford: Book Network International.

Africa, Middle East and Arab Countries

Foster, D. (2002). *The global etiquette guide to Africa and the Middle East: Everything you need to know for business and travel success*. New York: Wiley Global Etiquette Guides.

Gorges, M. (2008). *Geschäftserfolg im Iran* (1. Aufl.). Zürich: Orell Füssli.

Hackensberger, A. (2008). *Lexikon der Islamirrtümer* (1. Aufl.). Frankfurt a.M.

Hecht-Minshawi, B. (2008). *Business Know-how Golfstaaten: So wird Ihre Geschäftsreise zum Erfolg Kindle Edition* (1. Aufl.). REDLINE Verlag.

Nydell, M. K. (2012). *Understanding Arabs, A guide for modern times*. New York: Intercultural Press.

Richmond, Y., & Gestrin, P. (2010). *Into Africa: A guide to Sub-Saharan culture and diversity* (2nd ed.). Yale Richmond.

Brazil

Ragsdale, A. (2015). *Crossing the river: A life in Brazil*. Boston, MA: Intercultural Press.

Canada

Chesters, G. (2007). *Culture wise Canada: The essential guide to culture, customs & business etiquette*. London: Survival Books.

China

Fang, T. (1998). *Chinese business negotiation style*. International Business Series. Thousand Oaks, CA: Sage.

Granet, M. (2013). *Chinese civilization (The history of civilization)*. London: Routledge.

Jullien, F., & Lloyd, J. (2004). *Treatise on efficacy: Between Western and Chinese thinking*. Honolulu: University of Hawaii Press.

Lin-Huber, M. A. (2006). *Chinesen verstehen lernen* (2. aktualisierte Aufl.). Berne: Hogrefe AG.

Seitz, K. (2000). *China – eine Weltmacht kehrt zurück* (aktualisierte und erweiterte Auflage 2000). Berlin: Siedler.

Seitz, K. (2002). *CHINA – eine Weltmacht kehrt zurück*. Berlin: Berliner Taschenbuch Verlag.

Finland

Lewis, R. (2011). *Finland, cultural lone wolf* (Kindle edition). Intercultural Press.

France

Asselin, G., & Mastron, R. (2010). *Au Contraire!: Figuring Out the French* (Kindle edition) (2nd ed.). Boston: Intercultural Press.
Breuer, N. J. (2002). *Geschäftserfolg in Frankreich* (1. Aufl.). Bonn: Galileo Press.
Knorr, R. (2018). *The grown-up's guide to living in France* (3rd ed.). Ten Speed Press: Berkeley, CA.
PS: There are quite a few books entitled "Living in France". Make you pick!

Germany

Flippo, H. (2018). *When in Germany, do as the Germans do* (2nd ed.). New York: McGraw-Hill Book.

Great Britain

McAlpine, F. (2015). *Stuff Brits like: A guide to what's great about Great Britain*. London: Nicholas Brealey Publishing.

India

Bijapurkar, R. (2007). *We are like that only*. New Delhi: Penguin Group India.
Dalrymple, W. (1998). *The age of Kali*. London: HarperCollins Publishers.
Dehejia, V., & Subramanya, R. (2012). *Indianomix: Making sense of modern India*. Vintage Books.
Doniger, W. (2010). *The Hindus: An alternative history*. New York: Penguin Books.
Gandhi, M. K. (1925, 2008). *The story of my experiments with the truth*. Jaico Publishing House.
Guha, R. (2008). *India after Gandhi*. Pan Macmillan India.
Khilnani, S. (2016). *Incarnations: A history of India in fifty lives*. Farrar, Straus & Giroux.
Knappert, J. (1995). *Indian mythology*. London: Diamond Books.
Kolanad, G. (1994, 2005). *CultureShock! India*. Singapore: Marshall Cavendish.
Langworth, R. M. (2008). *Churchill in his own words*. London: Ebury Publishing.
Nair-Venugopal, S. (Ed.). (2012). *The gaze of the West and framings of the East*. New York: Palgrave Macmillan.
Rao, A. (2004). *Soteriologies of India and their role in the perception of disability*. Muenster: LIT Verlag.
Ramakrishna Rao, K., & Paranjpe, A. C. (2016). *Psychology in the Indian tradition*. New Delhi: Springer.
Roy, A. (2003). *The god of small things*. New Delhi: Penguin Books.
Sen, A. (2005). *The argumentative Indian*. London: Allen Lane.
Sinha, J. B. P. (1990). *Work culture in the Indian context*. New Delhi: Sage.
Sinha, J. B. P. (2014). *Psycho-social analysis of the Indian mindset*. New Delhi: Springer.
Tharoor, S. (1998). *From midnight to the millennium and beyond*. New York: HarperCollins.

Tharoor, S. (2016). *An era of darkness*. New Delhi: Aleph Book Company.
Theroux, P. (2011). *The Elephanta Suite*. London: Penguin Books.
Varma, P. K. (2005). *Being Indian: Inside the real India*. New Delhi: Penguin Books.

Israel

Shahar, L., & Kurz, D. (1995). *Border crossings: American interactions with Israelis*. Yarmouth: Intercultural Press.

Italy

Barzini, L. (1991). *The Italians* (New edition). London: Penguin.
Barzini, L. (1996). *The Italians*. New York: Touchstone.
PS: Barzini has written quite a few other books on cultural issues.

Japan

De Mente, L. B. (2012). *JAPAN: Understanding & dealing with the New Japanese way of doing business*. Seattle: CreateSpace Independent Publishing Platform.
Goshn, C., & Riès, P. (2006). *SHIFT: Inside Nissan's historic revival*. New York: Crown Business.
Hall, E. T., & Reed, M. (1990). *Hidden differences: Doing business with the Japanese* (Reprint). New York: Anchor.
Japan External Trade Organization. *Communicating with Japanese in business*. www.JETRO.go.jp

Korea

Kohls, L. (2001). *Robert, learning to think Korean: A guide to living and working in Korea* (Kindle Edition). Yarmouth: Intercultural Press.

Latin America and Mexico

Condon, J. C. (1997). *Good neighbours – Communicating with Mexicans* (2nd ed.). Yarmouth: Intercultural Press.
Sabath, A. M. (1999). *International Business Etiquette, Latin America: What You Need to Know to Conduct Business Abroad With Charm and Savvy*. Yarmouth: Intercultural Press.

Central Europe

Mochtarova, M. (2003). *Erfolgreiche Geschäfte im östlichen Mitteleuropa*. Hamburg: Springer.
Richmond, Y. (2000). *From da to yes – Understanding the East European*. Boston: Intercultural Press.

Netherlands

Vossestein, J. (2010). *Dealing with the Dutch: The cultural context of business & work in the Netherlands* (19th ed.). Amsterdam: KIT Publishers.

Russia

Yale, R. (2008). *From Nyet to Da, understanding the Russians* (4th ed.). Boston: Intercultural Press.

Sweden

Robinowitz, C. J. J., & Carr, L. W. (2011). *Modern-day Vikings—A practical guide to interacting with Swedes*. Boston: Intercultural Press.

Spain

Wattley-Ames, H. (1999). *Spain is different* (Kindle edition) (2nd ed.). Yarmouth: Intercultural Press.

Switzerland

Sitzler, S. (2013). *Grüezi und Willkommen – die Schweiz für Deutsche* (6th ed.). Berlin: Links Verlag.

South East Asia

Devin, E., & Braganti, N. L. (1988). *The travellers guide to Asian customs & manners*. New York: Meadowbrook.

USA

Althen, G., & Bennett, J. (2011). *American ways: A, cultural guide to the United States of America* (Kindle Edition) (3rd ed.). Boston: Intercultural Press.
Bennett, M. J. (2005). *American cultural patterns: a cross-cultural perspective*. Boston: Intercultural Press.
Gunduz, A. et alias. *Doing business in the United States—A handbook for Swiss business women*. see www.OSEC.ch
Pickens, J. W. (2003). *The art of closing any deal: How to be a master closer in everything you do* (Revised and updated). Business Plus.
Schmidt, P. L. (2007). *Understanding American and German business cultures*. Montreal: Meridian World Press.

Bridging Cultures in Everyday Life

5

Summary

In this chapter, we explain how you can transfer your intercultural learnings all by yourself into practice right away. With simple, yet effective methods you will be able to find an entry into an alien culture without much experience. Just follow our step-by-step approach based on our experience from numerous seminars and coaching in over 25 years.

The central point is to (re-)capture, recognize and develop your own image of a foreign culture. If you create a constructive image of that alien world and if you feel confident with it, you will have a solid and practical platform to build a trustful relationship over time, maybe even for life.

5.1 An Introduction: Historical Overview of Intercultural Education and Training

To the present day, the topic of interculturality in continuing education is treated like a stepchild—nice to have—but purely factual subjects always take precedence over softer topics.

The first concepts in intercultural training originated shortly before the WW II in the USA, primarily for US government organizations. Intercultural training courses in the US developed after the war in the 1950s and 1960s as American companies started to expand in Europe, Latin America, Japan, and Southeast Asia. In this

P. M. Haller et al., *Bridging Cultural Barriers*, Management for Professionals,
https://doi.org/10.1007/978-3-030-17130-8_5

context, the number of providers rose sharply—mostly coaches trained on the job who afterwards became facilitators.[1]

At that time, leaders in the USA became aware that language and culture skills were crucial to their image and their acceptance abroad. The consequences due to the lack of intercultural education are illustrated in the 1958 bestselling book "*The Ugly American*",[2] which is set in an imaginary land, but by which Vietnam is meant. One part of the book narrates a story in which an American diplomat holds a speech when handing over tractors gifted from USA to the farmers. The Vietnamese interpreter translates this as "*a gift from the great Russian brother*". "*The Ugly American*" became the epitome of the naivety of Americans in dealing with other cultures.

In Europe, intercultural communication and training did not develop until the late 1980s. In Germany, many universities and colleges in former East Germany were looking for attractive new courses after German reunification. Intercultural Communication and Management degree programs became wide-spread in Eastern Germany.

From the mid-nineties, with the increasing importance of the global economy, the field of intercultural training began to expand rapidly. At universities, the topic of intercultural management and communication became a core issue, and today there is almost no bachelor's or master's degree program that does not offer this study as a major or a minor.

At the start of intercultural training in the USA, it was, above all, individual trainers with practical experience who passed on their intercultural knowledge. As more and more universities got involved, the subject became more academic with numerous methods and concepts to teach this new discipline. As academic teaching at universities developed, a conflict between theory and practice arose.

In our view, both orientations complement each other and benefit from each other.

5.1.1 Intercultural Teaching Today

With the increasing economic networking in the world, the doctrine has moved away from national cultures. The subject has evolved from a macro view to diversity. Not only intercultural differences, but also gender roles are discussed. From the point of view of the companies and the authors' experience, the diversity of cultures is not perceived as a hindrance, but on the contrary is seen as a challenge that, if properly managed and nurtured, represents added value and a competitive advantage. Diversity today also includes the themes of gender roles, integration, equal opportunity and the social diversity of existing human capital in a company. Every major company today has a manager for diversity management.

[1]See Landis et al. (2004).

[2]See Leaderer and Burdick (1958).

5.2 Our Image of Man

From our personal experience in hundreds of intercultural trainings, intercultural encounters, and numerous international business trips and projects, we have developed an affective learning method that has given hundreds of participants of all levels from the industry and universities as well as the public sector an unbiased and open access to alien cultures and helped to build relationships. The key is the way to look at the world:

1. We assume that people with different origins communicate with differing maxims of thought and action but want to interact peacefully and constructively with each other.
2. The first impression always counts—at home, in India, in Australia ... all over the world. Everyone carries his or her view of the world with him or her: It is often recognizable, can open doors, build barriers or even close doors. This also means that people often can be associated with a specific culture by others, even before a single word has been spoken.
3. An open and positive world view opens the door to quick thinking, to intuition, helps to deal with difficult situations, avoids frustration, prejudices and the cliché trap.
4. An open world view leads to solutions and ways out of a dead end. An individual does not have to pretend to play a role, but he can be himself or herself and preserve naturalness and spontaneity.

We have been using this intuition and emotion-based principle for over 30 years in more than thousand trainings and workshops with professionals and executives, business teams, bachelor's and master's classes from a variety of universities.

In the following, we first explain our principles for further education according to our experience and how each person or even a group can transfer the learnings with a simple procedure.

▶ Just as you see and experience yourself in your own culture, you will also be seen and experienced by all other cultures.

5.3 Our Approach to Continuing Education and Coaching

We aim to bring together differing cultural perspectives and forms of communication from diverse cultural backgrounds to build a common, mutual understanding resulting in an improved cooperation between cultures and achieving higher levels of personal satisfaction and a sense of achievement.

This manual is directed in the broadest sense at interculturally interested and internationally active people from all cultures. It takes nothing for granted, because we know that every situation will always be new and different. To prepare for this in a positive way you need to have the courage to flexibly confront the unknown of an alien world combined with a total openness to your own world and culture.

5.4 A Self-learning Method

5.4.1 A Comprehensive Openness to Yourself

Whatever your intercultural knowledge and experience, openness, tolerance and respect for the alien culture are absolutely essential. This is a unique opportunity to share and process own intercultural experiences for fulfilling cross cultural encounters.

It is not the quantity and quality of intercultural experiences that is significant, but the ability to process cultural experiences and thereby gain access to people from other cultures, both those who were totally unknown to you before and those you did not understand or misunderstand in prior encounters. It is a never-ending lifelong learning process.

The key to intercultural communication relies on attentive and constructive observation of people from alien culture; how they speak, think and act. How they behave, alone or in their social environment.

Based on these observations, you will attempt to relate them to your own living conditions and culture. Based on your analysis and thoughts, as well as with the help of this book, you can seek to find a way to open doors to other cultures.

► The core of the character of a human being is his credibility and his authenticity. What he or she says must be consistent with his or her actions. Recognizing this is not always easy when dealing with other cultures, and often even difficult because the communication styles may be entirely different. Crossing these barriers to find the inner core of a stranger is the real secret and success of intercultural togetherness and cooperation.

5.4.2 How to Begin: Learning About Yourself

Take your time. If you are traveling to or have a project with China, do not start this exercise the night before. Intercultural learning is a long and ongoing process that requires a great deal of research, reflection about yourself and your own culture… and time to let it sink in. You will be asked to adjust your perspective and your views on your own and the alien culture. And the best ideas usually do not come sitting in front of a white sheet of paper, but maybe on a walk, after the brain has had time to process the input.

For the first time, you should schedule at least 2 h to write down your thoughts and review what they mean for your and a foreign culture.

You can also go through this process in twos or threes. The collection of information and discussion as well as the lessons of this work will thus be enriched, and learning will be faster, deeper.

5.4.3 The First Step Is Collecting Information

Take a blank sheet of paper and divide it into two parts, each with a heading for your culture and the foreign culture (Fig. 5.1):

Then, in a classic brainstorming, write your heart out; everything that comes to mind about your culture and this foreign culture. Do not take any thinking pauses—spontaneity is important. Experience shows brainstorming takes about 10 min. Only go to the second step when nothing else occurs to you.

In the following exercise we have taken Western culture with a focus on Northern Europe, and Asia, with a focus on China. All the information it contains is assembled from seminars and not invented by the authors. The examples at hand are just to demonstrate and illustrate the process (Fig. 5.2).

The output from brainstorming creates a clear picture of the following aspects.

5.4.3.1 The Level of My Knowledge

The first part of the work demonstrates what you know about the other country and its people. If you know little or nothing about a foreign culture, you have knowledge

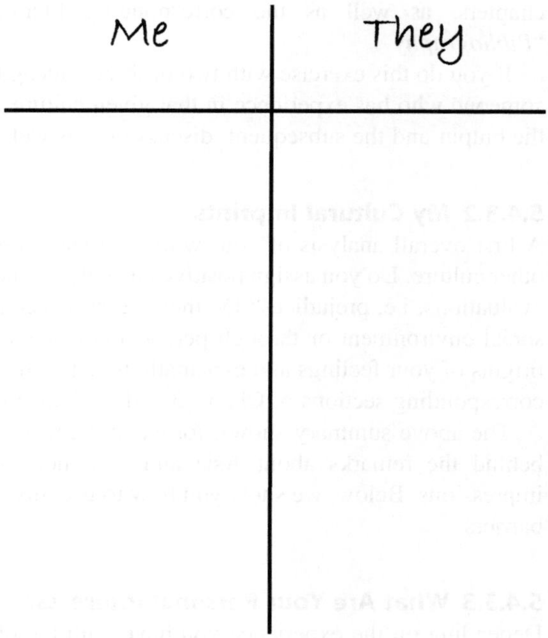

Fig. 5.1 Preparing a chart for a brainstorming

Fig. 5.2 Initial result of a spontaneous brainstorming with cultural characteristics

Me Western cultures	They Asian cultures
- Self centered	- work in teams
- direct communicators	- polite
- Safety oriented	- smiling
- Critical	- hierarchical
- methodogical thinkers	- can't say „no"
- liberal	- doers
- determined	- traditional
- sticking to decisions	- zealous
- honest	- (copycats)
- orderly	- cautions
- individualistic	- family
- ambitious	- sly
- quality is important	- curious
- planning ahead	- communiste
	- tough negotiations
	- dependent
	- decision making= black box

gaps. These can be filled with the help of this manual and the corresponding chapters, as well as the corresponding literature in our bibliography (see "*Bibliography*").

If you do this exercise with two or three colleagues or friends, perhaps even with someone who has experience in that given culture, the discussions will enrich both the output and the subsequent discussions, as well as the output.

5.4.3.2 My Cultural Imprints

A first overall analysis of your work will show how you think and feel about the other culture. Do you assign positive attributes to them or are these strongly negative evaluations, i.e. prejudices? Do these reactions come from the media? Or from the social environment or through personal contacts and experiences? Try to find the origins of your feelings and explanations as to why this may be so, in looking at the corresponding sections of Chaps. 3 and 4 of this manual.

The above summary shows, for example, that there is a lot of direct experience behind the remarks about Asia and that there are actually no strong negative impressions. Below, we show you how to use this information to overcome cultural barriers.

5.4.3.3 What Are Your Personal Interests?

Depending on the experience you have with the other culture as a businessman, a cultural enthusiast or a tourist, the focus will change in the subsequent stages of analysis.

The above summary of various brainstorming sessions indicates a high level of knowledge with a focus on business life. We have therefore taken the business world as the basis for processing the information.

5.4.4 The Second Step: Defining Key Cultural Features and Differences

What are the most salient features of the two cultures? Underline 3–4 characteristics that initially come to mind (Fig. 5.3).

5.4.5 The Third Step: Defining Potential Conflicts

When you have taken this step, try to be clear about the potential conflicts that may arise in the relationship between the two cultures or could create a barrier. Label the conflicting terms with a red flash (⚡) (Fig. 5.4):

This process makes you aware of the stumbling blocks that may arise in dealing with people and situations in a given foreign culture.

Fig. 5.3 Key criteria are underlined

Me Western cultures	They Asian cultures
- Self centered	- work in teams
- direct communicators	- polite
- Safety oriented	- smiling
- Critical	- hierarchical
- methodogical thinkers	- can't say „no"
- liberal	- doers
- determined	- traditional
- sticking to decisions	- zealous
- honest	- (copycats)
- orderly	- cautions
- individualistic	- family
- ambitious	- sly
- quality is important	- curious
- planning ahead	- communiste
	- tough negotiations
	- dependent
	- decision making= black box

Fig. 5.4 Criteria with conflict potential identified by a red flash

5.4.6 Transfer to Practice Using Communication as an Example

Here you begin to think fundamentally about the barriers in your area of interest and how you could overcome them. For example, regarding communication:

Looking at the Results from a Western Angle

Assume you come from a **Western culture** and are interested in language and communication. Then "*politeness*" will be a problem in Asia because you may find the smiling and the indirect handling of your questions perturbing, even dishonest. Therefore, read the more general information in Sect. 3.5.5 "*Use of Language*" or the more specific country information, i.e. in Sect. 4.13.5 "*Communication and Conflict Resolution*". There you will find out about the differences in communicating with each other and on how adjust your style to be successful in Asian cultures (Fig. 5.5).

Interpreting the Results from an Asian Point of View

Suppose you come from an **Asian culture, China for example**, **and you are dealing with a German**. In that case, "*direct communicators*" will be a problem for you. Read here in Sect. 4.10.2.3 "*Communication and Conflict Resolution*", Germany about the contrasts in linguistic interaction with each other. You will realize that Germans directness is not a verbal attack or insolence but is meant

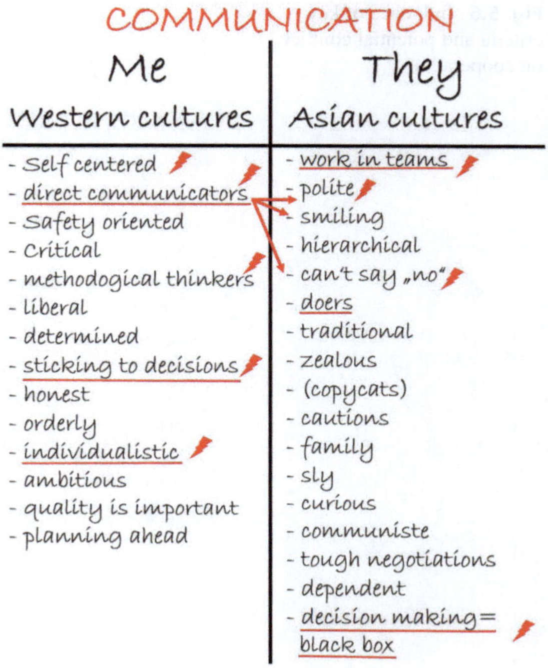

Fig. 5.5 Influence of key criteria and potential conflicts in cross-cultural communication

sincerely and may lead to a quicker understanding and agreement. So, you will be prepared and can also get into it immediately. But beware! It's a tightrope walk. German directness is factual only. If you get personal, this can be construed as an attack or insult. If you tell a German counterpart in a project meeting, "*You have not considered my original information at all*", it will quickly end in an escalation, because the German could find this to be an insult. Instead, if you say, "*I want to compare your suggestion with my guidelines*", you are still at the factual level and can have a productive conversation.

Factual discussions are customary in all Western cultures, but with many culturally adapted variations and nuances. Answers may be "*dressed up*" as a matter of courtesy. In England, if someone evaluates a project proposal as "*interesting*", it does not mean that the proposal is in principle accepted, but that it is rejected.

5.4.7 Transfer in Daily Business Using Cooperation as an Example

For the next example, we assume that you are on a business trip in a foreign culture and that professional cooperation is a central theme (Fig. 5.6):

Fig. 5.6 Influence of key criteria and potential conflicts on cooperation

What These Results May Mean for Someone with an Asian Background

If you are from an Asian culture, e.g. from **China**, the attributes "*self-centered*" and "*individualistic*" may be crucial to understanding the other side for a trustful cooperation. Because almost everything you do in business takes place in the group, you are used to all decisions being discussed and coordinated amongst the members of the team until everyone agrees. This may take more time than the Western partner is used to, or you may even exceed the deadline you had both agreed upon.

Your Western business partner may become nervous at this point because she or he does not understand the team-oriented process in China and may start using pressure to accelerate the decision process, resulting in frustrations on both sides.

You will have to explain to your Western partner how your teamwork functions, while at the same time reassuring him that you will do everything to meet his project target despite the delay—not an easy task. In the Western world an individual is used to deciding independently within the area of responsibility, and will, if necessary, impose his or her decision on the group just to make the deadline. In the individualistic Western world, time pressure on the individual weighs heavily. You will need a lot of persuasion to reassure her or him.

To overcome potential cross-cultural barriers, read Sect. 3.3 "*Worldviews*" and for China: Sect. 4.8.4 "*Cooperation in Business and Professional Life*" as well as the corresponding sectors of this book for the Western country you are working with.

What These Results May Mean for an American Project Manager

You are an **American** dealing with a Japanese colleague and are having difficulties getting feedback, particularly with regard to the deadlines in your project plan. You are getting no straight answers, which is making you nervous. You start to insist, and the tone is escalating. As time goes on, you get the impression that your Japanese partner is becoming difficult to speak to as he is adopting a distanced attitude.

You should be aware that your Japanese partner is still involved in an ongoing team process such as the one described in the example above. If you get to know Japan better, you will realize that your Japanese partners will do everything to meet deadlines and literally work day and night, regardless of contracts with the unions or laws. It is a matter of honor and loyalty to their own company and Japanese working ethics.

It will not be easy for you to deal with and accept it as it involves giving a lot of advanced credit and trust. As time goes on, you will gain confidence and be able to create a sound personal relationship!

For more information, see Sect. 4.13.7 "*Working together in Professional and Business Life*" for Japan and your country reference Sect. 4.19.5 "Cooperation in Professional and Business Life", USA, as to where the differences are, and the challenges you will face and how you should deal with them for a constructive cooperation.

The examples above are by no means a standard approach to find a successful entry into another culture or to solve a crisis in an international context. They are meant to be models to stir your own creativity to find your own way based on your knowledge and experience to better understand and respect their way to think and act, thus enabling you to build successful relations be it in France Italy, England, Russia, China or any given other culture.

5.4.8 Transfer Using the Example of Decision-Making and Leadership

A French Executive in Japan

Let's say you are a French executive who was transferred to Japan to head the local branch of your company. Decision making the Japanese will most likely be a black box for you.

You are used to making decisions which are then implemented by your employees. Now you suddenly have the feeling that your decisions are missing their mark; they are always acknowledged with "*hai*"—which you take as a "*yes*", but still, nothing is actually happening in the team. You try to follow up and intervene. Feelings of resistance crop up and you have the impression of dealing with a rubber wall. There is a danger of the situation escalating, that frustration will occur on both sides and that the working atmosphere will be affected.

Fig. 5.7 Influence of key criteria and potential conflicts in management and decision making

As amazing as this might seem, decisions are made from the bottom up in Japan. A team with the technical or marketing know-how will prepare a decision and submit it to the boss for approval. As a rule, the superior will also accept the proposal submitted and intervene only in absolute emergencies. Accepting this requires a lot of empathy and a great deal of trust in the team on your behalf. The book by Philippe Riès[3] about Carlos Ghosn as a leader in Japan offers a wealth of practical experience with case studies. For more details read Chap. 3 "**Access to other cultures—ways and possibilities**" especially Sect. 3.2 "*The Hofstede Indices*", as well as in the relevant country section of Chap. 4 "Cultures of our World" focusing on the segment "Cooperation in Work and Business".

A Japanese Executive in Germany

You are a **Japanese executive** transferred to Germany to head the branch office in Dusseldorf. For you "*individualistic*" is the decisive dimension.

In Japan, you were used to assigning a project to the team, e.g. product improvement, and then to waiting until the group leader came to you to seek approval for the unanimously approved solution of the team.

And now you are experiencing a total contrast; there are employees in your office asking you to intervene because the group is in disagreement and to make decisions about details that, in your experience, need to be solved in the group.

[3]Carlos Ghosn, Philippe Ries, John Cullen Shift, Inside Nissan's Historic Revival, Currency Doubleday, New York, 28.04.2004.

Western understanding, which is very much influenced by the USA today, is that every employee is an independent contractor, who should and must act independently in his area. Due to an insufficiently in clear delineation of the specific areas, conflicts of competence which the next higher instance must decide, arise. In many cases, the employees in Germany solve the problems among themselves, especially in work sessions, where all views are laid out and discussed.

Now in Germany, conflicts end up in your office. Let's say an employee was overruled by his direct superior, which he does not accept. Or an employee has the feeling that a colleague is interfering with his area of responsibility. In such extreme situations, you are required to make many individual, detailed decisions.

Please read Chap. 3 "*Access to Other Cultures—Ways and Means*" with focus on Sect. 3.2 "*The Hofstede Indices*", as well as the relevant country sections of Chap. 4 "*Cultures of our World*" with focus on "*Cooperation in Work and Business*".

A metaphor on leaders in the East and in the West:

In the Western world, the executive is the technical father figure; in the Asian world he is the social father figure.

The executive in the Western world is more of a technical leader, a role model for technical experience and competence. These are often the main reasons for a promotion to the next management level.

The executive in Asia is more of a social leader, a spiritual role model promoted because of his social experience and competence and recognized for these qualities by his people.

Grow into these respective roles if you want to be successful in alien cultures!

In this section we have shown the fundamental differences in dealing with each other across cultures. But every situation experienced can and will be different. Lifelong learning and mental flexibility and interest will lead you to success. Crossing cultures is a unique feeling of accomplishment.

5.5 The "Non-words"

In the experience of the authors there are two words which cropped up in many seminars:

1. . . . **are arrogant**: was contributed by participants who had either little experience with this culture and repeated a cliché they had picked up or participants suffering from or rejecting a cross cultural encounter. To the author this meant *I do not understand this culture*. Arrogance is a characteristic of an individual, but certainly not of a culture. The seminar often threw light on the matter and provided a solution to the participants who had expressed this feeling.

2. . . . **are corrupt**: (Please also refer to 3.9.4 *What is Corruption?*) Being corrupt is certainly not a characteristic of any culture in the world. It is the action of an individual or group of people or classes. Attributing corruption to a given culture is a result of undifferentiated media reporting. As a matter of fact, those pointing fingers at a country are often the bribe-givers. If you look at the map of Transparency International, it is evident that nobody is absolutely "*clean*". [4]

5.6 Intercultural Learning in a Group

The advantage of intercultural learning in a group is the social interaction amongst the members. Behavioral and attitudinal changes are addressed more clearly and thus also make the transfer more inspiring and perhaps more visible for each individual.

The transfer technique in this chapter can easily serve also for learning in small teams. It can actually be done by everyone in small groups of two to a maximum of four people.

For larger groups, it is advisable to book a preparation course[5] or to refer to relevant specialized literature.[6] A web seminar is possible, but face-to-face training is always preferable for personal interaction.

5.7 Ways to Memorize Intercultural Learnings

At the end of every intercultural seminar and workshop, the authors asked the groups to make a summary of significant take-aways to memorize and to transfer in their cross-cultural business interaction. They had a free choice of media, be it a poem, a motto, metaphor, a picture or even a role play. The author had some very touching and heartwarming experiences, as shown by the story below:

The Ideal Culture

Students from all over world in a master's program in International Management at a German University received a cultural integration seminar at the very beginning.

In one of the seminars a student from South America suddenly asked the facilitator: "*Is there an ideal culture?*" The author, somehow surprised by this question, answered after a while: "*Well, in my opinion it is the culture where you feel at ease, where you at home*". As soon as he had finished a student, an interpreter with Turkish roots raised in Germany jumped in and said: "*Yes, there are Turkish Turks and German Turks*". She had barely finished when a

[4] https://www.transparency.org/news/feature/corruption_perceptions_index_2017. Last viewed 05.11.2018.

[5] https://www.sietareu.org/activities/webinars Last viewed July 3, 2019

[6] Schwarz, Roger M., The Skilled Facilitator: A Comprehensive Resource for Consultants, Facilitators, Managers, Trainers, and Coaches, John Wiley & Sons, Hoboken, NJ, 25. 11.2016.

student, an engineer, replied: "*I am Turkish, but Germany is my home, I have been raised here and I feel at ease here*". A back-and-forth argument started without coming to a conclusion. It turned out, that though also raised in Germany, the interpreter, never felt at ease there and returned to Istanbul as an adult. The engineer, on the other hand, was at home in Germany.

Why am I telling you this story?

The interpreter-student became a very active member in group sessions and presented the following poem about how to integrate in Germany as a conclusion of their group sessions at the very end of the seminar. It has been translated literally from German and occasionally sounds a little odd, lacking in rhyme. But that was the purpose of the authors of the poem.

"Integration poem"

To adapt to Germany,
You should never miss punctuality.
But you should be competent in language, because going together
doesn't always mean we invite you too.
In your country nudity is not usual, so make a stop!
In front of a sauna with the sign "textile-free".[7]
No matter where you are, to be successful,
You sometimes have to say "no"!
The businessman must be individualistic.
Collectivism does not fit into the trade.
The German is thorough and factual,
Anyone who says "business goes fast" lied.
You should know Sunday is the day of rest,
Even if you want to party.
Sometimes you think the Germans are cold,
Have respect, that's the way they are.
They mean no harm, we have seen.
It can also be very nice, you have to confess.
Everybody knows for gluing you need paste,
Yes, maybe even Germany will become a football world champion!
We know that bit about paste does not fit into this poem,
Well, such a poem can only be by foreigners.
So long, Bayschke, Paka, Hoskahalin, Salaam and auf Wiedersehn
Too much of a good thing—we have to go now!

Hereafter we show you some examples for China to demonstrate the creativity of the groups and the variety of possible expressions and interpretations.

The first graph was made by a group composed of Western and Eastern Europeans (Fig. 5.8):

The Chinese letter "*He*" at the top stands for "*Harmony*" the basis for a successful relationship with Chinese partners. The "*WE*" underlines the group feeling, an essential element and attitude in cooperating. "*Give Information*" on the left and "*Relationship*" or "*Guanxi*" on the right indicate the central activities needed to bond a relationship.

[7]"*Textile free*" is the expression of being naked.

The example below was done by a German team in an inhouse seminar (Fig. 5.9): The Chinese letters from top to bottom read:

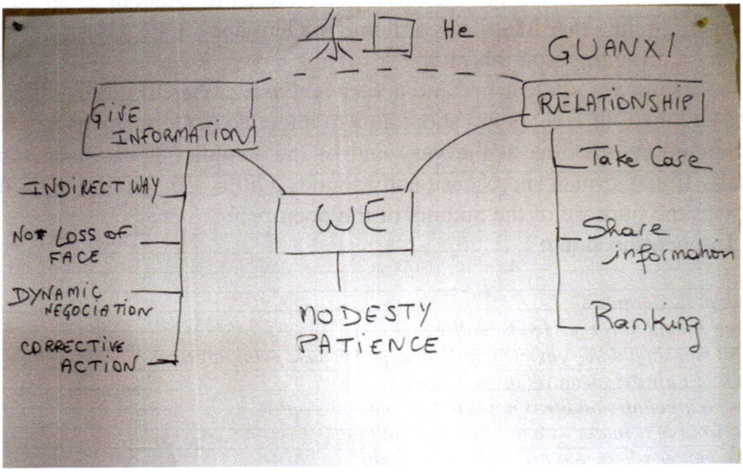

Fig. 5.8 China seen by Europeans

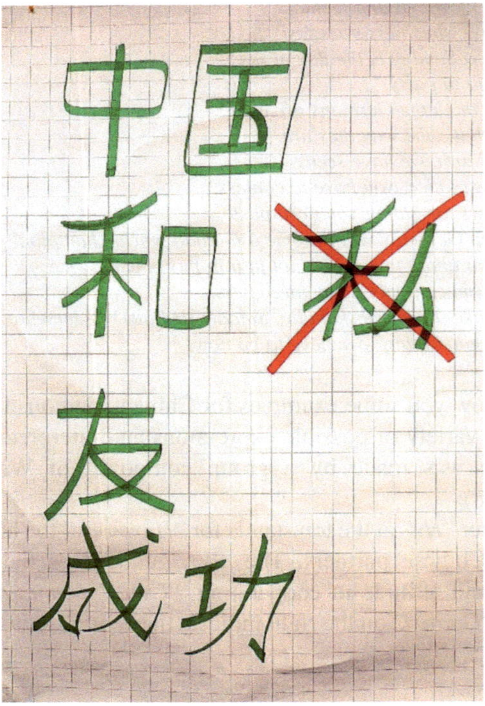

Fig. 5.9 China seen by a German inhouse team

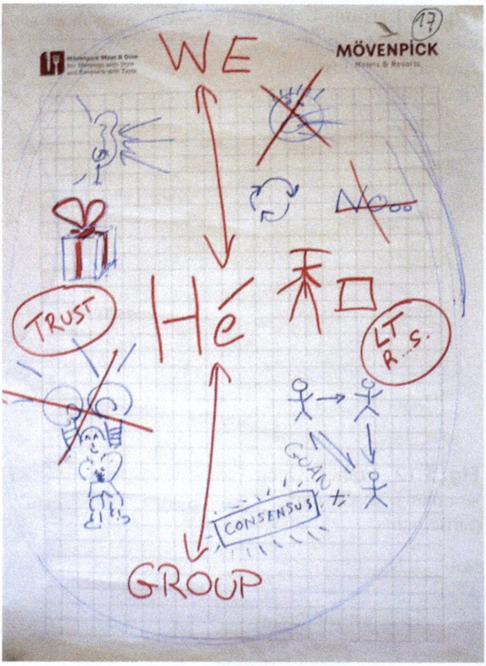

Fig. 5.10 China seen by Europeans from East and West

1. CHINA
2. HARMONY, PRIVATE (crossed out)
3. FRIENDSHIP
4. SUCCESS

The next conclusion chart on China was created by a team of European participants from the East and West (Fig. 5.10):

Here again "*Hé*", Harmony and the group are the central ideas. The illustrations around it are self-explanatory and suggest the dos and don'ts.

The last example on China was done by an in-house group in the German automotive industry (Fig. 5.11).

The illustration represents the Yin and Yang principle. Headline: How to co-operate successfully with Asians:

1. COMMUNICATION
   (a) Time
   (b) Do not lose sight of your target
   (c) Be yourself
2. RELATIONSHIP
   (a) Patience
   (b) Community
   (c) Composure
   (d) Respect

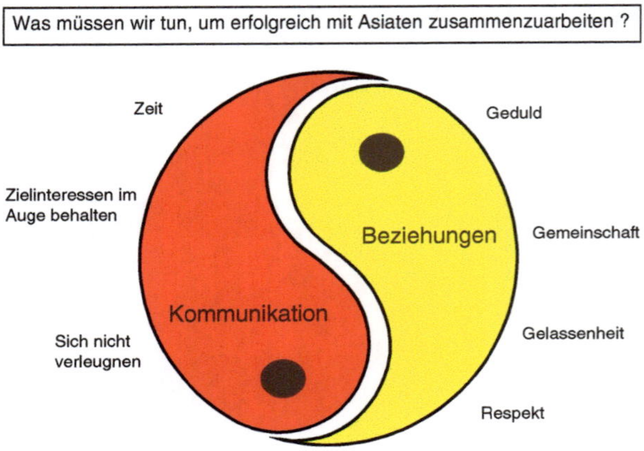

Fig. 5.11 China by an inhouse group in the automotive industry in Germany

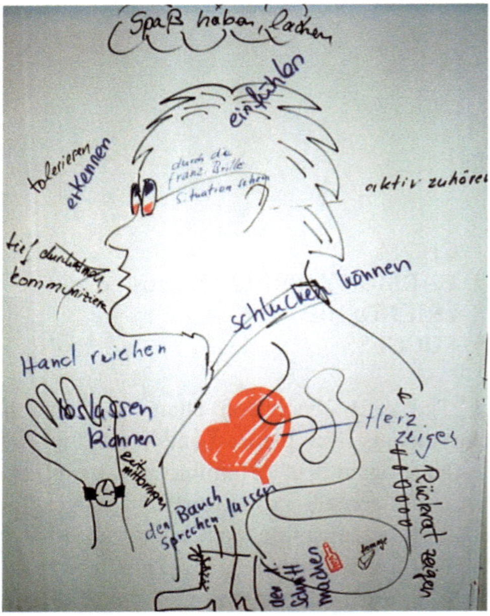

Fig. 5.12 France: Open seminar with German participants

This diagram made an effective desktop summary, especially for a person who had to deal with China on a daily basis.

The next example on France was done in an open seminar with mostly German participants (Fig. 5.12):

The pictures speak for themselves*: look at France through French glasses, use your heart and stomach*. The individual arguments used are*: Have fun, show empathy, tolerate, recognize, active listening, able to swallow a bitter pill, let go, show heart, use belly language, bring along some time and reach out.*

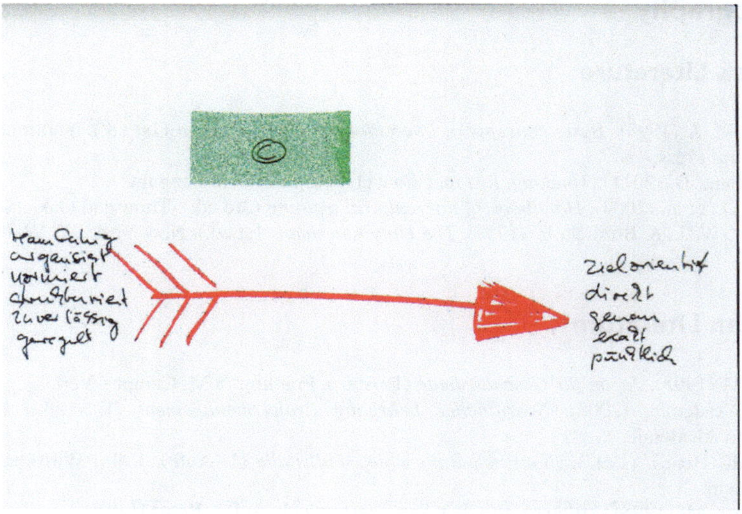

Fig. 5.13 Young German managers describing the essence of their own culture

The last example shows the self-evaluation of a German group of "*Young Tigers*", i.e. future managers about their own culture (Fig. 5.13):

The copy on the left reads:

1. Team minded
2. Organized
3. Normed
4. Structured
5. Reliable
6. Regulated

And the copy on the right reads:

1. Target oriented
2. Direct
3. Precise
4. Exact
5. Punctual

The author has never seen a more succinct summary of German characteristics than in this simple graph. Which is what the team working on it thought, too—hence the copyright!

Bibliography

English Literature

Bennet, M. J. (1998). *Basic concepts of intercultural communication* (1st ed.). Yarmouth: Intercultural Press.

Kahnemann, D. (2011). *Thinking, fast and slow* (1st ed.). London: Penguin.

Landis, D., et al. (2004). *Handbook of intercultural training* (3rd ed.). Thousand Oaks: Sage.

Leaderer, W. J., & Burdick, E. (1958). *The Ugly American* (1st ed.). New York: W. W. Norton.

German Literature

Gercik, P. (1995). *Japan für Geschäftsleute* (1. Aufl.). Frankfurt a.M: Campus-Verl.

Haufe Akademie. (2008). *Schriftlicher Lehrgang Projektmanagement* (1. Aufl.). Freiburg: Haufe Akademie.

Keim, H. (Hrsg.). (1992). *Planspiel, Rollenspiel, Fallstudie* (1. Aufl.). Köln: Wirtschaftsverlag Bachem.

Lin-Huber, M. (1998). *Kulturspezifischer Spracherwerb* (1. Aufl.). Bern: Huber.

Schilling, G. (2006). *Präsentieren mit Laptop und Beamer* (1. Aufl.). Berlin: Schilling.

Surmounting Cross Cultural Barriers in International Projectmanagement

6

You are a project manager, beginner or experienced, familiar with the technical side of the profession. Either you are starting an international project, or you have experienced a number of them and would like to preempt or get over stumbling blocks with the culture of your international partner.

In this chapter we concentrate on the cross-cultural side of issues in international project management with advice and hints on how to overcome cultural barriers. You will find many case studies to illustrate the points.

6.1 Current Standards for International Project Management

Projects are complex, special tasks with restrictions regarding time, costs and scope. They are often unique, innovative and risky. To manage this successfully, specific methods, tools and techniques are needed.

Projects have become a key tool over the last decades, standards have been developed to manage them effectively ensuring that project participants can refer to a common basis, procedures and terminology.

There are currently four leading standards which are accepted worldwide to manage projects:

1. Project Management Institute = PMI® based in the USA,
2. International Project Management Association = IPMA, based in Switzerland,

(continued)

P. M. Haller et al., *Bridging Cultural Barriers*, Management for Professionals,
https://doi.org/10.1007/978-3-030-17130-8_6

3. PRojects INControlled Environments = PRINCE II, a standard from Great Britain.
4. Agile Project Management as the newest project management technique emphasizing incremental development and high degree of self-organization. Agile Project Management is also linked in hybrid forms with the standards of PMI, IPMA and PRINCE II.

Of course, each of these standards do not reinvent project management. In the end, they differ only in the definition of procedures or assignments in a project organization.

The standard of the Project Management Institute—PMI®—is undoubtedly the best known globally and most widely used. It is mandatory in many international projects, e.g. in the Persian Gulf, Asia and North America, for multinational projects within global companies.

According to PMI®, project management is arranged in five process steps or phases, i.e. project initiation, planning, execution, monitoring/controlling and closing. Project initiation and planning lay the groundwork for the subsequent project process. The goal of this process is to produce an output, be it a software, a hardware or a feasibility study. The closing procedure at the end will deliver the results of the project process with reference to end-users, organizations, clients or markets. The graph and explanations below show the scope of this procedure (Fig. 6.1):

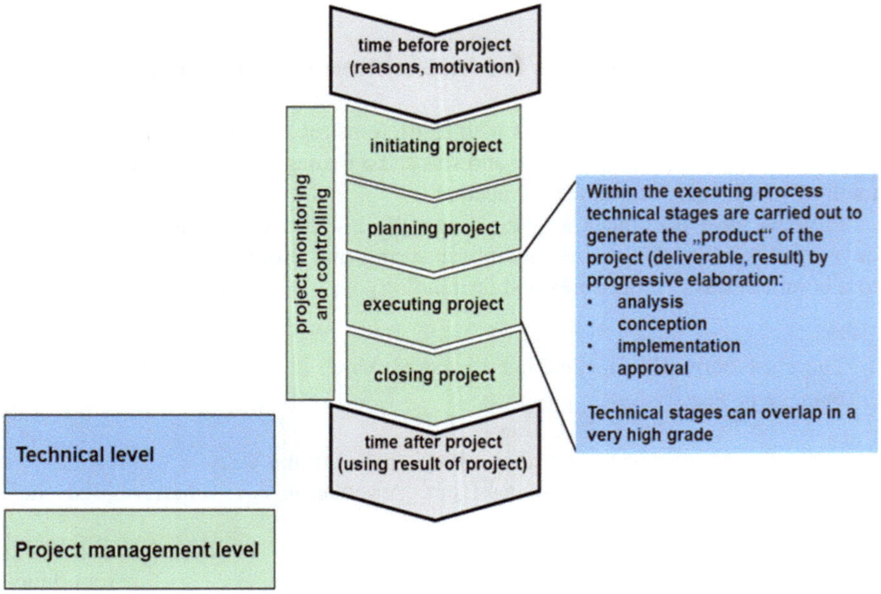

Fig. 6.1 Model showing involved process groups and the subsequent technical stages during the executing phase

Project Initiation sets the project's main aspects, clarifies main targets and gives a first rough outline of scope, contents, milestones and costs. At the end of this stage, a project charter is agreed upon, giving the project manager authority to plan and execute the project whilst delivering the expected results. The project charter is a binding agreement between the project manager and the sponsor as the decision maker.

Project Planning builds on the project charter and develops as detailed a project plan as possible. This entails learning in loops, which means that the project plan often has to be reworked and further refined as the project goes ahead.

Project Execution realizes the development of the project deliverable in progressive stages with technical phases such as analysis, conception, implementation and approval. Project execution is based on the project plan, which will often also be refined as work progresses.

Depending on the branch of an industry, technical terms may change names, i.e. a product development process (PDP) in the automotive sector may include phases such as functional and technical specifications, prototyping etc.

One or more phases in a given project may overlap; if this happens to a larger extent, it may result in using a mix of different methods combined with a high degree of self-organization, ongoing development and adaptation of techniques and methods.

Project planning and execution are regularly aligned and compared during the process by project monitoring and control.

Project Monitoring and Controlling During which the current status of the project is steadily monitored for corrective and/or preventive action to keep the project on track with reference to time, cost, scope, quality and risks.

Project Closing transfers the project deliverables, i.e. the end product to the organizational unit in charge, which will now manage the life cycle of the product that has been developed with subsequent approval procedures by the line management and lessons learned for the team.

Normally, international project management needs a greater degree of freedom so as to integrate all the people involved with different cultural backgrounds. Using methods rigidly based on just one cultural background could lead to misunderstandings amongst project stakeholders, frustrations because their input is not being considered, and ultimately even to failure.

► **Always tailor your project management methods to the cultural context you are working with.**

6.2 Answers to Your Questions When Your Project Is Crossing Borders

Summary
The content of this chapter follows the standard techniques and tools of project management while highlighting critical intercultural aspects. It will be easy for you to look up solutions for a particular issue without having to read through the whole chapter. The following numbering has to refer to the numbering of the following sections.

Please also refer to the index at the end of the book to make a selective search.

▶ **Motto: Methods remain the same, variances and diversity increase!**

6.3 Initiating an International Project in an Alien Environment

6.3.1 Why Key Targets Are Significant in International Projects

The more complicated goals are formulated, the harder it is to communicate these across language barriers. Briefing an international project team means simplifying goals to get them across clearly and to avoid misunderstandings. Here are some hints on how to prepare yourself:

1. Plan for sufficient time for the decision process. In hierarchical business cultures with many layers of decision makers, particularly in the Far East, more time is needed to coordinate the process.

2. The project goal is, as far as possible, worked out jointly in the project team. But bear in mind that in some cultures the decision makers will not be sitting in the meeting. Give these participants enough advance notice to clarify the goals with their superiors.
3. Adapt your style of communication to the cultures represented in the project. Speak slowly with non-native speakers of the project language. Don't hesitate to ask for feedback from the project team members repeatedly. Statements may be repeated to make sure that you have made yourself understood.

6.3.2 Target Circle: A Helpful Tool for Defining a Project in the Cross Cultural Context

The target circle as shown below has, in our experience, worked well for drafting the main targets of a project. This is illustrated by the following case study of the Europe-wide implementation of project management for a global player (Fig. 6.2):

European Launch of Project Management

The following example renders the implementation of standardized Project Management for a multinational company:

Why?

The goals were to avoid misunderstandings in the cross-border cooperation between the individual European branches of the company, reduce the complexity of the ever-increasing number of project inquiries causing time and cost to run high. International projects were to become significantly more effective in terms of cost, time, scope and quality of the result.

For Whom?

The key to success was defining stakeholders, especially the direct and indirect users of the product of the project. Those involved in this project were clients,

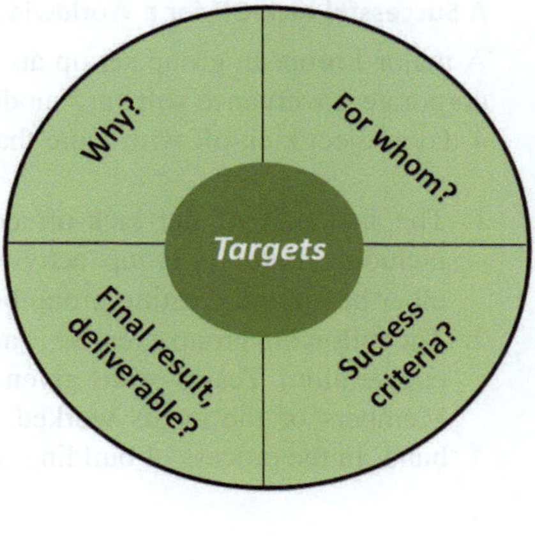

Fig. 6.2 Target circle

project managers, project staff, but also suppliers or investors in Germany, France, Spain, Italy, Belgium, the Czech Republic and Poland.

Final Result, Deliverable?

Project deliverable(s) may be more or less tangible or intangible, physically concrete or more abstract. Projects produce a wide spectrum—from the development of a feasibility study for a big factory, or a global roll-out of a new office system to the creation of new contents for a marketing strategy. If it is unique, complex and has limits regarding time, budget and scope, it is defined as a project.

The main deliverable of this Europe-wide implementation was project management itself with a standardized, documented process, training (if possible, in English), supported by project management software and accepted by all the cultures and subsidiaries concerned, as well as across all management levels.

Success Criteria?

The goal after 1 year of implementation was to have the new project management process in use for 80% of all projects across all European locations. It also included achieving a pre-set minimum of employee satisfaction to be measured using a reliable survey.

6.3.3 Project Kickoff: Discovering and Sharing Facts and Emotions

Project work becomes really productive when there is mutual personal understanding across cultures. Dealing with cultural issues at the initial stage will save time, cost and frustration. 50% of failures in international projects are mainly due to cross cultural misunderstandings rooted in prejudices and clichés. As soon as the first difficulty occurs, participants will, as a rule, attribute the problem to a cultural cliché. Anticipating the cultural barriers beforehand will save time and costs. Understanding across cultures may best achieved by gathering all the members in a kick-off once all the parties concerned have been identified.

A Successful Kick-Off for a Worldwide Software Project

A major European group set up an international project to implement a specific corporate governance software module in all its subsidiaries. For this purpose, a 4-day project kick-off with more than 200 people was organized in Canada.

1. The first part of the kick-off consisted of a 2-day intercultural workshop including outdoor group activities with the aim of getting to know each other better and creating group bonding across cultures.
2. The following group exercise is an example of how to build understanding and cooperation: Teams were given the task of building a tower with straws. Members of the teams worked in twos but were only allowed to use one hand. In the process of building one partner held the straw while the other one

applied the glue, the first one stuck the straw onto the tower and so on until the project was finished.
3. The workshop was based on several activities to deal with themes such as cultural differences in planning, the need for informal exchange and improvisation. The project team members got the key messages and solutions through practice.
4. The second part of the seminar concentrated on the technical briefing of the project itself.

6.3.4 Conditions On-Site: Frequently Unpredictable and Unexpected

On-site traffic conditions, availability of IT and telecommunications, travel times and the suitability of materials with reference to climatic conditions such as cold, heat, humidity, drought etc. may influence the success of international projects. Delivering a heavy machine in Pakistan during the monsoon season may be impossible if the roads are blocked by floods. Websites[1] offer valuable information on such topics. Involving a national expert may also be very helpful. Exploring the site personally to get an idea of the situation will certainly help to evaluate potential risks.

6.3.5 Achieving a Common Understanding of Time

Today, the standard is based on Universal Time Coordinated = UTC. This specifies a globally recognized standard.[2] When using English, remember to specify whether the time refers to **a.m.** or **p.m.**

Time zones and time differences should be taken into account to find the suitable time slots for telephone calls, conferences, etc.

6.4 Planning Communications Across Cultures

In an international project, team members and stakeholders often feel disconnected and overwhelmed by the sheer volume of information. Moreover, language difficulties and intercultural misunderstandings may occur. The following aspects need to be considered.

[1]https://weather.com/news/news/2018-05-02-pakistan-possible-global-record-high-april. Last viewed 23.10.18.

[2]https://www.timeanddate.com/. Last viewed 23.10.2108.

6.4.1 Dealing with Language Difficulties

Ensure from the beginning that there is a common understanding regarding project language and terminology. Check language skills (by telephone or with a questionnaire) to ensure that communications are clearly understood on both sides. To make understanding easier, simplify your language and reduce content and length of sentences. For example, if English is used, avoid complex sentences and use brief, pragmatic, everyday phrases. If necessary, employ an interpreter, but make sure in a prior briefing that he understands the technology of your business Sect. 4.8.3.2 "*The Interpreter as Alter Ego*".

6.4.2 Adjust Your Demands to the Available and Accessible Resources of Project Members

In countries with less developed economies, project members may have more than one task. They may face several jobs with differing priorities and may therefore need additional time to get down to your project. When estimating workloads or assessing deadlines, take their resources into account. Use such indicators as GDP or the productivity rate of a given country.

6.4.3 The NIH-Factor (Not-invented-Here)

The core problem in international projects is often the NIH syndrome (*Not Invented Here*). In other words: cultural differences are used to reject an idea. This may create almost insurmountable barriers for the execution and implementation of a project within a very short time. A vicious cycle begins. In our experience, the associated intercultural risks often represent more than 50% of project failures. The solution to internationalize your team is to develop ideas, concepts or even plans as a joint team. It then becomes theirs.

6.4.4 How You See Yourself Is How You Are Being Seen

The culture you have been socialized in travels with you around the world. Thus, a key aspect is your own awareness on how representatives of other cultures perceive you, what effect your behavior and communication has on them. Try to look at yourself from the other perspective. Use it to overcome obstacles, to create a common understanding and to build relationships and trust. The following example shows the pitfalls to watch out for when working with a German partner:

► **A German at Work** You have found, or you will find, that Germans often try to reach the perfect solution. They are normally bound by a very formal consensus culture with many meetings and a formal chain of command. This means that problems are frequently submitted and discussed with the direct superior. A German project member usually has a high extent of responsibility, experience and power to make decision at his level. Skipping hierarchy levels normally leads to distrust.

In many business cultures all over the world, problems are discussed with all hierarchical levels. In dealing with Germans, however, you would be well advised to solve problems at the level of the direct contact and not to jump hierarchies.

6.4.5 Communication Style: In Writing or Orally?

In most cultures, communication is characterized by talking informally person-to-person. In some instances, an email may be understood as impersonal or even considered to be offensive, e.g. in Latin cultures, where several follow-up emails are sent to stress the issue. Here you run the risk that your partner will withdraw and/or refuse to give feedback. Whatever the particular situation might be, oral communication is always preferable, as it helps to build and deepen relationships. In face-to-face conversations we can react directly, express nuances and modulate our voice to overcome potential conflicts. This, of course, does not exclude writing (e-mails, minutes, etc.), but relationships can only be shaped and deepened when we talk to each other and maintain personal contact.

Of course, exceptions prove the rule Sect. 3.5.5 "*Use of Language*" and Sect. 3.8.1 "*Business Communication: Verbally or in Writing*" For example, German culture is more of a written communication culture. Germans tend to believe that detailed e-mails will do the job (see Sect. 4.10.2.3 "*Communication and Conflict Resolution*").

6.4.6 Virtual Communication Cross Borders

Advanced web-based IT technologies offer an enormous media diversity to speed up and facilitate communications on a daily basis—face-to-face, video conferences, voice mail, document sharing via intranet, etc. The communication management plan will stipulate the various means of project communication to make project communication effective.

In complex and difficult communication situations, direct contact is normally indispensable, even if this involves more effort and travel costs. Personal relationships across cultures with project stakeholders, be it project teams, decision makers or superiors, or the lack thereof, can make or break project success. Nothing replaces personal contacts and direct communication. Traveling on-site may be cost intensive but is most effective for building relationships and getting to know local conditions. This takes a lot of time in most cultures as getting to know each other is done after business hours, at dinner in the evening or at other formal and informal social events such as karaoke in Asia. This helps to deepen trust and to build real teams.

6.4.7 Conversation Techniques: Discovering the Differences

There are three main types of conversation techniques:

1. **Talking directly**
   (a) This means straightforward, brief, precise communication, using statements and being fact-oriented. Talking directly leads to quick results and is appropriate for expert opinions, short briefings or recording the facts in the minutes of a meeting. On the other hand, talking too directly may also be perceived as rude and inappropriate.
2. **Talking indirectly**
   (a) For this conversation technique you not only need to be an active listener. Body language like nodding, etc. will emphasize positive interest. Paraphrase the statements of the other and repeat them in your own words. This will help to build empathy, trust and a sound relationship. Talking indirectly leads to a common understanding with fewer disagreements during negotiations, conflict resolution etc.
3. **Using open-ended questions**
   (a) Open questions create space to develop one's own and a joint mind set. They involve the counterpart and give him/her the possibility to participate actively. Open questions lead to more information and thus deeper input. Open questions lead to self-reflection when faced with unexpected and unprompted viewpoints.
   (b) Open questions are used in coaching and consulting processes. They are essential for building trust or really understanding interests. They are crucial for negotiations, conflict solving, understanding interests and diplomacy.

In international projects you will probably focus more on indirect and open-ended questions for communication. Being too direct may lead to a dead end in communication and harm or even destroy relationships. Most cultures all over the world use more indirect techniques in one or other form to communicate.

6.4.8 How to Get to the Point Across Borders

Some cultures get straight to the point, e.g. Germans. Others will package it more diplomatically in metaphors. In the international context we should emphasize indirect speech and open questions to build and deepen trust and create enduring relationships.

Being silent is also a form of conversation and can be a main part of communication as, for example, in Japan. Using and learning to read body language is vital especially when we deal with implicit messages in high-context cultures like China, the Arab countries etc.[3]

We recommend being more flexible in communication and to focus on building relationships by holding yourself back and emphasizing a more indirect and enquiring attitude to give the partner more room and possibilities to communicate.

That does not completely exclude straight talk, but that should be done selectively in the right context and at the appropriate moment. When you have to solve a critical issue with project staff, do it always in a one-on-one conversation so nobody loses face.

Reading and Understanding Body Language: Lessons from a Documentary

"*Le meilleur vin de Chine*"[4] ("The best Wine in China") is a documentary about French wine experts involved in project with Chinese partners in the Uygur region of China.

The language of the documentary is French, but even if you do not speak this language, you may draw your inferences by just watching the body language throughout the documentary. The story focusses essentially on cross cultural misunderstandings and escalating conflicts thereafter. There are several formal and informal scenes between the French and Chinese. From the facial expression and the body language it soon becomes evident whether a situation is positive or negative.

When the French partners are asking direct questions, the Chinese will often reply vaguely—"I wasn't prepared for that objection" or "I can't comment on that in detail before we discuss it with the boss." (a lady called Mrs. Li, member of the party).

They key difference between the two parties is that Mrs. Li has promised the management one million bottles of the best wine in China. The French calculation from the vineyards works out to 100,000 bottles at the very best. The French become more and more irritated, critical, harsh and direct. As a result, the Chinese leader Mrs. Li develops from a smiling to a distant person, doesn't look at the French partners, avoids direct eye-contact. The silences get longer and longer until the ultimate escalation—Mrs. Li explodes. She stands up, shouts "There is a lot of work to be done. There will be no meeting today and no meeting tomorrow", walks out, and slams the door.

The story ends well: Mrs. Li buys grapes from other producers to get the one million bottles and is awarded a national prize for a wine produced from her own vineyards.

The inner conflict is a classical one between the West and Asia Westerners follow a linear path to achieve the initial objective and rarely think about

[3]Pease Allan, Pease Barbara, The Definitive Book of Body Language: How to read others' attitudes by their gestures, Orion, 21.06.2018.

[4]https://www.filmsdocumentaires.com/films/532-le-meilleur-vin-de-chine. Last viewed 02.11.2018.

alternatives. It is an "*either . . .or*" attitude. With her "*as well . . . as*" attitude Mrs. Li is flexible, looks at other ways to fulfill her commitment to the party and ends up with a success. (see Sect. 4.8.4.1 "*China and the West—two Diametrically opposed Approaches to Life*", Fig. 4.3 "*Efficiency and Effectiveness in China and the West*").

Because the relationship turned sour, the Westerners were never able to get close enough to ask Mrs. Li "*What do you intend to do to achieve your target?*"

6.4.9 Dealing with Information Losses and Making Sure That You Are Being Understood

In international projects you may often be confronted with language barriers or "culturally coded messages". Unless you are in a face-to-face situation and trained, it will be difficult to read the indirect signals of body language and metaphoric expressions. The result is loss of information.

The following graph describes this schematically. In the classical sender-receiver model there are individual communication stages building on each other. A message is coded by the sender (verbally, non-verbally, in writing, through body language) and transferred via a media (telephone, video call, face-to-face meeting, email). The decoding by the receiver follows along the same lines. Each of these individual stages poses the danger of potential information losses and/or misinterpretations.

Suppose you are a project manager running a project in India and you only speak basic English. The ongoing project has performance problems. You try to solve them via email and telephone calls with the person in charge in India. The probability that information loss occurs is high. It may be that:

- Your pronunciation isn't well understood because of your accent.
- You have problems understanding the intonation or pronunciation of Indian English.
- Indians may not openly reject an idea or opinion. You may not notice that because you don't get the body language signals on the telephone.
- Your demands may overstrain your Indian partners because their infrastructure does not leave them with much leeway (Fig. 6.3).

What does all this mean for you? The more complex the situation, i.e. in contracting, negotiations or conflicts, the more necessary it is to have personal face-to-face contact.

In projects English is often used as the common language. In many cases, English may not be the first language of any of the parties involved. To avoid misunderstandings:

- Talk in short phrases.
- Avoid complex sentences.
- Talk very slowly particularly, when participants are not familiar with English.

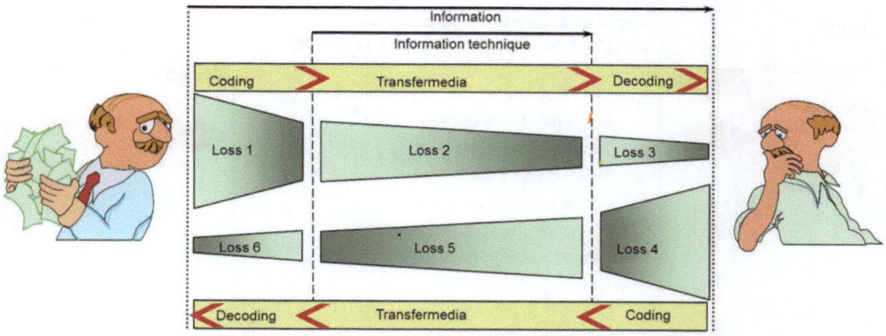

Fig. 6.3 Chain of information loss

- Make sure they can read your lips.
- Repeat frequently.
- Get feedback with repetitions and simple confirmations using other words/ synonyms.
- Never take a *yes* for granted.

Information Loss in a Global IT-Project

A global strategic IT-Project in a large enterprise was handed over to a new project manager, his predecessor having been promoted to a challenging career opportunity within the company.

Sub-project teams for the single-software modules had been installed in Brazil, South Korea, India, Germany, France and Spain. The former project manager used a tight communication style by calling the sub-project leaders frequently along with on-site visits every 3–4 months. He was not only known for his technical competence but also for caring for his staff.

The new project manager reached a dead end because his communication was concentrated mainly on emails. He reduced travelling as he had two young children and he wanted to spend more time with his family.

The result was a lack of visible leadership and a widening communication gap caused by increasing information losses and communication leaks.

Realizing this, the new project leader started a face-to-face project review with the core team to understand and reappraise what had happened. Thereafter, he designed a communication management plan returning to the former leadership style which had proven to be so successful.

Use always open questions:

1. To avoid information loss
2. To get the right information
3. To be clear on how to deal with the information given to you

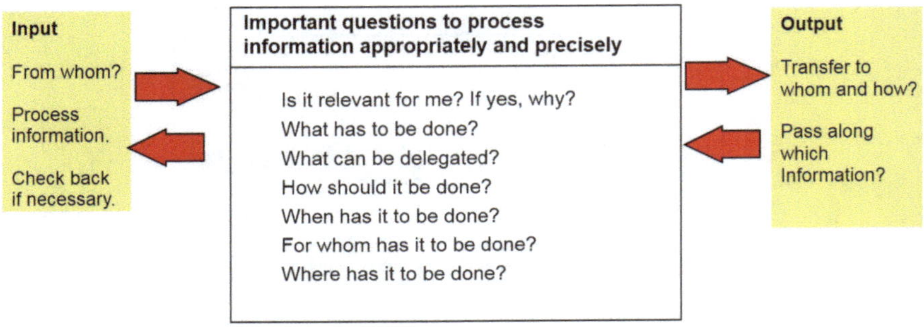

Fig. 6.4 Getting the information right!

4. To decide what to pass on, i.e. to other partners, stakeholders, etc.

Always ask yourself:

1. "What does this information mean for the project, for the stakeholders?"
2. "For the cultures involved?"
3. "How do I get the right information?"
4. "Is it motivating?"

The following graph contains a checklist with relevant key questions for both the sender and receiver (Fig. 6.4):

6.5 Stakeholder Management: Discovering Unusual Relationships

Stakeholders are individuals or groups of people whose interests are affected by an international project. Dealing with their interests in a positive way is a key success factor. Stakeholder management in international projects not only deals with cultural aspects but sometimes also with stakeholders whose role may not be apparent in a project, such as political parties, administrative authorities, religious representatives like priests or monks, and interpreters. Families may also be very important and powerful stakeholders.

► In psychological terms, stakeholders need and want to be understood and taken seriously even if their interests are often not absolutely rational but emotionally driven.

1. In Hungary or the Czech Republic, the term Warsaw has negative connotations because of the Warsaw pact, the defeat of the Hungarian revolt in the 1950s and the Prague Spring in the 1960s and its association with communist regimes. When

referring to Warsaw, call it the *"City of Warsaw"*. A minor detail perhaps, but it may make you win friends.
2. In China, emphasize and show respect for Chinese culture, Confucianism or inventions like paper etc. Chinese people are very proud of their millennia-old culture. Don't fall into the trap of Western clichés and prejudices (see Sect. 4.8.3.3 *"Saving Face and Face Saving Actions"*).
3. In Latin America show respect for indigenous history, especially when dealing with stakeholders with South American Indian roots. Dig into their history, ask a Mexican Indian about Aztec gods like Huitzilopochtli or Quetzalcoatl. Or start a conversation on the last Aztec king Cuauhtémoc. First of all, make sure that you get the pronunciation right. A quick search in the web will probably give you the solution.
4. King Bhumibol of Thailand died in 2016. Most Thais worshiped him like a god. Thai project members will appreciate you expressing sympathy and respect for the loss of their King.

► To be successful, make sure to involve all stakeholders from the very beginning, be empathic, intuitive and flexible in evaluating their specific personal and cultural needs. Be totally aware of which management style is being applied, hierarchical or individualistic Western!

6.5.1 Relationship Is a Fixed Cost Factor

In the Western World, relationships in Project Management are often considered just "*nice to have*". In most other cultures they are essential for the timely success of a project. Sometimes, as shown in the story below, you have to go a long way to find the key stakeholders in a complex constellation:

Tracing the Key Stakeholder Sometimes Takes a Longer Route

A development project in Eastern Europe for an international organization had the following wide array of stakeholders:

1. The German client and financier.
2. The German exporting contractor with the German project manager, his supervisor and his project team.
3. The partner institution on-site in Eastern Europe, the head of the partner institution, the wife of the head of the partner institution, a high-ranking government representative of the Eastern European country which was looking for ways to make contacts in Germany through the project.
4. The translator who had contacts with the government via her husband who was a government offical.

5. Staff of the executing German institution as well as the Eastern European institution on the ground, some of whom were friends with the translator, his daughter and the boss of the partner institution and some who were in adversarial roles.

Dealing with that highly complex and political constellation required a different approach from a Western style, with diplomatic skills combined with cross cultural competence.

The solution: The good relationship with the translator helped to save critical unexpected situations. Once, official security personnel just dropped into a project meeting in this Eastern country to put pressure on the German project manager. They assumed that he had contacts to politicians in Germany and wanted to use him as an intermediary to get more funds for their own purposes.

As you might expect, the German project manager gave a straightforward "no". The interpreter translated, but not directly. He provided an interpretation; had he translated rejection from the German directly there might have been obstacles to the ongoing project. The German side would have been accused of hampering the project.

Thanks to the good relationship between the German project manager and his interpreter, it was possible to solve this critical incident in a positive way, to avoid potential obstacles and a demotivating atmosphere with the project team.

Building relationships, particularly in Asia and Latin cultures takes time for personalized communication, for on-site-travel, staying overnight, dining out, maybe a joint sightseeing to a key spot of a given culture. To build confidence and trust will cost money, but you may be repaid by a smoothly running project. This is the lubricant in the gear-box of a project.

Deteriorating Project Quality in India

An Indian sub-project team was involved in a long-term software project. As the project leader who had done the job for 2 years had resigned, he had been replaced by a new colleague.

The predecessor had visited the sub-project in India regularly, not only for covering the technical side of the project in formal meetings but also for informal encounters. As a leader he was more of a father figure, giving him the platform to build good relationships with the line managers on-site in India.

The new project leader tried to run the project from Germany mainly via e-mail. Due to his missing presence the Indian team lacked leadership, lost orientation and felt unimportant.

When the new project manager realized the situation, he emphasized personal communication via telephone and video conferencing. He traveled every 3–4 months to India and did as his predecessor in taking more time in to meet people and to socialize. He also installed a deputy in the Indian team to make project management visible on the spot. Thereafter, the project was completed successfully.

6.5.2 Culturally Personalized Communication Management Plan

A communication management plan will document and guide you on how to manage and how to follow-up with all the parties involved. All stakeholder requirements need to be addressed. Your stakeholder analysis and project organization will serve as a basis and input for this plan.

In international projects stakeholder needs will most certainly be affected by their culture:

1. What is the management style like: hierarchical/collectivistic or transactional/individualistic[5] (Querverweis power distance)? How do you adapt your own management style?
2. What are the needs for communication: Mother tongue, command of the commonly used language in the project? Preferences for written or oral communication?
3. Topics to personalize conversations: i.e. family (Arab world), favorite pastimes, surroundings
4. Topics to avoid e.g. politics, religion

The following graph may serve as a checklist. You also may adapt the headings according to your individual needs to make sure it fits the particularities of your project (Fig. 6.5):

► A communication management plan considers and supports all aspects of cross border communication to avoid misunderstandings and loss of information.

6.6 The Meaning of Quality Across Cultures

Technical quality has standards regulated by local laws and norms. Yet, Quality does not have a universal signification and meaning. Quality is influenced by the specific characteristics of a given culture. Quality is also influenced by the availability of various resources as well as personal or business requirements. Developing a common understanding and definition of quality when working together with other cultures is an essential criterion to avoid misunderstandings. From a technical point of view, the technical means to produce quality are universal. Yet the following

[5]https://en.wikipedia.org/wiki/Transactional_leadership. Last viewed 12.11.2018.

Which Stakeholder	Which culture	Power-distance	Need in personal communication	Additional context info	Which info, how detailed, formal/ informal	How often	Which medium, communication channel	In charge
Decision Maker								
Sub-project Manager								
Supplier								
Head of department								
Interpreter								
....								

Fig. 6.5 Model of a communication management plan involving different cultures. Stakeholders are listed according to their rank and importance

examples give you an idea of how different cultures may perceive and evaluate quality.

6.6.1 German Quality

The German definition of quality is process- and system-based. Planning is supposed to be as perfect as possible, including all aspects in detail. Risks have to be avoided in advance to guarantee the best final quality. The understanding of quality is technical and functional.

6.6.2 Swiss Quality

The Swiss quality concept is characterized by the availability of few natural resources. This leads to a careful handling of the existing materials. In this sense, planning is understood as a means to produce perfect quality but also the careful handling of resources.

6.6.3 French Quality

Here the appeal of the final product is in the foreground. The design at the end is more important than the technology. Functionality requirements must be met but the product does not have to be a 100% perfect. What matters first and foremost is what the product looks like and the impression it creates.

6.6.4 Belgian Quality

Here quality is pragmatically defined due to the more limited financial and human resources available, i.e. a ratio of 1:10 compared to Germany. Achieving a 100% solution is an illusion, so you have to be satisfied with an 80% result. A Belgian marketing plan will never have the same in-depth quality, simply because Germans will most likely put a larger team on it against one person on the Belgian side.

6.6.5 Japanese Quality

The undisputed goal is the perfect product for the customer in terms of design and functionality. This leads to continued product improvement. The Japanese automotive industry, for example, has shown this over and over again in the last decades. Better equipped cars with more consumer-oriented features gave the Japanese automobile industry its competitive advantage.

6.6.6 Chinese Quality

In China, the understanding of quality has made quantum leaps in the last 20 years—from the basic quality that was resource-driven to the most advanced in many industries. The term is ultimately redefined daily. That is why it is particularly important to define the expected quality precisely in advance. Doing so prevents quality content from being just characterized by pragmatism or business acumen.

6.6.7 Understanding of Quality in the USA

The central quality criterion in the US is fitness for use. Does the product do its job or not? A house is built for a generation and not for centuries, i.e. a car will have to run for 4–5 years without any problems until the next model year. The cost-benefit ratio determines product quality. It is also important to deliver the scope as required. Overemphasizing quality would be unwanted *"gold plating"*.

Bridging a Quality Gap in Support and Resources

In a bilateral economic collaboration project in an Eastern European country in the 1990s, the project leader from Germany realized only on-site what the infrastructure equipment was like and what that would mean for the project.

1. For lunch there was thin soup with bread, for dessert tiny dried-up windfall apples from someone's little garden.
2. The meeting room was also the only training room, with only plywood panels for pinning and a classic blackboard. Pinboards were unknown.
3. Materials such as pentel pens or flipcharts with paper were unavailable.
4. Seating was cramped with participants sitting very close to each other.
5. The premises were on the fifth floor, the elevator was no longer safe and had to be used at one's own risk.
6. At this point, the German project leader changed his previous briefing for the service partners in the project because he realized that his requirements were over-exacting and could not be met by the East European partner.
7. The quality requirements were adjusted so that they could be provided locally in Eastern Europe.
8. Milestones were set with realistic and achievable objectives.
9. For necessary status feedback or upcoming decisions, the two-step information principle was introduced: During the first step all information is given to the international partner with sufficient lead-time to study and process the documents. In a second step all information is made acessible and distributed to all members of the staff involved in the project.

German Quality Standards Meet US Standards

A German supplier had developed a complex electronic component for the automotive industry. The product had just been launched successfully in the German market. The company now wanted to launch this technology in the USA. The specific technical needs of the US market were not looked into, as the German project team assumed that the German standards would automatically cover US requirements. Consequently, the entire project planning was based on this assumption and the key positions were filled in the project organization accordingly.

After the first contact with the US partner it became apparent that the American market had other, namely simpler, requirements. A back-and-forth discussion created resistance on the part of the Americans and ended in an escalation.

The solution was to go back to square one, change the project organization with key positions in the technical subprojects filled on an equal basis with American and German engineers. The simpler requirements of the US market were taken into account and the implementation ended in a success.

6.7 Project Charter: Clarify the Authority of the Project Leader Across Cultures

The project charter is the final document of a project launch giving the project leader authority to run the project until the final result is handed over. Authority in this context means clarifying the responsibilities and competences within the team and in allocating funds. The crucial competences needed in international projects are:

1. To get support from higher management to deal with differing management styles, and to involve, if necessary, higher management, e.g. the need to match levels in hierarchical cultures for meetings and decision making.
2. Having prior agreed upon clear procedures to solve conflicts at higher management levels whenever the competence of the project leader is exceeded.
3. An additional budget for dealing with intercultural issues. Personal face-to-face contacts with project team members, especially for the kick-off session, as well as travel expenditure for on-site reviews etc.

Project Charter for an International Engineering Project

A Swedish project manager in Stockholm led an international supplier project in mechanical engineering. The project steering committee was based in the headquarters in Germany. Sub-teams in Slovakia, Italy, China and India were responsible for several deliverables such as mechatronic components, software-modules or the circuit board.

The project launch had been very casual, initiated in a telephone call between the German bosses and the functional superior of the Swedish project leader in Stockholm. The decision was confirmed in two phrases within minutes after the call.

Project initiation lacked a binding agreement with agreed key data, clear assignments and defined competences. Thus, the project manager was not assigned a clearly defined role and authority. The result ended in general confusion. For the managers of the sub-projects it was unclear as to who was leading the project, because the German headquarters often intervened ad-hoc when they felt that something had to be done.

The Swedish project leader realized that the situation was unsatisfactory and started to solve it in several steps:

1. The project leader clarified his role with the decision makers in Germany and got his conditions accepted and the key data confirmed. He designed a project organization with formal communication channels and got it approved.
2. A workshop was carried out with the leader of the worldwide subprojects to identify the causes of the unsatisfactory situation and a project charter was defined.
3. As the project manager was the communication bottleneck, the responsibilities were newly defined between project manager and subordinate project leaders.

4. Bypasses and interferences between the decision makers and the operative level were eliminated to avoid confusion and frustrations.
5. The project charter cleared and confirmed these additional competences, i.e. travel budgets as well as a higher priority and therefore availability of all key resources involved in the project.
6. The now formally appointed Swedish project leader had a clear authority with the support of his management, giving him the platform to act freely.

Without this formally established charter the project would have ended in endless conflicts and poor results.

6.8 Snags in International Planning

6.8.1 How Detailed Should a Plan Be?

Planning right down to the last detail may create conflicts with other cultures. Project members may be overwhelmed because they lack resources or simply do not understand the necessity for these technical refinements. It may also be perceived as lack of trust or competence.

Creating a common understanding of planning and giving the cultures involved the freedom to adapt planning to their situation is a basic requirement of sound planning across cultures.

► **Leave empty spaces** for the cultures involved to express their specific needs.

6.8.2 How Long Should an International Planning Cycle Last?

The planning phase in international projects often needs more time; Geographical distance, language barriers, additional feedback loops need to be considered and redundancies eliminated. Cultures with decision-making processes involving many levels of hierarchies in planning cycles may take much more time. Make yourself familiar with the cultures involved and their decision-making processes before you start to plan and fix milestones.

Longer and more detailed planning cycles in some cultures, e.g. Japan, may also have the effect that execution is faster. Time is gained due to the fact that teams in Japan have a better and more detailed understanding of the implementation process, thus eliminating queries and delays in the preproduction or production phase.

6.8.3 Risk Analysis: Soft Factors May Be Half the Battle in Cross Cultural Projects

Risk management is an essential task in project management. According to PMI®,[6] risks are events which can happen, and which influence the result of a project negatively or positively. Risks listed in a project are mostly negative. The effect of a given risk depends on the probability of its occurrence and on its impact on the success of a project. The Western approach is linear and mostly tied to the hard factors, such as the technical aspects of a given project

In international projects risks are often underestimated. Culturally related soft factors may be just as important as the technical aspects. Therefore, you should examine and include these in your risk analysis, such as

1. Families and or social ties of key deciders in a project
2. Hierarchical versus cooperative lines of command
3. Different meaning of time and its implications
4. Different sense of quality, i.e. perfectionism versus pragmatism.
5. Attitude to professional life, "*live to work*" *or* "*work to live*"
6. Lacking cross cultural knowledge and sensitivity, "*walking all over*" *versus* "*walking along*"
7. NIH (not invented here), i.e. resistance to a project through non-involvement of the participants at the beginning
8. Communication style, direct versus diplomatic communication
9. Differing attitudes to environmental questions.
10. Meaning and influence of gender roles, social groups, age etc.

The French Client and the German Project Manager

An international project in the automotive sector was designed to develop a new wing mirror system for a French client. The German project leader used his preferred communication style, i.e. emails, mainly because communicating in English with the French client was difficult. He was also under the impression that the French disliked speaking English. When they did, their English was sometimes hard to understand (see Sect. 4.9.1.2 "*France and its Languages*"). This led to numerous misunderstandings which, in turn, caused increased customer complaints.

In a workshop, qualitative risks were listed and ranked as low, medium, or high with their corresponding likelihood of occurring and their impact. The main risk defined was the German project leader because of his lack of French language skills and his rare presence on-site in Paris. The analysis defined this as a decisive risk factor: lack of language skills and social contacts—and thus non-existent

[6]Details see PMBOK® GUIDE 6th edition Chapter 11 Risk Management page 395 onwards.

personal relationship with the French client (see Sect. 4.9.3 "*The Patron: Communication and Cooperation in Business Life*").

So, corrective action was taken. The current German project manager was replaced by an experienced person who spoke English as well as French, and who was willing to live temporarily in Paris to lead the project until its successful completion.

6.8.4 A Clear Work Structure Is Half the Battle

WBS (Work Breakdown Structure serves as the basis to produce the necessary additional sub-plans like schedules, cost structures, milestones, organizational charts etc. and to ensure a clearly structured project management process to deliver the expected results.

Depending on the complexity of the project and the desired results, the detailed breakdown may differ. A plan for an innovation may not be as detailed as one for a known product. Also, the skills and experience of the project staff will play a role; the more experienced the staff is in project management, the more detailed a breakdown structure will be.

WBS has to be complete while refining is an ongoing learning process. WBS is based on two major concepts:

1. **Object-oriented**, by breaking down the entire project into its individual deliverables, i.e. for a car development project you will include car body; driving system, control system and interior design. These are broken down again into other sub-deliverables.
2. **Phase-oriented**, which describes the technical process to reach the objective i.e. analysis, conception, implementation and approval.

Often both principles are combined to be called **mixed orientation**. In international projects, it will not always be necessary to break down a WBS to the work package level as is seen in the example below (see also Fig. 6.2 Target Circle):

A Virtual Project

Suppose you were leading a big international project in the engineering sector to set up a new paper manufacturing plant at your company's home base and install it turnkey, ready to operate, in a wooded area in Northern Mongolia.

If you based the WBS only on *phase-oriented* aspects you would miss out on the complexity of different technical aspects of the project, *the object- oriented* aspects, which have to be addressed in parallel. Typical deliverables would be:

1. The plant and building in Mongolia
2. The machine itself with mechanical modular components, power train and casing.

3. The logistics system with transport (ship, plane, etc.)
4. Incoterms, insurances, customs
5. Safety and security systems during transport
6. Technical conditions on site such as facilities, water and energy supply, etc.
7. Legal aspects in Mongolia.
8. Recruitment and training of Mongolian staff on-site
9. Customer service and support.

In defining these above deliverables, you will be able to assign clearly- defined responsibilities to the international team and give them the freedom to organize themselves in accordance with their technical and cultural needs.

► **Thinking in *deliverables*** is the basis of a proper project plan. First define what you are going to have when it is completed, and then do what has to be done to get the desired result.

The graph below is an example of how to create a WBS overview for a complex multinational project. It is an effective way to always have all the facets of the project at your fingertips—as a summary on your office pinboard or your desktop, as a checklist, and as a visual aid for stakeholders, staff-members etc. at presentations or meetings (Fig. 6.6).

Lost in Details

A German engineer had been in the printing machines business for 3 years when he was asked to take over a first-time development project for a new big, special printing machine. It involved sub-teams in India for software and Eastern Europe for the mechanical components. Having hardly any international experience in project management, he created the WBS the way he had been taught to at university. He broke down his WBS in great detail, with logical step-by-step sequences to realize the project perfectly. Moreover, he did the whole plan on his own, intending to brief his sub-project leaders and their teams once the plan was finished.

He was very diligent and created a WBS with more than 2000 work packages, all perfectly described and defined.

After the presentation, all the teams were totally lost in the details, leading to frequent misinterpretations. Even the German sub-team had some trouble understanding their compatriot. Milestones and deadlines were delayed, and the project was in danger of failing.

An external project coach was called in to help bring the project back on track. According to his assessment, project members from other cultures understood 20% or less of what was asked of them.

As a result, the WBS was simplified and

(a) Deliverables were outlined with details left to the sub-teams.

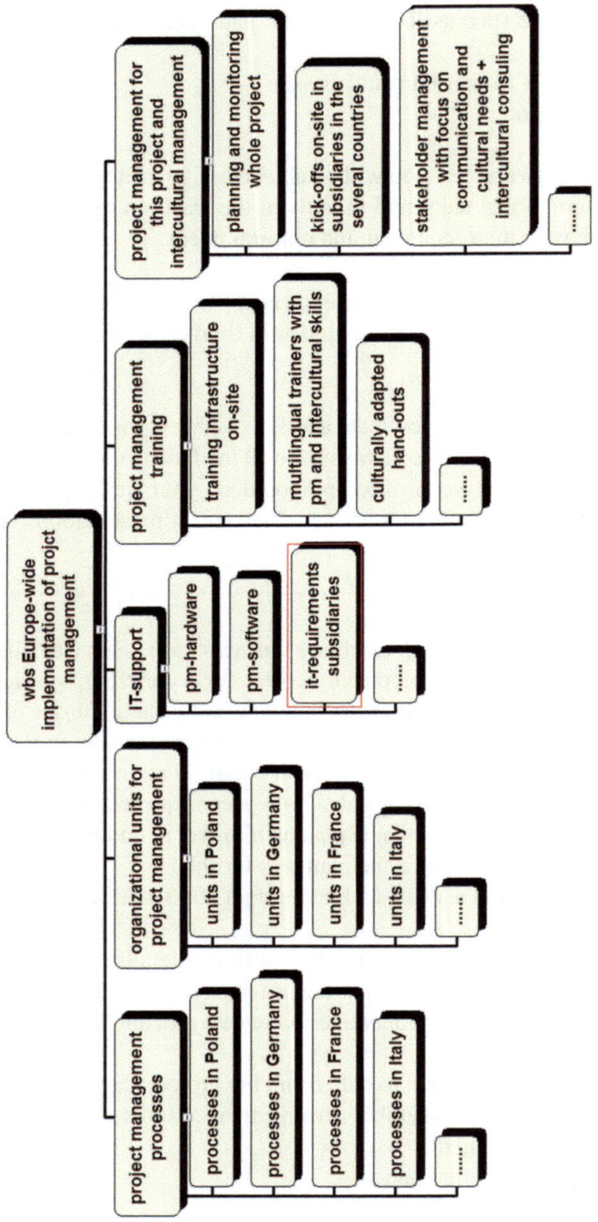

Fig. 6.6 WBS Europe-wide implementation of project management (draft)

(b) Objects were tailored to the needs of the sub-teams and transferred to their responsibility.
(c) Sub-teams got the freedom to plan for themselves within set major milestones and clearly defined objectives.
(d) A planning and cross culture workshop served to transfer and set the guidelines for this new approach.
(e) A monthly schedule of regular status reporting was established for the locations.
(f) Besides the status sheets sent by email there was also face-to-face communication, either onsite or via video conference or telephone.

6.8.5 Creating a Common Understanding of Detailed Planning

Many cultures are overwhelmed by too detailed scheduling. In cultures with hierarchical structures such as Japan, China or Central and Eastern Europe and in Africa or Arabian countries, you may consider the need for more time. Maybe you cannot plan in detail because you may not know the decision-makers and decision processes. However, when setting key data make it as personalized as possible by assigning them to specifically named individuals. If it is a group, e.g. in Asian countries, name the head.

Status Is Also Important

A German-Asian project in the public sector was set up to establish an in-house academy. The Asian partner was named Project Manager, the German was Project Coordinator.

The German Coordinator took the lead and developed detailed planning procedures which were perceived as too restrictive by the Asian Project Manager, resulting in a stalemate.

Part of the problem was that the German, in terms of hierarchy and title, was subordinate to the Asian Manager. To overcome this, he was upgraded from a simple Project Coordinator to Senior Project Manager by his German boss.

Both persons involved being on par, they started a meeting to get the plan rolling again. Milestones with sufficient total floats and clear intermediate goals for the Asian side were jointly developed, agreed upon and integrated into the detailed network plan on the German side. This served as a basis for a new masterplan (Fig. 6.7).

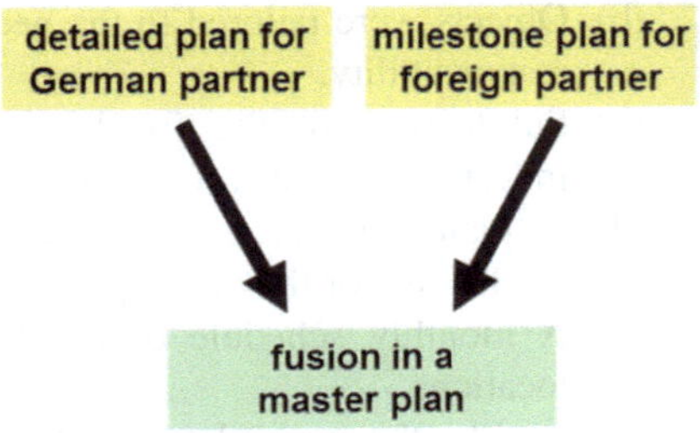

Fig. 6.7 Model for developing an integrated master plan

6.9 Tailoring International Project Organization to Cultural Needs

A project will bring together skilled professionals, all identified by name, to fulfill the objectives of the project. Projects must be coordinated alongside day-to-day business.

For the team members, a project organization may be a partially or totally new experience with new colleagues, new roles, new cultures, new challenges etc. The common instrument to define and document a project organization is a classical organization chart.

Special considerations for international projects:

(a) If at all possible, the different cultures should be equally represented in the project.
(b) The seniority principle, i.e. respect for the elderly, which is emphasized in many cultures must also be taken into account as part of the project organization. Putting a young, inexperienced, foreign project leader with a veteran Japanese department head may most likely be rejected. The same would apply to Eastern European or Arab cultures.

6.9.1 The Significance of SCRUM in International Projects

SCRUM is a term borrowed from football and rugby and is better known as agile project management. SCRUM and agile project management stand for a high degree of self-organization, flat hierarchies and rapidly created incremental developments of the project.

SCRUM criticizes classical project management as being too bureaucratic, inflexible and taking too much time. SCRUM was first applied in the software sector but has since expanded to other branches of industry.

From our point of view, SCRUM and agile project management are not absolutely new. SCRUM emphasizes self-organized cooperation in projects and a tight coordination process in the project team (SCRUM team). With *sprints,* incremental deliverables are developed and integrated in the project. *Sprints* normally last from

2 to 6 weeks. The incremental sprint result will be approved at the end of each sprint before the next one begins. A SCRUM board helps to coordinate work (derived from the Japanese Kanban[7] board) by disclosing processes and completed tasks.

(a) Team members from different cultures in international projects have special needs with regard to communication, leadership, and rules and rituals in teamwork. There is a need to adapt leadership and communication styles to whatever project management method is being used.
(b) A more open organizational and work structure rather than a detailed structure is generally preferable in international projects. SCRUM can serve this purpose; we can develop a draft or a generic milestone plan with open time boxes for deliverables and ask SCRUM teams to organize themselves in this structure adapted to their culture. It might even have a motivating effect!

6.10 Project Execution: Creating a Winning Team Across Cultures

During execution the team develops the product of the project in a continuous process.

(a) The project plan serves as reference for the technical work to be done. The plan will be adapted whenever necessary by comparing it to the current status. Deviations are analyzed, checked, and controlled, resulting in corrective and/or preventive action to bring the project back on track.
(b) As a project leader you will ensure that project tasks as well as each single team member are in line to achieve the expected results.

6.10.1 The Magic Triangle: Building Bridges Across Cultures

Besides the triple constraints—time, scope, cost—there is another magic triangle, that of project task, project team and individual project member. Cross cultural projects are more demanding in this respect as you will have to succeed in reconciling the irreconcilable.

(a) Transferring the complex **project task** with its objectives, work packages, milestones, status reports **to other cultures** with other perceptions of work, timing, cooperation, hierarchies, etc.
(b) Managing an **international project team** with its specific culturally defined communication patterns, its differing understanding of leadership and teamwork.

[7]https://en.wikipedia.org/wiki/Kanban_(development). Last viewed 24.10.18.

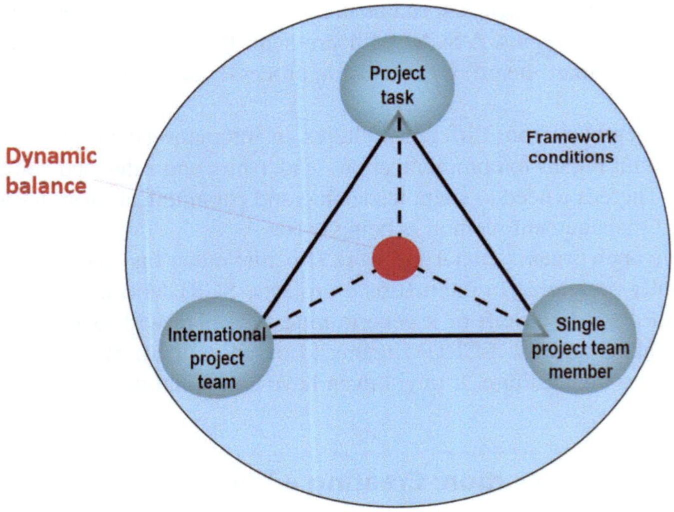

Fig. 6.8 Magic triangle of successful project implementation based on Ruth Cohn's theme-centered interaction

(c) Managing the **individual project team member**, who has his/her culturally driven needs.

It is all about bringing these three aspects together by asking yourself

▶ ***"Do I reflect sufficiently on the needs of the team and its individual members in my project?"***

The graph below is an illustration of how to deal with the irreconcilable. The red ball in the middle is an oscillating bullet which hangs on elastic strings. To keep the dynamic balance when moving between the three cornerstones you always have to keep the overall target in mind. What will be your assessment and solution if you have to decide between working in a virtual team with video conferencing and telephone calls instead of onsite travelling because of costs?

This model is known as theme-centered interaction by Ruth Cohn[8] who developed it in the 1960s to support working processes in groups (Fig. 6.8).

Remotivating an International Virtual Project Team

An international project with team members across the world developed a new control unit for a manufacturing machine in the automotive sector. Virtual communication, language barriers and lack of intercultural awareness led to misunderstandings and unsatisfactory intermediate results:

[8]https://www.ruth-cohn-institute.org/home.html. Last viewed 24.10.2018.

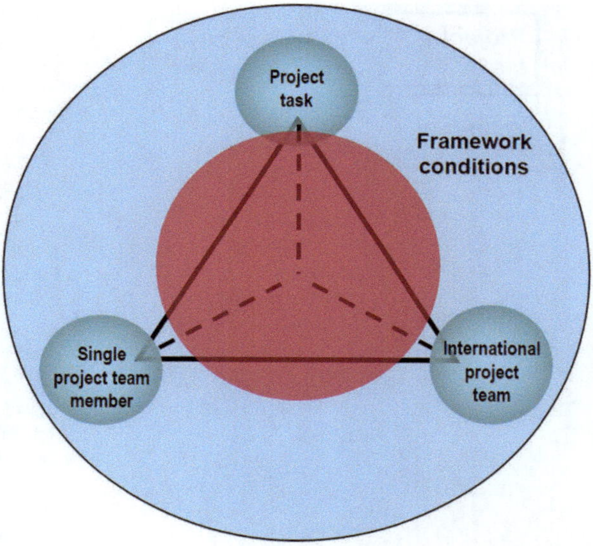

Fig. 6.9 Applying the theme-centered interaction model to an international engineering project

The project management methods used were locally interpreted in different ways and did not make the cultural hurdle.
The project leader was positioned and perceived as a facilitator rather than a real project leader.
Objectives and scope of the project were not defined precisely.
As time went on, the project team was increasingly demotivated: The members did not really grasp of the detailed aspects of the project as well as the why and what of the collaboration.

The graph below illustrates the dilemma: The theme-centered interaction model shows a diffused energy ball because of missing priorities, e.g. decisions (Fig. 6.9).

For the project team members and also other stakeholders it was not clear that they were moving in three interlinked areas of action (task, team, single member) and they disregarded their interdependencies. The binding element was missing—a project leader in command with the authority to bring everything together in reconciling the irreconcilable.

At a workshop the theme-centered interaction method was introduced. With this tool the interdependencies were discussed. The team members themselves developed a model aiming at bringing the project back on track. The anonymized graph below of the pin board shows the final project design resulting in specific recommendations:

(a) Specific actions are defined for the three dimensions as per the TCI model. *Project task* (orange cards), *Project team* (green cards) and *Single project team member* (blue cards).

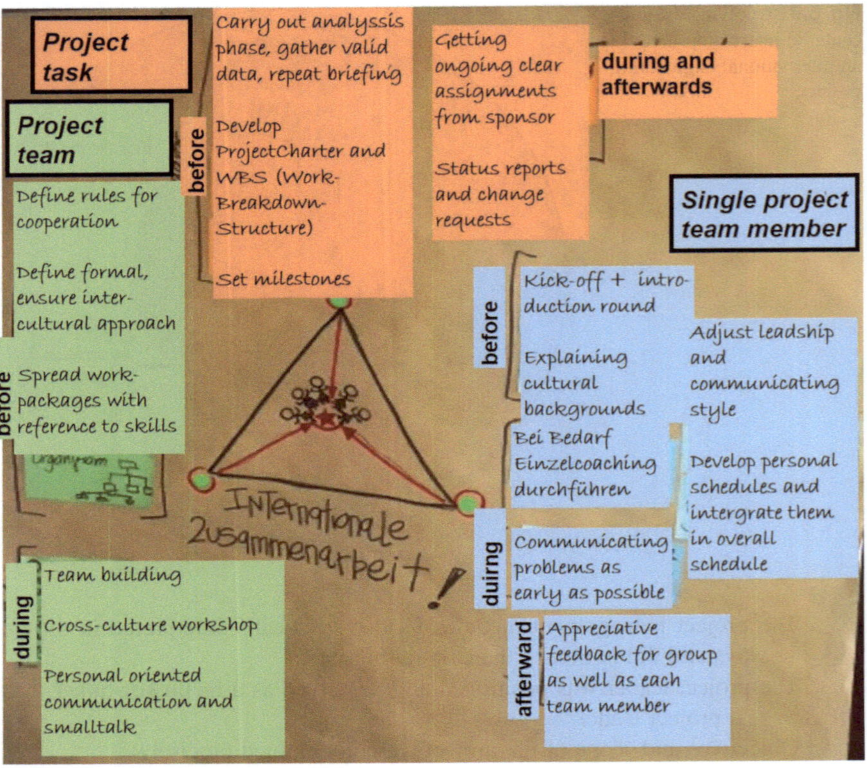

Fig. 6.10 Results of a theme-centered interaction workshop for an international project

(b) All actions were split up in *before, during* and *after*: Not only technical tips like create WBS were included but also interculturally driven tasks like ensure intercultural approach or explain cultural backgrounds.

(c) By re-designing the dynamic triangle in the center of the graph below these three dimensions were now interlinked. "*Internationale Zusammenarbeit!*" (*international cooperation*) provided the heading and summarized the learnings of the project team (Fig. 6.10).

6.11 Project Monitoring and Controlling: Make Yourself Understood by Simplifying

Planning and implementation of a project are directly connected with monitoring and controlling. Time, scope and cost are matched against the plan and adjusted if necessary.

In virtual intercultural and cross-border interfaces, simplified and tailored techniques help to demonstrate project process, aligning the cross-cultural project team and keeping the international project on track. This is seen below.

6.11.1 Milestone Trend Analysis: The Yardstick for International Understanding of Progress in Projects

Milestones correspond to the objective of simplification and this is perhaps why this trend analysis is one of the most widely used techniques in projects worldwide. It gains additional significance in international projects because milestones are pivotal, easy to communicate and understand for stakeholders from different cultures.

Milestones indicate which intermediate deliverables are to be achieved. They have a defined duration of zero and describe a status. To create a common understanding across cultures and language barriers, the description of the milestone should be self-explanatory, i.e. *rollout approved*, *kick-off done* etc.

Set milestones sparingly, otherwise they lose their function as orientation markers.

If you are not very familiar with this technique, you will find a brief explanation with the graph below (Fig. 6.11):

1. The milestone trend analysis is represented as isosceles triangle with two timelines showing the same time units from 0 to 20:
   (a) The horizonal *milestone baseline* axis serves to set the initially planned timing for the milestones
   (b) The vertical *reporting axis* serves to render the achievement status against the planned timing for the milestone
2. Milestone changes or shifts always refer to the project plan, i.e. the graph above shows that "milestone *concept approved*" was achieved 4 weeks later than planned. Thus, the following phases "*Implementation*" and "*final test approval*" will also be delayed accordingly.
3. Possible deviations from the plan may be underlined by red arrows as shown in the box of the above graph:
   (a) Milestone moving right means timing is getting off track.
   (b) Milestone moving straight down means status remains the same.
   (c) Milestone moving left means gaining time versus the planned milestone.
4. When a milestone has been achieved, it will lie on the diagonal "*completion axis*". If a milestone is on time as planned, it will be shown as a straight downward line from the planning axis until it meets the diagonal "*completion axis*".

This two-step principle will provide faster results when obtaining information on milestones in a cross-cultural context with differing management methods, different languages, differing teamwork:

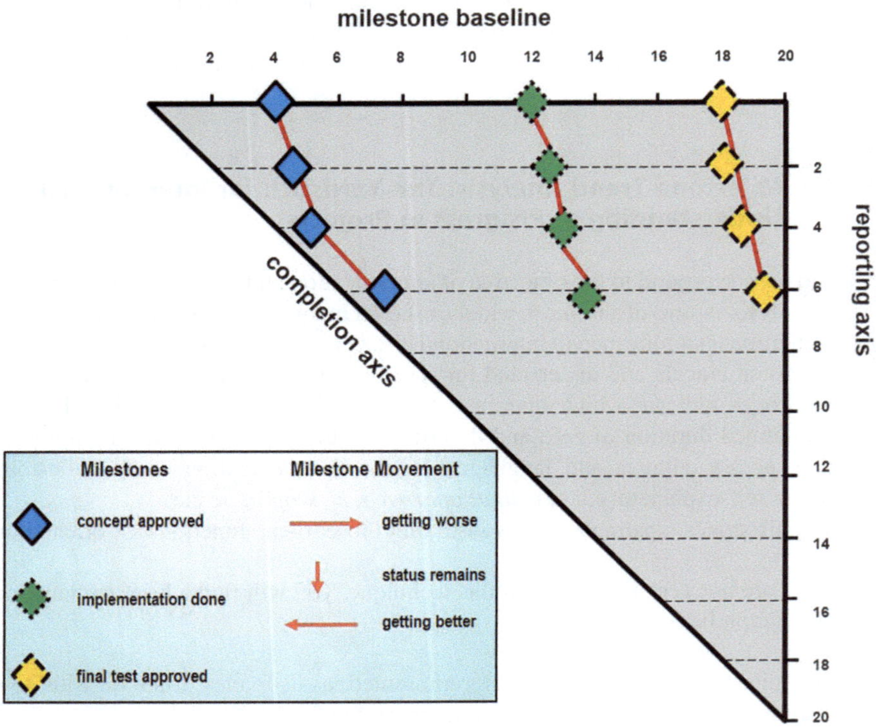

Fig. 6.11 Milestone trend analysis

1. Send an advance notice to the project partners regarding the kind of information is expected for the next milestone progress report.
2. Finetune the project progress for the given milestone for the trend analysis. Learn the ropes about cross cultural management and communication for this.

Refer to literature such as PMBOK[9] for further trend analyses, e.g. *the earned-value analysis*, which is increasingly being used in international projects.

Resetting of a Turk-Austrian Project

An Austrian project leader ran an infrastructure project in Turkey. He was not often on-site, felt rather uncomfortable in the Turkish culture and their very personal way of communication. Moreover, clear goals were missing. His challenge was to reset the ongoing project with its time and cost overruns. He learned how to go about it at an international project management training:

[9](PMBOK® Guide), 6th edition page 261 onwards.

(a) He set up a 3-day workshop in Istanbul with all teams. In addition to the technical, formal meetings he also took care to allocate time for socializing at dinners.
(b) Precisely defined milestones with responsibilities were discussed and agreed upon, i.e. who has to deliver which intermediate results and by when. Also, the approval procedure was agreed upon!
(c) Progress status was to be reported and controlled by an IT-supported milestone trend analysis accessible online to both the team and the decision makers.
(d) A culturally experienced project controller was appointed to implement complementary monitoring techniques such as *Earned-Value-Management*.

6.11.2 What Degree of Completion Should Your Plan Achieve?

The degree of completion helps to assess how far the project with its sub-projects have progressed, whether the project is still on time and if the goals for quality and budget can be reached. The degree of completion is also the basis for the earned value analysis mentioned above.

To obtain reliable results of the degree of completion requires a communication style that is adapted to the cultures involved. Whilst in some cultures a degree of completion can be questioned straightforwardly, this may be rather difficult in East Asia, India or in Arab countries with more refined and diplomatic ways to communicate. On-site reviews and face-to-face communication may get faster and better results.

Adapting Reporting in an Arab Country

An investment project to build new factory for consumer products was to be set up in Middle East. The project leader had already initiated the planning process as well as the kick-off. Because the start had been so successful, he thought that virtual communication would do the job for the follow-up. He established reporting via e-mail and project management software.

He soon discovered that status data such as degree of completion were invalid because of misunderstandings and lost information.

He started travelling again regularly on-site, got closer to people by informal contacts in the office. By asking back and forth questions he was in a better position to evaluate the validity of the given information. Showing his face was also a demonstration that he was the boss, status being an important criterion in Arab cultures.

6.11.3 Avoiding the Pitfalls of Contracts and Claim Management in Collectivist Cultures

In Japan, Arab countries and other collectivist cultures, the contract is a result of a profound personal relationship built up over a longer period of time. The relationship is of a greater value than the formal contract and is therefore more binding.

We know of German and Swiss companies doing excellent, win-win business with Japan or China for years without any contractual basis. The personal relationship is everything.

Claim management[10] is a tool for the client as well as for the supplier to resolve unforeseen happenings which may occur during a project and cannot be foreseen within a pre-defined management process. *Claim management,* which is widely recognized in the German or Anglo-American context, has a great potential for conflicts beyond the technical aspects. In a cross-cultural context with different languages, management and negotiation styles, and attitudes towards contracts (written contract versus personal relationship), the variables for potential conflict increase and may even lead to a rupture.

In many non-Western cultures, the trust and credibility given in a relationship is the binding element, as shown in the graph below (Fig. 6.12):

6.12 Closing a Project: Success Is Universal

If your project is a success, make it public. Let it to be known to all participants and stakeholders and praise their commitment and contribution. A feeling of success need not be culturally translated, just adequately communicated.

Evaluating and communicating the lessons learned in culturally appropriate terms is a key factor for motivation.

On the formal side, you will follow the closing procedures such as preliminary and final acceptance tests of the end product, approval procedures, final accounting, and contract termination as well as lessons learned.

► If ever you have to give critical feedback in project reviews, avoid direct personal criticism in public. Do it in one-on-one talks.

The International Project Review

An IT-based strategic international project was to implement a new quality assurance process covering the entire manufacturing area. It included a change in business processes, responsibilities as well as the functional organization units within a period of 3 years.

[10]Details see PMBOK® GUIDE 6th edition Chapter 12 *Procurement Management* page 459 and following.

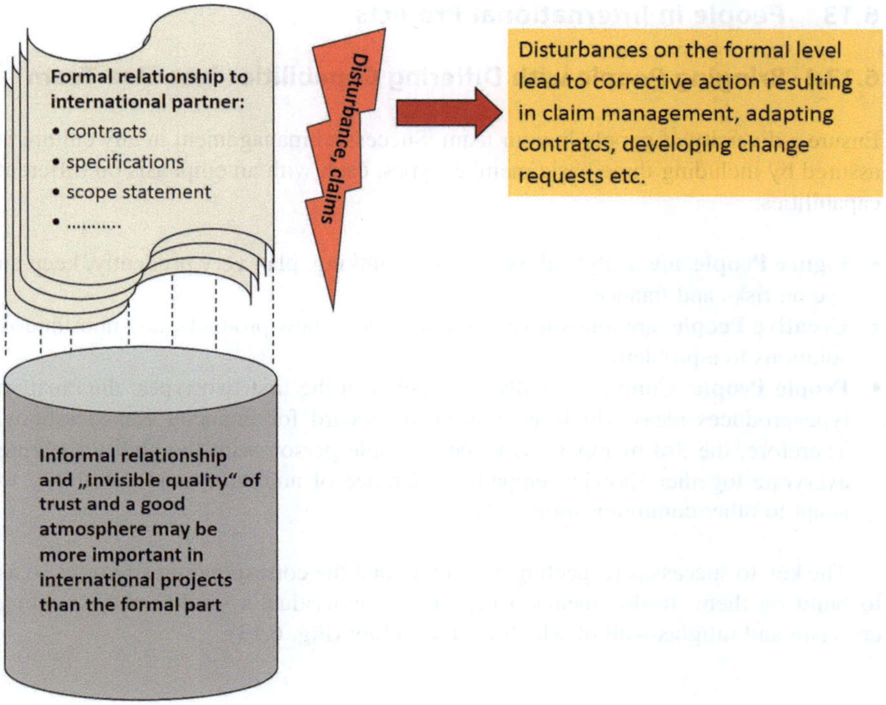

Fig. 6.12 Formal and informal ingredients in international projects

A worldwide project team was organized with members from China, Vietnam, India, France, Great Britain, Germany, Finland and the USA.

After 1.5 years, an intermediate project review was conducted for lessons learned and how to manage conflicts. Different communication styles between the West and Asia had led to technical misunderstandings and resistance on the Asian side.

With this in mind, the facilitator did the review face-to-face with about 80% of the team, the remaining team members having no time. Rules were agreed upon at the start, such as treating each other fairly and respectfully. Personal questions and critical issues were always dealt with in one-on-one talks.

Playing by the rules, the facilitator was able to create a motivating team atmosphere based on trust during this 2-day review.

6.13 People in International Projects

6.13.1 Bringing People with Differing Capabilities into One Team

Ensure a diversity of people in your team. Successful management in any culture is assured by including three basic member types, each with an emphasis on different capabilities:

- **Figure People**: are analytical, stringent in thinking, plan very prudently, keep an eye on risks and finances.
- **Creative People**: are innovative, with new ideas, new products, and unorthodox solutions to a problem.
- **People People**: Conflicts usually arise between the first two types; the creative type produces ideas which are thrown overboard for financial considerations. Therefore, the 3rd member has to be a people person with the ability to bring everyone together showing empathy, tolerance of ambiguity and the ability to adapt to other communication styles.

The key to success is respecting each other and the corresponding strengths so as to build on them. It also means accepting the individual's weaknesses, avoiding criticism and infights—all of which lead to failure (Fig. 6.13).

6.13.2 The Successful International Project Manager

The mind-map below is an overview of criteria for successful project management in an international context (Fig. 6.14):

6.13.2.1 The Ideal Cross Cultural Project Manager?

You are something of a diplomat with a cross cultural education, be it at home or on the job. You are capable of communicating without prejudices or reservations. Your feedback, both oral and written, is always culturally appropriate and acceptable. You have the patience to wait for an answer from a person whose English is not perfect, and you do not jump to conclusions. You are curious and empathetic, and you enjoy

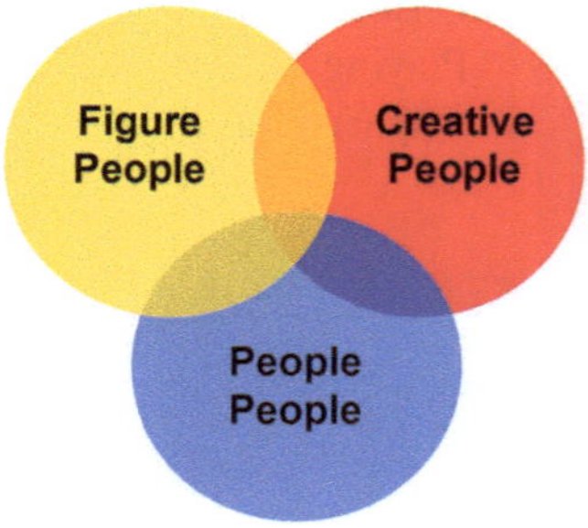

Fig. 6.13 Model of the characters in a perfect team

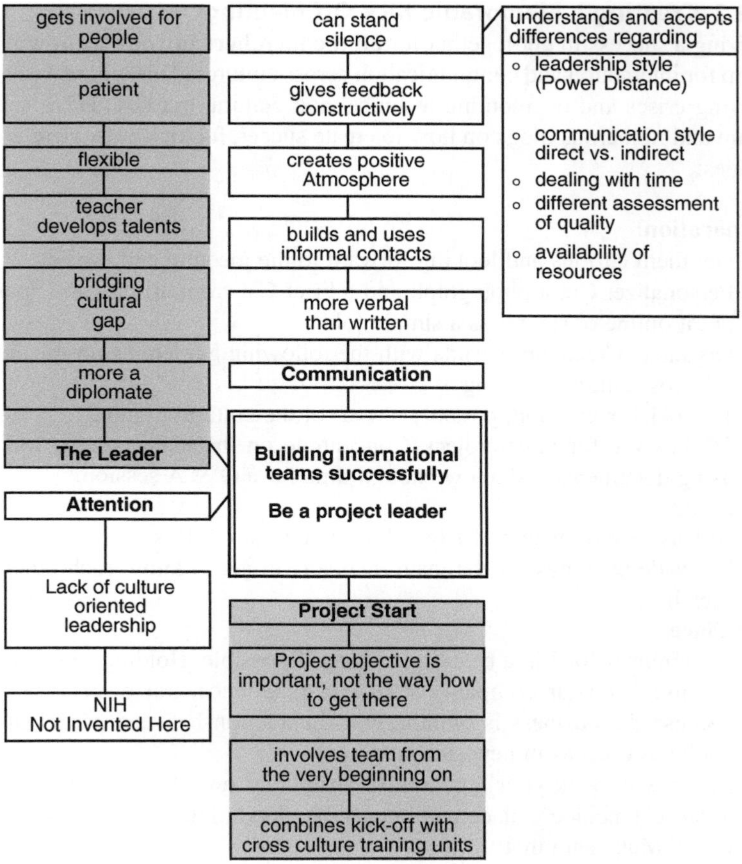

Fig. 6.14 Overview: criteria for international teambuilding

interacting with new and different people. You like to recognize and develop their talents. You are a teacher but not a lecturer! You can wait out ambiguous situations patiently. You have the flexibility to accept that things will not always go your way. Yet you never lose sight of your target and you are capable of realizing it with and through your team.

Nobody is perfect. There is a great likelihood that you may not match all the above characteristics. Don't worry, chose an assistant whose strengths lie in the areas you need. Let us say you are a seasoned Project Manager and have a perfect grasp of all the technical details. But somehow you feel that there is a need for more social contacts, which is not really your strength. In this case, find an empathic person, maybe even from the culture you are working with, as your second-in-command. Make sure you align your strengths instead of infighting about the weaker sides. If you can achieve it, your team will be unbeatable.

6.13.2.2 Creating a Memorable Kick-Off Meeting

Organizing a successful get-together for **all the members in your team** will build a platform for interaction and communication across cultures. This will serve as a basis for solving crises and overcoming technical and cultural hurdles. There is a lot of literature and numerous blogs on how to create successful kick-offs. Here are a few guidelines:

1. **Preparation**:
   (a) Get them curious and looking forward to the meeting and project.
   (b) Personalize: Get a photograph and a brief CV from all the participants and put it online or send it as a simple folder
   (c) Organize: Create an Agenda with the following guidelines for the contents:
   (d) 1/3 cross cultural training
   (e) 1/3 social interaction, possibly as part of the cultural training
   (f) 1/3 briefing for your project. Concentrate on the main issues. Add details using documents and allow enough time for a Q & A session.
2. **Duration**:
   (a) At least one or even better two days, maximum 3 days.
   (b) Set aside evenings for the team members to get to know each other and to socialize.
3. **The Place**:
   (a) A (seminar) hotel in a beautiful setting, if possible. Holding seminars on the premises of your company is, in our experience, not even a 2nd choice because the business is omnipresent. Interaction between participants may not be as open as in new surroundings.
   (b) Before you book your hotel, make absolutely sure that it is the right place, because a mediocre place will impact the mood of the participants, as well as yours. Make sure that:
      (i) The meeting room is big enough
      (ii) The seminar infrastructure is complete and the IT working
      (iii) The hotel rooms are comfortable
      (iv) The restaurants have a contemporary, maybe culturally oriented cuisine. Make sure that everybody likes it.
4. **Invitation**:
   (a) Put all this information online.
   (b) Make your future team members look forward to this event and stir their curiosity, possibly by including surprise elements in your program.
5. **The Meeting**:
   (a) Start off with a short, lighthearted speech, avoiding technical and business details and then let the program roll.
   (b) Move around in between people and groups all through the meeting. Make sure you give enough time for every member of your team.
   (c) Summing it up: Wrap up the essential takeaways from the kick-off in maximum 10 min. Remind them of maximum three key issues in your project. Don't lecture—motivate!

6. **Follow-Up**:
   (a) Put a resumé of the kick-off online with the key issues and takeaways
   (b) Let take and share photographs of the get-together in an online album.

This may not be your first international meeting and you may already have the experience and expertise to put it up yourself. If you are a beginner, consult any of the numerous blogs or corresponding literature.[11]

► **Involve a Cross Cultural Facilitator** You may be well advised to get an intercultural facilitator specializing in international team development to organize the program. Interactive games and cross-cultural information should be included to create a common understanding and team spirit.

This will relieve you of organizational tasks and you can devote your time to forging personal relationships.

► A successful kick-off is just the start, not a guarantee for success. It is a foundation to build on. It helps you concentrate on what constitutes success: CARING FOR YOUR PEOPLE

6.13.3 The Way to Get Decisions?

The Harvard Principles, which are discussed in Sect. 4.19.7.2 "*Negotiations*" help to evaluate any given situation in a negotiation or cooperation for a win-win solution. Here are a few suggestions for the road to success:

(a) Use open questions, train your listening capabilities and read body language to identify interests.
(b) Be aware of power factors and leverage them if needed. In international projects, we often have to deal with hierarchical management styles. The simplest way to solve critical issues is to escalate it to the next management level. However, if you do this, make sure both managers have rapport with each other. There may be informal influencers who have access to higher management levels. Before you tap them make sure that it does not backfire by hurting the direct partner's feelings.
(c) Define your problem briefly and succinctly with a simple question, i.e. "*Why isn't the Indian subproject-software-team delivering the expected results?*"

[11]Macchi, Margit E, The Trainer's Toolbox: The Secrets to Creating a Successful Seminar from Scratch, Stairway Press, 25.09.2018. von. (Autor).

6.13.4 Getting the Information for the Decision

A thorough stakeholder analysis will show you where to tap genuine sources for input for your decisions. The graph and table below are models for how to prepare your analyses for an overall picture and how to rank and approach key stakeholders in your project (Fig. 6.15):

This is how to proceed:

(a) Fill in the above list with the names and positions of your stakeholders. Include everybody who is involved or feels involved in your project—a government official or an NGO may be as important or even more important than the investor for getting the go-ahead.
(b) Thereafter, break down the stakeholders in groups, then identify groups or the single persons by name and position to assess the degree of influence and power they wield as clearly as possible and whether they support the project. Add information about your stakeholders such as culture, power orientation etc. to the list. Identify if you need to build up a personal relationship or if you can delegate it to a team member.
(c) Then, focus on the powerholders, whether stakeholders, friends or critical parties. Understand the interests involved and their cultural needs.
(d) Draft the organizational chart of the specific international project as well as the functional organization of the project partners, focusing on key persons. Align that with the assessment done in the stakeholder analysis. Make clear which role key-stakeholders have in the project organization and the functional organization. Understand which communication channels have to be strengthened.
(e) List the reasons for potential or actual problems and derive measures. Often, an important part of the solution will be powerholders who communicate formally or informally amongst themselves to get things done.
(f) Adapt and adjust your leadership style and communication to cultural needs.

Regaining Control Across the Finnish and Indian Border

An ERP-Project[12] based in Finland relied on data processed in India. There was only a rudimentary project plan. An organizational chart was missing, chain of command and milestones were not cleared. Therefore, deliverables from India were often delayed and data lacked quality.

An analysis showed that line manager of the Indian sub-project leader and her team had not been sufficiently involved.

Moreover, the superiors of the project manager had not understood the differing needs of international cooperation, i.e. face-to face interaction and on-site visits. They did not approve travelling expenses. Thus, a kick-off meeting never took place and communication was limited to emails and phone calls.

[12]ERP means *Enterprise Resource Planning* which stands for complex software systems like SAP or Navision to implement and monitor business processes more efficiently.

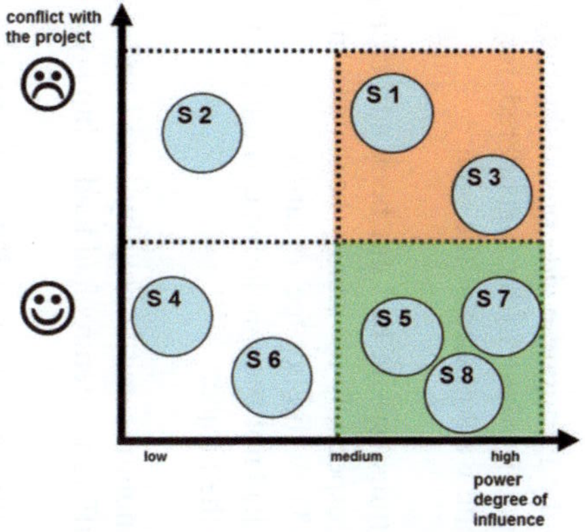

Stakeholder	Power and degree of influence	Describe influence	Culture	Power distance	Role in project	Communication needs	Additional context information	Describe affected interest (maybe conflict)	Measures
S1									
S3									
S7									
.....									

Fig. 6.15 Stakeholder analysis and communications planning

To get the project back on track, the Finnish project manager convinced his CEO that he needed his personal commitment, also with regard to funds so that the project could be completed successfully.

After getting his agreement, both traveled to India and set up a series of meetings. With the CEO on his side, he could arrange meetings with the whole Indian management as they were on par in terms of hierarchy.

At subsequent meetings the line manager, i.e. the superior of the Indian sub-project manager, was directly involved along with other functional managers connected to this project. Project details were negotiated and agreed upon. The presence of the Finnish top management and the project leader helped to start a positive and motivating relationship with the Indian partner.

To enhance cooperation further, the Finnish project manager travelled every 3–4 months to India.

Finding and Winning Your Stakeholders

A project led by a British service group was to build an entertainment park in the neighborhood of a medium-sized town in a rural region of Portugal to attract short-term business visitors and tourists. The plan was to have a kind of Portuguese Disneyland, creating an authentic but romanticized experience of daily Portuguese life.

The numerous stakeholder interests on the Portuguese side posed the biggest challenge. Family and neighborhood structures had to be considered for the project. A stakeholder analysis identified the weaknesses of the plan:

(a) The families and neighborhood structures on-site had not been sufficiently consulted. They didn't feel informed, especially the family heads and informal spokesmen of the neighborhood. They did not feel regarded.
(b) The staff of the Portuguese subsidiary had not been included enough because of their secondary, supporting role in the project

Again, the English project manager communicated largely by email and was unaware of the necessity to adjust to the different, hierarchical leadership style in Portugal.

In Portugal, family values and mutual support amongst each other are a basic value in this society, particularly in rural regions.

After realizing this, the British project manager started a turnaround:

(i) The project manager adapted his leadership and communication style.
(ii) With the lessons learned he set up an intermediate workshop onsite in Portugal with his Portuguese team to develop a joint plan on how to convince and involve stakeholders in the immediate vicinity of the entertainment park.

(iii) The project organization was adjusted. The Portuguese team was led by a newly appointed sub-project leader who acted as a deputy for the manager on-site when the project manager was not present.
(iv) As the next step, talks with stakeholder-families and community leaders were intensified to understand their needs and concerns.
(v) A joint event was organized for the residents. The project was first presented by the boss of the British group, then by the British project leader and by his Portuguese deputy. Then the local community leaders spoke to their people to persuade them to support the project. It ended with a big party with Fado and local food.
(vi) Thereafter, the project manager visited Portugal regularly to stay in touch with the project team and stakeholders.

6.14 Checklist for Success in International Projects

Take Care of the Soft Factors

1. Carry out a kick-off with the whole project team including a briefing as well as training for the cultures involved. Start a team building process. Get support from a specialized intercultural facilitator.
2. Make your team part of the solution: Be aware of the potential hurdles created by the *NIH-Factor* (not invented here). Involve, as early as possible, all the parties in the project process, be it at the start or at reviews.
3. Find and involve every stakeholder from the very beginning and build relationships with cultural awareness to get support for your project.
4. Create a suitable project organization with adequate technical support involving all the cultures concerned. Be culture sensitive, know and respect the other cultures and make sure you do not hurt their values and feelings. If you cause a mishap, learn to apologize according to the customs of a given culture (see Sect. 3.7 "*Behaviour in Case of a Conflict: Carry Out or Avoid*")
5. Personalize your communication style. Build your relationships with the teams and stakeholders and see it as ongoing task. Remember, all business is personal!
6. As an international project leader, be more of a diplomat than a technocrat.
7. Deepen your intercultural awareness, adapt your leadership style.

Tailor Methods to the Intercultural Context

1. Focus on a few clear and simple objectives. Clarify main goals precisely. Work along the lines of the target circle and create a project charter

(continued)

supported by the whole team. Get their consent through culturally adapted feedback loops.

2. Adjust project management methods and give team members leeway according to their cultural needs.
3. When using the core elements of project management, create open spaces within a general structure. Discuss and agree on the basic features of the underlying framework and key data.
4. Build a rough work breakdown structure and define broad work packages leaving room for the team members to contribute.
5. Discuss and set key milestones with the team to get their commitment.
6. Identify and be aware of the main risks deriving from the cross-cultural context. Put them in your plan.

Project Follow-Up

1. Set up a communication management plan containing the key elements for a successful communication across languages and cultures. Hold meetings regularly, either from time to time or as needed, if ever so possible face-to-face and onsite.
2. Take care of stakeholders and their interests with special attention to their culture.
3. Monitor risks, also those deriving from the cultures involved.
4. Use milestone trend analysis and be constantly aware of what this may mean in your cross-cultural context. Think first about the facts, then package them to get your message across cultural barriers.
5. Review and close a project with praise. And more praise! Celebrate the success! The joy of success is universal.

► **Become a Bridge Builder Across Cultures**
Develop your culture-oriented leadership continuously and be aware of it at all times when interacting with other cultures.

Learning interculturally also means the ability to learn from mishaps. If you are hurt, get over it and think twice before you reply. There is always a reason why your culture collided with your partner's. Finding the reasons behind it will lead to the solution.

Remember the key words are *"WE"*, *"thank you"* and *"I am sorry"*.

Achieving success in your own culture gives you satisfaction. Creating success across cultures is the ultimate fulfillment for a professional in project management.

Bibliography

English Literature

DeMarco, T. (1997). *The deadline* (1st ed.). New York: Dorset House Publishing.
Hall, E. T. (1959, 1981). *The silent language.* New York: Doubleday Anchor Books.
Kerzner, H. (2009). *Project management. A systems approach to planning, scheduling and controlling* (10th ed.). Hoboken: Wiley.
Mulcahy, R. (2018). *PMP® exam prep* (9th ed.). RMC Publications, Inc.
Nägele, U. (2014). *Lighthouses and warning buoys in the field of international project management.* https://www.xing.com/profile/Ulrich_Naegele3?sc_o=mxb_p
Project Management Institute (PMI®). (2017). *A guide to the project management body of knowledge (PMBOK® Guide)* (6th ed.). Newton Square: Project Management Institute.
https://www.scrumguides.org/scrum-guide.html
http://agilemanifesto.org
Watzlawick, P., et al. (2011). *Pragmatics of human communication.* New York: W.W. Norton & Company, Inc.

German Literature

Kompetenzbasiertes Projektmanagement (PM3). (2012). *Handbuch für die Projektarbeit, Qualifizierung und Zertifizierung auf Basis der IPMA Competence Baseline Version 3.0* (5th ed.). GPM Deutsche Gesellschaft für Projektmanagement.
Meier, H. (Hrsg.). (2015). *Internationales Projektmanagement* (1st ed.). Herne: NWB Verlag.
https://www.xing.com/profile/Ulrich_Naegele3?sc_o=mxb_p
http://bit.ly/themenzentrierte_interaktion
https://www.projektmagazin.de/artikel/qualitaet-im-internationalen-projekt-zielfuehrend-managen_1090785
https://www.projektmagazin.de/artikel/fuehrung-internationalen-projekten-einflussfaktor-machtdistanz_913140

Résumés/CV of Authors

Vinita Balasubramanian

INTERCULTURAL TRAINING &
CONSULTING
Balasubramanian@gmx.de

Professional Experience

Freelance intercultural trainer and facilitator for teams and processes and one-on-one consultant for international leadership. Clients include Robert Bosch GmbH, Daimler AG, Allianz, Continental ADC, Merck, WMF with assignments in Germany, India, Italy, France, Turkey, Switzerland and Austria.

Court and therapy Interpreter for German, English and Tamil

Adjunct Faculty: University of Esslingen (Intercultural Communication), visiting lecturer at Jena and Berlin Universities, Anglia Ruskin University Cambridge UK

Teacher-Trainer in Adult Education for the Federal State of Baden-Württemberg, Germany

P. M. Haller et al., *Bridging Cultural Barriers*, Management for Professionals,
https://doi.org/10.1007/978-3-030-17130-8

Educational and Professional Qualifications

- Ongoing PhD research: 'Gap Factors in Communication in Indian-German Virtual Engineering-IT Teams' (working title)
- 2012: Certified Civil and Commercial Mediator (LSM, UK)
- 2009: Certificate in Intercultural Training (LTS, England)
- 2005–2006: Certificate in Change Management (Synnecta, Germany)
- 2001: Certificate for Intervention Techniques (Embassy, England)
- 1999: Certificate for Teaching English for Business Purposes (LCCI, England)
- 1978: Certified and Court-appointed Translator and Interpreter for German, English and Tamil
- 1969–1974: M.A. in English Literature, University of Madras, India

Publications

- 2013: Interview SIETAREUROPA journal, March 2013 issue
- 2010: 'Living and Working in India' (Original title: 'Leben und Arbeiten in Indien'), V&R Verlag
- 2009: 'Preparing for a Secondment to India' (Original title: 'Umgang mit der funktionierenden Anarchie: Vorbereitung auf die Entsendung nach Indien'), University of Heidelberg

Languages

English, German, Tamil, Hindi, basic Italian
Seminars and Workshops held in German or English.

Michael C. Ferrier

British of Scottish/Dutch parentage
Born 12 July 1936

1954
Graduate of Stowe Private School, Buckingham, UK.
1955
Trainee Clifford Bloxham,
Medium sized London Advertising Agency.
1959
Shell International London.
Advertising Dept. product development,
Magazine Editor, Advertising Manager Shell Holland, and Shell Switzerland.
1966
McCann Erickson World Wide.
Esso account coordinator Europe.
Opened Zurich Office.
Deputy Manager Paris office.
Chairman Canadian Company.
Regional Director Latin America,
Regional Director Europe,
Regional Director Africa and The East.
1995
Retired.
Professor IUM, Monaco (10 years)
(Subjects: Marketing, International negotiations, Cross- Cultural understanding.)
Operated annual Next Entrepreneurs competition.
Advised both the Monegasque and (later) Cayman Islands Governments.
Lectured at various international forums, and for Chamber of Commerce.
Writer of two biographies and five novels (Amazon.com)
Rotarian.
Lived in:
London, Paris, Zurich, Amsterdam, Brussels, Toronto, Mexico City, San Jose (Costa Rica), Caracas, and Hong Kong.
Languages.
(a) English, French, Dutch, German, Spanish

Michael C. Ferrier.
PO Box 719, Camana Bay, Grand Cayman, Cayman Islands KY1-9006
Email: Mike.ferrier.ky@gmail.com.

Peter M. Haller

Cross Culture Coaching ©
Roosstrasse 66
8105 Regensdorf
Switzerland
pm.haller@bluewin.ch
Swiss, born 17.04.1936.

Professional Overview

Starting in business in the late 50s, my entire professional experience is based on on-the-job training. Marketing and advertising were in its infancy. I owe my business and basic cultural knowledge to the 20 years of working in management positions in Europe and Japan for two large American advertising agencies with blue chip clients like, Coco-Cola, Exxon, General Motors, Gillette, Miele, Nestle, Unilever, etc.

At the age of 50, I started my career as consultant and coach, at first in international marketing. However, I soon discovered that the young people I was training had the latest techniques in marketing. What was missing was competence in dealing with people in other cultures. Soon cross culture coaching and facilitating became my vocation, handing down my experience to young executives. I began to lecture and train on international projects across the continents. Today my training experience covers participants from most cultures of our world.

In looking back at my professional life, I am grateful for all those rewarding encounters with people from cultures around the world, both positive and negative, which brought me forward.

Education and Basic Business Experience

1955: Diploma of Senior Commercial High School in Aarau, Switzerland
1955–1962: Training in Industry. Publishing and Banking in Switzerland

Work History

1963–1985: Consultant and general manager in international advertising agencies for consumer and investment goods in Switzerland, France, Belgium, Germany and Japan.

1985–1994: Consultant for international market expansion for medium sized Swiss companies

As of 1994: Facilitator and Coach for large multinational companies mainly in Germany for expatriation and teambuilding with France, US, China, Japan, Russia and Switzerland

Lecturer at the Export-Academy in Reutlingen, Germany covering topics like International Marketing and Cross Cultural Management to build management training centers with Universities in China, Vietnam, Russia, Belarus, Lithuania, Ukraine, Hungary, Slovakia, Palestine, Tunisia.

Lecturer in Bachelor courses at Private Hochschule für Wirtschaft in Bern and in Master Classes in International Management at the University of Nürtingen

Languages

Fluent: German, French and English
Good: Spanish, Italian, and Dutch
Basic: Japanese

Ulrich Naegele PMP®

Project Management Professional, Agile Coach, Trainer, Facilitator
info@ulrich-naegele.de

More than 25 years of experience and activity for global companies and for leading education providers in international and national projects, M. A. in Economics, Pedagogy, and Political Science

Professional Experience
Project management and intercultural expert. Trainer, facilitator for international/national projects, project teams, decision makers and other stakeholders.

Clients are leading companies in the engineering, services, administration and IT-sector, i.e. Hella + other big automotive suppliers, Bundespresseamt, Haufe Akademie, Danone, Export Academy, Carl Duisberg Gesellschaft.

Assignments in Eastern Europe, France, Germany, Switzerland, Scandinavia.

Lecturer for Intercultural Management and International Project Management

Universitys of Stuttgart, Karlsruhe, Nürtingen, Jena, Donaueschingen

Educational and Professional Qualifications

- From 2005: Diverse certificates: Project Management Professional PMP®, Systemic Consultant, SCRUM Master, Product Owner.
- Since 2003: Freelance consultant, project management professional, intercultural expert, trainer, coach, facilitator for global companies and for leading education providers
- 1999–2002: ExperTeam AG, consultant, trainer, coach, facilitator for project management, organizational development, intercultural management
- 1993–1998: International project management for Eastern and Middle Eastern Europe, Intercultural management, facilitation, evaluation. Diverse organizations as Carl Duisberg Society or Export Academy.
- 1996: M.A. in Economics, Pedagogy, and Political Science.
  Thesis topic: Personal development in the intercultural context

Publications

- 2014: Lighthouses and warning buoys in the field of international project management
  https://www.xing.com/profile/Ulrich_Naegele3?sc_o=mxb_p
- 2013: Praxishandbuch Interkulturelles Management, Springer
- Since 2010: Various publications in www.projektmagazin.de, i.e. Leadership in International Projects, Quality in International Projects, Project Review
- 2008: International Projects, Project Organization. Fare course handouts Haufe Akademie.

Languages

English, German, French, basics in Spanish and Italian

Raeid Meri

Focus on Man and Encounters
email raeid@walkthechange.de
web www.walkthechange.de
Place of birth Bonn
Nationality German, Jordanian

Education and Qualifications

- Intercultural Trainer und Coach
- Experience Educator
- Businessman
- Computer Scientist

Key Areas in Trainings and Coaching

- Intercultural training with the goal to develop a holistic understanding of the thinking and behavior of people from other cultures
- Seminars for action-oriented team development with the aim of increasing trust, motivation and success
- Project Management
- Communication training
- Conflict management
- Experience-oriented personality and orientation development

Professional Experience/Areas of Expertise

- 15 years management experience in the areas of Consultation, Marketing, Distribution and Product Development in various DAX corporation and start-ups. i.e. Head of Education Marketing at Deutsche Telekom AG (2000–2008).
- Since 2012, Independent Trainer und Coach with emphasis on Team and Personal Development, Intercultural Management and Communication.
- Lecturer and Intercultural Trainer at the German-Jordanian-University in Amman, Jordan.

- Experienced manager on major marketing and sales projects, including the development of strategies and products for the opening of new on business areas (e.g. Education Market, Online Marketing, Cloud Technology.)
- Own cultural focus on Germany and the Middle East
- Multicultural experience in about 100 countries on all continents.
- Volunteer for several non-profit NGOs (e.g. CARE, Caritas) in Germany and the Near East
- Participation and creation of various projects to support refugees and disadvantaged people (e.g. Sameplace)

Work Languages

- German, Arabic, English

Adiza Ujo

No: 13, 3rd Avenue
FHA Gwarimpa
Phase II Abuja
+234(0)82116373
adizaujo@yahoo.com

Professional Overview
I am a passionate environmental advocate committed to ending littering in Nigeria and providing engagement opportunities from waste. I am dogged and resilient about finding sustainable solutions to environmental issues that plague my community.

I am an astute entrepreneur with strong project management skills and the ability to develop ideas

A good manager of people and resources and a great team player with the ability to fuel team spirits and achieve set goals and targets.

Education

1. Master in International Affairs and Diplomacy (MIAD)
   (a) Ahmadu Bello University Zaria 2006
   (b) Usmanu Danfodiyo University Sokoto 2004

Work/Employment History

- March 2018 till May 31, 2018
  Political and Economic Assistant to the Ambassador Embassy of the Socialist Republic of Vietnam Abuja, Nigeria
- June 2016 till Dec 2017
  English language Teacher to Diplomats Abuja, Nigeria
- September 2015 till present
  Convener/Initiator, (Stewards of the Environment for Sustainable Change Initiative) *Stop Don't Drop* Abuja, Nigeria
- January 2011 till present
  CEO/Business Development Manager, Pools R Us Ltd, Abuja, Nigeria

Languages

- Fluent in English speaking writing and reading,
- Advanced speaker of Hausa
- Basic speaker of German and Portuguese

Susan R. Berger

Susan would like to be visited at her website:
https://www.imdb.com/name/nm2048282/

Index

P. M. Haller et al., *Bridging Cultural Barriers*, Management for Professionals,
https://doi.org/10.1007/978-3-030-17130-8

MIX
Papier aus verantwortungsvollen Quellen
Paper from responsible sources
FSC® C105338

If you have any concerns about our products,
you can contact us on
ProductSafety@springernature.com

In case Publisher is established outside the EU,
the EU authorized representative is:
Springer Nature Customer Service Center GmbH
Europaplatz 3, 69115 Heidelberg, Germany

Printed by Libri Plureos GmbH
in Hamburg, Germany